D0948548

DATE DUE

Psycholinguistics

The Free Press, New York

COLLIER-MACMILLAN LIMITED, LONDON

Psycholinguistics

SELECTED PAPERS BY

Roger Brown

with

ALBERT GILMAN

ERIC LENNEBERG

ABRAHAM BLACK

ARNOLD HOROWITZ

COLIN FRASER

URSULA BELLUGI

DAVID MCNEILL

COURTNEY CAZDEN

CAMILLE HANLON

THE FREE PRESS
A DIVISION OF THE MACMILLAN COMPANY
866 Third Avenue, New York, N.Y. 10022

COLLIER-MACMILLAN CANADA LTD., TORONTO, ONTARIO

Library of Congress Catalog Card Number: 73-95296

printing number
1 2 3 4 5 6 7 8 9 10

To Mary June

Preface

It is now eighteen years since the Social Science Research Council brought together three linguists and three psychologists for an interdisciplinary conference that led quite directly to the creation of the field of psycholinguistics. If the interaction of two kinds of specialists is to result in the creation of a new field, the field must combine the two specialties in one way or another. But in what way? The possibilities, surveyed in advance, would seem to be indefinitely numerous—which makes it interesting that psycholinguistics has, from the first, meant the importation of linguistic science into psychology and never the importation of psychological science into linguistics. Why is there this asymmetry? Very possibly there is a general law for hybrid fields, of which psycholinguistics is an instance, but I do not know enough about other hybrid fields to make a general argument and can only attempt an explanation of our own case.

I used to think that psychology took from linguistics because linguistics was the more "advanced" field; "advanced" perhaps meaning here "nearer the truth about its subject matter," or "with more practical accomplishments to its credit," or simply "more technical." I do not think this anymore. Linguistics has, after all, solved very few practical problems, and while it is certainly technical, more so now than ever, I do not know that it is more technical than such psychological specialties as learning theory, visual sensation, and decision theory. I am also not at all sure that linguistics is nearer the truth about its subject matter, but I do think it always seems so and that that is the main reason why it is imported rather than importing.

Linguistics must seem nearer its truth than does psychology because linguists as a group make a more compact monolithic impression; they are closer than we to agreement on their problems, their methods, and their answers. The outsider, never entirely sure that he understands the specialty, takes the degree of consensus as an index of approximation to truth. And of course it could be and, in the case of linguistics, may still prove to be but there is reason to consider other possible explanations. Professional linguists in the United States are a smaller group than professional psychologists, about one-sixth the size, and so linguists come closer to being a connected network in which information and attitudes are evenly spread. Psychologists are diverse as well as numerous; our professional association has twenty-six divisions and we are in fact divided at least twenty-six ways by content, methods, and professional activities. It is possible then that comparative size and diversity of interest will alone account for the fact that linguistics is a more compact field than psychology and therefore more easily imported.

There is one remaining fact that tells heavily against the view that linguistics is nearer its truth than is psychology. The comparatively good consensus found at any one period has not been preserved over time. When the SSRC held its conference, the structural linguistics of Bloomfield, Fries, Trager, Pike, Wells, Bloch, and others held sway. In the late 1950's and early 1960's the structuralists were attacked and, in the opinion of most younger linguists, thoroughly discredited by the transformationalists, under the leadership of Noam Chomsky. In the middle 1960's the first version of transformational linguistics was drastically revised by Chomsky, Postal, Katz, and others. Now, in the late 1960's, a much more drastic revision is in progress with James McCawley, John R. Ross, and George Lakoff leading the way.

With a fifteen-year perspective it becomes clear that linguistics has its schools consecutively whereas psychology has its schools contemporaneously and that fact alone would account for the import–export balance in psycholinguistics. How different things would be if all psychologists were Skinnerians!

The fact that linguistic theory changes, and does so at a rapid clip, poses real difficulties for the psychologist who wants to use linguistic theory in his own work. What one discipline wants from another—in interdisciplinary work—is always The Word. "Don't tell me your troubles tell me your results," is the borrower's real attitude. It is not a possible attitude for the psycholinguist in 1969. We can only use linguistics by participating very fully in its intellectual struggles and making our own principled decisions about what can be used at any given time. I think psycholinguistics is one of the very few hybrids in all of behavioral science that has penetrated to the hard truth that a dilettante interest in another field is not enough to support interdisciplinary work.

The present collection of papers, spanning the fifteen years from 1954 to 1969, reflects the changes in linguistic theory that have occurred in that time. Such an early paper as "A Study in Language and Cognition" draws upon structural linguistics, whereas the recent paper "Derivational Complexity and Order of Acquisition in Child Speech" reflects the transformational linguistics of the mid 1960's. Between these two papers there is a contrast not only in the kind of linguistics used but also in the seriousness of the use. Across the full span one has the impression that the interpenetration of linguistics and psychology increases.

The original intention behind this collection was to put together in one place and in revealing sequence the main papers we have done on child speech before beginning work on a research monograph on child speech to which these papers are preliminary. This set of papers appears as "Part One. The Development of a First Language." As a set it seemed a bit small for a book so I added the other psycholinguistics papers, on miscellaneous topics, that I like best, and these constitute "Part Two. Psycholinguistic Processes in Adult Life."

PREFACE

For the majority of the papers I had the help of one or more co-authors. I am grateful to all of them for permission to assemble this collection. They are: Albert Gilman, Eric Lenneberg, Abraham Black, Arnold Horowitz, Colin Fraser, Ursula Bellugi, David McNeill, Courtney Cazden, and Camille Hanlon. Ursula Bellugi is now Ursula Bellugi–Klima.

I would like also to thank Miss Esther Sorocka for help with the original versions of many of the papers as well as with the preparation of this collection for the press.

R.B.

Contents

PART ONE

THE DEVELOPMENT OF A FIRST LANGUAGE

PART TWO

PSYCHOLINGUISTIC PROCESSES IN ADULT LIFE

Figures

Tables

Psycholinguistics

THE DEVELOPMENT OF A FIRST LANGUAGE

A first language is acquired normally in early childhood and the papers in this section are about child speech. An interest in the speech of children, one that goes beyond the usual extra-scientific interest in all aspects of the development of one's own children, is scarcely normal and needs to be accounted for. My long-term research associate, Colin Fraser, once expressed it this way. We had had a particularly wearing day listening to someone's two-year-old talk and also scream. "Eeh" (Fraser has a Scottish dialect). "It's not as if we enjoyed listening to children, is it?" I had to agree that it wasn't, it was never that. What made children's language interesting to us, and makes it so still, are certain mysteries. Probably there is some dominating mystery behind any program of research that stretches over a period of years. It is a good thing to confess to these since they give direction to a path that may otherwise seem erratic. We know the mystery must be there because the pellet-sized presumed truths laid down by a succession of research reports cannot alone account for the researcher's labors.

The mystery dominating the first few papers in this section and also the first (and contemporaneous) paper of the second section is the nature of the influence of language on thought. The efforts reported were rather directly inspired by the thesis of Benjamin Whorf that language is not merely a means of expression but is a kind of mold that shapes the minds of the children who learn it as a first language. The absolute dominion of this mystery yields in the later papers to another. How is it possible for a child to extract from the finite sample of speech he happens to hear a latent structure that will enable him to construct indefinitely numerous new sentences, sentences he has never heard and which even may never have been spoken by anyone? This question was made salient for all of us by the development at the Massachusetts Institute of Technology of transformational generative grammar by Noam Chomsky and his associates. They put sharply in focus the remarkable terminal state that is the regular outcome of language development. As the first great question gradually yielded to the second there were attendant and understandable shifts of focus in our research. In content, from semantics to grammar. In method, from cross-sectional experimental studies to longitudinal naturalistic studies.

Glancing back over the trail at this point the two mysteries still loom as mountains unscaled. We refuse to feel daunted by that fact. After all it took Karl von Frisch something like thirty years to understand the "language" of the honey bee. It cannot be supposed that the language of children constitutes a simpler subject.

[1]

How Shall a Thing be Called?

When adults name things and persons for children they incidentally transmit the texture or grain of their reality. They do this by choosing for some referents names that categorize very broadly and, for some referents, names that categorize very narrowly. That is what this paper is about. It does not exhaust its subject if we understand its subject to be the function of names in tuning one consciousness to another. In English, for instance, any name once introduced may be made definite or indefinite so as to reflect the immediate consciousness of a speaker. "Let me have a dime" requests any instance of a class, but "Let me have the dime" refers to some particular instance which has been made the focus of attention—perhaps a certain coin among many in a handful of change. "Let me have the car" may refer to that car which is most salient in this household, the family car, whereas "Let me have a car" is a request for some instance of a class of vehicle. And, of course, all mothers speak of *the sky, the moon, the sea,* referents unique in their world, whereas they speak of *a tree, a chair, a book,* referents present in many instances.

This paper was first published in *Psychological Review*, Vol. 65, No. 1 (1958), 14–21. Reprinted by permission of the author.

THE MOST DELIBERATE PART of first-language teaching is the business of telling a child what each thing is called. We ordinarily speak of *the* name of a thing as if there were just one, but in fact, of course, every referent has many names. The dime in my pocket is not only a *dime*. It is also *money*, a *metal object*, a *thing*, and, moving to subordinates, it is a *1952 dime*, in fact a *particular 1952 dime* with a unique pattern of scratches, discolorations, and smooth places. When such an object is named for a very young child how is it called? It may be named *money* or *dime* but probably not *metal object, thing, 1952 dime,* or *particular 1952 dime*. The dog out on the lawn is not only a *dog* but is also a *boxer*, a *quadruped*, an *animate being;* it is the *landlord's dog*, named *Prince*. How will it be identified for a child? Sometimes it will be called a *dog*, sometimes *Prince*, less often a *boxer*, and almost never a *quadruped*, or *animate being*. Listening to many adults name things for many children, I find that their choices are quite uniform and that I can anticipate them from my own inclinations. How are these choices determined and what are their consequences for the cognitive development of the child?

Adults have notions about the kind of language appropriate for use with children. Especially strong and universal is the belief that children have trouble pronouncing long names and so should always be given the shortest possible names. A word is preferable to a phrase and, among words, a monosyllable is better than a polysyllable. This predicts the preference for *dog* and *Prince* over *boxer, quadruped,* and *animate being*. It predicts the choice of *dime* over *metal object* and *particular 1952 dime*.

Zipf (1935) has shown that the length of a word (in phonemes or syllables) is inversely related to its frequency in the printed language. Consequently the shorter names for any thing will usually also be the most frequently used names for that thing, and so it would seem that the choice of a name is usually predictable from either frequency or brevity. The monosyllables *dog* and *Prince* have much higher frequencies according to the Thorndike-Lorge list than do the polysyllables *boxer, quadruped,* and *animate being*.

It sometimes happens, however, that the frequency-brevity

principle makes the wrong prediction. The thing called a *pineapple* is also *fruit*. *Fruit* is the shorter and more frequent term, but adults will name the thing *pineapple*. Similarly they will say *apple, banana, orange,* and even *pomegranate;* all of them longer and less frequent words than the perfectly appropriate *fruit*. Brevity seems not to be the powerful determinant we had imagined. The frequency principle can survive this kind of example, but only if it is separated from counts like the Thorndike-Lorge of over-all frequency in the printed language. On the whole the word *fruit* appears more often than the word *pineapple* (and also is shorter), but we may confidently assume that, when pineapples are being named, the word *pineapple* is more frequent than the word *fruit*. This, of course, is a kind of frequency more directly relevant to our problem. Word counts of general usage are only very roughly applicable to the prediction of what will be said when something is named. What we need is referent-name counts. We don't have them, of course, but if we had them it is easy to see that they would improve our predictions. Bananas are called *banana*, apples *apple*, and oranges *orange* more often than any of them is called *fruit*. The broad frequency-brevity principle predicts that *money* and *dime* will be preferred to *metal object, 1952 dime,* and *particular 1952 dime*, but it does not predict the neglect of the common monosyllable *thing*. For this purpose we must again appeal to imagined referent-name counts, according to which dimes would surely be called *dime* or *money* more often than *thing*.

While the conscious preference for a short name can be overcome by frequency, the preference nevertheless, affects the naming act. I have heard parents designate the appropriate objects *pineapple, television, vinegar,* and *policeman;* all these to children who cannot reproduce polysyllabic words. Presumably they use these names because that is what the referents are usually called, but the adult's sense of the absurdity of giving such words to a child is often evident. He may smile as he says it or remark, "That's too hard for you to say, isn't it?"

Some things are named in the same way by all adults for all children. This is true of the apple and the orange. Other

5

things have several common names, each of them used by a specifiable group of adults to specifiable children. The same dog is *dog* to most of the world and *Prince* in his own home and perhaps on his own block. The same man is a *man* to most children, *policeman* to some at some times, *Mr. Jones* to the neighborhood kids, and *papa* to his own. Referent-name counts from people in general will not predict these several usages. A still more particular name count must be imagined. The name given a thing by an adult for a child is determined by the frequency with which various names have been applied to such things in the experience of the particular adult. General referent-name counts taken from many people will predict much that the individual does, but, for a close prediction, counts specific to the individual would be needed.

The frequencies to which we are now appealing have not, of course, been recorded. We are explaining imagined preferences in names by imagined frequencies of names. It is conceivable, certainly, that some of these specific word counts might be made and a future naming performance independently predicted from a past frequency. Probably, however, such frequencies will never be known, and if we choose to explain particular naming performances by past frequencies we shall usually have to infer the frequency from the performance.

BEYOND THE FREQUENCY PRINCIPLE

A frequency explanation is not very satisfying even when the appeal is to known frequencies. The question will come to mind: "Why is one name more common than another?" Why is a dog called *dog* more often than *quadruped* and, by some people, called *Prince* more often than *dog*? Perhaps it just happened that way, like driving on the right side of the road in America and on the left in England. The convention is preserved but has no justification outside itself. As things have worked out, coins are usually named by species as *dime*, *nickel*, or *penny* while the people we know have individual names like *John*, *Mary*, and *Jim*. Could it just as easily be the other way around? Might we equally well give coins proper names and introduce people as types?

The referent for the word *dime* is a large class of coins. The name is equally appropriate to all members of this class. To name a coin *dime* is to establish its equivalence, for naming purposes, with all other coins of the same denomination. This equivalence for naming purposes corresponds to a more general equivalence for all purposes of economic exchange. In the grocery one dime is as good as another but quite different from any nickel or penny. For a child the name given an object anticipates the equivalences and differences that will need to be observed in most of his dealings with such an object. To make proper denotative use of the word *dime* he must be able to distinguish members of the referent category from everything else. When he learns that, he has solved more than a language problem. He has an essential bit of equipment for doing business. The most common names for coins could not move from the species level to the level of proper names without great alteration in our nonlinguistic culture. We should all be numismatists preparing our children to recognize a particular priceless 1910 dime.

Many things are reliably given the same name by the whole community. The spoon is seldom called anything but *spoon*, although it is also a piece of *silverware*, an *artifact*, and a *particular ill-washed restaurant spoon*. The community-wide preference for the word *spoon* corresponds to the community-wide practice of treating spoons as equivalent but different from knives and forks. There are no proper names for individual spoons because their individuality seldom signifies. It is the same way with pineapples, dimes, doors, and taxicabs. The most common name for each of these categorizes them as they need to be categorized for the community's nonlinguistic purposes. The most common name is at the level of usual utility.

People and pets have individual names as well as several kinds of generic name. The individual name is routinely coined by those who are disposed to treat the referent as unique, and is available afterwards to any others who will see the uniqueness. A man at home has his own name to go with the peculiar

7

privileges and responsibilities binding him to wife and child. But the same man who is a one-of-a-kind *papa* to his own children is simply a *man* to children at large. He is, like the other members of this large category, someone with no time to play and little tolerance for noise. In some circumstances, this same man will be given the name of his occupation. He is a *policeman* equivalent to other policemen but different from *bus drivers* and *Good Humor men*. A policeman is someone to "behave in front of" and to go to when lost. To the kids in the neighborhood the man is *Mr. Jones*, unique in his way—a crank, bad tempered, likely to shout at you if you play out in front of his house. It is the same way with dogs as with people. He may be a unique *Prince* to his owners, who feed and house him, but he is just a *dog* to the rest of the world. A homeless dog reverts to namelessness, since there is none to single him out from his species. Dimes and nickels have much the same significance for an entire society, and their usual names are fixed at this level of significance. People and pets function uniquely for some and in various generic ways for others. They have a corresponding variety of designations, but each name is at the utility level for the group that uses it. Our naming practices for coins and people correspond to our nonlinguistic practices, and it is difficult to imagine changing the one without changing the other.

The names provided by parents for children anticipate the functional structure of the child's world.[1] This is not, of course, something parents are aware of doing. When we name

---

[1] The equivalence of dimes and their distinctiveness as a class from nickels and pennies is strongly suggested by the appearance of individual coins as well as by their names. Variations in size, weight, and hue are far greater between classes than within a class. This, of course, is because coins are manufactured in accordance with a categorical scheme which is also represented in our names for coins. It is possible, then, that a child might structure coins in the culturally approved manner if he never heard them named at all. However, we cannot be sure that an untutored child would not put all shiny new coins into one class and all the dingy specimens into another. When the referents are not manufactured articles but are such things as dogs, people, flowers, and insects, it is clear that autochthonous factors in perception do not force any single scheme of categorization. The names applied must be the child's principal clue to the locally functioning scheme.

a thing there does not seem to be any process of choice. Each thing has its name, just one, and that is what we give to a child. The one name is, of course, simply the usual name for us. Naming each thing in accordance with local frequencies, parents unwittingly transmit their own cognitive structures. It is a world in which *Prince* is unique among dogs and *papa* among men, *spoons* are all alike but different from *forks*. It may be a world of *bugs* (to be stepped on), of *flowers* (not to be picked), and *birds* (not to be stoned). It may be a world in which *Niggers*, like *spoons*, are all of a kind. A division of caste creates a vast categorical equivalence and a correspondingly generic name. *Mr. Jones* and *Mr. Smith* do not come out of racial anonymity until their uniqueness is appreciated.

Adults do not invariably provide a child with the name that is at the level of usual utility in the adult world. An effort is sometimes made to imagine the utilities of a child's life. Some parents will, at first, call every sort of coin *money*. This does not prepare a child to buy and sell, but then he may be too young for that. All coins are equivalent for the very young child in that they are objects not to be put into the mouth and not to be dropped down the register, and *money* anticipates that equivalence. A more differentiated terminology can wait upon the age of store-going. Sometimes an adult is aware of a child's need for a distinction that is not coded in the English lexicon. A new chair comes into the house and is not going to be equivalent to the shabby chairs already there. A child is permitted to sit on the old chairs but will not be permitted on the new one. A distinctive name is created from the combinatorial resources of the language. *The new chair* or *the good chair* is not to be assimilated to *chairs* in general.

Eventually, of course, children learn many more names for each thing than the one that is most frequent and useful. Sometimes a name is supplied in order to bring forward an immediately important property of the referent. A child who starts bouncing the coffee pot needs to be told that it is *glass*. Sometimes a name is supplied to satisfy the child's curiosity as to the place of a referent in a hierarchy of categories. Chairs are *furniture* and so are tables; carrots are a *vegetable*

9

but apples are not. Probably, however, both children and adults make some distinction among these various names. *The name of a thing, the one that tells what it "really" is, is the name that constitutes the referent as it needs to be constituted for most purposes.* The other names represent possible recategorizations useful for one or another purpose. We are even likely to feel that these recategorizations are acts of imagination, whereas the major categorization is a kind of passive recognition of the true character of the referent.

THE CHILD'S CONCRETE VOCABULARY

It is a commonplace saying that the mind of a child is relatively "concrete" and the mind of an adult "abstract." The words "concrete" and "abstract" are sometimes used in the sense of subordinate and superordinate. In this sense a relatively concrete mind would operate with subordinate categories and an abstract mind with superordinate categories. It is recorded in many studies of vocabulary acquisition (e.g. International Kindergarten Union, 1928; Smith, 1926) that children ordinarily use the words *milk* and *water* before the word *liquid;* the words *apple* and *orange* before *fruit; table* and *chair* before *furniture; mamma* and *daddy* before *parent* or *person;* etc. Very high-level superordinate terms like *article, action, quality,* and *relation,* though they are common in adult speech (Thorndike and Lorge, 1944), are very seldom heard from preschool children (International Kindergarten Union, 1928). Presumably this kind of vocabulary comparison is one of the sources of the notion that the child's mind is more concrete than the mind of the adult.[1] However, the vocabulary

[1] From the facts of vocabulary acquisition alone it is not possible to draw safe conclusions about cognitive development. Such conclusions rely on something like the following set of assumptions. A subject, whether animal or human, is ordinarily credited with a cognitive category when he extends some distinctive response to new instances of the category and withholds it from noninstances. Words, when used to denote new referents, are such a distinctive response. If children speak words they probably can make correct denotative use of them, and so the presence of the word in a child's vocabulary may be taken as evidence that he posses-

of a child is not a very direct index of his cognitive preferences. The child's vocabulary is more immediately determined by the naming practices of adults. The occasion for a name is ordinarily some particular thing. In the naming it is categorized. The preference among possible names seems to go to the one that is most commonly applied to the referent in question. That name will ordinarily categorize the referent so as to observe the eqivalences and differences that figure in its usual utilization. There are not many purposes for which all liquids are equivalent or all fruits, furniture, or parents; and so the names of these categories are less commonly used for denotation than are the names of categories subordinate to them. It is true that words like *article*, *action*, *quality*, and *relation* are rather common in adult written English, but we can be sure that these frequencies in running discourse are not equaled in naming situations. Whatever the purposes for which all articles are equivalent, or all actions or qualities, they are not among the pressing needs of children.

It is not invariably true that vocabulary builds from concrete to abstract. *Fish* is likely to be learned before *perch* and *bass; house* before *bungalow* and *mansion; car* before *Chevrolet* and *Plymouth* (Smith, 1926). The more concrete vocabulary waits for the child to reach an age where his purposes differentiate kinds of fish and makes of cars. There is much elaborately concrete vocabulary that is not introduced until one takes courses in biology, chemistry, and botany. No one has ever proved that vocabulary builds from the concrete to the

ses the category to which the word makes reference. The instances of the category are presumed not to be differentiated by the child unless he uses words for such differentiations. If all of these assumptions are made it would seem to follow that the direction of vocabulary growth (from subordinate to superordinate or vice versa) reveals the direction of cognitive development. When the assumptions of such an argument are explicitly stated, it is clear that they are too many and too doubtful. Obviously words may be spoken but not understood; objects may be differentiated by nonlinguistic response even though they are not differentiated linguistically. However, it is not my purpose here to quarrel with these assumptions but rather to show that, even when they are accepted, the facts of vocabulary growth do not compel the conclusion that cognitive development is from the concrete to the abstract.

11

abstract more often than it builds from the abstract to the concrete. The best generalization seems to be that each thing is first given its most common name. This name seems to categorize on the level of usual utility. That level sometimes falls on the most concrete categories in a hierarchy (proper names for significant people), and vocabulary then builds toward the more abstract categories (names for ethnic groups, personality types, social classes). Utility sometimes centers on a relatively abstract level of categorization (fish) and vocabulary then builds in both directions (perch and vertebrate). Probably utility never centers on the most abstract levels (thing, substance, etc.), and so probably there is no hierarchy within which vocabulary builds in an exclusively concrete direction.

In the literature describing first-language acquisition (McCarthy, 1946) there is much to indicate that children easily form large abstract categories. There are, to begin with, the numerous cases in which the child overgeneralizes the use of a conventional word. The word *dog* may, at first, be applied to every kind of four-legged animal. It sometimes happens that every man who comes into the house is called *daddy*. When children invent their own words, these often have an enormous semantic range. Wilhelm Stern's (Stern and Stern, 1920) son Günther used *psee* for leaves, trees, and flowers. He used *bebau* for all animals. Lombroso (Werner, 1948) tells of a child who used *qua qua* for both duck and water and *afta* for drinking glass, the contents of a glass, and a pane of glass. Reports of this kind do not suggest that children are deficient in abstracting ability. It even looks as if they may favor large categories.

There are two extreme opinions about the direction of cognitive development. There are those who suppose that we begin by discriminating to the limits of our sensory acuity, seizing each thing in its uniqueness, noting every hair and flea of the particular dog. Cognitive development involves neglect of detail, abstracting from particulars so as to group similars into categories. By this view abstraction is a mature rather than a primitive process. The contrary opinion is that the primitive stage in cognition is one of a comparative lack of differentiation. Probably certain distinctions are inescapable; the difference between a loud noise and near silence, between a bright contour and a dark ground, etc. These inevitable discriminations divide the perceived world into a small number of very large (abstract) categories. Cognitive development is increasing differentiation. The more distinctions we make, the more categories we have and the smaller (more concrete) these are. I think the latter view is favored in psychology today. While there is good empirical and theoretical support (Gibson and Gibson, 1955; Lashley and Wade, 1946; Lewin, 1935) for the view that development is differentiation, there is embarrassment for it in the fact that much vocabulary growth is from the concrete to the abstract. This embarrassment can be eliminated.

Suppose a very young child applies the word *dog* to every four-legged creature he sees. He may have abstracted a limited set of attributes and created a large category, but his abstraction will not show up in his vocabulary. Parents will not provide him with a conventional name for his category, e.g., *quadruped*, but instead will require him to narrow his use of *dog* to its proper range. Suppose a child calls all elderly ladies *aunt*. He will not be told that the usual name for his category is *elderly ladies* but, instead, will be taught to cut back *aunt* to accord with standard usage. In short, the sequence in which words are acquired is set by adults rather than children, and may ultimately be determined by the utility of the various categorizations. This will sometimes result in a movement of vocabulary toward higher abstraction and sometimes a movement toward greater concreteness. The cognitive development of the child may nevertheless always take the direction of increasing differentiation or concreteness.

The child who spontaneously hits on the category four-legged animals will be required to give it up in favor of dogs, cats, horses, cows, and the like. When the names of numerous subordinates have been mastered, he may be given the name *quadruped* for the superordinate. This abstraction is not the same as its primitive forerunner. The schoolboy who learns the word *quadruped* has abstracted from differentiated and named subordinates. The child he was abstracted through a failure to differentiate. Abstraction after differentiation may be the mature process, and abstraction from a failure to differentiate the primitive. Needless to say, the abstractions occurring on the two levels need not be coincident, as they are in our quadruped example.

SUMMARY

Though we often think of each thing as having a name—a single name—in fact, each thing has many equally correct names. When some thing is named for a child, adults show considerable regularity in their preference for one of the many possible names. This paper is addressed to the question: "What determines the name given to a child for a thing?" The first answer is that adults prefer the shorter to the longer expression. This gives way to the frequency principle. Adults give a thing the name it is most commonly given. We have now come full circle and are left with the question, "Why is one name for a thing more common than another?"

It seems likely that things are first named so as to categorize them in a maximally useful way. For most purposes Referent A is a spoon rather than a piece of silverware, and Referent B a dime rather than a metal object. The same referent may have its most useful categorization on one level (*Prince*) for one group (the family) and on another level (*dog*) for another group (strangers). The categorization that is most useful for very young children (*money*) may change as they grow older (*dime* and *nickel*).

With some hierarchies of vocabulary the more concrete terms are learned before the abstract; probably the most abstract terms are never learned first, but it often happens that a hierarchy develops in both directions from a middle level of abstraction. Psychologists who believe that mental development is from the abstract to the concrete, from a lack of differentiation to increased differentiation, have been embarrassed by the fact that vocabulary often builds in the opposite direction. This fact need not trouble them, since the sequence in which words are acquired is not determined by the cognitive preferences of children so much as by the naming practices of adults.

References

GIBSON, J. J., and GIBSON, ELEANOR J. Perceptual learning: differentiation or enrichment? *Psychol. Rev.*, 1955, 62, 32–41.

INTERNATIONAL KINDERGARTEN UNION. *A study of the vocabulary of children before entering the first grade.* Baltimore: Williams & Wilkins, 1928.

LASHLEY, K. S., and WADE, MARJORIE. The Pavlovian theory of generalization. *Psychol. Rev.*, 1946, 53, 72–87.

LEWIN, K. *A dynamic theory of personality.* New York: McGraw-Hill, 1935.

McCARTHY, DOROTHEA. Language development in children. In L. Carmichael (Ed.) *Manual of child psychology.* New York: Wiley, 1946.

SMITH, M. E. An investigation of the development of the sentence and the extent of vocabulary in young children. *Univer. Iowa Stud. Child Welfare*, 1926, 3, No. 5.

STERN, CLARA, and STERN, W. *Die Kindersprache.* Leipzig: Barth, 1920.

THORNDIKE, E. L., and LORGE, I. *The teacher's word book of 30,000 words.* New York: Bureau of Publications, Teachers College, Columbia University, 1944.

WERNER, H. *Comparative psychology of mental development.* Chicago: Follett, 1948.

ZIPF, G. K. *The psycho-biology of language.* Boston: Houghton Mifflin, 1935.

[2]

Linguistic Determinism and the Part of Speech

When you count in Japanese you use not only numerals (*ichi*, *ni*, *san*, etc.) but also counters which are a subclass of nouns. Some of these counters are class terms. For example, there is a class term *-mai* used for counting flat thin things such as sheets, newspapers, and handkerchiefs. There is a term *-hon* (or, in some cases, *-pon* or *-bon*) for thin, long things such as pencils, sticks, and cigarettes. For most animals, fish, and insects the counter is *-hiki* (or *-biki* or *-piki*) but for large domesticated animals like horses, cows, dogs, and cats the counter is *-too*. The words actually used in counting are compounded from numerals and counters. Three insects would be *sanbiki*; three pencils *sanbon*, three sheets of paper *sammai*. The student of Japanese whose native language is English is likely to find this system fascinating and to be awakened by it to a problem of language and cognition. When one language makes grammatical use of a meaning-based class that does not function in the same way in another language, is there some corresponding difference in the cognitive processes of speakers of the two languages? That is the general question to which this paper is addressed.

This paper was first published in *The Journal of Abnormal and Social Psychology* Vol. 55, No. 1 (July 1957), 1–5. Reprinted by permission of the author.

LINGUISTIC DETERMINISM AND THE PART OF SPEECH

This paper was prepared for a conference on "Linguistic Meaning" held at Yale University in May of 1956. Noam Chomsky was there and I heard about transformational grammar for the first time. Following Chomsky's talk there was an exchange that went something like this:

Brown: "It sounds to me as if a transformational grammar might be what children learn when they learn their first language."

Chomsky: "Oh, do you think so?"

IN RECENT YEARS the anthropologists Whorf (1956), Lee (1938), and Hoijer (1954) have put forward the view that language is a determinant of perception and thought. The nature of the determining influence exerted by the vocabulary of a language is quite clear (Brown, 1956), but it is less easy to see how the grammatical features of a language can affect cognition. Yet it is just the grammatical differences between languages that are most striking and it is their determining force that the anthropologist has stressed. This paper undertakes to show how one kind of grammatical practice, the allocation of words to one or another part of speech, does affect cognition.

The words of a language can be collected into classes of formal equivalents which are called the parts of speech. Fries (1952) has shown that English nouns, for example, are words acceptable in sentence frames of the type "(The) —— is (are) good." Native speakers of English will find it possible to insert *concert* or *cow* or *truth* in that frame but will find *very* or *of* grammatically impossible. Fries has used other sentence frames to separate out verbs, adjectives, and adverbs. In French, nouns can be further subdivided into formal gender classes. In Navaho there are more than twenty formal classes for words naming different kinds of objects. All of these word classes are defined by linguistic science in terms of the combinatorial possibilities of forms in a language without reference to the meanings of forms.

So long as these classes are defined in purely formal terms

they do not suggest important cognitive differences. That suggestion comes in when we add the semantic correlates of the classes. The native speaker of English is likely to think of the parts of speech in semantic terms. Nouns name substances; verbs name processes; and adjectives name qualities. The genders of certain European languages are usually called masculine, feminine, and neuter, and these are semantic characterizations. The object classes of Navaho are usually described as words naming round objects, words naming long, thin objects, words naming granular substances, etc. The linguistic determinists in anthropology believe that the semantic character of the form classes fixes the fundamental conception of reality in a language community and that differences on this level correspond to different *Weltanschauungen*.

At the same time the science of descriptive linguistics refuses to define its word classes in semantic terms. Fries (1952) has shown that for the English parts of speech such definitions are always either unclear or overextended. We all know the English teacher's characterization of the noun as the name of a person, place, or thing. The terms *person* and *place* are reasonably clear, but do not apply to such nouns as *truth*, *odor*, and *thought*. The meaning of *thing* is so unclear that we cannot tell whether or not odor and thought are things. No one has been able to provide clear semantic definitions that will serve to distinguish every English noun from every verb, adjective, and adverb. It is well known that the "masculine" and "feminine" genders in the European languages include names for objects having no sex. In Navaho, too, the object classes do not show perfect semantic consistency. In short, the semantic definitions of the form classes ignore many exceptions and are unsuitable for the purposes of linguistic science.

When the linguistic scientist sets up his descriptive categories he quite naturally looks for attributes of exceptionless validity, and there are not such semantic attributes for the English parts of speech. However, the layman may operate, in this area as in so many others, with conceptions that take account of probabilistic as well as certain associations. It may be that nouns *tend to have* a different semantic from verbs, and that the native speaker detects this tendency while he is in the process of learning the language. To answer these questions examination was made of the nouns and verbs of young children learning English to see whether there was a semantic distinction between the two parts of speech. The distinction proved to be much clearer than it is in the vocabulary of English-speaking adults. The second step was an experiment to find out whether the children were aware of the semantic distinction between nouns and verbs and whether they made any use of the distinction.

THE NOUN AND VERB IN CHILDREN'S SPEECH

Harvard pre-school sessions were visited for about a month. There were eight children in each class; two of the classes were limited to children between four and five years while a third class accepted those between three and four. As an observer, the author sat on the side-lines and let the pre-school life swirl about him, recording verbatim all the conversation he could hear. From these records, he made vocabulary lists classified into the parts of speech. It was his impression, on examining this vocabulary, that the nouns and verbs of children were more nearly consistent with the classroom semantic definitions than are the nouns and verbs of adults. Nouns commonly heard were *truck*, *blocks*, and *teacher*. There were no uses of *thought* or *virtue* or *attitude*. These observations suggested that as the form classes grow larger they decline in semantic consistency. Perhaps children develop firm, and temporarily reliable, notions about the semantics of nouns and verbs. These notions may stay with them as adults even though they retain only a probabilistic truth.

To compare the character of adult and child vocabularies, the first thousand most frequent words from the Thorndike-Lorge (1944) list of adult usage were examined, and also the first thousand most frequent words from the Rinsland (1945) list of the vocabulary of children in the first grade. The Rinsland list is based on 4,630 pages of conversation, plus more than a thousand letters and stories. The Rinsland list is much the same as lists compiled independently by the Child Study Committee of the Kindergarten Union (1928) and by Horn (1925).

The first set of contrasts deals with two reduced lists; nouns found among the first thousand for adults but not for children, compared with nouns among the first thousand for children but not for adults. The set of nouns having clearest "thing" character would seem to be those that are called "concrete" and it is a commonplace to describe the language of children as more concrete than that of adults. One sense of the pair "concrete–abstract" is the same as "subordinate–superordinate." The more abstract term, the superordinate, includes in its denotation the denotation of the concrete or subordinate term, but extends beyond it. Superordinate-subordinate relations between the two lists were all in one direction. The adult list included *action, article, body, experience,* and at least seven others which were superordinate to many words on the children's list. There were no nouns on the children's list superordinate to those on the adult list.

The concrete noun with the smaller denotation is likely to be more picturable than its superordinate, and picturability is another common sense of "concrete." Of course the concrete noun, like the abstract, names a category rather than a particular instance. However, some categories have a more or less characteristic visual contour and size while others do not. Visual contour is a defining attribute for *table*, but not for *thing* or *experience*. Of the adult nouns, 16 per cent named categories having a characteristic visual contour, while 67 per cent of the children's nouns were of this kind. Nouns like *apple, barn,* and *airplane* name categories for which size is a defining attribute, while nouns like *affair, amount,* and *action* do not. On the adult list, 39 per cent of the nouns were of the former kind, while 83 per cent of the children's nouns had size implications. It appears that children's nouns are more likely to name concrete things (in the sense of naming narrow categories with characteristic visual contour and size) than are the nouns of adults.

Two lists of verbs were compared: those among the first 1,000 for adults but not for children, and those among the first 1,000 for children but not for adults. The question here was the percentage of verbs naming animal (including human) movement. Of the adult verbs, 33 per cent were of this kind, while 67 per cent of the children's verbs named actions. The common notion that verbs name actions seems to be truer for the vocabulary of children than for the vocabulary of adults.

These studies of word lists confirm the impression that the nouns and verbs used by children have more consistent semantic implications than those used by adults. It remains a question whether children are, in any sense, aware of these implications. There are many ways in which such awareness could be useful to one learning the language. Adults often try to convey the sense of a word by speaking it in the presence of the object or event named. All such single namings are ambiguous. The adult who says "water" while looking at a glass of water may cause a child to attend to the glass itself as a container, to the glass as a transparent material, to the liquid character of its contents, to the height of the liquid, to the state of containment, and so on. Selection of the non-linguistic attributes that govern proper denotative use of the word *water* cannot be guaranteed by a single naming. Repeated pointings can, of course, establish the invariant circumstances governing use of the word. If there were nothing to suggest to the child the probably relevant features of the nonlinguistic world, discovery of linguistic meanings would be a very laborious affair. However, a new word is ordinarily introduced in a way that makes its part-of-speech membership clear: "Look at the *dog*" or "See him *running*." If a part of speech has reliable semantic implications it could call attention to the kind of attribute likely to belong to the meaning of the word. A child who had absorbed the semantics of the noun and verb would know, the first time he heard the word *dog*, that it was likely to refer to an object having characteristic size and shape, whereas *running* would be likely to name some animal motion. The part-of-speech membership of the new word could operate as a filter selecting for attention probably relevant features of the nonlinguistic world. It seemed that one could learn whether children experience any such filtering of attributes by introducing to them newly invented words assigned to one or another part of speech, and then inquiring about the meanings the words appeared to have.

In the children's speech that had been recorded, nouns and verbs were given proper grammatical treatment. In addition, the children made correct use of a subclass of nouns—the mass nouns. These are words like *dirt, snow, milk,* and *rice* which are given different grammatical treatment from such particular nouns as *barn, house,* and *dog.* For example, when *some* is used with *barn* the noun is in the plural—*some barns,* whereas a mass noun would be in the singular—*some rice.* The semantic difference between these two classes of noun is suggested by the designations "mass" and "particular." Mass nouns usually name extended substances having no characteristic size or shape, while particular nouns name objects having size and shape. Many nouns can function in either a mass or particular way with attendant shifts in the speaker's view of the referent. *Some cake* is a chunk of a mass while *some cakes* are either cupcakes or layer cakes arranged in a row. Many words in the vocabulary of psychology have this double potentiality. Although the personologist deplores such usage, the layman speaks of someone having "a lot of personality" or "very little temperament." The professional insists that personality is not an undifferentiated substance of which one can have more or less. Personalities are like cupcakes—all of a size and one to a customer—with only their frostings to make them unique.

In the speech of the pre-school children *milk,* and *orange juice,* and *dirt* were the most common mass nouns. These were always given correct grammatical treatment. No one said *a milk* or *some dirts.* I decided to work with three functional classes: the particular noun, the mass noun, and the verb.

METHOD

The experiment involved three sets of four pictures each. One of these sets will be described in detail. The first picture in the set shows a pair of hands performing a kneading sort of motion, with a mass of red confetti-like material which is piled into and overflowing a blue-and-white striped container that is round and low in shape. The important features of the picture are the kneading action, the red mass, and the blue-and-white round container. The motion would ordinarily be named with a verb (like *kneading*), the mass with a mass noun (like *confetti*), and the container with a particular noun (like *container*). It was assumed that children would have no readily available names for any of these conceptions. Each of the remaining three pictures of this set exactly reproduced one of the three salient features of the first picture, either the motion, the mass, or the container. In order to represent the motion a second time it was necessary to show also a mass and a container. However, the mass was here painted yellow so as not to duplicate the original, and the container was of a different size, shape, and color from the original. The other two sets of pictures involved different content, but always an action, a mass substance, and a particular object. In one case, the first picture showed hands cutting a mass of cloth with a strange tool. In the third set, hands were shown emptying an odd container of a slushy sort of material.

In overview, the following use was to be made of the three sets of pictures. Children were to be shown the first picture in conjunction with a new word identifiable either as a verb, a mass noun, or a particular noun. Then they would be shown the remaining three pictures of the set and asked to point out the one that pictured again what had been named in the first picture. It was anticipated that when the new word was a verb they would point to the picture of motion, when it was a particular noun they would point to the container, and when it was a mass noun they would point to the extended substance.

Three word stems were used: *niss*, *sib*, and *latt*. If the stem was to function as a verb, the experimenter would begin by asking: "Do you know what it means to sib?" (Children do not always answer "no" as they ought.) "In this picture" (first picture of a set) "you can see sibbing. Now show me another picture of sibbing" (presenting the other three pictures of the set). If the stem was to function as a particular noun, the experimenter began: "Do you know what a sib is?" and proceeded in consistent fashion. If the word was to function as a mass noun, the experimenter began: "Have you ever seen any sib?" and went on accordingly.

Each child saw all three sets of pictures and heard each of the word stems; one of them as a particular noun, one as a mass noun, and one as a verb. The combinations of word stem, part-of-speech membership, picture set, and order of presentation were all randomly varied. There were sixteen children in all, half of them between three and four years, and half between four and five. They were all acquainted with the experimenter by the time the experiment was performed. The procedure was very like the familiar business of looking at a picture book and naming the things seen and was accepted by the children as a kind of game. The game was always played with one child at a time.

RESULTS AND DISCUSSION

When a new word was introduced as a verb, ten of the sixteen children picked out the picture of movement. When the word was a particular noun, eleven of sixteen selected the picture of an object; and when the word was a mass noun, twelve of sixteen selected the extended substance. Of the fifteen responses that were not correct, four were simply failures to answer because of some distraction from the task. The results are summarized in Table. 2–1. A simple test was

Table 2–1. Picture Selections for Words Belonging to Various Parts of Speech

Category Depicted	Verbs	Particular Nouns	Mass Nouns
Actions	10	1	0
Objects	4	11	3
Substances	1	2	12
No response	1	2	1

made to determine the significance of the differences in the pictures selected by children when the new word was a verb, when the word was a particular noun, and when it was a mass noun. For example, the selections made when the word was a verb were dichotomized into pictures of actions and all others. These frequencies for verbs were compared with like frequencies for the choices made when the words were either particular or mass nouns. In other words, the test was to determine whether action pictures were more likely to be selected as referents for new words introduced as verbs than for new words introduced as nouns. Comparable tests were made to see whether particular nouns were associated with pictures of objects and mass nouns with substances. All three of the resultant 2×2 tables yielded differences beyond the .005 level of significance when the Fisher-Yates test was applied.

It is well known that children will sometimes do what an adult wishes in a task of this kind though they do not understand the task as the adult does. Consequently, the qualitative results may be more persuasive than the quantitative. In the first trial with the first child, for instance, I showed the picture of cloth being cut by an odd tool and said that there was a "sib" in the picture. Then went on with: "Can you show me another sib?" and while I still fumbled with the other three pictures, my subject swung around and pointed to the steam valve on the end of the radiator saying, "There's a sib." The pictured tool looked very like the steam valve. In another case, I showed the picture of confetti-kneading and said, "There is some latt in this picture," whereupon my subject said: "The latt is spilling." And it was.

Recent experiments with phonetic symbolism (Brown, Black and Horowitz, 1955) and metaphor (Brown, Leiter, and Hildum, 1957) indicate that semantic rules are not always arbitrary. A word can suggest its meaning because the sound is an echo of the sense or because the word had a prior meaning which is related to the new meaning. The present study suggests that most words have an additional kind of "appropriateness" stemming from their grammatical character. While the part-of-speech membership of a word does not give away the particular meaning, it does suggest the general type of that meaning, whether action, object, substance, or whatever. In learning a language, therefore, it must be useful to discover the semantic correlates of the various parts of speech; for this discovery enables the learner to use the part-of-speech membership of a new word as a first clue to its meaning. The present experiment with very young children who are learning English indicates that in this language, at least, the semantic implications of the verb, mass noun, and particular noun are discovered by native speakers. It now seems quite probable that speakers of other languages will also know about the semantics of their grammatical categories. Since these are strikingly different in unrelated languages, the speakers in question may have quite different cognitive categories. It remains to be determined how seriously and how generally thought is affected by these semantic distinctions.

SUMMARY

Descriptive linguistics defines the parts of speech in strictly formal or syntactical terms. Nevertheless, the parts of speech usually have distinct semantic characteristics. These characteristics do not hold for all members of the various parts of speech, however, and so cannot serve to define the parts of speech for the purposes of linguistic science. Human beings are generally adept at picking up imperfect probabilistic implications, and so it may be the case that native speakers detect the semantic nature of the parts of speech of their language. It was shown that the nouns used by young English-speaking children were more reliably the names of things and their verbs more reliably the names of actions than is the case for the nouns and verbs used by English-speaking adults. It was shown experimentally that young English-speaking children take the part-of-speech membership of a new word as a clue to the meaning of the word. In this way, they make use of the semantic distinctiveness of the parts of speech. It seems likely that speakers of languages other than English will also have detected the semantic characters of their parts of speech. There is a sense, then, in which this grammatical feature of a language affects the cognition of those who speak the languages. Differences between languages in their parts of speech may be diagnostic of differences in the cognitive psychologies of those who use the languages.

References

BROWN, R. W. Language and categories. Appendix to J. S. Bruner, Jacqueline J. Goodnow, and G. A. Austin, *A study of thinking.* New York: Wiley, 1956.

BROWN, R. W., BLACK, A. H., and HOROWITZ, A. E. Phonetic symbolism in natural languages. *J. abnorm. soc. Psychol.*, 1955, **50**, 388–393.

BROWN, R. W., LEITER, R. A., & HILDUM, D. C. Metaphors from musical criticism. *J. abnorm. soc. Psychol.*, 1957, **54**, 347–352.

BUCKINGHAM, B. R., & DOLCH, E. W. *A combined word list.* Boston: Ginn, 1936.

FRIES, C. C. *The structure of English.* New York: Harcourt Brace, 1952.

HOIJER, H. (Ed.) *Language in culture.* Chicago: University of Chicago Press, 1954.

HORN, E. The commonest words in the spoken vocabulary of children up to and including six years of age. In National Society for the Study of Education, *Twenty-fourth yearbook.* Bloomington, Illinois: Public School Publishing Company, 1925.

INTERNATIONAL KINDERGARTEN UNION, CHILD STUDY COMMITTEE. *A study of the vocabulary of children before entering the first grade.* Washington, D. C.: The Int. Kindergarten Union, 1928.

LEE, DOROTHY D. Conceptual implications of an Indian language. *Phil. of Sci.*, 1938, **5**, 89–102.

RINSLAND, H. D. *A basic vocabulary of elementary school children.* New York: Macmillan, 1945.

THORNDIKE, E. L., and LORGE, I. *The teacher's word book of 30,000 words.* New York: Bur. of Publ., Teachers College, Columbia Univer., 1944.

WHORF, B. L. *Language, thought, and reality: selected writings.* Cambridge: Technology Press, 1956.

[3]

Control of Grammar in Imitation, Comprehension, and Production

Students of child language know that imitation is often *assimilatory:* the child hearing a sentence beyond his present competence does not exactly reproduce what has been modeled but rather produces something resembling the model that is within his present competence. At a certain time if you ask a child to imitate *Why can't a dog talk?* he will come back with *Why a dog can't talk?* If you ask him to imitate *John, who called, is her brother* he will come back with *John is her brother.* Results like these suggest that imitation must work through the grammatical knowledge of the imitator and cannot extend beyond it. One of the interesting results of the experiment reported in the present paper is the demonstration that children can, in some circumstances, correctly imitate sentences that they do not understand, preserving, for instance, grammatical distinctions they seem unable to analyze'in a test of comprehension. Apparently, accurate imitation of sentences does

This paper was written in collaboration with Colin Fraser and Ursula Bellugi. It was published in *Journal of Verbal Learning and Verbal Behavior* Vol. 2, No. 2 (August 1963), 121–135. Reprinted by permission of the authors.

not presuppose the ability to make a complete analysis of everything in the sentences. Exactly how much analysis must be possible
we still do not know.

"MOST WRITERS AGREE that the child under-
stands the language of others considerably before he actually
uses language himself." This sentence is from Dorothea
McCarthy's comprehensive review (1954, p. 520) of research
on the speech of children, and the sentence is certainly an
accurate summary of what most writers have written. It is also
an accurate summary of what parents believe that they have
observed. We will separate out several senses of the thesis,
review the relevant evidence, and report some new data bearing
on the understanding and production of grammatical features
in speech.

The assertion that understanding precedes production can
be taken to mean that *some* utterances are ordinarily understood before *any* utterances are produced. There is strong
empirical support for this thesis if we are willing to accept the
production of an appropriate response as evidence that an
utterance has been understood. There are just two kinds of
appropriate response that have been commonly reported for
children. When an utterance makes reference the child sometimes identifies the referent; when an utterance is intended to
be an imperative the child sometimes performs the designated
action. Gesell and Thompson (1934), for instance, tested
understanding of the questions: "Where is the cup?" "Where
is the shoe?" "Where is the box?" by placing the child before
a table on which rested a cup, a shoe, and a box and noting
his identifying responses. Bühler and Hetzer (1935), in testing the child's understanding of such commands as "Get
up" and "Lie down" and "Give that to me," required that the
designated actions be performed. Appropriate responses of
these two kinds are regularly obtained from normal children
before any intelligible speech is heard. Indeed, Lenneberg
(1962) has demonstrated linguistic comprehension of a high

order in an eight-year-old child who is completely anarthric (speechless). In addition, the chimpanzee Gua, who was raised by the Kelloggs (1933), could, at the age of nine months, make appropriate reaction to some seventy utterances though she never learned to speak at all. The Hayeses' chimpanzee, Viki, eventually approximated the sounds of several words but before she could do this she seemed to understand many utterances (Hayes, 1951).

The fact that some utterances usually seem to be understood before any recognizable utterances are produced is a generalization of little significance. The responses that suggest comprehension of an utterance include such very simple actions as orientation of the head, reaching, and grasping. It is not remarkable that some of these responses, those that are congenial to the child or animal, should come under the control of speech stimuli when the organism is not able to perform any of the culturally patterned articulatory movements that constitute speech. Any infant that can clap its hands can appear to its parents to understand "Pat-a-cake"; any animal that can run to its food dish can appear to its owner to understand "Come and get it." Certainly speech can operate as a signal for various nonverbal responses in many organisms that do not produce any speech.

The thesis that understanding precedes production is more interesting in a second form: Particular utterances or features of an utterance are ordinarily understood before the same utterances or features are produced. Our experiment is concerned with this version of the thesis in the case of particular features that are grammatical. Ervin and Miller, in their review of research on the development of language (1963) find that only a few studies have been made which bear, directly or indirectly, on the problem of the development of passive control of grammatical patterns. Neither these studies nor the ordinary observations made by parents provide evidence adequate to establish the thesis that passive control or understanding precedes productive use.

A monograph by Kahane, Kahane, and Saporta (1958) illustrates one sort of evidence. Working from previously published materials on children learning French, English, or

German, the authors find that the verbal categories of tense, voice, aspect, and agreement are understood before they are marked in speech. For example, one child is reported to have said "This mine" on a certain occasion and on another occasion "Glenna on bus." There is no verb in either utterance and no marking for tense. However, the parents of the child suggest that the first utterance really means "This *is* mine" and the second, "Glenna *was* on a bus." The Kahanes and Saporta take the parents' word for it and credit the child with understanding a distinction of tense that he is not yet marking. The authors do not go on to say that the child would understand distinctions of tense in the speech of another person but that is a reasonable extension of their position.

How do parents arrive at a gloss for a child's utterance such as "Glenna was on a bus" for "Glenna on bus?" Presumably there was situational support for the linguistic expansion. Perhaps the person named was at home when the child spoke but, on the previous day, had been on a bus. In these circumstances the parents would have said, "Glenna was on a bus" and what the parents would have said is what the child is presumed to have meant. The inference may be correct but it is not appropriate for determining whether understanding does or does not precede expression. When children first begin to combine words, these combinations are "telegraphic" (Brown and Fraser, 1963) and so grammatically incomplete. If whenever a child produces such an incomplete sentence he is to be credited with understanding the complete sentence that an adult would have produced in his circumstances, then the child's understanding must necessarily seem to be in advance of his production. To make an empirical test of the assertion that understanding precedes production one must look for evidence of understanding in the behavior of the child and not simply for the absence of linguistic expression from the child combined with an interpretation by his parents.

Parents, including linguists and psychologists, often see, in their own children, behavior that they take to be evidence of a grammatical understanding that surpasses production. A child who never produces the kind of question that places the verb before the subject may nevertheless appropriately answer

"Yes" (or "No") to such a question as "Are you hungry?" Before concluding that the child understands the significance of the verb–subject word order, however, one should try the effect of the single word "Hungry?" spoken with rising interrogative intonation or even without the intonation. A child who never produces a sentence containing both an indirect and a direct object may nevertheless respond appropriately to: "Bring your game to me." Again, however, one cannot tell whether the grammatical feature has been understood unless appropriate variations are tried. Would the child's response change if one were to say: "Bring me to your game"? Parents do not do control experiments of this kind.

The set of sentences used by Gesell and Thompson in connection with a cup, a shoe, and a box is well designed to test understanding of the substantive words *cup*, *shoe*, and *box*. In the sentence frame "Where is the ——?" they permute the three nouns, and the response pattern reveals whether the variable element has been understood. These sentences do not test understanding of the interrogative pronoun *where* since this word is constant across all sentences. Most controlled tests of comprehension focus on the content words, especially on nouns and adjectives. However, there is an occasional exception in the literature that points the way to a test of grammatical comprehension. Gesell and Thompson, for example, have asked children to "Put the block *in* the cup." and have also asked them to "Put the block *over* the cup." By making a function word a variable they obtain evidence on the understanding of such words. No one seems to have compared this kind of evidence for the passive control of grammar in normal children with evidence of active or productive control in the same children, and we have done an experiment to fill the gap.

When we tried to think of tests of the productive control of grammar we found that production might mean any one of three things. (1) It could mean the spontaneous performance of grammatically contrasting utterances in the absence of any identifiable controlling stimuli. To find out whether particular productions of this kind had or had not occurred, an investigator would need to have the record of a child's total speech output and that is never possible. A systematic study of production must work with controlling stimuli of some kind, and here there are two possibilities: (2) The controlling stimuli could be model performances of the utterances under investigation, in which case the subject's productions would be imitations; or (3) the controlling stimuli could be reference conditions appropriate to the emission of the utterances, in which case the subject's performances would qualify as evidence of understanding, but the evidence would be appropriate speech rather than appropriate pointing. This third performance we will call *Production* and abbreviate as *P*; the performance that follows a model utterance we will call *Imitation* and abbreviate as *I*. The experiment we have done compares understanding or *Comprehension* (*C*) with production in the sense of *P* and also with production in the sense of *I*, but not with spontaneous production. Which kind of production it is that has been supposed to follow understanding, we cannot tell.

OPERATIONS FOR TESTING *IMITATION*, *COMPREHENSION*, AND *PRODUCTION*

Consider now a concrete problem drawn from those we have devised to test *Comprehension*, *Imitation*, and *Production*. We begin with a pair of sentences: "The sheep is jumping" and "The sheep are jumping." These two sentences are identical except for the auxiliary verb, which is marked for a singular subject in the first sentence and for a plural subject in the second. Ordinarily in English the noun would also be marked (for example: "The dog is jumping" as opposed to "The dogs are jumping"), and so there would be redundancy in the grammatical marking of number. We selected the irregular noun *sheep* so as to eliminate this redundancy and isolate a single grammatical variable.

For each of the two sentences there is an appropriate picture (see Figure 3–1). In both pictures there are two sheep and a small hurdle. In one picture a single sheep jumps while the other looks on; in the other picture both sheep jump. It is necessary to have two sheep in both pictures so that a subject cannot simply match each sentence with its correct picture by noting whether the picture contains one sheep or more than one. This is necessary because the grammatical contrast presented does not encode the number of sheep present but the number of sheep performing a certain action.

Figure 3–1. Pictures Illustrating a Grammatical Contrast. Left, "The sheep is jumping"; Right, "The sheep are jumping."

There are three tasks: *I*, *C*, and *P*. For the *Comprehension* task (*C*) the experimenter shows the two pictures and names them, but without revealing which name belongs to which picture. The experimenter then speaks one of the sentences and asks the subject to point to the picture named. The experimenter then speaks the other sentence and asks the subject to point once more. The subject is not asked to speak at all. His appropriate response that can give evidence of comprehension is selective pointing.

In the *Imitation* procedure (*I*) no pictures are used. The experimenter speaks two sentences that are grammatically equivalent to the two used in *C* (e.g., "The sheep is walking"; "The sheep are walking"). The subject is then asked to imitate these, one at a time, following repetitions by the experimenter. Since we want to know whether the subject will imitate the features of the sentences that are crucial for correct pointing in the *C* procedure, we score, in the *I* task, only the subject's retention of the contrasting *is* and *are*. His rendering of other parts of the utterance does not affect his score.

In the *Production* procedure (*P*) pictures are once again used—new pictures to match a pair of sentences grammatically equivalent to those used in the other tasks ("The sheep is eating"; "The sheep are eating"). The subject is twice told the names of the two pictures but not which name goes with which picture. The *I* and *C* tasks by their very nature require the experimenter to speak the contrasting sentences twice each. The *P* task does not by its nature necessitate a repetition of the sentences, but we introduced this feature into the *P* procedure in order to equate, across tasks, the subject's exposure to each grammatical contrast. After repeating the names of the pictures the experimenter points to one picture at a time and asks the subject to name it. As with the *I* procedure we score only the grammatical contrast in the subject's rendition of the sentences, but to be scored correct for *P* the contrast has to be appropriately matched with the pictures.

HYPOTHESES

Imitation (I), Comprehension (C), and *Production (P)* will, in this paper, be called *procedures* or *tasks*. The experimental materials, we shall see, are made up of ten different grammatical contrasts, and these will be called *problems*. The contrast we have described, between the singular and the plural marked by *is* and *are*, is one such problem. Each of the ten problems was administered in all three tasks or procedures.

The rough prediction that comprehension will be superior to production can be somewhat refined if we think about the psychological operations that would seem to be required for *I, C*, and *P*. For all three tasks the subject must notice and retain the critical difference between the two sentences that make a pair. For the sample sentences we have been considering the contrast between *is* and *are* must be attended to and identified as a change that matters, as accidental variations of articulation and tone do not matter. A correct performance on all tasks depends upon common operations of perception, attention, and memory; the quality of these operations may depend on the nature of the sentence contrast, on its embeddedness, its familiarity, the number of redundant features, and the total length of the sentences. There is reason to expect, therefore, that the order of difficulty of the ten grammatical problems should be similar in all three tasks.

There is reason to expect that the three tasks across all ten problems will show consistent differential difficulty. To perform correctly on I it would seem that a subject must not only perceive the contrast between the two sentences but must also have sufficient motor control of speech to produce the difference. To perform correctly on C, the subject must perceive the difference between the sentences and also the difference between the two pictures and know how the referential contrast is related to the grammatical contrast; he must have motor control of pointing but need not have motor control of the speech contrast. The P task requires all the operations of both I and C, save only the pointing that is required for C. P, then, would seem to be more complex than I since P entails more operations than I. P would seem to be more complex than C since it requires control of speech rather than pointing. If the likelihood of successful performance is inversely related to the number of psychological operations that must be performed in near simultaneity and to the complexity of these operations, then P should be more difficult than either I or C. In terms of the number of correct answers, then, we might expect $I > P$ and $C > P$. However, it is possible that the referential contrast offers situational support for the sentence contrast; without the pictures it may be difficult to pick up the difference in the sentences. This possibility would lead us to expect $P > I$ and $C > I$.

There are still other ways of thinking about the psychological operations underlying the three tasks. Perhaps imitation is not a purely perceptual-motor task; perhaps it usually works through the meaning system. Decroly (circa 1934), for instance, has argued that a child can only distinguish those words to which he gives a meaning, and since perceptual differentiation is necessary for imitation, imitation cannot succeed when understanding is absent. One might argue for the same prediction in a different way: perhaps, in imitation, one ordinarily decodes a sentence, retains it as a meaning, and then encodes it for production. It may be difficult to retain sentences in any form other than as meanings. This argument, like Decroly's, predicts $C > I$.

There is another possibility. Speech is a much simpler system than reference, (Brown, 1958, pp. 202–216). Speech can be analyzed into a small number of distinctive features on both the acoustic and articulational levels. The total domain of reference does not yield to any such simple systematic

Table 3–1. Possible Outcomes and Reasons for Expecting Each One

$I > C$	*Imitation* depends only on the perceptual-motor organization of speech, whereas *Comprehension* depends on reference, and reference is more complex than speech.
$C > I$	*Imitation* is not a purely perceptual-motor task but depends upon *Comprehension*, either for the perceptual differentiation of sentences or for their retention.
$I > P$	*Production* entails all the operations of *Imitation* and, in addition, depends upon knowledge of referential distinctions.
$P > I$	The presence of the pictures in *Production* facilitates the perceptual differentiation and retention of the sentences.
$C > P$	*Comprehension* and *Production* entail the same operations except that, whereas *Comprehension* calls for control of pointing, *Production* calls for control of speech and pointing is simpler than speech.
$P > C$	No reason why this should be so.

analysis. Consequently, we would expect control of the speech system to be more complete than control of the reference system, and that is the case since most adult speakers perfectly control speech but are far from knowing all the referential rules of their language. A sampling of referential problems of the kind used in our experiment would be likely to include some that children do not control, though these children may already control, perceptually and motorically, all the distinctive features of speech. If this were the case, then we should expect $I > C$.

There are three tasks. If we consider them in pairs and think only of the relation "more correct than" ($>$) then there are six possible outcomes. It is possible to think of a reason or a combination of reasons that will predict any of these except $P > C$. These two tasks are identical except that, where C

requires selective pointing, P requires selective speech and it is difficult to conceive of speech as easier than pointing. It seems almost inevitable that $C > P$ and this prediction may be what some writers have meant when they said that comprehension precedes production. When the thesis is operationalized in this way an obviousness is exposed that goes undetected in vaguer formulations. However, if we understand the thesis to say that $C > I$ then it is not obvious since one can argue with at least equal conviction for $I > C$. The thesis does not predict the relative difficulty of I and P. The six possible relations of inequality for the tasks I, C, and P are listed in Table 3–1 opposite the reasons for expecting each one. The experiment was done to find out which of the possible outcomes would occur.

METHOD

The Imitation–Comprehension–Production (ICP) Test

The test involves ten grammatical contrasts. A grammatical contrast is always created by the use of two utterances which are identical but for some grammatical feature. Subjects were

Table 3–2. Sample Utterances (Set A) and Scoring for the ICP Test

Practice items

The girl with the big hat.	The boy with the blue belt.
The girl playing with the doll.	The bunny eating the carrot.
The cat with the brown face.	The dog with the black tail.
The boy playing with the truck.	The mouse eating the cracker.

1. Mass noun/Count noun.
   Utterances: Some mog/A dap.
               Some pim/A ked.
   Scoring: *Some*/*A* + any nonsense syllables or appropriate English words.

2. Singular/Plural, marked by inflections.
   Utterances: The boy draws/The boys draw.
               The kitten plays/The kittens play.
   Scoring: Noun without inflection and verb with -*s*/Noun with -*s* and verb
               without inflection.

3. Singular/Plural, marked by *is* and *are*.
    Utterances: The deer is running/The deer are running.
        The sheep is eating/The sheep are eating.
    Scoring: *Is/Are*.

4. Present progressive tense/Past tense.
    Utterances: The paint is spilling/The paint spilled.
        The boy is jumping/The boy jumped.
    Scoring: *Is* and verb with -*ing*/No auxiliary and verb with -*d*.

5. Present progressive tense/Future tense.
    Utterances: The girl is drinking/The girl will drink.
        The baby is climbing/The baby will climb.
    Scoring: *Is* and verb with -*ing*/*Will* and verb without inflection.

6. Affirmative/Negative.
    Utterances: The girl is cooking/The girl is not cooking.
        The boy is sitting/The boy is not sitting.
    Scoring: Absence of *not*/Presence of *not*, + some assertion.

7. Singular/Plural, of 3rd-person possessive pronouns.
    Utterances: His wagon/Their wagon.
        Her dog/Their dog.
    Scoring: *His* or *her*/*Their*.

8. Subject/Object, in the active voice.
    Utterances: The train bumps the car/The car bumps the train.
        The mommy kisses the daddy/The daddy kisses the mommy.
    Scoring: Noun$_1$ + active form of verb + noun$_2$/Noun$_2$ + active form of verb + noun$_1$.

9. Subject/Object, in the passive voice.
    Utterances: The car is bumped by the train/The train is bumped by the car.
        The daddy is kissed by the mommy/The mommy is kissed by the daddy.
    Scoring: Noun$_1$ + verb + *d* + *by* + noun$_2$/Noun$_2$ + verb + *d* + *by* + noun$_1$.

10. Indirect object/Direct object.
    Utterances: The girl shows the cat the dog/The girl shows the dog the cat.
        The boy brings the fish the bird/The boy brings the bird the fish.
    Scoring: Any verb + noun$_1$ + noun$_2$/Any verb + noun$_2$ + noun$_1$.

required to process the grammatical distinctions in each of the three ways described above.

Examples of the ten grammatical contrasts presented in the ICP Test are listed in Table 3–2 together with the criteria for scoring them. These ten problems were selected because previous work (Brown and Fraser, 1963) had shown that complete productive mastery of the contrasts involved was not common in children before about four years and because pictorial representations of the differences of reference were possible.

We constructed six examples of each linguistic contrast, i.e., six pairs of utterances for each of the ten contrasts. The number of morphemes in the paired utterances necessarily varied from one grammatical contrast to another, but the six examples of any one contrast are of the same length. For all utterances, words familiar to young children are used: *cat, dog, mommy, daddy, boat, truck, fall, jump*, etc. The Mass noun/Count noun contrast utilizes nonsense syllables for the reason that the referential contrast between such real words as *some milk* (mass noun) and *a cup* (count noun) is clear on the lexical level. In such a case a subject would not need to know that when a noun in the singular can be preceded by *some* that that noun must be a mass noun, and that when a noun can be preceded by *a* the noun must be a count noun. However, when the utterances are ''some tiss'' and ''a heg,'' only the grammar of mass nouns and count nouns can guide a subject to the selection of an extended substance as *tiss* and a bounded object as a *heg*. The twelve nonsense syllables required for the Mass noun/Count noun problems were rated by adults as relatively easy to pronounce (pronunciability ratings of less than 3.50 in Appendix E of Underwood and Schulz, 1960).

For each grammatical contrast there are two utterance-pairs for *I*, two for *C*, and two for *P*. Tasks *C* and *P* involve a contrast of reference and so there are pictures to illustrate the utterances assigned to these procedures. The Massachusetts Institute of Technology Illustration Service made brightly colored line drawings on 7 × 5 in. white cards. All details of the drawings were specified by the investigators following the general principle that the representations of paired utterances should be identical in every respect except the one coded by the grammatical contrast. The two pictures making a pair usually involve the same creatures and things and actions but differ in subject–object relations, in the apparent time of an action, or in the number of creatures performing an action.

In addition to the grammatical contrast items the ICP Test includes four practice items involving utterances that contrast in their substantive words, e.g., "The cat with the brown face" and "The dog with the black tail." The corresponding pictures are of the two different animals. With these items the experimenter instructed the subject in the three procedures: *I*, *C*, and *P*.

All of the pictures were mounted in loose-leafed photograph albums. The pictures were inserted between a sheet of backing material and a transparent cover; this proved to be a good way to preserve them from excited and sticky fingers. The pictures belonging to a contrasting pair were mounted side by side in such a way that there was no consistent relationship on any problem between the order in which a verbal contrast was given and the positions (left or right) of the pictures.

Subjects

From a pretest we learned that children four years of age or older performed correctly on *I*, *C*, and *P* with most of the problems. To insure that the performances should not generally be perfect we needed to work with children under four years and the pretest suggested that three years was the lowest age at which the test procedures would usually be possible. Accordingly, we worked with children whose ages ranged from thirty-seven to forty-three months, the mean being forty months. They were twelve monolingual English-speaking children, six boys and six girls, attending one or another of four Cambridge, Massachusetts, preschools. In order to obtain twelve children who completed the test it was necessary to attempt the test with fifteen children, and so our sample selects in favor of the cooperative child.

Order of Tasks and Problems

We wanted to be certain that consistently correct responses should be possible only for subjects having control of the grammatical contrasts presented. A subject ought not to be able to infer correct responses from the positions of the pictures, the order of the problems, the order in which he was asked to respond to the parts of the contrast, or from any interrelationship among these variables. We also wanted our comparison of the quality of performance on *I*, *C*, and *P* to be free of practice effects. To make sure of these things we used counterbalanced and randomized orders.

Table 3–3. Order of Tasks and Problems Correct for Each Subject

			Order of Tasks[a]			Problems correct			
Subject	Age	Sex	1st	2nd	3rd	Imita-tion	Compre-hension	Pro-duction	Total
E	3;5	F	C(A)	I	P(B)	18	15	12	45
C	3;6	F	I	P(A)	C(B)	17	17	10	44
L	3;7	F	P(B)	C(A)	I	18	14	6	38
F	3;1	F	C(B)	I	P(A)	17	11	8	36
G	3;5	M	C(A)	(B)	I	17	9	6	32
K	3;3	M	P(A)	C(B)	I	13	11	4	28
D	3;5	F	I	P(B)	C(A)	15	9	3	27
B	3;5	M	I	C(B)	P(A)	13	8	3	24
J	3;6	M	P(B)	I	C(A)	10	10	2	22
I	3;2	M	P(A)	I	C(B)	12	3	2	17
H	3;3	F	C(B)	P(A)	I	7	8	1	16
A	3;1	M	I	C(A)	P(B)	9	6	0	15

[a] Letters in parentheses after C and P indicate use of Set A or Set B.

Each child was to do a full set of problems with each of the three tasks. It was necessary to continue with a given task until the full set of problems was completed since a pretest demonstrated that changes back and forth among the tasks confused the subject. Since the order in which a task was presented might affect the level of performance, each of the six possible task-orders was used with two children. The scheme can be seen in Table 3–3.

Of the six utterance-pairs constructed for each grammatical contrast, two pairs were to be used in *I*, and for these pairs no pictures had been drawn. Pictures had been prepared for the remaining four pairs since these were to be used in *C* and *P*.

While great care was taken to make equivalent all pairs that involved the same contrast, it seemed unwise always to use one set of utterances and pictures in *C* and the other set in *P*. Consequently, we divided the pictures and the utterances, matching them into sets A and B; the utterances of Set A appear in Table 3-2. For half of the subjects *C* was done with Set A and *P* with Set B; for the other half of the subjects the assignment of the sets was reversed. This scheme can be seen in Table 3-3

Within a task each child received the individual problems in a different random order though the same random order was used across tasks for a given child. There was one departure from randomness in these orders: the Subject/Object contrasts in the active voice were always given last. The same pictures were used for this contrast and for that in the passive voice, and we wanted to make sure that the active-voice problems had no opportunity to affect performance on the passive-voice problems. In a revised edition of the ICP Test, which we now use, this minor inconsistency has been eliminated by adding enough pictures to provide different sets for the active-voice and passive-voice problems.

Each single problem involved two utterances and both utterances were pronounced twice by the experimenter on all tasks. The first pronunciation simply presented the contrast, and the order in which the paired utterances were spoken was randomly determined. For tasks *I* and *C* the posing of a problem necessitates a second pronunciation (e.g., "Show me: 'The sheep are jumping.' ") but, for task *P*, the problems can be posed without a second pronunciation (e.g., "What is the name of this picture?"). A second pronunciation was, however, included in the *P* task so as to equate exposure to sentences across tasks. The second pronunciation in the *P* task immediately followed the first and reversed the order of the utterances in the first. For problems 1, 7, 8, 9, and 10 in Table 3-2 the order in which the paired items were posed was randomly determined in all tasks. The remaining problems (2, 3, 4, 5, and 6) were always posed, in all tasks, in a fixed order. Each of these contrasts involves a simple affirmative sentence with a singular subject and a verb in a present tense. If this sentence were presented first we thought it possible that the subject might point correctly and then, ignoring the grammatical contrast in the second sentence, point correctly again by exclusion. To guard against such a possibility the crucial utterance in each of these contrasts was presented first and the simple base form second.

Procedure

All testing was done in the preschools in small rooms with only the child and two experimenters present. One experimenter, who had previously visited the schools to become acquainted with the children, administered instructions and the test materials and encouraged and cajoled when necessary; the other experimenter made a written record of the child's responses and operated a Wollensak T-1500 tape-recorder, which recorded the entire session.

Before performing any of the three tasks, the subject was shown a colored picture-book and encouraged to talk about the pictures. This helped the child to overcome any reluctance to talk and provided a small sample of the child's spontaneous speech. To explain each of the three tasks (*I*, *C*, and *P*) and to test the subject's understanding of each task, the experimenter always began with the four practice items. To each subject the experimenter administered the tasks, the problems within a task, and the items within a problem in accordance with a predetermined schedule. The techniques of administration are described above as "Operations for Testing *Imitation*, *Comprehension*, and *Production*."

It was most expedient to continue testing a child in one session for as long as he proved cooperative and attentive. Three children succeeded in completing the entire performance in only one session each. Normally, however, two or three sessions on successive school days were necessary to take a child through all three tasks. With a few unavoidable exceptions, it was possible to make breaks in performance coincide with breaks between tasks. After performing both halves of an item, the subject, whether or not he had answered correctly, was encouraged by the experimenter with some such remark as: "That's the way." Nonverbal rewards were not used. For the *I* task, in which there were no pictures to hold the child's attention, a "divided attention" technique was sometimes necessary. The subject was allowed to hold some simple toy and the experimenter would administer an item whenever the child was not engrossed in the object.

RESULTS

Scoring

There were two records of each experimental session; one on tape and one written on the scene. The scorers took advantage of the information in both records. The criteria for scoring each problem appear in Table 3–2; a response was marked "correct" if it completely satisfied these criteria, and was otherwise marked incorrect. On the *C* task a subject sometimes pointed quickly, then reflected and corrected himself; the last definite pointing is the one we always scored. Two scorers independently scored all of the data (720 items). They agreed on 713 items or about 99 per cent of the total. The seven disagreements, which were almost evenly distributed among the three tasks, were resolved by discussion.

Quantitative Findings

Table 3–3 shows the age and sex of each subject, the order in which each performed the three tasks, and the number of problems correct for each task and for all tasks combined. Even within the restricted age range represented, there was a correlation between age and total score: $\rho = 0.48$, p slightly above 0.05. The girls did somewhat better than the boys, but the difference was not significant.

Before comparing performances on the three tasks we must report several preliminary analyses. Six subjects performed task *C* with Set A of the materials and task *P* with Set B and six subjects did the reverse. A two-way analysis of variance, Groups by Tasks, showed that neither the difference between the two groups ($F = .35$, $df = 1/30$) nor the interaction of Groups and Tasks ($F = .07$, $df = 2/30$) was significant. Therefore we will ignore in subsequent analyses the sets of materials used.

Table 3–4 shows the mean scores of subjects who did each of the tasks as the first task, the second task, or the third task. It is clear that order had no consistent effect on either I or C. On P, there was a slight tendency for subjects who performed P as their second task to do better than those who performed P first, and for those who did P last to score higher than those who did it second. However, it could not be demonstrated that this tendency was statistically significant. Three different analyses were performed: a two-way analysis of variance, Tasks by Order; a Kruskal-Wallis nonparametric analysis of variance covering P as the first, the second, and the third

Table 3–4. Mean Task Scores and Order of Performing Tasks

	Imitation	Compre-hension	Production
As 1st Task	13.50	10.75	3.50
As 2nd Task	14.25	9.75	5.00
As 3rd Task	13.75	9.75	5.75

task, with p being multiplied by $\frac{1}{6}$ to take account of the fact that the order obtained is the one to be expected if practice on the other tasks facilitates performance on P (see Chassan, 1960); and a Randomization Test comparing P as first task with P as third task. In none of these did order produce a p of even 0.10. Therefore, we shall ignore in subsequent analyses the order in which tasks were performed.

Because all three tasks involve operations of perception, attention, and memory, we predicted that the difficulty of the problems would be similar from task to task. In Table 3–5 the task scores for each problem appear. On any one problem the maximum possible score is 24 since there were always 2 items responded to by 12 subjects. The Spearman rank correlations for the difficulty of problems from task to task are: $\rho_{IC} = 0.64$ ($p > 0.05$); $\rho_{CP} = 0.72$ ($p < 0.05$); $\rho_{IP} = 0.68$ ($p < 0.05$).

In Table 3–1 we listed the six possible relations of inequality among the tasks, and now we can report which ones occurred. There might, of course, have been no significant inequalities among I, C, and P, but the Groups by Tasks analysis of variance reported above showed that there were significant differences among the tasks ($F = 16.05$, $df = 2/30$, $p<0.01$). We did t-tests between pairs of tasks (IC, CP, and IP) and found that all were significant with $p<0.01$. The mean number of correct responses of subjects on I was 13.83; on C, 10.08; and on P, 4.75. In short $I > C > P$. In Table 3–3 it can be seen

Table 3–5. Task Scores on Grammatical Problems in Order of Increasing Total Difficulty

Problem	Imita-tion	Compre-hension	Pro-duction	Total
Affirmative/Negative	18	17	12	47
Sing./Pl., of 3rd-person poss. prons.	23	15	8	46
Subject/Object, in active voice	19	16	11	46
Pres. Prog. tense/Future tense	20	16	6	42
Sing./Pl., marked by *is* and *are*	20	12	7	39
Pres. Prog. tense/Past tense	17	13	6	36
Mass noun/Count noun	12	13	1	26
Sing./Pl., marked by inflections	14	7	1	22
Subject/Object, in passive voice	12	7	2	21
Indirect Object/Direct Object	11	5	3	19

that this order holds with striking consistency for individual subjects. For all 12, $C > P$ and, for 9, $I > C$. In Table 3–5 it can be seen that the order held true for all but one of the grammatical problems; on that one (Mass noun/Count noun) C was higher than I by one point.

Guessing on the Tasks

On a very abstract level the three tasks, I, C, and P, make identical demands on the subject. In each task the experimenter provides two stimuli (s_1 and s_2) and requires two appropriately matched responses (r_1 and r_2). For I the stimuli are the two model utterances and the responses are the subject's pronunciations of the critical features of these two utterances in an order matching the order of the models. For C the two stimuli are again the two utterances, and the responses are pointing appropriately first to one picture and then to the other. For P the stimuli are provided by the experimenter pointing to the pictures, one at a time, and the responses are the subject's pronunciations of the critical features of the utterances corresponding to the pictures. The problem in all cases is to match r_1 to s_1, and r_2 to s_2.

For an adult subject the first pointing in any item of the C task (e.g., "Show me: 'The sheep are jumping.' ") would be a choice between two alternatives and the second pointing would be completely determined by the first. Consequently, for an adult subject the probability (p) of guessing a correct answer on any item in the absence of grammatical knowledge would be 0.50. This is a substantial probability, and since there do not seem to be comparable opportunities for a chance success on I and P, where the responses are speech, it may seem that chance gives an advantage to the C scores.

However, our three-year-old subjects did not handle the C task as adults would. On the practice materials, which involved familiar lexical distinctions, all the children did point first to one picture and then to the other, but this was because they were giving the correct answers.

On the grammar contrasts, too, when they saw the solution they pointed first to one picture and then to the other. However, when they did not see the solution, they often pointed twice to the same picture, acting as if the second pointing were completely independent of the first. They sometimes pointed simultaneously at both pictures, and one subject, on one occasion, gave an unscorable response. The probability of a chance success for these subjects was clearly less than 0.5. A case can be made for assuming it was 0.25 and a case can be made for assuming it was 0.11; neither case is perfectly satisfactory.

On the I and P tasks, too, there must have been some possibility of obtaining a chance success. The two relevant responses, r_1 and r_2, were twice produced by the experimenter just before the subject was asked to respond. If the subject randomly selected for production some number of words from those pronounced by the experimenter, then the subject would occasionally hit on the right combination to score a success. However, there is nothing to guide us in selecting an exact model for such a process. On the other hand, whenever the subject did produce first the one half of the grammatical contrast (r_1) and then the other half (r_2), the probability that these would occur in the correct order was 0.5, just as p was 0.5 when the subject pointed first to one picture (r_1) and then to the other (r_2). We have pulled out all the cases for each task in which both r_1 and r_2 were produced; the numbers appear in Table 3–6. Expansion of the binomial for $p = 0.5$ shows that

Table 3–6. Cases in which the Two Relevant Responses (r_1 and r_2) Were Produced

	Imitation	Compre- hension	Production
Total cases	167	168	68
Correct	166	121	57
Correct-incorrect	165	74	46

the numbers correct are well above chance on all tasks. It is possible to argue that there are likely to be as many lucky guesses included in the correct responses as there are unlucky guesses which appear as incorrect responses. If one subtracts the number incorrect from the number correct to obtain an estimate of the number of successes not obtained by chance, the order $I > C > P$ is preserved and the differences are still all significant with $p = 0.02$ or less.

The comparison of cases in which both r_1 and r_2 were produced disregards the differential probabilities involved in producing, if one had no knowledge of the grammatical contrast involved, two relevant points as opposed to two relevant utterances. The probabilities would certainly favor pointing. Table 3–6 indicates that response production came nearer to guaranteeing success on P and on I than it did on C. However, some such difference would seem to be intrinsic to the tasks in question and so we conclude that insofar as the tasks can be made comparably difficult, the order of control for three-year-olds is $I > C > P$.

Qualitative Findings

For the student of language acquisition who seeks to discover the grammatical operations that are developmentally prior to attainment of the rules followed by adult speakers, the procedures of the ICP Test will be useful. The incorrect responses to several problems in the present test are sufficiently regular to suggest the nature of the underlying operations. We will describe a single example.

Consider the Subject/Object contrast in the passive voice. While young children probably do not very often hear sentences in the passive voice they very frequently do hear all the individual morphemes involved; they hear *is*, *-ed*, and *by* if not *is chased by*. The *C* score for the passive-voice problems was only five correct. Evidently the sense of the passive construction cannot be guessed from a knowledge of its constituent elements. How do children process this construction when they do not correctly understand it?

Consider a sample pair of sentences: "The girl is pushed by the boy" and "The boy is pushed by the girl." When, for the *P* task, the experimenter pointed to the picture in which the girl was doing the pushing and asked for its name, the subject sometimes said: "The girl is pushed by the boy" and then, for the other picture, the subject spoke the other sentence. This is an incorrect response that perfectly preserves the form of the sentences but exactly reverses the correct pattern of application to the pictures. Five subjects responded in this way, and five is a large number when we recall (Table 3–6) that there were only eleven such reversals on *P* in all the data. In addition these five reverse responses seemed to be made with high confidence. What incorrect rule would generate such a performance?

In active-voice sentences, subject and object appear in that order, whereas in passive-voice sentences the order is object and subject. Suppose that the three-year-old processes each passive-voice sentence as though it were in the active voice.

"The girl is pushed by the boy" is not computed as: Object–Verb in the passive–Subject, but rather as: Subject–Verb in the active with odd appurtenances–Object. The odd appurtenances are *is*, *-ed*, and *by* which the subject may take to be signs of some uncommon tense like "will have pushed." Processing the sentence in this way would enable the subject to maintain the generality of the usual rule of English word order in which the subject precedes the object.

With the Subject/Object contrast in the passive voice we turned up a revealing pattern of evidence by accident. If an investigator wanted to use the ICP procedures to test hypotheses about particular aspects of grammatical operation, he could easily design problems that would be revealing by intention.

DISCUSSION

We predicted that the order of difficulty of the ten problems would be similar from task to task for the reason that all three tasks involve operations of perception, attention, and memory which should be affected by the nature of the sentences provided. The order of difficulty was indeed similar from task to task but there does not seem to be any single dimension of the contrasts that will account for the order. The contrast Singular/Plural marked by inflections may be harder than the contrast Singular/Plural marked by *is* and *are* because the bound morphemes are less well marked acoustically than are the free morphemes. The Subject/Object contrast may be easier in the active voice than in the passive voice because children hear fewer passive-voice sentences than active-voice sentences. Probably the order obtained for the problems is a complex resultant of many factors that increase difficulty including the perceptual obviousness of the contrast, the amount of redundancy in the contrast, the length of the total sentences, and the frequency with which the construction has been heard. It should be possible to investigate the importance of these variables with problems designed to that purpose.

Of the possible outcomes listed in Table 3–1, those that occurred are: $I > C$, $I > P$, and $C > P$. These occurrences reflect some credit on the ideas that led to their prediction and some discredit on the ideas that led to the prediction of their opposites. Because $I > C$ rather than $C > I$, it would seem that imitation is a perceptual-motor skill not dependent on comprehension. It would seem, in addition, that the highly systematic speech system is under more complete control at three years than is the less systematic and more complex referential system.

The conclusion that imitation is a perceptual-motor skill that does not work through the meaning system is supported by certain details in the data. Consider, for example, the Indirect object/Direct object contrast in such a pair as: "The woman gives the bunny the teddy" and "The woman gives the teddy the bunny." In five cases when subjects were given this problem, with appropriate pictures for the P task, they transformed the original sentences so as to express the indirect object with a prepositional phrase. They pointed correctly but instead of saying, "The woman gives the bunny the teddy" they said, "The woman gives the teddy to the bunny"; the latter construction is probably the more familiar of the two. If on the I task, these subjects had decoded the sentences into meanings, as they do on the P task, the same transformation ought to have occurred. It never did occur. On the I task the subject either correctly reproduced the originals or made errors that were not transformations. It seems reasonable to conclude that the imitation performance did not work through the meaning system.

Because $I > P$ occurred and $P > I$ did not, it would seem that increasing the number of psychological operations to be performed in near simultaneity increases the difficulty of the task. It would seem, in addition, that the presence of the referential contrast either does not have a facilitating effect on the perception and retention of the sentence contrast or else that the effect is less powerful than the one that results from increasing the number of operations. We have already concluded that imitation is a perceptual-motor performance and that speech is a simpler system than reference. It is consistent now to add that the sentences of the test could usually be differentiated and retained without the support of reference.

Because $C > P$ occurred and $P > C$ did not, it would seem that the motor control of speech is more complicated than the motor control of pointing. We could not imagine that the contrary of this proposition would be true, and so this prediction was labelled obvious and the obvious worked out. How stands the thesis that understanding precedes production in the development of child speech? The thesis is true if by production we mean task P, since C scores were higher than P scores. This outcome suggests that children learn a lot about the referential patterning, the stimulus control of grammatical forms, before they produce these forms. This learning which precedes the linguistic response may be a purely s-s registration of the correspondence between constructions produced by others and the circumstances of production, but, as our operation for testing comprehension shows, it need not be. Understanding could be s-r learning in which the r is some nonlinguistic response such as pointing. Production occurs when the appropriate linguistic response begins to appear, conforming to a stimulus pattern that may originally have been established in connection with nonlinguistic responses.

The thesis that understanding precedes production is false if by production we mean task I, since C scores were lower than I scores. It is very possible, however, that this latter outcome would reverse with still younger children. The longest sentences of the ICP Test were only eight morphemes long, which means they were easily within the sentence-programming span of three-year-old children. However, the much shorter span of children at about 2:6 should compel such younger children, in the I task, to "reduce" the model sentences of the ICP Test. Brown and Fraser (1963) have shown that such reductions are accomplished by dropping the function words of the sentence, leaving a "telegraphic" string of nouns and verbs. The function words are the essential elements in which the sentences of the ICP Test contrast. Perhaps, then, 2-year-olds will omit these words in I and yet show by correct pointings on C that they can internally process more words than they can "print out." Such an outcome would suggest the existence of a longer span for internal sentence computation than for sentence production. We are now trying to adapt the ICP procedures to that least docile of subjects, the child between two and three.

SUMMARY

The familiar assertion that, in language development, understanding precedes production was tested for ten grammatical contrasts with twelve three-year-old children. Understanding was operationalized as the correct identification of pictures named by contrasting sentences. Production was operationalized in two ways: (a) as the correct imitation of contrasting features in sentences without evidence of understanding; and (b) as the correct production of contrasting features in sentences applied appropriately to pictures. Production, in the second sense, proves to be less advanced than understanding in three-year-old children. However, production in the sense of imitation proves to be more advanced than understanding in three-year-olds.

References

BROWN, R. *Words and things*. New York: Free Press, 1958.
BROWN, R., AND FRASER, C. The acquisition of syntax. In C. N. Cofer and Barbara S. Musgrave (Eds.) *Verbal behavior and learning: Problems and processes*. New York: McGraw-Hill, 1963.
BUHLER, C., AND HETZER, H. *Testing children's development from birth to school age*. New York: Farrar and Rinehart, 1935.
CHASSAN, J. B. On a test for order. *Biometrics*, 1960, **16**, 119–121.
DECROLY, O. Comment l'enfant arrive à parler. *Cahiers de la centrale* (Centrale du P.P.S. de Belgique), circa 1934, **8**, 1–306.
ERVIN, SUSAN M., AND MILLER, W. Language development. In Child Psychology, *Yearb. nat. Soc. Stud. Educ.*, 1963.

GESELL, A., AND THOMPSON, H. *Infant behavior.* New York: McGraw-Hill, 1934.

HAYES, CATHY. *The ape in our house.* New York: Harper, 1951.

KAHANE, H., KAHANE, R. AND SAPORTA, S. *Development of verbal categories in child language.* Bloomington, Indiana: Indiana University Res. Ctr. Anthrop. Folklore, Ling., 1958.

KELLOGG, W. N., AND KELLOGG, LOUISE A. *The ape and the child.* New York: McGraw-Hill, 1933.

LENNEBERG, E. H. Understanding language without ability to speak: A case report. *J. abnorm. soc. Psychol.*, 1962, **65,** 419–425.

MCCARTHY, DOROTHEA. Language development in children. In L. Carmichael (Ed.) *Manual of child psychology.* New York: Wiley, 1954.

UNDERWOOD, B. J., AND SCHULZ, R. W. *Meaningfulness and verbal learning.* Philadelphia: Lippincott, 1960.

[4]

Explorations in Grammar Evaluation

Why reprint this paper? It fails to solve the problem it sets: definition of an explicit and quantitative criterion by which one might judge one candidate-grammar, written to fit a particular corpus of child speech, superior to another candidate-grammar. The failure is understandable; the goal was much too ambitious. The effort seems worth reprinting because it clarifies the problems involved in discovering the grammar implicit in a child's utterances. In addition, I have a hunch that the indices, so crudely formulated in this paper, will have a more refined future in computational linguistics.

Since the paper quite conclusively demonstrates that it is not possible to prove that any given grammar is the right grammar for a sample of child speech, how does it happen that quite a few of us, nevertheless, went on to attempt the writing of such grammars? It happens because the demonstration was based, in part, on a mis-

The paper was written for a conference on the acquisition of language sponsored by the Social Sciences Research Council and held at M.I.T.'s Endicott House. Ursula Bellugi and I edited the report of the conference ("The acquisition of language," *Monographs of the Society for Research in Child Development*, 1964, Vol. 29, No. 1, Serial No. 92, 79–92) and I guess one could say that this report set the contemporary study of child language on its slightly shaky legs. Colin Fraser and Ursula Bellugi were co-authors of the paper. Reprinted by permission of the authors.

conception that could be corrected. In this paper candidate-grammars are evaluated only in terms of their ability to predict future sentences (or generate grammatical sentences) without predicting sentences that will not occur (or generating ungrammatical sentences). But much more can be, and ordinarily is, demanded of a generative grammar. In particular, such a grammar is expected to assign each sentence a correct structural description. Shortly after the present paper was published we learned that there are data in the spoken discourse of child and parent from which quite a bit can be learned about the structural descriptions that it is appropriate to assign child sentences. When grammars are required to fit these data, or to generate these descriptions, they are much harder to write and are also more likely to be correct. It is no longer easy to think of numerous equally good alternative grammars. Less easy but still possible. The grammars written remain far from fully determinate. The test of their rightness and, in general, of the rightness of interpretations of child speech is going to be the same as the test of any theory. Not some quantitative index but the degree of congruence with what is known and the relative ability to unlock the unknown will choose among grammars.

IN THE 1961 EDITION of Gleason's *An Introduction to Descriptive Linguistics* the following paragraph appears:

The difference between a description of a corpus and of a language is partly a matter of scope. A corpus consists of a few thousand sentences. A language might be considered as consisting of a very large number of sentences—all those, either already spoken or not yet used, which would be accepted by native speakers as "belonging" to that language. Even the largest corpus can be only an infinitesimal portion of the language (pp. 196–197.)[1]

In the summer of 1961 we collected 26 hours of speech in one week from a 24-month-old boy whom we are calling Abel. In

[1] This statement does not represent Gleason's final opinion but is for him, as for us, the starting point of an extended argument. In chapter 13 of *An Introduction to Descriptive Linguistics* (1961) the reader will find Gleason's full discussion of the relation between language and grammars.

26 hours Abel produced 2,081 different utterances. These utterances are a corpus and Abel is a native speaker. The problem is to find Abel's *language*.

Here are fragments of two additional paragraphs from Gleason:

A second corpus of roughly comparable scope should also exemplify a similarly high percentage of the pertinent constructional patterns. This being the case, the greater part of the grammatical features of either corpus should be shared by the other.

This gives a test for a grammar. It is only necessary to elicit another sample, independent of the first. If the grammar fits the new corpus equally well, it is highly probable that it is correct (p. 201).

A grammar is a set of generalizations induced from given data but going beyond the given data. Consequently a grammar makes predictions. From things already said, a grammar predicts things likely to be said and things not likely to be said. For the linguist working with adults an important test of the grammar written from one corpus is its ability to anticipate the sentences of a new corpus. This test is also available to the student of child speech.

The prediction test has never been made precise. The linguist in the field does not write down alternative grammars, generate predictions, and keep track of outcomes. He works at a single grammar, revising it so as to accommodate new data, but never subjecting it to an explicit, comparative, quantitative evaluation. Is such an evaluation possible? We are able to imagine some relevant calculations, and, being empirical mathematicians who do not know what numbers will do until they do it, we decided to work through some exercises with Abel's utterances.

The transcribed utterances were divided into two sets: one consisted of the utterances produced in fifteen hours (the fifteen-hour corpus) and the other of utterances produced in eleven hours (the eleven-hour corpus). The division was made in such a way as to guarantee that the two sets were similar to one another in the proportions of speech taken from each day and from each time of day. It was our plan to study first the fifteen-hour corpus and, from this study, to write grammatical rules whose predictions would be tested against the utterances obtained in the eleven-hour corpus.

We began with a restricted grammar written from a subset of the utterances in the fifteen-hour corpus. The subset consisted of all two-word utterances created from a list of seventy-nine words which were selected because they occurred frequently and in a variety of contexts. The restricted grammar was written from and designed to generate all of the two-word utterances using the given lexicon of seventy-nine words in the fifteen-hour corpus, and it was tested by its ability to anticipate such utterances in the eleven-hour corpus. The subset of utterances was chosen so as to reveal with maximal clarity certain problems that arise in the evaluation of any grammars written from the speech of very young children.

The lexicon of seventy-nine words appears as Table 4–1. On the distributional evidence (see Brown and Fraser, 1963) of the fifteen-hour corpus the seventy-nine words were placed

Table 4–1. The Sample Lexicon

a	blanket	cookie	George	need	shovel	this
Abel	block	cup	get	nice	sock	throw
all	boat	Da	glass	no	some	two
another	book	Daddy	hat	on	soup	up
away	box	down	here	one	sweep	want
Baby	bubble-drink	draw	in	orange	swim	water
ball	bye-bye	eat	jump	paper	table	where
bathtub	cake	eye	man	pencil	telephone	
bed	car	find	milk	penny	tiger	
bell	chair	firetruck	Mommie	pillow	that	
big	clean	for	more	ring	the	
bike	coffee	fork	my	see	there	

in thirteen syntactic classes. There were five residual words which had little in common with the members of any syntactic class or with one another, and these must be dealt with individually. Adult speakers of English use a terminal sibilant inflection to pluralize regular count nouns and to mark the third-person present indicative of regular verbs. Abel sometimes used such an inflection, but he would add it to mass nouns as well as to count nouns and to any verb in any person.

We provided for these possibilities by allowing a terminal [s] to occur with any member of four syntactic classes: count nouns, mass nouns, transitive verbs, intransitive verbs. This rule has the effect of entering each noun and verb into a lexicon twice and so brings the total number of words to 128. The classified lexicon appears as Table 4–2.

Table 4–2. The Lexicon Distributed among Word Classes

Word Class	Lexicon
Definite articles (Art$_d$)	*my, the, two*
Indefinite articles (Art$_i$)	*a, another*
Descriptive adjectives (Adj)	*big, nice*
Count nouns (N$_c$)	*ball, bathtub, bed, bell, bike, blanket, block, boat, book, box, cake, car, chair, cookie, cup, eye, firetruck, fork, glass, hat, jump, man, orange, pencil, penny, pillow, ring, shovel, sock, table, telephone, tiger* (Plus -*s*)
Mass nouns (N$_m$)	*bubble-drink, coffee, milk, paper, soup, water* (Plus -*s*)
Proper nouns (N$_p$)	*Abel, George, Baby, Mommie, Daddy, Da*
Intransitive verbs (V$_{in}$)	*sweep, swim* (Plus -*s*)
Transitive verbs (V$_t$)	*clean, draw, eat, find, get, need, see, throw, want* (Plus -*s*)
Locatives (Loc)	*here, there*
Demonstrative pronouns (Pro$_d$)	*this, that*
Prepositions 1 (Pr$_1$)	*away, down, up*
Prepositions 2 (Pr$_2$)	*in, on*
Qualifiers	*all, more, some*
Others	*where, for, bye-bye, no, one*

In order to determine how Abel combined the lexical items to form two-word utterances, we constructed the matrix of Table 4–3 in which the thirteen classes and five residual words are listed on each axis. The abscissa is the word in initial position, and the ordinate the word in second position. An " × " means that one or more combinations of the type indicated occurred (e.g., Art$_d$ + N$_c$), and a blank that no combinations of the type indicated occurred (e.g., N$_c$ + Art$_d$).

From this matrix it is possible to write a rule for each class and each residual word describing the classes and words that have followed it and those that have preceded it. These rules may be considered a two-word grammar which produces all of the 371 two-word combinations of the designated lexicon. In addition, of course, the grammar generalizes the distributional facts of the 371 utterances since it permits the formation of all utterances of a given type if at least one utterance of that type has actually occurred.

It was then possible to determine the total number of combinations predicted by the rules. For example: there are three definite articles (*my*, *the*, and *two*). The first rule says that each of these can occur with any count noun (32 in the singular and 32 in the plural, or 64). Multiplying 3×64 yields 192 possible combinations of the type: $\text{Art}_d + \text{N}_c$. The three definite articles can also occur with all of the six mass nouns in either the singular or plural, and the result is 3×12, or 36 additional sentences. Finally, the grammar says that the three articles can occur with the six proper nouns, which is 18 more. The total number of utterances predicted by the first rule is then: $192 + 36 + 18$, or 246. Proceeding in this fashion through all the rules, we found that the grammar as a whole generates 13,154 different utterances.

We looked next at the utterances of the 11-hour corpus selecting out all of the two-word combinations made up from the original lexicon. There are 90 exact repetitions of utterances from the original 371; 105 utterances predicted by the grammar but not in the original set; eight not predicted by the grammar. Clearly this grammar predicts most of the events of the second set that fall within its purview. Is it then a good grammar? Is it a better description of Abel's behavior than some other possible description?

We decided first to compare the grammar with a maximally general and simple prediction, a prediction of all possible combinations of two forms drawn from the lexicon. The total number of possible combinations is 16,384, and this figure includes 3,230 combinations not predicted by the grammar. For the obtained utterances of the second set the total-combinations rule predicts all 203 whereas the grammar predicts $203 - 8$, or 195.

As a third comparison we decided to consider the obtained

Table 4-3. The Matrix of Two-Word Combinations

Word	Art_d	Art_i	Adj	N_c	N_m	N_p	V_{in}	V_t	Loc	Pro_d	Pr_1	Pr_2	Qual	Where	For	Bye-bye	No	One
Art_d				X	X	X				X								
Art_i				X														
Adj				X	X		X	X										
N_c	X	X	X	X	X	X	X	X	X	X	X	X	X	X		X	X	X
N_m	X		X	X	X	X	X	X	X	X		X	X	X		X	X	X
N_p	X			X	X	X	X	X	X	X	X	X	X	X	X	X	X	
V_{in}			X						X	X			X					
V_t			X	X	X	X	X	X	X	X			X					
Loc											X							
Pro_d												X	X					
Pr_1				X	X								X				X	X
Pr_2				X	X								X					
Qual																	X	X
Where											X							
For														X				
Bye-bye																	X	
No																		
One									X	X								

Note.—"X" indicates that utterances of this type occurred.

371 utterances of the first set as predictors of the second set. What happens if we simply say that Abel does with two-word combinations in one corpus what he does with such combinations in the other corpus. In the second set there are 90 exact repetitions of utterances in the first set, and these are the only utterances predicted; the remaining 113 are not predicted. The numbers for the various kinds of combinations appear in Table 4–4.

Table 4–4. Two-Word Combinations in the 15-hour Corpus and in the 11-hour Corpus

15-hour Corpus

Number of forms in lexicon	128
Obtained combinations	371
Combinations grammar predicts	13,154
All possible combinations	16,384
Possible combinations not predicted by grammar	3,230

11-hour Corpus

Number of forms in lexicon	128
Obtained combinations	203
Exact repetitions	90
Predicted by grammar but not repetitions	105
Not predicted by grammar but obtained	8

Clearly it is to the credit of a grammar if occurring utterances are predicted, and to its discredit if occurring utterances are not predicted. On first thought, then, we might express the value of a grammar as the ratio of occurrences predicted to occurrences not predicted. The three ratios for the grammar, the total-combinations rule, and the original list rule appear in Table 4–5 under the heading "Ratio A."

The total-combinations rule has the largest ratio, of course, since it predicts everything conceivable. The grammar is next best, and the first set of utterances is least good. This index alone must therefore be insufficient since it would always lead us to prefer the same description—all possible combinations of items. This first ratio (A) offers a translation of one requirement of a grammar—production of all grammatical sentences

—which is rendered as prediction of all obtained utterances. However there is a second requirement of a grammar—production of no ungrammatical sentences. We will try rendering this second requirement as: prediction of no utterances that do not occur.

Clearly it is to the credit of a grammar if utterances not occurring are not predicted. But what is the number of utterances not occurring and not predicted? We decided to

Table 4–5. Possible Grammar-Evaluating Ratios

Ratio A—Prediction of All Grammatical Sentences

Value$_A$ of grammar	= Occurrences, predicted/Occurrences, not predicted			
Grammar	=	195/8	=	24.38
All possible combinations	=	203/0	=	∞
First set of utterances	=	90/113	=	.80

Ratio B—Prediction of No Ungrammatical Sentences

Value$_B$ of grammar	= Nonoccurrences, not predicted/Nonoccurrences, predicted			
Grammar	=	3,222/12,959	=	.25
All possible combinations	=	0/16,181	=	0
First set of utterances	=	15,900/281	=	56.58

interpret this notion as utterances conceivable in terms of the designated lexicon and the limitation on length, but yet not predicted by the grammar and not occurring in the sample. In the present case there are 3,230 such conceivable utterances (predicted by the rule of total combinations) which were not predicted by the grammar. Of these 3,230, only eight were obtained, and so 3,230 − 8, or 3,222, is the number of utterances not predicted and not occurring. Because these utterances are to the credit of the grammar, we entered them as the numerator of ratio B.

Utterances not occurring but predicted are to the discredit of a grammar. The present grammar predicted a total of 13,154 combinations, and, of these, 195 occurred. This leaves 13,154 − 195, or 12,959 combinations that were predicted but failed to occur. Because this number tells against the grammar, it is entered as the denominator of the new ratio.

A ratio of this second kind was also calculated for the total-combinations rule. For this rule there are no nonoccurrences not predicted since all conceivable combinations are predicted. There are very many nonoccurrences that are predicted (16,181). The numerator, which expresses the fact that non-occurrences cannot be to the credit of this rule, causes the ratio for the total-combinations rule to have a value of zero. The total-combinations rule which does a perfect job of producing all grammatical (obtained) sentences is no good at all when it comes to not producing ungrammatical sentences.

Consider now the same ratio B for the list of utterances from the first set. There are very many combinations which do not occur and are not predicted (15,900), and a relatively small number of predictions that fail (281). The first set of utterances which is not very good at producing all grammatical sentences is the best of the three at not predicting ungrammatical sentences. Note that if the ratios were calculated for the total corpus the value of ratio B for the list would be infinity, since there would be no nonoccurrences predicted.

Table 4–6. Values of the Three Descriptions for the Two Ratios

Description	Ratio A	Ratio B
Grammar	24.38	.25
Total combinations	∞	0
First set of utterances	.80	56.58
		(∞ for total corpus)

Ratios A and B operationalize the two requirements of a generative grammar, and the summary of Table 4–6 shows how the three descriptions stand with respect to both requirements. A grammar is good in the degree that it is able to generate all the utterances that occur without generating any that do not occur. The rule of total combinations perfectly satisfies the former requirement but completely fails to satisfy the latter. The first set of utterances perfectly satisfies the second requirement but completely fails to satisfy the first requirement. Only the grammar can, in some degree, meet both requirements, and that is a reason for preferring the grammar to either the rule of total combinations or the first set of utterances as a description of what Abel knows. However, from the 15-hour corpus one could write a large number of grammars alternative to the one presented here but equally well adapted to the data of that corpus. Let us see why this is so.

Consider the grammatical rule: $N_c + N_c$. This rule permits any count noun to go with any count noun, and since there are 64 count nouns in the lexicon (including both singular and plural forms) the rule generates 64 × 64, or 4,096 combinations. The rule is a generalization of a small number of such actual occurrences as "baby boat," "book bed," and "chair Mommie." What rules other than the rule $N_c + N_c$ will cover these occurrences? At one extreme there is the rule that simply summarizes the obtained utterances: Nouns-occurring-in-first-position (No_1) + Nouns-occurring-in-second-position (No_2). This rule exactly describes utterances of a certain type in the 15-hour corpus, but it does not generalize at all and so will fail to anticipate the utterances of the 11-hour corpus. What generalized rules other than $N_c + N_c$ might be written?

In principle one could write general rules in terms of any categories into which No_1 and No_2 can be placed. Suppose that all the No_1 happened to begin with the letter "p" and all of the No_2 with the letter "q". One could generalize the facts as: $N_p + N_q$. This degree of distributional consistency with regard to a grammatically irrelevant attribute is not likely to exist in any real corpus. However, there would always be some degree of consistency in terms of initial letters or final letters or length-of-word that could be generalized into a predictive rule.

In writing rules for Abel, we only consider word categories that had a grammatical function in adult English and count nouns are one such category. However there are other noun categories. The majority of the combinations $No_1 + No_2$ are made up of an initial noun naming some animate being (N_{an}) and a subsequent noun naming something inanimate (N_{inan}). It seems likely that these combinations are "telegraphic" versions of a possessive construction. In adult English it is necessary, for syntactic reasons, to distinguish N_{an} from other sorts of nouns. Suppose then that we were to drop the $N_c + N_c$ rule from Abel's grammar and replace it with the rule: $N_{an} + N_{inan}$.

Since N_{an} are much less numerous in Abel's lexicon than are N_c, the new rule would greatly reduce the number of predicted combinations. Since most of these predicted combinations did not occur in the 11-hour corpus, the denominator of ratio B would go down and the value of ratio B would go up. However, the new rule fails to generate a few of the utterances in the 15-hour corpus that are generated by the old rule. For example, "book bed" and "chair Mommie" are covered by $N_c + N_c$ but not by $N_{an} + N_{inan}$. In the 11-hour corpus, too, a few utterances occur which the old rule covered but which the new rule does not cover. These then become "occurrences, not predicted," and they must be added into the denominator of ratio A. The result is that this ratio goes down. In the above example, then, one cannot simultaneously maximize both ratios. The cost of making the grammar less general is to make it less adequate to the facts.

It is not logically necessary that a less general rule be less adequate to the facts. If all of the members of No_1 in both corpuses had been animate nouns and if all the members of No_2 had been inanimate nouns, then the rule $N_c + N_c$ and the rule $N_{an} + N_{inan}$ would have been equally adequate though unequally general. In such circumstances the choice is clear—the less general formulation is to be preferred. However these circumstances are rare with Abel's utterances. The usual case is that improving the value of the grammar in terms of one criterion entails a certain cost in terms of the other criterion.

We have explored these problems of evaluation for grammars written from all of Abel's utterances as well as for grammars written from only the subset of two-word utterances. When all the utterances of the 15-hour corpus are considered, the size of the lexicon increases and the range in utterance length is from one to four words. With these increases the number of possible combinations runs into billions. It is possible to write a grammar that will cover all of the obtained utterances and yet will fall far short of generating this set of possible combinations. But the least general grammar that is adequate to all the utterances generates many millions of possibilities. If we insist on generating all utterances, on using only categories that are relevant to grammar, and on preferring the least general set of rules that will meet these conditions, the choice of a grammar becomes reasonably determinate. Perhaps this is what we should do. It would mean crediting Abel with a machinery for generating millions of utterances. He may have such machinery. However, it is not obvious that one should insist on covering every obtained utterance when the cost of doing so is to predict astronomically large numbers of utterances that have not been obtained.

Here is a final quotation from Gleason (1961). "The occurrence of a sentence in a carefully elicited corpus is prima-facie evidence that the sentence does 'belong' to the language, but nothing more. Informants do make mistakes. Occasionally very bad sentences will occur" (p. 197). The linguist in the field commonly exempts his grammar from the obligation to cover certain ones of the utterances that have actually been obtained. If we allow ourselves to exclude utterances from Abel's 15-hour corpus, we can write less general grammars. But by what criteria does one select the utterances to be excluded?

An utterance produced by a child may be either a construction or a repetition. Only constructions should be consulted in formulating grammatical rules since these rules are intended to model the construction process. However, Brown and Fraser have argued that in the normal case of the child at home one cannot usually determine whether an utterance is a construction or a repetition. The basic difficulty is that one never knows exactly what a child has heard, and so any utterance, except certain errors, might be a repetition. If we had a rule for distinguishing constructions from repetitions in spontaneous speech, we would exclude repetitions from the corpus but the rule is hard to find.

Some of Abel's utterances immediately followed adult utterances which they closely resembled. Such seeming imitations are almost certainly repetitions rather than constructions, and we have excluded them in writing grammars. However a repetition need not immediately follow its model.

When an utterance does not resemble anything that has immediately preceded it in the speech of others, how can one tell whether it is a construction or a well-practiced repetition of some earlier model?

Suppose we have a set of two-word utterances such that all the members have one word in common and the remaining words, which are not identical across the utterances, are drawn from the same part-of-speech. Abel produced many such sets. One of them is: "Big blocks," "Big boat," "Big car," "Big cookie," "Big fish," "Big man," "Big pockets." It seems likely that at least some of these two-word utterances have been constructed. It seems likely because the set establishes a very simple and definite pattern (*Big* + Noun) which makes new constructions very easy. We do not find it difficult to believe that Abel has abstracted this pattern and can commute nouns in the open position.

Abel also produced the two-word utterance: "Coffee cup." There were no other utterances of the type: *Coffee* + Noun, and none of the type: Noun + *cup*. There were, however, utterances of the type: Noun + Noun. It is possible that Abel constructed "Coffee cup" on that abstract model, but we feel that it is more likely that he has learned "Coffee cup" as a prefabricated whole, a repetition of a common adult utterance.

Some utterances, then, can be assigned to a recurrent type such that the type is partially defined by a particular word or words. Other words can only be assigned to recurrent types which are defined entirely in terms of word classes. We have a hunch (it is no more) that utterances which fall into the narrower, more concrete patterns are more likely to be constructed than utterances which can only be placed in abstract patterns. This hunch ultimately concerns what we think it reasonable to suppose that a 24-month-old child has learned to do.

Using the narrow sort of recurrence as a ground for excluding material from the 15-hour corpus, we have found it possible to write grammars that generate these more regular utterances of the corpus and only predict some thousands of utterances beyond those obtained. Such grammars, of course, fail to generate the many less regular utterances.

Some of us believe that the grammars which exclude the more intractable utterances come nearer to describing Abel's actual constructional competence than do the grammars that generate everything. However the exclusion criterion was fixed by pure hunch. A case can be made that it is just the odd utterance, the one that does not fall into any narrow recurrent type, that is most likely to have been constructed. The grammar-evaluation problem has not been solved.

Perhaps our problem has begun to seem rather "scholastic" —in the medieval sense. Is it sensible to worry about whether a child who has produced 2,000 utterances has a rule system for producing 50,000 utterances or 50,000,000 utterances? This problem seems particularly "scholastic" when you consider that the rule system would be likely to change before the child had time to turn out more than a fractional part of the supposed possibilities. However, you will grant that it can be reasonable and even practically important to determine whether a child knows how to add numbers. Suppose that the child cannot tell us anything about the addition process—and most children cannot. All he can do is operate with numbers. How would we decide whether or not he knew how to add?

The operation of addition predicts an infinite set of occurrences and an infinite set of nonoccurrences. If a child knows how to add, he will be prepared to say: "2 plus 2 are 4"; "12 plus 83,120 are 83,132"; "750 plus 91 are 841"; etc., and not to say: "2 plus 5 are 6"; "15 plus 19 are 22"; etc. We never hear a child say more than a triflingly small number of the acceptable utterances; yet we do not hesitate, on the basis of such evidence, to credit him with knowledge of addition. Furthermore most children will occasionally make a mistake; they will occasionally produce an incorrect sum. When that happens we do not feel that we must adjust our conception of the rules in the child's head so as to generate the unpredicted occurrence. We confidently exclude the difficult case from the corpus and decide that he knows how to add but sometimes makes computational errors. How do we come to be so confident here and so uncertain in the case of grammar?

The addition rule predicts more precisely than does a grammar. Given the numbers to be summed it generates the particular outcome. The chances of doing that if you have not got the correct rule are small, and that may be why we feel confident that the rule is right. A grammar, given the words to be made into a sentence, would in some extremely simple cases predict a particular outcome. Usually, however, the grammar would only generate a set of possible outcomes. For the particular sentence one must go beyond grammar to meaning and the motivation of a speaker. One difference between addition and grammar, then, seems to be in the precision of prediction.

There are rules other than the grammatical which only generate possibilities, rules that do not generate particular outcomes. Consider the rules for bidding in contract bridge. These rules do not tell us what a particular player will bid on a particular occasion, but they do permit one set of bids and proscribe another set. The class of permitted bids narrows with the accumulation of prior bids; if someone has bid "three diamonds," it is no longer acceptable to bid "two diamonds." However there is always more than one acceptable response.

Of course there are guides to intelligent bidding which do prescribe particular bids. In the case of language the particular sentence can only be prescribed by considering semantics and motivation in addition to grammar. The particular bid in bridge can only be prescribed by considering the hand the player holds as well as the rules of the game. The rules of bidding in themselves do not require that a bid be sensible, only that it be drawn from the population of lawful bids.

Suppose a player had not told us the rules of bidding, and most players could not easily do so. The player can only play, and we must judge whether he possesses the rules we have in mind. Even though these rules do not predict the particular bid, if the player repeatedly drew his bids from the class of possibilities, we would come to believe that he possessed the rules. I think we would not be convinced quite so quickly as in the case of addition, but it would not take very many games to persuade us that the player had the rules. If he then made a mistake, perhaps bidding "two diamonds" when it is not permitted to do so, we would not revise our conception of his knowledge so as to incorporate this deviant case. We would instead decide that he knew the rules of proper bidding but lost track of the prior bids. How so?

There is a critical difference between the adding child or the bridgeplayer and the sentence-producing child. The child who has mistakenly said "2 plus 5 are 6" will sometimes correct himself or will accept our correction and agree that 2 plus 5 are 7. The bridgeplayer, if he is told that someone has already bid "three diamonds," will apologize for his "two diamonds" and offer instead an acceptable bid. We can be confident that these actions must be excluded from the corpus because they elicit a characteristic reaction from the person producing them. They are judged to be incorrect and so are separated out from the other sums or bids. The rule system identifies certain behavior as unlawful and the subject also identifies it as unlawful. It is very improbable that this would happen if our formulation of his rules were mistaken. It is chiefly because of this coincidence between the boundaries defined by the rules and the boundaries marked out by the subject that we can be so confident in attributing to him knowledge of bridge or of addition.

The linguist working with an adult informant gets reactions to utterances as well as the utterances themselves. The informant will sometimes stop and strike out an utterance following it with a corrected version. The linguist can test his hypotheses about the grammatical system by constructing possibly acceptable sentences and asking for judgments of grammaticality. The linguist is able to get judgments of the acceptability of behavior, and this is the kind of data that is so decisive for the adding child and the bridgeplayer. Can such data be obtained from very young children?

With Abel we were not successful in eliciting judgments of grammaticality. Of course there was no point in asking him whether an utterance was "grammatical" or "well-formed." We experimented with some possible childhood equivalents. The first step was to formulate tentative grammatical rules, and the next to construct some utterances that ought to have been acceptable if the rules were correct and other utterances that ought not to have been acceptable. For Abel "The cake" should have been grammatical and "Cake the" ungrammatical. How to ask? The experimenter said: "Some of the things I will say are silly and some are not. You tell me when I say something silly." Abel would not. If Abel had a sense of grammaticality, we were unable to find the word that would engage it. When do children begin to make judgments of grammaticality? We plan to find out.

How stands the problem of evaluating grammars written for the speech of children? There are two basic criteria: the grammar should generate as many as possible of the utterances that will be produced while generating as few as possible of the utterances that will not be produced. It is ordinarily the case that changing the grammar so as to better its performance with respect to one criterion entails a cost in that the change worsens the performance of the grammar with respect to the other criterion. It is not ordinarily possible to optimize performance on both criteria at the same time. There is no good rationale for pursuing one criterion to the neglect of the other. We might aim at achieving some minimal excellence in terms of both criteria but the setting of the acceptable levels would be quite arbitrary. It would be as if we tried to decide how many addition problems a child must solve correctly and how few incorrectly if he is to be credited with a knowledge of addition. A decision would be arbitrary and unsatisfactory.

The way out of this dilemma in the case of addition and also in the case of the linguist writing a grammar for adult speech is to obtain *reactions* as well as *actions*, reactions which judge the acceptability of actions. With one 24-month-old boy we could not obtain such reactions. Perhaps they can be obtained from older children. Children who are first combining words may not have a sense of grammaticality, and it may never be possible to settle on the best general description of their speech output.

Judgments of grammaticality and nongrammaticality are data for a grammar to fit; data in addition to occurrence and nonoccurrence. These additional data greatly reduce the number of conceivable grammars and so increase our confidence in any one that fits. It may be possible to obtain from children other kinds of data that will help to select among grammars, possibly data on the perception or comprehension of speech or data on imitation.

The psychologist working on computer simulation of cognitive processes has the same problem we have. If he simulates some single simple problem-solving performance, he cannot feel very sure that his simulation is similar to the information-processing of the human being because there will be a large number of alternative equally-adequate simulations. If the simulator increases the range of data he can generate, the number of alternative simulations will decrease and confidence in any one that works will increase. Of course with a greater range of data it is more difficult to create satisfactory generative rules. For the grammars of children, we have been setting ourselves too easy a task. We have not required very much of these grammars, and so they have not been very difficult to invent. But, also, there have been too many alternatives and no clear ground for choosing among them.

References

BROWN, R., and FRASER, C. The acquisition of syntax. In C. N. Cofer & Barbara S. Musgrave (Eds.), *Verbal behavior and learning: Problems and processes.* New York: McGraw-Hill, 1963.

GLEASON, H. A., JR. *An introduction to descriptive linguistics.* (Rev. ed.) New York: Holt, Rinehart & Winston, 1961.

[5]

Three Processes in the Child's Acquisition of Syntax

In 1962 Ursula Bellugi, Colin Fraser, and I began a longitudinal study of the development of English in two children: Adam and Eve; a third child, Sarah, was added somewhat later. This paper was the first to be based on the longitudinal study. It reports three major phenomena that were evident almost at once. I notice today that the paper has a certain light-heartedness which reflects the optimism we then felt that language learning would soon yield up its secrets. There are brief comments to be made about each of the three processes discussed.

The telegraphic character of early English sentences (when the child's average utterance is between two and three morphemes long) is one of the well-substantiated facts in this field and it seems, in the light of recent studies of other languages, to be a universal feature of linguistic development. It is, however, only a fact and it still awaits a really convincing explanation.

The fact that adults often respond to a child's telegraphic sentence with glosses which do not exactly imitate the originals but

This paper was written for a special issue of the *Harvard Educational Review* Vol. 34, No. 2 (1964), 133–151, devoted to *Language and Learning*. Ursula Bellugi was co-author. Reprinted by permission of the authors.

rather *expand* them into well-formed sentences is also well established. The function of such expansions is not established. In this paper, at the end of the section on the expansion process, we express the intention of doing an experiment to contrast the effects of expansion training with simple exposure to English. Such an experiment was done by our associate, Courtney Cazden. The results are reported in the immediately following paper in this volume ("The Child's Grammar from I to III"): they were negative. Expansions were not demonstrated to have any special efficacy. That is where the evidence is but I do not believe this is the last we shall hear of expansions. They seem so ideally devised to teach that it is hard to believe they do not do so.

In the third section there are two errors to be corrected and one point to clarify. In discussing the modifier rule in Table 5–5 we say that it is "generative," and that we meant by this that it is "a model of the mechanism by which Adam and Eve generated such utterances." This is an erroneous use of "generative" (from "generative grammar") that was common in psycholinguistics at that time. Generative grammar is not intended to be a representation of an actual mechanism of speech production.

Certain data in Table 5–9, including such sentences from Adam as *Mommy get it ladder*, in which a pronoun occurs alongside a noun it ought to have replaced, seemed to us to be evidence of the developing unity or integration of noun phrases. A later more complete analysis has corrected this interpretation. What we have in Table 5–9 are certain errors of morpheme segmentation; *get-it*, for instance, was simply a verb to Adam. The correct interpretation appears in "The Child's Grammar from I to III."

In connection with the modifier constructions of Table 5–5 we point out that in three studies of child speech (those of Martin Braine; Susan Ervin and Wick Miller; and our own) this construction has turned out to be extremely common. The modifier construction is similar to the Pivot-Open construction reported by Braine and Ervin, and several students of child speech have hailed the Pivot-Open construction as the universal first-step in syntax. We did not mean to say anything of the kind. In fact, Adam's speech at this time went well beyond a Pivot-Open grammar and, so far as I have ever been able to see, the published data of Braine and Ervin also are not very well described by such a grammar.

SOME TIME in the second six months of life most children say a first intelligible word. A few months later most children are saying many words and some children go about the house all day long naming things (*table, doggie, ball*, etc.) and actions (*play, see, drop*, etc.) and an occasional quality (*blue, broke, bad*, etc.). At about eighteen months children are likely to begin constructing two-word utterances; such a one, for instance, as *Push car*.

A construction such as *Push car* is not just two single-word utterances spoken in a certain order. As single word utterances (they are sometimes called holophrases) both *push* and *car* would have primary stresses and terminal intonation contours. When they are two words programmed as a single utterance the primary stress would fall on *car* and so would the highest level of pitch. *Push* would be subordinated to *car* by a lesser stress and a lower pitch; the unity of the whole would appear in the absence of a terminal contour between words and the presence of such a contour at the end of the full sequence.

By the age of thirty-six months some children are so advanced in the construction process as to produce all of the major varieties of English simple sentences up to a length of ten or eleven words. For several years we have been studying the development of English syntax, of the sentence-constructing process, in children between eighteen and thirty-six months of age. Most recently we have made a longitudinal study of a boy and girl whom we shall call Adam and Eve. We began work with Adam and Eve in October of 1962 when Adam was twenty-seven months old and Eve eighteen months old. The two children were selected from some thirty whom we considered. They were selected primarily because their speech was exceptionally intelligible and because they talked a lot. We wanted to make it as easy as possible to transcribe accurately large quantities of child speech. Adam and Eve are the children of highly-educated parents, the fathers were graduate students at Harvard and the mothers are both college graduates. Both Adam and Eve were single children when we began the study. These facts must be remembered in generalizing the outcomes of the research.

While Adam is nine months older than Eve, his speech was only a little more advanced in October of 1962. The best single index of the level of speech development is the average length of utterance and in October, 1962, Adam's average was 1.84 morphemes and Eve's was 1.40 morphemes. The two children stayed fairly close together in the year that followed: in the records for the thirty-eighth week Adam's average was 3.55 and Eve's, 3.27. The processes we shall describe appeared in both children.

Every second week we visited each child for at least two hours and made a tape recording of everything said by the child as well as of everything said to the child. The mother was always present and most of the speech to the child is hers. Both mother and child became very accustomed to our presence and learned to continue their usual routine with us as the observers.

One of us always made a written transcription, on the scene, of the speech of mother and child with notes about important actions and objects of attention. From this transcription and the tape a final transcription was made and these transcriptions constitute the primary data of the study. For many purposes we require a "distributional analysis" of the speech of the child. To this end the child's utterances in a given transcription were cross classified and relisted under such headings as: "A +noun"; "Noun +verb"; "Verbs in the past"; "Utterances containing the pronoun it," etc. The categorized utterances expose the syntactic regularities of the child's speech.

Each week we met as a research seminar, with students of the psychology of language,[1] to discuss the state of the construction process in one of the two children as of that date. In these discussions small experiments were often suggested, experiments that had to be done within a few days if they were to be informative. At one time, for instance, we were uncertain whether Adam understood the semantic difference between putting a noun in subject position and putting it in object

[1] We are grateful for intellectual stimulation and lighthearted companionship to Dr. Jean Berko Gleason, Mr. Samuel Anderson, Mr. Colin Fraser, Dr. David McNeill, and Dr. Daniel Slobin.

position. Consequently one of us paid an extra visit to Adam equipped with some toys. "Adam," we said, "show us the duck pushing the boat." And, when he had done so: "Now show us the boat pushing the duck."

Another week we noticed that Adam would sometimes pluralize nouns when they should have been pluralized and sometimes would not. We wondered if he could make grammatical judgments about the plural, if he could distinguish a correct form from an incorrect form. "Adam," we asked, "which is right, 'two shoes' or 'two shoe'?" His answer on that occasion, produced with explosive enthusiasm, was "Pop goes the weasel!" The two-year-old child does not make a perfectly docile experimental subject.

The dialogue between mother and child does not read like a transcribed dialogue between two adults. Table 5-1 offers

Table 5–1. A Section from Adam's First Record

Adam	Mother
See truck, Mommy.	
See truck.	
	Did you see the truck?
No I see truck.	
	No, you didn't see it?
	There goes one.
There go one.	
	Yes, there goes one.
See a truck.	
See truck, Mommy.	
See truck.	
Truck.	
Put truck, Mommy.	
	Put the truck where?
Put truck window.	
	I think that one's too large to go in the window.

a sample section from an early transcribed record. It has some interesting properties. The conversation is, in the first place, very much in the here and now. From the child there is no speech of the sort that Bloomfield called "displaced," speech about other times and other places. Adam's utterances in the early months were largely a coding of contemporaneous events and impulses. The mother's speech differs from the speech that adults use to one another in many ways. Her sentences are short and simple; for the most part they are the kinds of sentences that Adam will produce a year later.

Perhaps because they are short, the sentences of the mother are perfectly grammatical. The sentences adults use to one another, perhaps because they are longer and more complex, are very often not grammatical, not well formed. Here for instance is a rather representative example produced at a conference of psychologists and linguists: "As far as I know, no one yet has done the in a way obvious now and interesting problem of doing a in a sense a structural frequency study of the alternative syntactical in a given language, say, like English, the alternative possible structures, and how what their hierarchical probability of occurrence structure is." (Maclay and Osgood, 1959) It seems unlikely that a child could learn the patterns of English syntax from such speech. His introduction to English ordinarily comes in the form of a simplified, repetitive, and idealized dialect. It may be that such an introduction is necessary for the acquisition of syntax to be possible but we do not know that.

In the course of the brief interchange of Table 5-1 Adam imitates his mother in saying: "There go one" immediately after she says "There goes one." The imitation is not perfect; Adam omits the inflection on the verb. His imitation is a reduction in that it omits something from the original. This kind of imitation with reduction is extremely common in the records of Adam and Eve and it is the first process we shall discuss.

IMITATION AND REDUCTION

Table 5-2 presents some model sentences spoken by the mothers and the imitations produced by Adam and Eve. These were selected from hundreds in the records in order to illustrate some general propositions. The first thing to notice is that the imitations preserve the word order of the model sentences. To be sure, words in the model are often missing

Table 5–2. Some Imitations Produced by Adam and Eve

Model Utterance	Child's Imitation
Tank car	Tank car
Wait a minute	Wait a minute
Daddy's brief case	Daddy brief case
Fraser will be unhappy	Fraser unhappy
He's going out	He go out
That's an old time train	Old time train
It's not the same dog as Pepper	Dog Pepper
No, you can't write on Mr. Cromer's shoe	Write Cromer shoe

from the imitation but the words preserved are in the order of the original. This is a fact that is so familiar and somehow reasonable that we did not at once recognize it as an empirical outcome rather than as a natural necessity. But of course it is not a necessity, the outcome could have been otherwise. For example, words could have been said back in the reverse of their original order, the most recent first. The preservation of order suggests that the model sentence is processed by the child as a total construction rather than as a list of words.

In English the order of words in a sentence is an important grammatical signal. Order is used to distinguish among subject, direct object, and indirect object and it is one of the marks of imperative and interrogative constructions. The fact that the child's first sentences preserve the word order of their models partially accounts for the ability of an adult to "understand" these sentences and so to feel that he is in communication with the child. It is conceivable that the child "intends" the meanings coded by his word orders and that, when he preserves the order of an adult sentence, he does so because he wants to say what the order says. It is also possible that he preserves word order just because his brain works that way and that he has no comprehension of the semantic contrasts involved. In some languages word order is not an important grammatical signal. In Latin, for instance, "Agricola amat puellam" has the same meaning as "Puellam amat agricola" and subject-object relations are signalled by case endings. We would be interested to know whether children who are exposed to languages that do not utilize word order as a major syntactic signal preserve order as reliably as do children exposed to English.

The second thing to notice in Table 5–2 is the fact that when the models increase in length there is not a corresponding increase in the imitation. The imitations stay in the range of two to four morphemes which was the range characteristic of the children at this time. The children were operating under some constraint of length or span. This is not a limitation of vocabulary; the children knew hundreds of words. Neither is it a constraint of immediate memory. We infer this from the fact that the average length of utterances produced spontaneously, where immediate memory is not involved, is about the same as the average length of utterances produced as immediate imitations. The constraint is a limitation on the length of utterance the children are able to program or plan (Brown and Fraser, 1963). This kind of narrow span limitation in children is characteristic of most or all of their intellectual operations. The limitation grows less restrictive with age as a consequence, probably, of both neurological growth and of practice, but of course it is never lifted altogether.

A constraint on length compels the imitating child to omit some words or morphemes from the mother's longer sentences. Which forms are retained and which omitted? The selection is not random but highly systematic. Forms retained in the examples of Table 5–2 include: *Daddy, Fraser, Pepper*, and *Cromer; tank car, minute, briefcase, train, dog*, and *shoe, wait, go*, and *write; unhappy* and *old time*. For the most part they are nouns, verbs, and adjectives, though there are exceptions, as witness the initial pronoun *He* and the preposition *out* and the indefinite article *a*. Forms omitted in the samples of Table 5–2 include: the possessive inflection *–s*, the modal auxiliary *will*, the contraction of the auxiliary verb *is*, the progressive inflection *–ing*, the preposition *on*, the articles *the* and *an*, and the modal auxiliary *can*. It is possible to make a general characterization of the forms likely to be retained that distinguishes them as a total class from the forms likely to be omitted.

Forms likely to be retained are nouns and verbs and, less often, adjectives, and these are the three large and "open" parts-of-speech in English. The number of forms in any one of these parts-of-speech is extremely large and always growing. Words belonging to these classes are sometimes called "contentives" because they have semantic content. Forms likely to be omitted are inflections, auxiliary verbs, articles, prepositions, and conjunctions. These forms belong to syntactic classes that are small and closed. Any one class has few members and new members are not readily added. The omitted forms are the ones that linguists sometimes call "functors," their grammatical *functions* being more obvious than their semantic content.

Why should young children omit functors and retain contentives? There is more than one plausible answer. Nouns, verbs, and adjectives are words that make reference. One can conceive of teaching the meanings of these words by speaking them, one at a time, and pointing at things or actions or qualities. And of course parents do exactly that. These are the kinds of words that children have been encouraged to practice speaking one at a time. The child arrives at the age of sentence construction with a stock of well-practiced nouns, verbs, and adjectives. Is it not likely then that this prior practice causes him to retain the contentives from model sentences too long to be reproduced in full, that the child imitates those forms in the speech he hears which are already well developed in him as individual habits? There is probably some truth in this explanation but it is not the only determinant since children will often select for retention contentives that are relatively unfamiliar to them.

We adults sometimes operate under a constraint on length and the curious fact is that the English we produce in these circumstances bears a formal resemblance to the English produced by two-year-old children. When words cost money there is a premium on brevity or to put it otherwise, a constraint on length. The result is "telegraphic" English and telegraphic English is an English of nouns, verbs, and adjectives. One does not send a cable reading: "My car has broken down and I have lost my wallet; send money to me at the American Express in Paris" but rather "Car broken down; wallet lost; send money American Express Paris." The telegram omits: *my, has, and, I, have, my, to, me, at, the, in.* All of these are functors. We make the same kind of telegraphic reduction when time or fatigue constrain us to be brief, as witness any set of notes taken at a fast-moving lecture.

A telegraphic transformation of English generally communicates very well. It does so because it retains the high-information words and drops the low-information words. We are here using "information" in the sense of the mathematical theory of communication. The information carried by a word is inversely related to the chances of guessing it from context. From a given string of content words, missing functors can often be guessed but the message "my has and I have my to me at the in" will not serve to get money to Paris. Perhaps children are able to make a communication analysis of adult speech and so adapt in an optimal way to their limitation of span. There is, however, another way in which the adaptive outcome might be achieved.

If you say aloud the model sentences of Table 5–2 you will find that you place the heavier stresses, the primary and secondary stresses in the sentences, on contentives rather than on functors. In fact the heavier stresses fall, for the most part, on the words the child retains. We first realized that this was the case when we found that in transcribing tapes, the words of the mother that we could hear most clearly were usually the words that the child reproduced. We had trouble hearing the weakly stressed functors and, of course, the child usually failed to reproduce them. Differential stress may then be the cause of the child's differential retention. The outcome is a maximally informative reduction but the cause of this outcome need not be the making of an information analysis. The outcome may be an incidental consequence of the fact that English is a well-designed language that places its heavier stresses where they are needed, on contentives that cannot easily be guessed from context.

We are fairly sure that differential stress is one of the determinants of the child's telegraphic productions. For one thing, stress will also account for the way in which children reproduce polysyllabic words when the total is too much for them. Adam, for instance, gave us 'pression for expression and Eve gave us 'raff for giraffe; the more heavily-stressed syllables were the ones retained. In addition we have tried the effect of placing heavy stresses on functors which do not ordinarily receive such stresses. To Adam we said: "You say what I say" and then, speaking in a normal way at first: "The doggie will bite." Adam gave back: "Doggie bite." Then we stressed the auxiliary: "The doggie will bite" and, after a few trials, Adam made attempts at reproducing that auxiliary. A science fiction experiment comes to mind. If there were parents who stressed functors rather than contentives would they have children whose speech was a kind of "reciprocal telegraphic" made up of articles, prepositions, conjunctions, auxiliaries, and the like? Such children would be out of touch with the community as real children are not.

It may be that all the factors we have mentioned play some part in determining the child's selective imitations; the reference-making function of contentives, the fact that they are practiced as single words, the fact that they cannot be guessed from context, and the heavy stresses they receive. There are also other possible factors: for example, the left-to-right, earlier-to-later position of words in a sentence, but these make too long a story to tell here (Brown and Fraser, 1963). Whatever the causes, the first utterances produced as imitations of adult sentences are highly systematic reductions of their models. Furthermore, the telegraphic properties of these imitations appear also in the child's spontaneously produced utterances. When his speech is not modeled on an immediately prior adult sentence, it observes the same limitation on length and the same predilection for contentives as when it is modeled on an immediately prior sentence.

IMITATION WITH EXPANSION

In the course of the brief conversation set down in Table 5-1, Adam's mother at one point imitates Adam. The boy says: "There go one" and mother responds: "Yes, there goes one."

She does not exactly reproduce the model sentence of the child but instead adds something to it or expands it. What she adds is a functor, the inflection for third-person on the verb, the very form that Adam had omitted when he imitated his mother.

One of the first things we noticed when we began to study child speech several years ago was the frequency with which adults imitated children. Indeed they seemed to imitate more often than did the children themselves. We later came to realize that adult imitations are seldom exact reproductions; they are usually expansions. The mothers of Adam and Eve responded to the speech of their children with expansions about thirty per cent of the time. We did it ourselves when we talked with the children. Indeed we found it very difficult to withhold expansions. A reduced or incomplete English sentence seems to constrain the English-speaking adult to expand it into the nearest properly formed complete sentence. Table 5–3 lists a few sample expansions from the hundreds in the records.

Table 5–3. Expansions of Child Speech Produced by Mothers

Child	Mother
Baby highchair	Baby is in the highchair
Mommy eggnog	Mommy had her eggnog
Eve lunch	Eve is having lunch
Mommy sandwich	Mommy'll have a sandwich
Sat wall	He sat on the wall
Throw Daddy	Throw it to Daddy
Pick glove	Pick the glove up

The first thing worthy of attention in the expansions of Table 5–3 is the fact that the words spoken by the mother preserve the order of the words in the child's sentences. To be sure, words and inflections are added but they are fitted in—before, and after and between the words the child used; they are not generally permitted to disturb the order of the child's words. It is as if these latter were taken as constants by the mother, constants to which some sentence had to be fitted. She acts as if she were assuming that the child means everything he says, all the words and also their order, but as if he might also mean more than he says. From the mother's point of view an expansion is a kind of communication check; it says in effect: "Is this what you mean?"

The second thing to notice about Table 5-3 is the character of the forms added to the child's utterances. They include the auxiliaries *is* and *will;* the prepositions *in, on, to,* and *up;* the verb forms *is, have, had,* and *having;* the articles *a* and *the;* the pronouns *her, he,* and *it.* For the most part, the words added are functors and functors are of course the words that the child omits in his reductions.

The interaction between mother and child is, much of the time, a cycle of reductions and expansions. There are two transformations involved. The reduction transformation has an almost completely specifiable and so mechanical character. One could program a machine to do it with the following instructions: "Retain contentives (or stressed forms) in the order given up to some limit of length." The expansion accomplished by Adam's mother when she added the third-person inflection to the verb and said "There goes one" is also a completely specifiable transformation. The instructions would read: "Retain the forms given in the order given and supply obligatory grammatical forms." To be sure this mother-machine would have to be supplied with the obligatory rules of English grammar but that could be done. However, the sentence "There goes one" is atypical in that it only adds a compulsory and redundant inflection. The expansions of Table 5-3 all add forms that are not grammatically compulsory or redundant and these expansions cannot be mechanically generated by grammatical rules alone.

In Table 5-3 the topmost four utterances produced by the child are all of the same grammatical type; all four consist of a proper noun followed by a common noun. However, the four are expanded in quite different ways. In particular the form of the verb changes: it is in the first case in the simple present tense; in the second case the simple past; in the third case the present progressive; in the last case the simple future. All of these are perfectly grammatical but they are different. The second set of child utterances is formally uniform in that each one consists of a verb followed by a noun. The expansions are again all grammatical but quite unlike, especially with regard to the preposition supplied. In general, then, there are radical changes in the mother's expansions when there are no changes in the formal character of the utterances expanded. It follows that the expansions cannot be produced simply by making grammatically compulsory additions to the child's utterances.

How does a mother decide on the correct expansion of one of her child's utterances? Consider the utterance "Eve lunch." So far as grammar is concerned this utterance could be appropriately expanded in any of a number of ways: "Eve is having lunch"; "Eve had lunch"; "Eve will have lunch"; Eve's lunch," etc. On the occasion when Eve produced the utterance, however, one expansion seemed more appropriate than any other. It was then the noon hour, Eve was sitting at the table with a plate of food before her, and her spoon and fingers were busy. In these circumstances "Eve lunch" had to mean "Eve is having lunch." A little later when the plates had been stacked in the sink and Eve was getting down from her chair the utterance "Eve lunch" would have suggested the expansion "Eve has had her lunch." Most expansions are not only responsive to the child's words but also to the circumstances attending their utterance.

What kind of instructions will generate the mother's expansions? The following are approximately correct: "Retain the words given in the order given and add those functors that will result in a well-formed simple sentence that is appropriate to the circumstances." These are not instructions that any machine could follow. A machine could act on the instructions only if it were provided with detailed specifications for judging appropriateness and no such specifications can, at present, be written. They exist, however, in implicit form in the brains of mothers and in the brains of all English-speaking adults and so judgments of appropriateness can be made by such adults.

The expansion encodes aspects of reality that are not coded by the child's telegraphic utterance. Functors have meaning but it is meaning that accrues to them in context rather than in isolation. The meanings that are added by functors seem to be nothing less than the basic terms in which we construe reality: the time of an action, whether it is ongoing or completed, whether it is presently relevant or not; the concept of possession and such relational concepts as are coded by *in*, *on*, *up*, *down*, and the like; the difference between a particular instance of a class ("Has anybody seen *the* paper?"); and any instance of a class ("Has anybody seen *a* paper?"); the difference between extended substances given shape and size by an "accidental" container (*sand*, *water*, *syrup*, etc.) and countable "things" having a characteristic fixed shape and size (*a cup*, *a man*, *a tree*, etc.). It seems to us that a mother in expanding speech may be teaching more than grammar; she may be teaching something like a world-view.

As yet it has not been demonstrated that expansions are *necessary* for learning either grammar or a construction of reality. It has not even been demonstrated that expansions contribute to such learning. All we know is that some parents do expand and their children do learn. It is perfectly possible, however, that children can and do learn simply from hearing their parents or others make well-formed sentences in connection with various nonverbal circumstances. It may not be necessary or even helpful for these sentences to be expansions of utterances of the child. Only experiments contrasting expansion training with simple exposure to English will settle the matter. We hope to do such experiments.

There are, of course, reasons for expecting the expansion transformation to be an effective tutorial technique. By adding something to the words the child has just produced one confirms his response insofar as it is appropriate. In addition one takes him somewhat beyond that response but not greatly beyond it. One encodes additional meanings at a moment when he is most likely to be attending to the cues that can teach that meaning.

INDUCTION OF THE LATENT STRUCTURE

Adam, in the course of the conversation with his mother set down in Table 5–1, produced one utterance for which no adult is likely ever to have provided an exact model: "No I see truck." His mother elects to expand it as "No, you didn't see it" and this expansion suggests that the child might have created the utterance by reducing an adult model containing the form *didn't*. However, the mother's expansion in this case does some violence to Adam's original version. He did not say *no* as his mother said it, with primary stress and final contour; Adam's *no* had secondary stress and no final contour. It is not easy to imagine an adult model for this utterance. It seems more likely that the utterance was created by Adam as part of a continuing effort to discover the general rules for constructing English negatives.

In Table 5–4 we have listed some utterances produced by Adam or Eve for which it is difficult to imagine any adult model. It is unlikely that any adult said any of these to Adam or Eve since they are very simple utterances and yet definitely

Table 5–4. Utterances Not Likely to be Imitations

My Cromer suitcase	*You naughty are*
Two foot	*Why it can't turn off?*
A bags	*Put on it*
A scissor	*Cowboy did fighting me*
A this truck	*Put a gas in*

ungrammatical. In addition it is difficult, by adding functors alone, to build any of them up to simple grammatical sentences. Consequently it does not seem likely that these utterances are reductions of adult originals. It is more likely that they are mistakes which externalize the child's search for the regularities of English syntax.

We have long realized that the occurrence of certain kinds of errors on the level of morphology (or word construction) reveals the child's effort to induce regularities from speech. So long as a child speaks correctly, or at any rate so long as he speaks as correctly as the adults he hears, there is no way to tell whether he is simply repeating what he has heard or whether he is actually constructing. However, when he says something like "I digged a hole" we can often be sure that he is constructing. We can be sure because it is unlikely that he would have heard *digged* from anyone and because we can see how, in processing words he has heard, he might have come by *digged*. It looks like an overgeneralization of the regular past inflection. The inductive operations of the child's mind are externalized in such a creation. Overgeneralizations on the level of syntax (or sentence construction) are more difficult to identify because there are so many ways of adding functors so as to build up conceivable models. But this is difficult to do for the examples of Table 5-4 and for several hundred other utterances in our records.

The processes of imitation and expansion are not sufficient to account for the degree of linguistic competence that children regularly acquire. These processes alone cannot teach more than the sum total of sentences that speakers of English have either modeled for a child to imitate or built up from a child's reductions. However, a child's linguistic competence extends far beyond this sum total of sentences. All children are able to understand and construct sentences they have never heard but which are nevertheless well-formed, well-formed in terms of general rules that are implicit in the sentences the child has heard. Somehow, then, every child processes the speech to which he is exposed so as to induce from it a latent structure. This latent rule structure is so general that a child can spin out its implications all his life long. It is both semantic and syntactic. The discovery of latent structure is the greatest of the processes involved in language acquisition and the most difficult to understand. We will provide an example of how the analysis can proceed by discussing the evolution in child speech of noun phrases.

A noun phrase in adult English includes a noun but also more than a noun. One variety consists of a noun with assorted modifiers: *The girl; The pretty girl; That pretty girl; My girl*, etc. All of these are constructions which have the same syntactic privileges as do nouns alone. One can use a noun phrase in isolation to name or request something; one can use it in sentences, in subject position or in object position or in predicate nominative position. All of these are slots that nouns alone can also fill. A larger construction having the same syntactic privileges as its "head" word is called in linguistics an "endocentric" construction and noun phrases are endocentric constructions.

For both Adam and Eve, in the early records, noun phrases usually occur as total independent utterances rather than as components of sentences. Table 5–5 presents an assortment of such utterances at Time 1. They consist in each case of some sort of modifier, just one, preceding a noun. The modifiers, or, as they are sometimes called, the "pivot" words, are a much smaller class than the noun class. Three students of child speech have independently discovered that this kind of

Table 5–5. Noun Phrases in Isolation and Rule for Generating Noun Phrases at Time 1

A coat	More coffee
A celery*	More nut*
A Becky*	Two sock*
A hands*	Two shoes
The top	Two tinker-toy*
My Mommy	Big boot
That Adam	Poor man
My stool	Little top
That knee	Dirty knee

$$NP \rightarrow M + N$$

M → a, big, dirty, little, more, my, poor, that, the, two.

N → Adam, Becky, boot, coat, coffee, knee, man, Mommy, nut, sock, stool tinker-toy, top, and very many others.

---

* Ungrammatical for an adult.

construction is extremely common when children first begin to combine words (Braine, 1963; Brown and Fraser, 1963; Miller and Ervin, 1964).

It is possible to generalize the cases of Table 5–5 into a simple implicit rule. The rule symbolized in Table 5–5 reads: "In order to form a noun phrase of this type, select first one word from the small class of modifiers and select, second, one word from the large class of nouns." This is a "generative" rule, by which we mean it is a program that would actually serve to build constructions of the type in question. It is offered as a model of the mental mechanism by which Adam and Eve generated such utterances. Furthermore, judging from our work with other children and from the reports of Braine and of Miller and Ervin, the model describes a mechanism present in many children when their average utterance is approximately two morphemes long.

We have found that even in our earliest records the M + N construction is sometimes used as a component of larger constructions. For instance, Eve said: "Fix a Lassie" and "Turn the page" and "A horsie stuck" and Adam even said: "Adam wear a shirt." There are, at first, only a handful of these larger constructions but there are very many constructions in which single nouns occur in subject or in object position.

Let us look again at the utterances of Table 5–5 and the rule generalizing them. The class M does not correspond with any syntactic class of adult English. In the class M are articles, a possessive pronoun, a cardinal number, a demonstrative adjective or pronoun, a quantifier, and some descriptive adjectives—a mixed bag indeed. For adult English these words cannot belong to the same syntactic class because they have very different privileges of occurrence in sentences. For the children the words do seem to function as one class having the common privilege of occurrence before nouns.

If the initial words of the utterances in Table 5–5 are treated as one class M then many utterances are generated which an adult speaker would judge to be ungrammatical. Consider the indefinite article *a*. Adults use it only to modify common count nouns in the singular such as *coat*, *dog*, *cup*, etc. We would not say *a celery*, or *a cereal*, or *a dirt*; *celery*, *cereal*, and *dirt* are mass nouns. We would not say *a Becky* or *a Jimmy*; *Becky* and *Jimmy* are proper nouns. We would not say *a hands* or *a shoes*; *hands* and *shoes* are plural nouns. Adam and Eve, at first, did form ungrammatical combinations such as these.

The numeral *two* we use only with count nouns in the plural. We would not say *two sock* since *sock* is singular, nor *two water* since *water* is a mass noun. The word *more* we use before count nouns in the plural (*more nuts*) or mass nouns in the singular (*more coffee*). Adam and Eve made a number of combinations involving *two* or *more* that we would not make.

Given the initial very undiscriminating use of words in the class M it follows that one dimension of development must be a progressive differentiation of privileges, which means the division of M into smaller classes. There must also be sub-division of the noun class (N) for the reason that the privileges of occurrence of various kinds of modifiers must be described in terms of such sub-varieties of N as the common noun and proper noun, the count noun and mass noun. There must eventually emerge a distinction between nouns singular and nouns plural since this distinction figures in the privileges of occurrence of several sorts of modifiers.

Sixteen weeks after our first records from Adam and Eve (Time 2), the differentiation process had begun. By this time there were distributional reasons for separating out articles (*a, the*) from demonstrative pronouns (*this, that*) and both of these from the residual class of modifiers. Some of the evidence for this conclusion appears in Table 5–6. In general

Table 5–6. Subdivision of the Modifier Class

(A) Privileges Peculiar to Articles

Obtained	Not Obtained
A blue flower	*Blue a flower*
A nice nap	*Nice a nap*
A your car	*Your a car*
A my pencil	*My a pencil*

(B) Privileges Peculiar to Demonstrative Pronouns

Obtained	Not Obtained
That my cup	*My that cup*
That a horse	*A that horse*
That a blue flower	*A that blue flower*
	Blue a that flower

one syntactic class is distinguished from another when the members of one class have combinatorial privileges not enjoyed by the members of the other. Consider, for example, the reasons for distinguishing articles (Art) from modifiers in general (M). Both articles and modifiers appeared in front of nouns in two-word utterances. However, in three-word utterances that were made up from the total pool of words and that had a noun in final position, the privileges of *a* and *the* were different from the privileges of all other modifiers. The articles occurred in initial position followed by a member of class M other than an article. No other modifier occurred in this first position; notice the "Not obtained" examples of Table 5–6A. If the children had produced utterances like those (for example, *blue a flower, your a car*) there would have been no difference in the privileges of occurrence of articles and modifiers and therefore no reason to separate out articles.

The record of Adam is especially instructive. He created such notably ungrammatical combinations as "a your car" and "a my pencil." It is very unlikely that adults provided models for these. They argue strongly that Adam regarded all the words in the residual M class as syntactic equivalents and so generated these very odd utterances in which possessive pronouns appear where descriptive adjectives would be more acceptable.

Table 5–6 also presents some of the evidence for distinguishing demonstrative pronouns (Dem) from articles and modifiers (Table 5–6B). The pronouns occurred first and ahead of articles in three-and-four-word utterances—a position that neither articles nor modifiers ever filled. The sentences with demonstrative pronouns are recognizable as reductions which omit the copular verb *is.* Such sentences are not noun phrases in adult English and ultimately they will not function as noun phrases in the speech of the children, but for the present they are not distinguishable distributionally from noun phrases.

Recall now the generative formula of Table 5–5 which constructs noun phrases by simply placing a modifier (M) before a noun (N). The differentiation of privileges illustrated in Table 5–6, and the syntactic classes this evidence motivates us to create, complicate the formula for generating noun phrases. In Table 5–7 we have written a single general formula for producing all noun phrases at Time 2 [NP→(Dem)+ (Art)+(M)+N] and also the numerous more specific rules which are summarized by the general formula.

Table 5–7. Rules for Generating Noun Phrases at Time 2

$NP_1 \rightarrow Dem + Art + M + N$ $NP \rightarrow (Dem) + (Art) + (M) + N$

$NP_2 \rightarrow Art + M + N$

$NP_3 \rightarrow Dem + M + N$

$NP_4 \rightarrow Art + N$ ( ) means class within

$NP_5 \rightarrow M + N$ parentheses is optional

$NP_6 \rightarrow Dem + N$

$NP_7 \rightarrow Dem + Art + N$

By the time of the thirteenth transcription, twenty-six weeks after we began our study, privileges of occurrence were much more finely differentiated and syntactic classes were consequently more numerous. From the distributional evidence we judged that Adam had made five classes of his original class M: articles, descriptive adjectives, possessive pronouns, demonstrative pronouns, and a residual class of modifiers. Generative rules of Table 5–7 had become inadequate; there were no longer, for instance, any combinations like "A your car." Eve had the same set except that she used two residual classes of modifiers. In addition nouns had begun to subdivide for both children. The usage of proper nouns had become clearly distinct from the usage of count nouns. For Eve the evidence justified separating count nouns from mass nouns, but for Adam it still did not. Both children by this time were frequently pluralizing nouns but as yet their syntactic control of the singular–plural distinction was imperfect.

In summary, one major aspect of the development of general structure in child speech is a progressive differentiation in the usage of words and therefore a progressive differentiation of syntactic classes. At the same time, however, there is an integrative process at work. From the first, an occasional noun phrase occurred as a component of some larger construction. At first these noun phrases were just two words long and the range of positions in which they could occur was small. With time the noun phrases grew longer, were more frequently used, and were used in a greater range of positions. The noun phrase structure as a whole, in all the permissible combinations of modifiers and nouns, was assuming the combinatorial privileges enjoyed by nouns in isolation.

In Table 5–8 we have set down some of the sentence positions in which both nouns and noun phrases occurred in the speech

Table 5–8. Some Privileges of the Noun Phrase

Noun Positions	Noun Phrase Positions
That (*flower*)	That (*a blue flower*)
Where (*ball*) go ?	Where (*the puzzle*) go ?
Adam write (*penguin*)	Doggie eat (*the breakfast*)
(*Horsie*) stop	(*A horsie*) crying
Put (*hat*) on	Put (*the red hat*) on

of Adam and Eve. It is the close match between the positions of nouns alone and of nouns with modifiers in the speech of Adam and Eve that justifies us in calling the longer constructions noun phrases. These longer constructions are, as they should be, endocentric; the head word alone has the same syntactic privileges as the head word with its modifiers. The continuing failure to find in noun phrase positions whole constructions of the type "That a blue flower" signals the fact that these constructions are telegraphic versions of predicate nominative sentences omitting the verb form *is*. Examples of the kind of construction not obtained are: "That (that a blue flower)"; "Where (that a blue flower)?"

For adults the noun phrase is a subwhole of the sentence, what linguists call an "immediate constituent." The noun phrase has a kind of psychological unity. There are signs that the noun phrase was also an immediate constituent for Adam and Eve. Consider the sentence using the separable verb *put on*. The noun phrase in "Put the red hat on" is, as a whole, fitted in between the verb and the particle even as is the noun alone in "Put hat on." What is more, however, the location of pauses in the longer sentence, on several occasions, suggested the psychological organization: "Put . . . the red hat . . . on" rather than "Put the red . . . hat on" or "Put the . . . red hat on." In addition to this evidence the use of pronouns suggests that the noun phrase is a psychological unit.

The unity of noun phrases in adult English is evidenced, in the first place, by the syntactic equivalence between such phrases and nouns alone. It is evidenced, in the second place, by the fact that pronouns are able to substitute for total noun phrases. In our immediately preceding sentence the pronoun "It" stands for the rather involved construction from the first sentence of this paragraph: "The unity of noun phrases in adult English." The words called "pronouns" in English would more aptly be called "pro-noun-phrases" since it is the phrase rather than the noun which they usually replace. One does not replace "unity" with "it" and say "The *it* of noun phrases in adult English." In the speech of Adam and Eve, too, the pronoun came to function as a replacement for the noun phrase. Some of the clearer cases appear in Table 5–9.

Table 5–9. Pronouns Replacing Nouns or Noun Phrases and Pronouns Produced Together with Nouns or Noun Phrases

Noun Phrases Replaced by Pronouns	Pronouns and Noun Phrases in Same Utterances
Hit ball	Mommy get it ladder
Get it	Mommy get it my ladder
Ball go ?	Saw it ball
Go get it	Miss it garage
Made it	I miss it cowboy boot
Made a ship	I Adam drive that
Fix a tricycle	I Adam drive
Fix it	I Adam don't

Adam characteristically externalizes more of his learning than does Eve and his record is especially instructive in connection with the learning of pronouns. In his first eight records, the first sixteen weeks of the study, Adam quite often produced sentences containing both the pronoun and the noun or noun phrase that the pronoun should have replaced. One can here see the equivalence in the process of establishment. First the substitute is produced and then, as if in explication, the form or forms that will eventually be replaced by the substitute. Adam spoke out his pronoun antecedents as chronological consequents. This is additional evidence of the unity of the noun phrase since the noun phrases *my ladder* and *cowboy boot* are linked with *it* in Adam's speech in just the same way as the nouns *ladder* and *ball*.

We have described three processes involved in the child's acquisition of syntax. It is clear that the last of these, the induction of latent structure, is by far the most complex. It looks as if this last process will put a serious strain on any learning theory thus far conceived by psychology. The very intricate simultaneous differentiation and integration that constitutes the evolution of the noun phrase is more reminiscent of the biological development of an embryo than it is of the acquisition of a conditional reflex.

References

BRAINE, M. D. S. The ontogeny of English phrase structure: the first phase. *Language*, 1963, 39, 1–13.

BROWN, R., and FRASER, C. The acquisition of syntax. In C. N. Cofer & Barbara S. Musgrave (Eds.), *Verbal behavior and learning: Problems and processes.* New York: McGraw-Hill, 1963.

MACLAY, H., and OSGOOD, C. E. Hesitation phenomena in spontaneous English speech. *Word*, 1959, 15, 19–44.

MILLER, W., and ERVIN, SUSAN M. The development of grammar in child language. In Ursula Bellugi & R. Brown (Eds), The acquisition of language. *Monogr. Soc. Res. Child Develpm.*, 1964, 29, No. 1, Serial No. 92.

[6]

The Child's Grammar from I to III

The "I to III" of the title is not an eccentric way of referring to chronological age. It is not possible to talk about the "child's grammar" at a particular age because individual children progress at such markedly different rates. Some sort of index is needed that is responsive to grammatical development as a whole and can be used to identify a child's level regardless of the child's age. The mean length of utterance is that sort of index. In the first few speaking years the index rises steadily for all normal children. We have used the numerals I to V to designate five benchmarks evenly spaced in terms of mean length of utterance across a long period of development. A given numeral represents for the three children of our longitudinal study (Adam, Eve, and Sarah) a particular mean length of utterance, the same for all three.

With our I to V system one naturally falls into the habit of speaking of Stage I and Stage II and so on. There is no harm in that so long as we recognize that these are imposed stages, laid upon continuous data by the investigator as an analytic convenience.

This paper is the first extended report of the results of the longitudinal study. It was co-authored by Courtney Cazden and Ursula Bellugi, and it makes reference to the dissertation research of both these investigators. The paper was prepared for the second annual Minnesota Symposium on Child Psychology, and it was published (1969; pp. 28–73) in the volume of that title edited by John P. Hill. Reprinted by permission of the authors.

Our numerals "I" to "V" do not designate real stages, fitted to major discontinuities or system transformations, in the data. These latter may exist and eventually be defined, but I to V, for now, are like a set of intervals, of constant size, imposed by a statistician on a continuum of annual incomes.

A GROUP OF US AT HARVARD are engaged in a longitudinal study of development of grammar in three pre-school children. One of the children, Eve, is the daughter of a graduate student, Adam is the son of a minister who lives in Boston, and Sarah is the daughter of a man who works as a clerk in Somerville. Eve's and Adam's parents have college educations; Sarah's parents have high school degrees. The principal data of the study are transcriptions of the spontaneous speech of the child and his mother (occasionally also the father) in conversation at home. For each child we have at least two hours of speech for every month that he has been studied; sometimes as much as six hours. Sarah's records are entirely transcribed in a phonetic notation that includes stress and intonation. The other children's records are not in phonetic notation except at a few points where some particular hypothesis made the notation necessary.

Figure 6-1 identifies an initial developmental period which has been the focus of our analyses thus far. The initial period has been defined in terms of the means and ranges of utterance length, terms external to the grammar. The period begins, for all three children, when the mean was 1.75 morphemes and ends when the mean was 4.0 morphemes. The longest utterance at the lower bound of the interval was 4 morphemes; at the upper bound, 13. Mean length of utterance is useful as a rough term of reference for developmental level in this early period but it grows more variable and less useful with age.

As can be seen from Figure 6-1, the children were not of the same chronological age when the study began: Eve was eighteen months; Adam and Sarah were twenty-seven months. We selected these three children from some thirty considered on the basis of matched initial performance rather than age.

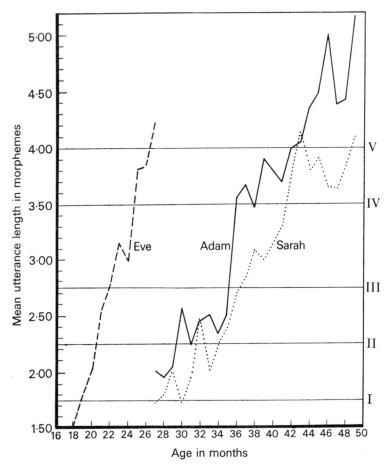

Figure 6–1. Mean Utterance Length and Age in Three Children.

At the end of the period for analysis, Eve was twenty-six months, Adam forty-two months, and Sarah forty-eight months. In terms of the utterance length the rates of development of the three children may be ordered: Eve, Adam, Sarah. The research is directed at two general questions. What does the child know of the structure of English at successive points in his development? By what processes does he acquire his knowledge? The most explicit, comprehensive, and systematic form in which adult knowledge of grammar has been represented is the generative transformational grammar (Chomsky, 1957; 1965). A generative grammar is a system of rules that derives an infinite set of well-formed sentences and assigns them correct structural descriptions. The most demanding form in which to pose the question of the child's knowledge of structure at any time is to ask for a generative grammar that represents his knowledge. We are attempting to write such grammars for the three children at each of five points in the initial developmental period. These points are marked with lines and Roman numerals in Figure 6–1; they fall at nearly equal intervals across the period. For the grammars we make detailed distributional analyses of seven hundred utterances from each child.

A complete annotated grammar is between fifty and a hundred pages long, and so none is presented here. We do, however, present portions of a single grammar, the one written for Adam at III, to illustrate the kinds of knowledge such a grammar is designed to represent. Then, using Adam III as a kind of temporary terminus, we provide a descriptive overview of developments in the first period. Following this we offer more detailed discussions of two specific developments: segmentation into morphemes and the construction of wh questions. Finally we review what we have learned about the role of "training variables" in grammar acquisition.

A PORTION OF ADAM III

The sentence *Where those dogs goed?* was not actually created by Adam in III; it is a composite that illustrates more of the interesting features of his grammar than does any single sentence he actually formed. Let us follow the derivation of this composite sentence using the grammar constructed for Adam at III.

The grammar is a set of mechanical procedures or algorithms for generating sentences and assigning structural descriptions to them. The generation in question is "logical" rather than "psychological," in the sense that the grammar does not constitute a model of practical processes by which sentences might actually be produced or understood. The grammar is psychological in that it is supposed to *represent* Adam's knowledge about the organization of sentences, and it is presumed that this knowledge somehow enters into actual production and comprehension.

The structure of grammatical knowledge is not given in any direct and simple way in spontaneous speech. It is worked out from spontaneous speech by a process of inference that is far from being either mechanical or certainly correct. The process is something like trying to fit together the pieces of an immense jigsaw puzzle and something like the process of trying to decipher an unknown Minoan script but not at all like the process of doing experiments in a psychological laboratory. We operate on the general assumption that the child's terminal state of knowledge is of the kind represented by current transformational grammars (e.g., Chomsky, 1965; Katz & Postal, 1964; Klima, 1964). However, we do not simply attribute to each sentence that the child produces the analysis that would be appropriate to that sentence if it were produced by an adult; if we were to do that, the inquiry would be largely vacuous. Insofar as the child's particular sentence—and all related sentences—depart from adult forms, the grammar is tailored to the departures. The most informative departures are analogical errors of commission, such as *goed* in the sample sentence. Harder to interpret, but still important, are errors of omission, such as the absence of the auxiliary *did* from the sample sentence. Omissions in a sentence are at least easy to detect, but omissions in the distributional range of a form are harder to detect and harder to interpret since it is necessary to weigh the probability that an omission is simply a consequence of the size of the sample that has been taken. Finally, all the errors that occur must be considered in comparison with conceivable errors that do not occur. Even this full procedure will not render the construction completely determinate in all respects. The indeterminacies are tentatively resolved by assigning the usual adult representation insofar as that representation does not depend on forms that have never appeared in the child's speech. We shall be able to illustrate most aspects of this process in what follows.

The Phrase Structure Level

A phrase structure rule in adult grammar rewrites a single symbol into symbol(s) distinct from the one rewritten. Roughly speaking, the phrase structure represents the adult's sense of hierarchical grouping in a sentence—the feeling that a sentence cracks or breaks up into natural major constituents which in turn break up into natural smaller constituents. It also represents such basic sentence relations as are called, in traditional grammar, subject of a sentence, predicate of a sentence, object of a verb, and so forth. The phrase structure includes everything essential for a complete semantic interpretation, but it does not necessarily order elements as they are ordered in the ultimate surface structure.

Table 6-1 gives the phrase structure portion of the derivation of the sentence "Where those dogs goed?" This derivation, and every derivation, begins with the symbol S for *sentence*, not because Adam is supposed to have a generic intention to compose a sentence which precedes the composition of any particular sentence, but because the grammar is a kind of extended definition of the meaning of *sentence*. The first rule of the phrase structure rewrites S into Nominal and Predicate and a set of abstract morphemes symbolized as imp, wh, and neg. These last three represent the germs from which, respectively, imperatives, interrogatives, and negatives can be developed. The abstract morphemes do not stand for any particular words but provide the occasion in adult grammar for transformations that result in a great variety of imperative, interrogative, and negative expressions. The abstract morphemes are in parentheses; sentences need not be

Table 6–1. Phrase Structure Rules and a Derivation

Rules of Phrase Structure	Derivation of "Where those dogs goed?"
1. S→([imp/wh]) (neg) Nominal– Predicate	S wh–Nominal–Predicate
2. Predicate →[MV/Cop]	wh–Nominal–MV
3. MV→Vb (Comp)	wh–Nominal–Vb–Comp
4. Vb→(Aux) V (Prt)	wh–Nominal–Aux–V–Comp
5. Aux→[Vᶜ/B+ing/Past]	wh–Nominal–Past–V–Comp
6. Comp→[Adverb/Nominal (Adverb)]	wh–Nominal–Past–V–Adverb
7. Cop→B–Pred	
8. B→[be/β]	
9. Pred→[Det/Nominal/Adverb]	
10. Adverb→[Loc/Adv/Prep Phr]	wh–Nominal–Past–V–Loc
11. Loc→[somewhere/Adv/Prep Phr]	wh–Nominal–Past–V–somewhere
12. Prep Phr→Prp[Nominal/Adv]	
13. Nominal→[something/NP]	wh–NP–Past–V–somewhere
14. NP→(Det) N	wh–Det–N–Past–V–somewhere

Key: Symbols do not all have exact equivalents in the terminology of traditional grammar so translations are only suggestive. The exact sense of each symbol is given by the grammar itself.

( ) : optionality
[x/y] : mutual exclusivity of x and y
Adv : adverb
Adverb : adverbial
Aux : auxiliary
B : *be* or β
B+ing : progressive aspect
β : should contain *be* form but does not
Comp : complement
Cop : copula
Det : determiner or descriptive adjective
imp : imperative
Loc : locative adverbial
MV : main verb

N : noun
neg : negative
NP : noun phrase
Past : past tense
Pred : predicate adjectival,
    nominal, or adverbial
Prp : preposition
Prep Phr : prepositional phrase
Prt : particle
S : sentence
Vᶜ : catenative verb
V : verb
Vb : verbal
wh : interrogative

either imperative, interrogative, or negative. In the derivation of a declarative affirmative sentence none of the abstract morphemes is selected. The imp and wh symbols are in brackets to indicate that the symbols are mutually exclusive; a sentence is not simultaneously imperative and interrogative. The second rule of the phrase structure makes a fundamental division among predicates. The symbol Cop (for *copula*) expands either as a form of *be* or as β, which ultimately has no phonological representation (Adam produces sentences such as *That my book* which should contain a *be* form but do not). Sentences with Cop are sometimes called equational sentences. The verb (or its absence) is followed in such sentences by a noun phrase (NP) functioning as predicate nominative or an adverbial (Adverb) or a descriptive adjective (included in Det which means *determiner*). Sample sentences are *That's a clock, Doggie is here, Doggie big*. The main verb (MV) form of the predicate may, if the verb is a transitive, be followed by a NP functioning as direct object which may in turn be followed by some sort of adverbial (Adverb). Intransitive verbs take adverbials but not direct objects.

In Rule 4 the auxiliary (Aux) is introduced and in Rule 5 it is rewritten. These rules are somewhat different from the rules that represent adult use of the adult auxiliary. What kinds of distributional facts about Adam's speech suggest the rules we have written? Adam's Aux is introduced into MV but not Cop; the adult auxiliary would be introduced into both. The adult rule represents the fact that adults combine *be* forms with Past (e.g., *was*) and with auxiliary verbs (e.g., *I want to be*) and with progressive (B+ing) aspect (e.g., *He is being good*) as well as combining main verbs with these operations. Adam, on the other hand, never combined *be* with auxiliary operations. The division between equational and main verb sentences lies deep in Adam's grammar precisely because he includes Aux in the one and not the other.

In Rule 5 Aux is rewritten as three constituents: catenative verbs (V^c) such as *wanna, gonna*, and *hafta*; the progressive aspect (B+ing) which produces such forms as *walking* and *eating*; the Past morpheme which produces such forms as *walked* and also *feeled*. Why are the three constituents collected together and placed before the V? The description is not in accord with the surface characteristics of Adam's relevant sentences, for, although the catenatives do precede verbs on the surface, the progressive and past inflections are affixed to the ends of verbs. At a later point in the grammar, in the transformational component, there has to be a rule that transposes stems and affixes so as to produce the correct surface order. In that case why set them wrong in the first place? For several reasons. In the first place, as a means of representing the relation of mutual exclusion which obtains among the three auxiliary elements in Adam's speech. He never combines two or more auxiliaries to say such things as *I was eating* or *I wanted to eat*, though adults of course do. Deeper motivation for the Aux constituent derives from the requirements of the transformational component. In the construction of imperatives, for example, Adam never uses an auxiliary. He says *Please read* but not *Please reading* or *Please wanna read* or *Please readed*. It is convenient to be able to exclude all of the possibilities at once by forbidding the use of all auxiliaries in imperatives and for that you need an Aux constituent. Behind the convenience, of course, is the fact that catenative verbs, progressives, and pasts are distributed in sentences as if they were, on some level, one thing.

These are some of the considerations that shape the first five rules. How does one use the rules to construct a derivation? The derivation of a sentence is, essentially, the pathway through the rules that will yield the sentence. There must be such a pathway for every sentence and none for non-sentences. One constructs a derivation by applying the rules to successive strings, making those (permitted) choices which will in the end produce the intended sentence. In Table 6–1, the first step of the derivation might be read, "the symbol S is rewritten, by Rule 1, as 'wh-Nominal-Predicate.' " Since the intended sentence is to be an interrogative, wh is chosen from among the optional abstract morphemes. The intended sentence is to contain a main verb (*go*) and so MV is selected by Rule 2. The sentence will also contain a locative, and since these develop out of the complement (Comp), that constituent must be added by Rule 3. There is to be a Past auxiliary, and Rules 4 and 5 accomplish its selection.

And so the derivation proceeds. The last line, sometimes called the "preterminal" string, still does not look much like the sentence *Where those dogs goed?* Instead of the interrogative word *where*, we have the abstract interrogative morpheme wh and the locative "somewhere." This last is not the word *somewhere* but rather is a dummy element standing for an unknown, or unspecified, locative. The *where* interrogative will be derived by transformation from the wh element and the dummy locative. The preterminal string contains, in place of the lexical items *those, dog,* and *go*, symbols for the categories (or parts of speech) to which these items respectively belong: Det, N, and V. In the next level of the grammar the category symbols will be replaced by appropriate lexical items, and the result will be a terminal string: "wh–those–dog–Past–go–somewhere."

The Subcategorization Level

If determiners, nouns, and verbs from the lexicon were allowed freely to replace the category symbols Det, N, and V in the preterminal string underlying the sample sentence, the results would often be ungrammatical. In addition to *those dogs go*, we might have *a dogs go, those Adam go, the stone knows*, and what not. There are, in English, restrictions on the co-occurrence of lexical items forbidding many of the combinations that the phrase structure rules alone permit. These restrictions have traditionally been formulated in terms of lexical subcategories. For example, among nouns, those that may take determiners are said to belong to the subcategory of common noun, such as *dog*. Nouns that may not take determiners are proper nouns, such as *Adam*. Nouns are also subcategorized on other principles; count nouns (including *dog*) may be pluralized, whereas mass nouns (e.g., *air*) may not. How is subcategorization to be represented in the present grammar? We shall illustrate the general character of the rules with reference to one constituent of the sample sentence, the subject Nominal, which is represented in the preterminal string as Det-N and in the surface sentence as *those dogs*.

Each entry in the lexicon of the language is going to be assigned certain syntactic features (such as +ct for count nouns) that represent certain distributional potentialities of the lexical items. In addition, the lexical category symbols in the last line of the phrase structure derivation—such as Det, N, and V—are going to expand into complex symbols that also contain syntactic features. The complete complex symbol will be a kind of grappling hook with a set of syntactic features constituting a denticulate surface shaped to retrieve only the right kind of item from the lexicon.

The complex symbol is, first of all, marked with the name of the major category (e.g., +N). In the lexicon all nouns (e.g., *dog* in the subcategorization rules and derivation, Table 6–2)

Table 6–2. Subcategorization Rules and a Derivation

Subcategorization Rules

Lexical Category	Categorical Contexts	Other Syntactic Features
N→[+N]a	N→[+Det___] ; [–Det___]	N→[+ct] ; [–ct]
		N→[+no] ; [–no]
Det→[+Det]b		Det→[___[+ct]N] ;
		[___[–ct]N]
		Det→[___[+no]N] ;
		[___[–no]N]

Derivation

Preterminal string	wh–Det–N–Past–V–somewhere
Complex symbol expansion	N→[+N, +Det___, +ct, +no]
	Det→[+Det, ___[+ct]N, ___[+no]N]
Replacement by lexical items	*dog*, [+N, +Det___, +ct, +no]
	those, [+Det, ___[+ct]N, ___[+no]N]

a Lexical entry : *dog*, [+N, +Det___, +ct, ±no]
b Lexical entry : *those*, [+Det, ___[+ct]N, ___[+no]N]

are assumed to be similarly marked. Now we have the first level of subcategorization, sometimes called strict subcategorization. This involves the assignment to each complex symbol of syntactic features which are simply its frames or contexts stated in category symbols. It is as if one were to scan the preterminal string, to take note of the fact that each category occurs in the context of certain other categories, and then to enter those category contexts which restrict the selection of lexical items. In our own example the symbol N occurs in the context Det＿. When, therefore, N is replaced by a particular noun from the lexicon, that noun must be of the kind that may be preceded by a determiner—in fact, by a common and not by a proper noun. The facts can be expressed by assigning the complex symbol for N the contextual feature [+Det＿], by assigning all common nouns in the lexicon (including *dog*) this same feature, and by adopting a replacement rule which allows the complex symbol for N to be replaced by only those lexical items with matching syntactic features.

From Rule 14 of the phrase structure we know that *in general*, which means across all sentences, determiners are optional before nouns. In the particular sentence under derivation, however, there is to be a determiner before the noun, and that fact must enter into the derivation. The need for specification of a contextual feature arises only, but always, where there is in the phrase structure an optional environment for a lexical category. Contextual features are needed at several points in Adam's grammar. By assigning verbs the contextual features +＿NP and −＿NP, for instance, it is possible to retrieve transitive verbs when they are required and intransitives when they are required.

At the next level in the expansion of the complex symbol, syntactic features are added which are not defined in terms of the categories of the preterminal string. In the case of the nouns in a sentence the syntactic features are context-free— that is, they are selected without reference to other complex symbols in the sentence. The syntactic features added to the symbols for determiners and verbs are context-sensitive—they are selected with reference to markers already added to nouns. Such rules are sometimes called selection rules. By this arrangement other words are made to agree with nouns rather than nouns with them. For English, in general, and also for Adam III, the selectional dominance of the noun is not just a convention, but it is rather a representation of certain facts about sentences.

The symbol N in our present derivation acquires the marker +ct rather than −ct and the marker +no rather than −no.

It is then equipped to retrieve a count noun from the lexicon, a noun marked +ct as *dog* is in Table 6–2. Lexical entries for nouns will not be marked +no but rather ±no, to indicate that they may be pluralized, or else −no, to indicate that, like *air*, they may not be pluralized. These markers, and in addition a marker that indicates whether a noun is human (+hum) or not, are needed for nouns in Adam III.

The symbol Det acquires syntactic features in a context-sensitive manner, taking its lead, as it were, from the head word in the noun phrase. Since that head word, the N, has the features +ct and +no, the determiner to accompany it must have features which comprise a matrix to the noun's patrix. Det requires the features [__[+ct]N] and [__[+no]N]; the features require that the determiner drawn from the lexicon be one able to modify count nouns in the plural.

The fully expanded complex symbols for our sentence (there would be one for V as well as N and Det) serve to select lexical entries. The general lexical rule (which need not be stated in the formal grammar, since it constitutes part of the definition of derivation) is, Where a complex symbol is not distinct from a lexical entry the latter can replace the former. The lexical entry for *dog* is one of those common count nouns that can replace the symbol for N in the present derivation, and *those* is among the entries that can replace the symbol for Det. These processes are illustrated in the rules and derivation in Table 6–2.

The Transformational Level

The phrase structure and subcategorization levels together comprise what has been called the base structure of a grammar. In a derivation the base structure yields a structured string of morphemes such as wh–[those dog]$_{Nominal}$[Past–go]$_{Vb}$ –somewhere; this string contains only some of its labeled bracketings. Transformational rules map such underlying strings into new structured strings that are closer to actual sentences. Transformations delete, substitute, and permute elements—as phrase structure rules cannot. Roughly speaking, transformations represent the feeling native speakers have that the members of a certain set of sentences are related to their counterparts in another set by a single function.

Table 6–3. Transformation Rules and a Derivation

Transformation Rules[a]

XIV. Wh incorporation for MV sentences:

wh–Nominal–Vb(Nominal)–somewhere $\Rightarrow$ wh + somewhere–Nominal–Vb (Nominal)

XIX. Affixation of Past[b]:

χ^1–[Past]$_{Aux}$–V–χ^2 $\Rightarrow$ χ^1–V+ Past–χ^2

Derivation

Base: wh–[those dog]$_{Nominal}$[Past–go]$_{Vb}$–somewhere

XIV: wh + somewhere–those–dog–Past–go

XIX: wh + somewhere–those–dog–go + Past

---

[a] The numbers assigned the rules are those they carry in the full grammar.
[b] χ^1 and χ^2 simply stand for any other sentence constituents.

Adam III includes twenty-four transformational rules. Some of the grammatical functions they perform are: agreement in person and number for subject and verb; agreement in number for subject and predicate nominative; creation of such elliptical possessives as *yours* and *mines*; and deletion of subject *you* from imperatives. In the derivation of our sample sentence, transformations are needed to transpose an affix and stem and to incorporate *somewhere* into wh. The rules and the steps in the derivation appear in the list above. A transformational rule describes the structure of the kind of string to which it is applicable; there will generally be an indefinite number of strings that satisfy that structural description. In an actual derivation it is a particular string that is transformed.

The Morphophonemic Level

Rules on this level really belong to the phonological component, but to bring the derivation of our composite sentence to a recognizable form we need to use two of them. They are: xv, wh + somewhere→*where*, and xxiv, $[\chi]_v$ + Past→χ + −*ed*. Rule xxiv results in the erroneous form *goed*. The occurrence of this error marks the absence from Adam III of the adult morphophonemic rule, $[go]_v$ + Past→*went*. In terms of the conventions with which we are working, then, the error in question is a superficial one. It can be corrected by adding a single rule which does not disturb the remainder of the grammar in any way.

Now that we have a general picture of the children's competence at III, let us characterize in a general way developments between I and III.

OVERVIEW OF DEVELOPMENTS BETWEEN I AND III

Figure 6–1 indicates that there are large differences in rate of linguistic development among Adam, Eve, and Sarah but the order of events is, for these three unacquainted children, strikingly uniform. So much so that it is possible to describe developments between I and III in a way that is true of all. This is not to say that there are no differences among the children. One that is especially consistent and interesting concerns the rate of production of ungrammatical and anomalous forms. Adam produced these at about four times the rate of either girl—he spoke of "talking crackers," said his nose could "see," addressed the microphone as if it were a person, and said, "It's went," "Why I can't do that," and "That a my book." The girls were more literal and, except for telegraphic omissions, more often grammatical. From other data we have seen and from what parents tell us, there is evidently great individual variation among children on this dimension; probably it explains the very different notions of language development that particular psychologists derive from their own children. When the girls made errors, they were the same kinds of errors that Adam made. For that reason we have assumed that the induction and hypothesis-testing involved is common to the three and simply more copiously externalized by Adam. He gives us a richer print-out, and so we more often cite evidence from his records than from the girls'.

Types of Sentences

From I to III the children seem to be working chiefly on simple sentences. This is not to say that all or even most of the children's *utterances* were complete simple sentences. It is rather to say that the most complex constructions they produced were simple sentences, that they never (or almost never) conjoined or embedded simple sentences. We do not find such sentences as *John and Mary laughed, The man you saw is here*, or *I want you to eat.*

In saying that the children from I to III seemed to be working on the structure of simple sentences it is necessary to make explicit the fact that we do not intend to make two related but stronger claims: We do not claim that in I and III the children learned nothing about conjoining and embedding; it is possible, after all, that some restriction on performance prevented them from revealing in spontaneous speech all that they had learned. Nor do we say that the children's knowledge of the simple sentence was complete before they started to embed and conjoin; that is clearly untrue. In III there were a few instances of embedding, and at that point all three children still had a great deal to learn about simple sentences. Auxiliary elements were only occurring singly; there were no combinations. There were no passives and only the simplest reflexes of negativity. There were no tag questions, and indeed, well-formed yes-no questions of all kinds were missing. Clearly, embedding and conjoining do not wait upon the development of complete knowledge of simple sentences.

What sorts of simple sentences were the children working on from I to III? Declarative-affirmative sentences, of course, but we shall leave till last the description of these, since most of the knowledge involved is not specific to them but is common to all sentences. In addition to declarative-affirmative sentences, the children were working on negatives, imperatives, and interrogatives. We saw in Adam III that these are developed, in transformational grammar, from the abstract morphemes neg, imp, and wh. From the beginning of our records, that is, from I, the children gave evidence of understanding the meaning of these morphemes. What they lacked was the transformational rules which develop surface structures expressing these morphemes. These rules were missing entirely in I. In III there were eight to twelve transformational rules serving this purpose, only a fraction of the adult rules, and some of them were not proper adult rules at all.

René Spitz (1957) says that the child begins at about fifteen months to shake his head as an intentional negative signal, usually having the sense of resistance to some attempt to influence him. In I, we find this signal and also the word *no* used to resist imperatives and to answer yes-no questions. We also find *no* added initially to several kinds of utterance: *No fall, No put, No picture in there*, and so forth; this seems to be the child's own invention. In II and III the *no* forms were supplemented by *can't, won't*, and *don't*. It seems unlikely to us that these were related transformationally, as they are in the adult language, to *can, will*, and *do*—unlikely because the affirmative modal auxiliaries had not appeared at this time. The forms seemed simply to be a set of preverbal forms introduced by obligatory transformation when the neg morpheme was in the base structure of a sentence with a main verb.

Imperative sentences in adult grammar are derived by transformation out of underlying strings containing the morpheme imp and having *you* as subject and *will* as auxiliary. This analysis is motivated by such adult sentences as, *Go chase yourself* and *Come here, will you?* Neither reflexives (*yourself*) nor tags (*will you*) occurred in early child speech, and so the facts justifying the adult analysis were lacking. In the recording sessions at home one could often be quite sure that a child's sentence had an imperative meaning, but there was nothing in the surface form of his imperative sentences that could serve as a reliable sign of this meaning. To be sure, such sentences were often produced without explicit subject, as are adult imperatives, but the children also very often omitted the subjects of sentences clearly intended to be declaratives. What happened between I and III was that the subjectless sentence came to be ever more nearly restricted to the imperative, but it was not exclusively imperative even in III. In addition, there were a few words the child learned to use after I (especially *please* and *gimme*) which may be confidently interpreted as imperative markers.

Very few of the linguistic reflexes of imperativity developed, then, in this first period, but from the start in I there were indications that the child understood the imperative meaning. This evidence on the responsive side lay in the child's compliance with or (at least as often) resistance to the force of a parental imperative. On the performance side the evidence lay in the child's occasional persistence in using certain constructions again and again to accomplish some effect in a resistant adult.

Interrogatives are of two basic types: yes-no questions and wh questions. We shall leave for a later section the description of wh questions. From I to III the child's yes-no questions were identifiable by rising intonation but not, consistently, by any other feature. It was as if he asked, "Yes or no?" by speaking any sentence or sentence fragment with questioning intonation. Well-formed yes-no questions, with the subject and the first member of the auxiliary transposed, appeared later than III.

The grammatical structure of declarative affirmative simple sentences is represented almost entirely by the base component of a grammar, the phrase structure and subcategorization rules. All of this structure is relevant also to negatives, imperatives, and interrogatives, but these three kinds of sentence include something more—rules in the transformational component. There are several kinds of knowledge represented by the base component: relations within a sentence, a hierarchy of constituents, and subcategorizations or co-occurrence restrictions. We shall say something about each of them.

Basic Sentence Relations

The basic relations are those called subject of the sentence, predicate of the sentence, and object of the verb. So far as our

117

materials permit us to judge, the child's knowledge of these relations (which, in English, are chiefly expressed by order) undergoes no development. He seems to express the relations he means to express from the very start. At any rate, there are few detectable errors in all the records. In most utterances it is clear that the intended subject and object are the constituents found in subject and object position—for instance, *I dump trash out, I making coffee, You need some paper*. It is unlikely that the child intended to convey the reversed relations, *Trash dump me out, Coffee making me, Some paper need you*. There are in the records a handful of exceptions in which the intended object seems to be in subject position—*Paper find, Daddy suitcase go get it, Paper write*—but these are the only exceptions in thousands of well-ordered sentences.

The precision with which the child expresses basic sentence relations is important, since these relations are probably linguistic universals and so may themselves be organizations preformed in the human brain. Perhaps subject and object relations are to the child what nut-burying is to the squirrel, an innate pattern requiring only a releaser to set it in operation. Perhaps, but we shall not want to draw that conclusion until we have more data. The children we have studied scrupulously preserve sentence word order not only with respect to basic relations but also with respect to the order of articles, adjectives, auxiliary verbs, adverbs, and all other words. In imitation tasks they omit words but seldom confuse order. This may be a general feature of imitation in children or perhaps only a feature of the imitation of speech. The accurate expression of sentence relations by children learning English may, therefore, be a kind of incidental consequence of the fact that English expresses these relations by word order. We should like to know how well the relations are expressed by children learning a language that expresses subject and object relations by case endings (see Slobin, 1966, for some evidence concerning Russian).

Constituents

The Aux is a constituent that developed in the period I–III. In I, all main verbs occurred in unmarked generic form. In II and III, the same set of operations on the verb developed in all three children: the progressive, the past, and a set of semi-auxiliary verbs we called catenatives. Most prominent among the catenatives are *gonna*, *wanna*, and *hafta*. The three operations on the verb are represented as a constituent Aux for reasons already described.

The constituent NP was present even in I but underwent consolidation and elaboration between I and III. The constituent status of the NP even in I is attested to by the fact that the children quite consistently responded to questions in *Who* or *What* with some sort of NP. This equivalence in the exchanges of discourse is evidence that the many particular NP's were organized together. In adult speech, the NP has four principal functions in simple sentences: in equational sentences it serves as subject and as predicate nominative, and in main verb sentences as subject and direct object. For the children, the NP had these four functions from the start. At any rate some sort of NP served each function, but, whereas an adult will use every sort of NP in all positions, in the children's speech at I, each position seemed to require a somewhat different formula for the NP. Subjects of equational sentences were often impersonal pronouns (especially *that* and *it*), but predicate nominatives never were. Subjects of main verbs were almost always names of persons or animals, whereas direct objects were almost always names of inanimate things. Subject NP's in both kinds of sentence, at I, never consisted of more than one morpheme—a simple pronoun or noun. Object and predicate nominative NP's at I were, on the other hand, somewhat more complex; they might consist of two nouns (e.g., *Adam book*) or a determiner and noun (e.g., *my book*). If we write a grammar that stays close to the sentences actually obtained at I, we must include four distinct versions of NP, which makes a fragmentary grammar strangely unlike the adult form. One of the things that happened between I and III was that the four NP's came to resemble one another closely enough so that a single NP symbol, one rewritten by a single set of rules, could be entered in all four positions. In addition, the NP grew in complexity in all positions.

There are, finally, constituents that had still not developed by III. These include the adverbials Time and Manner. There were occasional time and manner expressions in the children's speech by III, but they were few. Most importantly, the children at III were not giving grammatically appropriate answers to time (*When*) and manner (*How*) questions. Of the adverbials, the locative is by far the first to develop. It is clearly present even in I.

Strict Subcategorization

The progressive inflection (*-ing*) emerged for all three children between I and III. In adult English, this inflection is not used with all verbs. So-called "process" verbs (*sing, walk, eat,* and so forth) freely take the progressive, whereas "state" verbs (*need, equal, know,* and *like*) do not. To say *I am singing the song* is quite correct, but *I am knowing the song* is strange. The process-state subcategorization of verbs can be represented, in an English grammar, in the expansion of the complex symbol for V. A choice is made between two features which represent contexts at the level of the phrase structure, the features $[+[be+ing]\_]$; $[-[be+ing]\_]$.[1] These features are entered also in relevant verbs in the lexicon. The interesting fact is that these rules were already needed for the children's grammar at III because the children observed the subcategories and made no mistakes of the type *I liking candy* or *I wanting a book*. Such mistakes were not absent simply from the samples used for the grammars; they were absent from all data over the full range I–V.

David McNeill (1966) has argued that children must have innate knowledge of a hierarchy of subcategories corresponding to whatever hierarchy may prove to be a linguistic universal. The complete absence of subcategorization errors in connection with the progressive inflection seems to support McNeill's position—or, at any rate, does so if the following interpretation of his position is acceptable.

If we ask what could possibly be universal and therefore

---

[1] The form be+ing refers to English grammar, whereas the form used earlier, B+ing, refers specifically to the grammar of the children in this study.

innate about the process-state distinction, the answer must surely be the underlying semantic principle. The distributional facts, such as the rule for -*ing*, are known to be specific to particular languages. How could an innate process-state distinction forestall inflectional errors? Something like this would have to be true: As the meaning was learned of each new verb like *walk*, *eat*, *need*, and *like*, the semantic entry would have to include all innate subcategorization features as well as individual elements of meaning. In short, *walk* would from the first be tagged as a "process" and *need* as a "state."

When at a later time the child attended to distributional facts peculiar to English, such as the fact that some verbs are inflected with -*ing* and some not, he would have a set of ready hypotheses to explain the cleavage. He would test to see whether it was governed by one or another of the pre-established, universal subcategorizations. And of course the process-state subcategorization defines the proper dotted line for -*ing*. It is somewhat as if a child learning to recognize coins kept track of all the attributes that are ever significant in a coinage system—color, weight, size, design, texture, and so forth. Then when he first encountered the distributional facts of monetary exchange, such as the fact that two coins of one kind equal one of another, he would quickly see which of the perceptual attributes he had been keeping track of were useful.

The absence of error in connection with a semantically principled subcategorization is one prediction of the "innateness" hypothesis, and this prediction is confirmed in the case of the progressive. However, one easily thinks of other predictions that are not confirmed. The division of nouns into mass and count subcategories is semantically based and as likely to be universal as the process-state division, but the children were, at V, still making some errors in their use of the noun subcategories. Some subcategorizations in English are unprincipled (i.e., they have no semantic base)—for example, the verb subcategories that take regular and irregular inflections for Past. Not surprisingly, children make many mistakes in cases like these, where rote learning of the subcategory membership of each verb is really the only possibility. In fact, errors in this connection are often heard in the elementary school years; they are to be expected. But if the children have innate subcategories, should they not, on first encountering unprincipled cleavages, act as if they expected one or another of the innate principles to govern the cleavage? On first encountering the fact that some verbs take -*ed* and some do not, a child ought to test the hypothesis that all of the former verbs might be processes and the latter states, the hypothesis that the former might be transitives and the latter intransitives, and so forth. There is no trace of anything of the kind in our data.

The full story is too long to tell, but our present best guess is that the absence of error with -*ing* is not to be attributed to innate subcategorization. And, in general, we have not found any reason to believe that subcategories are innate other than the usual reason—it is exceedingly difficult to determine how they are learned.

Noncategorical Syntactic Features

Plural number in English is marked by inflection of the noun; this inflection, like the progressive, was entirely absent in I and often present by III. The expression of number in English is vastly more complicated than the expression of something like progressive aspect. For example, there must be agreement in number between a head noun and its determiners, between a subject noun and a predicate nominal, and between a pronoun and its antecedent noun. Number and person together, as features of a subject noun, determine the form of the verb: *walks* or *walk*, *is* or *are*. In Adam III, number is introduced in the base structure in the form of two context-free syntactic markers in the complex symbol for the noun: [+no] and [−no]. There are related markers for the complex symbol of Det and for many lexical items. There are three transformations and several morphophonemic rules.

The development of number in the three children illustrates nicely the difference between deep and superficial acquisition of a grammatical feature. In terms of chronological age,

Eve began to inflect nouns some fourteen months earlier than did Sarah. However, when Eve first used plurals she made many mistakes in all aspects of number agreement, whereas Sarah, from the start, made almost no mistakes. What this means is that in Eve's grammar, number first appears as a low-level morphophonemic rule which, in effect, says that nouns have an optional pronunciation with a terminal sibilant. The introduction of this rule leaves the rest of Eve's grammar undisturbed. For Sarah, number enters in the base structure and effects complex changes in the total grammar. So we see that Eve was not always so far in advance of Sarah as the simple mean length of utterance index alone would indicate. And we see that acquisitions that may look alike if only certain words or endings are examined may look very unlike when the total distributional pattern is examined.

In summary of this overview, it is correct to say that the child's early grammar comprises a base structure not very different from that of the adult grammar and a syntactic transformational component that is rudimentary in III and almost totally absent in I. This is not the same as saying that children directly speak base-structure sentences. It is not clear what that statement could mean since morphophonemic and phonetic rules are required to make sentences of the underlying strings. But the underlying strings themselves seem to be chiefly those that can be generated by the base.

SEGMENTATION INTO MORPHEMES

In order to learn grammar, a child must segment the speech he hears into morphemes because morphemes are the ultimate units of grammatical rules. There are short-run regularities that can be formulated in smaller units, the segmental phonemes, but the long-run regularities that render an infinite number of meanings constructable and interpretable cannot be formulated in terms of phonemes.

It may be useful to imagine an erroneous segmentation into morphemes and what its consequences would be. Consider the following set of utterances that a child might easily hear:

My book, Your book; My bike, Your bike; My birthday, Your birthday. If we let a slash mark represent a morpheme cut, then this segmentation is erroneous; *Myb/ook, Yourb/ook; Myb/ike, Yourb/ike; Myb/irthday, Yourb/irthday.* These morphemes look odd in print, but they represent sound combinations that are, in English phonology, easily pronounceable—think of *scribe* and *orb*, *Ike* and *oops*.

Suppose the child who has segmented in the above fashion goes on to store the contexts of each morpheme to the (unintentional and unconscious) end of discovering general and meaningful construction rules. The result may be represented in part as:

myb, [__*ook*, __*ike*, __*irthday*]
yourb, [__*ook*, __*ike*, __*irthday*]
ook, [*myb*__, *yourb*__]
ike, [*myb*__, *yourb*__]

Myb and *yourb* have identical context entries distinct from the entries for *ook* and *ike*, the latter two being themselves identical. In these circumstances it would be reasonable to infer the existence of two morpheme classes ($C_1 \rightarrow myb$, *yourb*; $C_2 \rightarrow ook$, *ike, irthday*) and of a construction signifying possession which is created by selecting class members in proper sequence (C_1–C_2). These inferences founded on a mistaken segmentation do not lead anywhere. For the small set of utterances that preserve the artificial co-occurrence of certain morphemes and a subsequent /b/ phoneme, the segmentation would appear to work. Given *my b/rake* and *my b/and*, the child could construct *your b/rake* and *your b/and* with approximately correct meaning. However, outside this artificial range his false morphemes would not work. He would not hear *the ook, the ike, the irthday* or *myb pencil, myb doggie, yourb Mommy*. And he would find unanalyzable such new possessives as *my pencil, my doggie, my Mommy, your pencil*, and *your doggie.*

Compare the results of a correct segmentation. The context entries would look like this:

my, [__*book*, __*bike*, __*birthday*]

your, [__*book*, __*bike*, __*birthday*]
book, [*my* __, *your* __]
bike, [*my* __, *your* __]

One morpheme class would represent a start on possessive pronouns, and the other a start on count nouns. A construction rule written in terms of these classes correctly anticipates *your brake* from the occurrence of *my brake*, *my band* from *your band*, and so on in an indefinite number of cases. Furthermore, the tentative morphemes *book*, *bike*, *birthday*, *my*, and *your* will recur with approximately the same meaning in such new constructions as *the book*, *my old hat*, and *your good friend*. A correct segmentation is repeatedly confirmed by its continuing ability to unlock regularities and structural meanings. An erroneous segmentation is a false trail winding off into the desert.

Judging from our materials, and from what we know of the materials of others, morpheme segmentation errors such as *myb pencil* or *the ook* are uncommon. It is easy to overlook the segmentation problem in child speech because there is so little evidence that it exists. The evidence we found in the fine structure of our data suggests that segmentation is a real problem in the sense that it is something a child learns but that it is also a problem for which he has highly effective solution procedures.

For example, Adam produced in an early record the sentence *It's big*. What was the status in Adam's grammar of the form *'s* (or *is*)? In adult grammar, *is* is a morpheme distinct from such other morphemes as *it* and *big* and organized closely with *am* and *are* as forms (allomorphs) of the verb *be*. We find in Adam's records certain errors of commission suggesting that *is* was differently organized for him. He produced hundreds of well-formed equational sentences with *it* as subject, but he also produced a large number of odd ones. The following are representative: *It's fell* (Sample 14), *It's has wheels* (Sample 21), *It's hurts* (Sample 17), and *It's went on the top* (Sample 22). The form *is* has no place in these sentences and seems to have been imported into them as an onhanger of *it*. Perhaps, then, the adult polymorphic form *its* was a single unanalyzed

125

morpheme for Adam. How does this hypothesis fare when tested against all the relevant evidence?

Suppose the hypothesis were wrong, and Adam was, in fact, learning to organize *is* in the correct, adult way. What errors ought he then to have made? Since *is*, as a form of *be*, is closely related to *am* and *are*, we should expect the several forms to have occasionally displaced one another in Adam's sentences through disregard of the features of the subject noun phrase that are supposed to select them. There ought to have been such errors as *I is*, *we is*, *I are*, and *he am*. There were no such errors in Adam's early records, and that fact supports the conclusion that *is* was not at first organized as a form of *be*.

In certain contexts *is* is obligatory: in such reduced equational sentences as *it big*, and in sentences with a verb inflected for progressive aspect, such as *it going*. When Adam began sometimes to produce an audible *is* in such contexts, he did not, for many months, always do so. On the same page of a protocol, it is quite usual to find otherwise identical sentences with and without *is*. Of course, adults too do not always sound all their segmental phonemes, but this particular reduction, from *it's* to *it*, is not one that adults make. Its occurrence in Adam suggests that for him *it's* and *it* were just varying pronunciations of one morpheme.

The range of *is* in Adam's early records was restricted in an important way. The word *it* is an impersonal pronoun and substitutes for impersonal noun phrases. When such noun phrases themselves occur as subjects of equational sentences and with verbs inflected for progressive aspect, an adult uses *is*—for example, *The top is big; The top is spinning.* In such cases, during the many months when we believe *it-s* was organized as a single morpheme, Adam always failed to produce *is*—that is what should happen if our hypothesis is correct. If, on the contrary, *is* were a separate morpheme, the difference between its invariable absence with noun phrase subjects and its only occasional absence with *it* as subject would be unaccountable.

There is another revealing restriction of range. If *it's* were simply a variant of *it*, then it ought to have occurred sometimes in all the sentence positions that *it* ever fills. As the third column of Table 6–4 shows, *it* was an object of a verb

Table 6–4. The Forms *It* and *It's* in Early Adam Samples

Samples	It *as Subject,* Is *Required as Verb*[a]		It *as Subject,* Is *Forbidden as Verb*[b]		It *as Object,* Is *Forbidden to Occur*[c]
	Is *Absent*	Is *Present*	Is *Absent*	Is *Present*	Is *Absent*
5–7		1			73
8–10		2	1		106
11–13		4	2		89
14–16	4	6	8	2	94
17–19	3	33	2	10	132
20–22	3	54		18	112

[a] For example, *It's big; It's going.*
[b] For example, *It hurts; It went.*
[c] For example, *Get it; Put it there.*
[d] No sentences with *is* present appeared in the sample.

more often than it was a subject. An adult would never use *it's* as a pronoun object, but our hypothesis about *it's* predicts such errors for Adam. If *it's* were a simple variant of *it*, he ought to have formed such sentences as *get it's* and *put it's there.* As the third column of Table 6–4 shows, he never made such errors.

The forms *it* and *it's* were in perfect complementary distribution. This is not a phonologically conditioned complementary distribution of the kind that obtains for the several forms of the regular plural inflection in English. In the phonologically conditioned case the several forms are perfectly predictable, so the variation among them is always redundant, and the descriptive linguist (e.g., Gleason, 1961; Harris, 1942; Hockett, 1947; Nida, 1948) considers the forms to be allomorphs of one morpheme. The complementary distribution that obtains for *it* and *it's* seems to be conditioned by grammatical role (sentence subject versus verb object), and in such cases the linguist does not necessarily conclude that the forms are allomorphs or variant forms.

Many languages use inflectional forms to signal the role of a word in a larger construction. When nouns are involved (the most familiar instance), we speak of cases. Subject and object case (or nominative and accusative) are marked in Sanskrit, Latin, Greek, Finnish, and many other languages (Gleason, 1961). In English, nouns are not inflected for case; nominative and accusative forms are distinguished by word order (e.g., *John saw Mary* versus *Mary saw John*). However, Adam used *it* and *it's* as if *'s* or *is* were a nominative case ending. If *it* and *it's* were organized in this way, then *is* was a separate morpheme, and we are incorrect in suggesting that *it's* was a single form, a variant of *it*. The possibility is an interesting one. Since case is a common syntactic device in the languages of the world, it is reasonable to suppose that case should be among the hypotheses about linguistic structure that the human mind would be disposed to entertain and test (Chomsky, 1965; Fodor, 1966). Much of the distributional data available to Adam would seem to have confirmed this hypothesis, and he might reasonably have organized the facts about *it* and *it's* in this way until more data motivated reorganization. However, for various reasons that cannot be detailed here, it is quite clear that Adam's *is* was not functioning as a case ending. The conclusion that best fits all the evidence is that *it* and *it's* were allomorphs of a single morpheme, their occurrence conditioned by grammatical role.

Errors of segmentation were rare in Adam, Eve, and Sarah, but *it's* was not the only case. The clearer instances[1] include: *I'm, that-a, drop-it, get-it, put-it, want-to, have-to, going-to, another-one, what-that,* and *let-me.* These pairs have two characteristics which, taken together, distinguish them from pairs that were correctly analyzed. The first characteris-

---

[1] Brown and Bellugi (1964) previously interpreted some portions of the relevant evidence in other ways. For instance, errors like *That a my boot* and *That a your car* were thought to indicate that Adam had adopted a mistaken rule permitting articles to precede every sort of nominal other than pronouns. Such errors as *drop it book* and *get it pencil* suggested that Adam, in learning to substitute pronouns for noun phrases, was making both explicit. In certain points of detail, previously overlooked, the view here that *that-a, drop-it,* and *get-it* were all unanalyzed single morphemes provides a closer fit to the data than do the previous interpretations.

tic is a phonetic one. *It's, wanna, lemme, put-it,* and, indeed, all pairs in the set are regularly run together by adults as if they were in fact single words (Heffner, 1949). This is to say that the morpheme boundary is not in these pairs marked in any way whatever—the pairs all lack the open juncture phoneme (/+/) which marks the majority of morpheme boundaries in English. Perhaps, then, children are usually able to avoid segmentation errors because they regularly cut the stream of speech at just those points were /+/ occurs. This, however, is not a simple claim.

How are children able to recognize /+/? It is not a phonetically simple feature. To be sure, when detectable pauses occur in a sentence, it is usually at morpheme boundaries; pause is thus considered one of the phonetic manifestations of /+/. The difficulty is that pause is only an intermittent feature. How is /+/ identified more generally?

Consider the pairs *nitrate* and *night-rate*, *slyness* and *minus*, *mark it* and *market*. There need be no actual pause in either member of a pair, but still there is an audible difference in the amount of aspiration on the /t/, in the duration of the vowel /ay/, and in the release of /k/. For each pair there is a phoneme that takes two somewhat different forms. In order to be able to classify the related but different sounds as single phonemes and so to simplify description, the linguist creates the junctural phoneme /+/ and assigns to it the phonetic features distinguishing a pair (Harris, 1951). The phonemic transcriptions will then look like this: /nayt+reyt/, /slay+nĭs/, /mark+ət/, /naytreyt/, /maynĭs/, /markət/. It follows that the phonetic values of /+/ are a disjunctive set and elaborately so. It follows also that /+/ is not itself a segment at all, since aspiration, duration, and the like have no existence apart from particular vowels and consonants. The open juncture, in short, is an invention of linguistic science designed to simplify language description. How could a child possibly learn to recognize /+/ and use it to segment the speech he hears?

The /t/ one hears in *night rate* occurs also at the ends of words (e.g., *night* or *right*) and so can occur terminally in complete utterances, whereas the /t/ of *nitrate* is never terminal. Similarly, the /ay/ of slyness can be terminal (as in *sly* or *die*), but the /ay/ of *minus* cannot. And, in general, that form of a phoneme which is found within utterances at morpheme boundaries is found also in final position in total utterances, but the form found within utterances internal to a morpheme is never final in a total utterance. A child might learn that. He might learn also to give special status to utterance-internal consonants or vowels that assumed the forms they ordinarily assumed in utterance-final position. In fact, he might learn to make morpheme cuts at just these points and to make contextual entries in terms of the resultant units.

When a child first begins to produce polymorphemic utterances, he has for some time been producing single-morpheme utterances. Suppose that he has made independent entries for all of these—both the one-morpheme utterances like *dog* and the polymorphemic utterances like *my dog*; at this point, the polymorphemic utterances might simply have the status for him of longer words. Suppose now that an internal analysis routine is activated which involves retrieving two entries at a time and comparing them, phonemically, from left to right. Suppose, further, that he returns to storage pairs with unlike first phonemes but retains for further analysis pairs that start out identically. Let him then make a tentative morphemic cut at the first point of phonemic divergence in the pair. Let him finally look up the resulting segments to see if there are already independent entries for them—as there usually would be if they were morphemes—and mark as morphemes just those segments having prior entries. If he picked a pair like br/eak and br/ing, he would cut them as indicated, would find no prior entries for any of the segments, and would not mark them as morphemes. However, a pair like *my/dog* and *my/cat* would yield segments with prior entries, and a child who started with this pair might soon discover that cuts yielding morphemes by his original criteria regularly coincided with terminal vowels and consonants (or, one might say, with / + /). Thereafter he could make segmentation cuts wherever terminal phonemes occurred without regard to either identical sequences or prior entries. By this account, the value of / + / is discovered from its correlation with more primitive criteria.

It is possible, however, that the terminal vowels and consonants are themselves the most primitive criterion of morpheme segmentation.

Although errors of segmentation seem only to occur across boundaries unmarked by open juncture in adult speech, it is far from the case that every such unmarked boundary will give rise to an error of segmentation. Adults will run together *Pop's here* as well as *It's here*. But Adam organized *is* as a feature in the pronunciation not of any noun but only of the pronoun *it*. Probably the important factor here is the second characteristic, which helps to define the pairs erroneously organized as single morphemes. Each such pair was characterized by a high transition probability in the speech mothers addressed to their children. After the first member, the second was more frequent by far than any other morpheme. Nouns like *Pop* or *Adam* sometimes appeared as subjects of equational sentences, but they also often appeared as subjects of main verbs—too often, apparently, for Adam to make the mistake of thinking *is* belonged to the nouns. *It*, on the other hand, appeared hundreds of times a day as the subject of equational sentences but seldom, surprisingly seldom, as the subject of any other verb. The high transitions in these pairs have nothing to do with grammar, of course, but are simply accidental statistical features of mother-child interaction. They demonstrate that bias in the language sample to which a child is exposed can, in an extreme case, result in a partly erroneous formulation of the underlying grammar.

It is important to make it perfectly clear that the evidence for segmentation errors is not simply, or even primarily phonetic. We are not relying on the fact that Adam's version of *it's* often sounded like *iss* or that his rendering of *want to* sounded like *wanna*. The important evidence is distributional: the fact that Adam said *It's hurts*, for instance, and that he said *I want to play* but never *I want you to play*. When, at length, the children corrected their few segmentation errors and reconstrued the forms of *be* and articles, the evidence was again distributional and in some cases dramatically clear. In the case of Adam's *a*, for example, the form appeared for nineteen samples in only a restricted portion of its proper

Table 6–5. Systematic Relations among Questions and Answers

Constituents to Be Specified	Normal Questions[a][b]	Occasional Questions[a][c]	Possible Answers[a]
Subject nominal	*Who* will read the book ?	*WHO* will read the book ?	*John* will read the book.
Object nominal	*What* will John read ?	John will read *WHAT* ?	John will read *the book.*
Predicate nominal	*What* is that ?	That is *WHAT* ?	That is *a book.*
Predicate	*What* will John do ?	John will *do WHAT* ?	John will *read the book.*
Locative adverbial	*Where* will John read ?	John will read *WHERE* ?	John will read *in the library.*
Time adverbial	*When* will John read ?	John will read *WHEN* ?	John will read *this evening.*
Manner adverbial	*How* will John read ?	John will read *HOW* ?	John will read *slowly.*

[a] Wh words and the substitutes for them are italicized.

[b] The derivation of normal questions follows: Base : Wh—John—will—read—something ; Preposing and Wh incorporation : Wh+something—John—will—read ; Transposition : Wh+something—will—John—read ; Morphophonemic : What—will—John—read.

[c] Words with all letters capitalized receive heavy stress and rising intonation.

range—chiefly with *that* as pronoun subject.[1] Then, in Samples 20 and 21, the full range quite suddenly filled out, and *a* appeared with noun phrases in isolation, noun phrases functioning as subjects of sentences, noun phrases in locative questions, and so forth. We do not yet know what causes reconstruction of forms at one time rather than another.

TRANSFORMATIONS IN WH QUESTIONS

Wh questions are those using an interrogative word from the set *who, whom, what, where, when, why*, and *how*. Contemporary generative grammars of English (e.g., Katz and Postal, 1964; Klima, 1964) do not all derive wh questions in just the same way, but they all do use transformational rules to represent the systematic relations between these questions and the declaratives that answer them. Wh questions begin to appear in good quantity and variety at Level III; indeed, the composite sentence derived with rules from Adam III was such a question. The question here is whether there is, in the form of these questions, evidence directly supporting the notion that the child acquires implicit knowledge of the kind represented by the transformational rules of the adult grammar. The brief discussion here is drawn from a full research report (Brown, 1968) which presents the evidence for all wh questions in all the protocols from I through V.

Table 6–5 sets out some adult questions and answers so as to expose the systematic relations among them. Consider first the two middle columns. Each question in "normal" form stands alongside a semantically equivalent, but less frequent "occasional" form, in which the wh word is in final position and is to be spoken with heavy stress and rising intonation. If someone said, "John will read the telephone book," one might respond, "John will read *what*?"—this response is an occasional form. The occasional form for the subject nominal—the first entry—is unlike the others in the

---

[1] The form appeared also with a few strictly transitive verbs where, as with *that*, it seems to have been a feature of pronunciation. Representative errors are: *have a two minute, get a one.*

column in that the wh word appears initially, its normal position.

The occasional forms (except the subject nominal) are all related to their normal counterparts by the same function. In describing the function let us take the occasional form as the base or starting point. The normal form can be created from the occasional in two steps: The first would move the wh word from final position to initial position; we call this preposing. The second would interchange the subject of the sentence and the auxiliary; we call this transposing. The same two steps will generate all the questions of the second column from their respective counterparts in the first column. Essentially, these two steps are the transformational rules used in adult grammar to derive wh questions. The main difference is that normal questions are not derived from actual occasional questions but from underlying strings that are similar to the occasionals.

Consider now the sentences of the last column, which are examples of well-formed answers to the questions standing opposite them. Question and answer differ in the words that are italicized in each case and only in these words. The italicized words in the answers may be said to stand in place of the italicized wh words—in the *exact* place, the very sentence locus of the wh word, for the occasional questions. The normal questions, we know, shift the place of the wh word. The material italicized in the answer is the material most directly responsive to the question. Indeed it is the only essential part of the answer. "What will John read?" "*The book.*" "When will John read?" "*This evening.*" In fact, each interrogative word is a kind of algebraic x standing in the place of a particular constituent of the sentence, the constituent identified in the left column of Table 6-5. The wh word asks for specification of that constituent. It marks the spot where information is to be poured into the sentence, and the form of the wh word—whether *who, what, where,* or *when*—indicates the kind of information required.

A transformational grammar of adult English can represent the systematic relations of Table 6-5 in the following way. Associated with each of the sentence constituents there is a stand-in element symbolized as "someone," "something," "somewhere," "sometime," and "somehow." The derivation of a wh question begins in the phrase structure with the selection of the interrogative morpheme wh. Then, from the constituent which is to be specified in a well-formed answer, the stand-in element is selected, rather than some particular NP, Loc, or whatever. The phrase structure derivation terminates in an underlying string which is just like the string for the occasional question except that the stand-in element stands where the interrogative words stand in the occasional questions of Table 6–5. In the derivation of normal questions, a first transformation preposes the stand-in element and incorporates it into wh, and a second transformation transposes the order of the subject NP and the first member of the auxiliary. A morphophonemic rule rewrites the wh + stand-in component as the appropriate interrogative word: wh + something as *what*: wh + someone as *who*; wh + somewhere as *where*, and so forth. The derivation rules and sample strings are represented in the note to Table 6–5.

Production of a Hypothetical Intermediate

The composite sentence derived by Adam III was *Where those dogs goed?* and not *Where did those dogs go?* How is Adam's form related to the derivation of the normal adult form? It is a sentence that would be produced by the rules in the note to Table 6–5 if the second transformation, the one that transposes subject and auxiliary, were simply omitted, and if the morphophonemic rules followed upon the preposing transformation alone. In short, Adam seems to have given phonetic form to a structure that is generated by the adult grammar as a hypothetical intermediate, a structure not actualized as a question by adults. The composite form is, in this respect, representative of all Adam's wh questions in III and for many months after III. Eve and Sarah both also constructed these preposed wh questions, though not in such quantity as did Adam. Table 6–6 represents the relation between the children's version of various wh questions and the two varieties of well-formed adult questions.

Table 6–6. The Child's Wh Question as a Hypothetical Intermediate in Adult Grammar

Occasional Questions[a]	Child's Questions[b]	Normal Questions[c]
WHO will read the book ?	Who will read the book ?	Who will read the book ?
John will read WHAT ?	What John will read ?	What will John read ?
That is WHAT ?	What that is ?	What is that ?
John will do WHAT ?	What John will do ?	What will John do ?
John will read WHERE ?	Where John will read ?	Where will John read ?

[a] Words with all letters capitalized receive heavy stress and rising intonation.
[b] Derivable from occasional questions by preposing.
[c] Derivable from occasional questions by preposing and transposing.

A Transformation in Discourse

The derivation rules loosely described in the note to Table 6–5 and presented in explicit form in Adam III presuppose the establishment of such major sentence constituents as NP and Loc, since the stand-in elements are associated with these constituents. As seen earlier in the Overview of Developments between I and III, there was good evidence of the existence of these constituents from early in the records. The most persuasive evidence was the children's ability to answer *who* and *what* questions with noun phrases and *where* questions with locatives. We also reported in the Overview that adverbials of time and manner did not seem to be organized as constituents in I to III, since the children did not make grammatically appropriate answers to *when* and *how* questions. If the responsive constituents were not organized as such, then *when* and *how* questions could not be derived in the children's grammar by the kinds of rules we have proposed. It is consistent, therefore, to find that Adam in III was still not making *when* and *how* questions.

In another respect, Adam's performance in III seems not to have been consistent with the rules. He produced a large number of *why* and *why not* questions. But in all of the prior sixteen samples he had only once answered a *why* question in a way that could possibly be considered appropriate. In this case, then, we seem to have the construction of the question occurring before there is any evidence on the responsive side that the relevant grammatical organization exists.[1] We have also, incidentally, a demonstration that, in language development, comprehension need not always precede production.

When we look at Adam's *why* and *why not* questions in their actual discourse setting, we find something unexpected and interesting: they were often closely related to an immediately antecedent declarative from his mother. Table 6–7 contains a set of mother's declaratives and Adam's *why* responses. Some

Table 6–7. *Why* and *Why Not* Questions from Adam 17–19 with Apparent Bases

Mother's Declaratives	Adam's Questions
Why	
He was playing a little tune	Why he play little tune?
I see a seal	Why you see seal?
You bent that game	Why me bent that game?
Well, because she wanted to	Why she want to?
I think it's resting now	Why it's resting now?
Why Not	
I guess I'm not looking in the right place	Why not you looking right place?
Because you weren't careful	Why not me careful?
I don't see any	Why not you see any?
You can't dance	Why not me can't dance?
You're going to have to buy another one and give it to Ursula because you're breaking that one	Why not me break that one?

of the differences between members of these pairs are not peculiar to *why* questions. For instance, the telegraphic reduction process that eliminates *was*, *-ing*, and *a* from the adult sentence is quite general in child speech. Setting aside such nonspecific differences, Adam's questions are a simple function of his mother's antecedent declaratives: the word *why*

[1] Adult *why* questions cannot be derived in a way directly parallel to other wh questions. We have not gone into the details because they do not alter the fact that Adam produced such questions when his responses gave no evidence that he could analyze them correctly with respect to either grammar or semantics.

is placed in front of the declarative. Table 6–7 also has a set of questions in *why not*, and these, too, have apparent bases in the mother's speech. Setting aside a few details, what happens is that the words *why not* are added in front of the mother's negative declaratives. In creating these questions, Adam seems to have been operating with a rule very like the preposing transformation.

Where did Adam's *why* and *why not* transformations come from? Once in a long while, his mother produced a *why* question as a direct follow-up of a declarative and repeated in her *why* question the proposition expressed in the declarative. Probably Adam was attempting to imitate this performance, but his imitation did not come out right. Suppose the antecedent declarative were "He can't dance." Mother would follow this with "Why can't he dance?" Adam's version, on the other hand, would be "Why he can't dance?" Mother not only preposed *why*, she also transposed the subject and auxiliary in the manner of the adult grammar. Adam only preposed. Probably he copied according to his present understanding—as children also do when they pretend to drive a car or read a newspaper. Perhaps his imitation took the form it did because that form was close to the general operation that Adam was using with his other wh questions.

So we do have some evidence that the knowledge represented by transformation rules in the derivation of wh questions was learned by the children. They did not simply start to produce well-formed questions at a given point in time. All three children first produced a simpler form that would result from the application of just one of the two transformations required. And Adam—always the one to make interesting errors—also created *why* questions in circumstances that suggest the application of the same single transformation to declarative bases supplied by his mother.

THE ROLE OF TRAINING VARIABLES

Whatever the processes by which children acquire grammar, their primary data come from the speech they hear. Part of our work has consisted of attempts to isolate antecedents in the child's linguistic environment which may affect the rate or quality of the child's development. By antecedents we do not mean global variables like social class, but specific features of parental speech and parent-child interaction.

We have learned something about the effects of two aspects of variation in the speech to which a child is exposed: variation in the frequency with which particular constructions are produced or "modeled," and variation in the frequency with which particular reactions are made to a child's utterances.

The work has progressed through three phases: first, discovery of relations between parental speech and rate of language development in our three subjects; second, a manipulative experiment with different subjects to test a hypothesis derived from those observations; and third, more detailed analyses of relations within our longitudinal data.

Preliminary Observation and an Experiment

When we began work several years ago, one of the first things we noticed was the frequency with which parents responded to the young child's telegraphic utterance[1] by echoing what the child said and filling in the missing functors. If the child said *Eve lunch* or *Throw Daddy*, the parent often responded with the nearest complete sentence appropriate in the particular situation—*Eve is having lunch* or *Throw it to Daddy*. Brown and Bellugi (1964) called such responses "expansions," and suggested that they might provide optimal data for the acquisition of grammar. It was not their intention to suggest that the child learned grammar by storing the expanded versions of his telegraphic utterances, since he could not in this way learn more than the finite set of sentences he had at some time attempted to produce. Brown and Bellugi recognized that expansions were only data, and that grammatical knowledge was a system of general rules some-

[1] We have not in this paper discussed the telegraphic aspect of the child's early sentences, since that was a major topic of such earlier papers as Brown and Fraser (1963) and Brown and Bellugi (1964). In I, II, and III, however, the speech of the three children was extremely telegraphic.

how derived from data. They argued, however, that the data provided by expansions were maximally relevant and seemed to be delivered with ideal timing.

At the same time, we have always realized that the relevance and timing of particular forms of interaction may have no importance for the acquisition of grammar. It is quite possible that the adult need do nothing but "model" the language—that is, provide samples of well-formed speech. When evidence is limited to natural observations, it is not possible to separate the effect of expansions from the effect of the amount of well-formed speech that the child hears. The mothers of Adam and Eve responded to the speech of their children with expansions about thirty per cent of the time. Sarah's overall language development was slower, and her mother expanded fewer of Sarah's utterances. But Sarah's mother also talked less to her child in general. In our samples of three parents, expansion rate and general volubility varied together, and their effects on language acquisition could not be teased apart.

A manipulative experiment was designed to separate these two aspects of the child's language environment and to compare their effects (Cazden, 1965). The subjects were twelve Negro children, aged twenty-eight to thirty-eight months. They were all attending a private day-care center in Boston, where thirty children under three and a half years were cared for by one adult. Four matched trios were formed on the basis of the child's chronological age, talkativeness, and initial level of language development as judged by his mean length of utterance during an orientation period. Within each trio the children were randomly assigned to one of three treatment groups: expansion, modeling, or control.

The expansion group received forty minutes per day of intensive and deliberate expansions. The modeling group received exposure to an equal number of well-formed sentences that were not expansions. One of two tutors trained for this research talked with each child in these two groups in an individual play session every school day for three months. The sessions were held in two small rooms normally used only for naps; both were equipped with toys and books selected to stimulate conversation. The play sessions were monitored at regular intervals during the three-month period to ensure the separation of the critical interaction variables. Children in the control group received no treatment, but they were brought into the treatment rooms every few days so that they stayed familiar with the materials and the tutors.

Tape recordings were made of each child's speech at the beginning, middle, and end of the three-month period. The tapes were transcribed by a secretary who was trained by a linguist on our staff and who was ignorant of the treatment assignment of the children. The transcriptions were then coded according to strict rules. The dependent variables were six measures of language development: one was a test of the child's ability to repeat sentences, and five measured aspects of the child's spontaneous speech—mean length of utterance in morphemes, noun phrase index, verb complexity, copula index, and type-of-sentence index (the last four indexes were devised for this research).

Two statistical analyses were used to test the hypothesis that expansions would be the most effective treatment. First, the six dependent variables were considered separately. A two-way analysis of variance (treatment x tutor) was computed for the post-test scores on each measure separately, with the pretest scores on that same measure as a covariance control. Then, in order to compare the children on their overall growth on the six measures considered together, growth was operationally defined as the sum of the child's six gain score ranks, and Friedman's nonparametric two-way analysis of variance was used to test the significance of group differences. In neither analysis was there any evidence that expansions aid the acquisition of grammar. Contrary to our hypothesis, modeling was the most effective treatment.

Before speculating on possible explanations for these results, we need to examine what happens when forms of interaction which naturally co-occur are experimentally separated. Originally, we assumed that modeling without expansion had no positive features of its own, but this turns out not to be the case. If a child says *Dog bark* when a dog is indeed barking, the expanding adult says *Yes, the dog is barking*. The non-expanding adult who desires to maintain a reasonable discourse sequence—as our tutors did—has to contribute a related idea, such as, *Yes, he's mad at the kitty* or *Yes, but he won't bite.* Thus, a treatment which focuses on grammatical structure confines the adult to expanded echoes of the child and limits the ideas to the child's presumed meaning, whereas a treatment that focuses on the idea extends that idea beyond the presumed meaning of the child and introduces more varied words and grammatical elements to express those related ideas. In natural conversation, parents often provide both grammatical expansions and semantic extensions. Our tutors were asked not to do this, in order to keep the distinctions between the experimental treatments as sharp as possible.

Three reasons can be suggested for the results. Cazden originally proposed that richness of verbal stimulation might be more important than the grammatical contingency of the adult response. If we consider the learning of syntactic rules to be akin to concept formation, then learning may be aided by variation in non-criterial attributes—for instance, the particular noun stem in the case of inflection for plurality. If the process of first language learning is akin to construction of scientific theory, in which hypotheses are tested against available data, then a meager set of data may be disadvantageous. We have seen that bias in the mother-to-child sampling of the possibilities of English grammar caused Adam to make the segmentation error revealed in such a sentence as *It's fell.*

Miller and McNeill (1969) suggest an alternative explanation. When an adult attempts to expand a child's telegraphic utterances far more often than parents spontaneously do, some of the expansions probably misinterpret the child's intended meaning. Instead of facilitating the acquisition of grammar, such erroneous expansions may mislead the child and interfere with his learning.

Still a third explanation is possible, separately or in conjunction with either of the previous two. Artificial elevation of the expansion rate may depress attentional processes in the child. We know from many current studies of child development that stimuli of a certain degree of novelty—not too familiar and not too strange—command the greatest attention. The acquisition of language should be facilitated by those environmental events that enhance the child's attention to the adult's utterance and to relevant features of the verbal and nonverbal context in which it is spoken. In these particular experimental treatments, a greater degree of novelty may have been attained in the modeling treatment. We do not consider this experiment conclusive; all we can say is that the benefits of expansions remain unproved.

Training Variables in the Longitudinal Data

In the last two years we have gone back to the longitudinal data on Adam, Eve, and Sarah to look more carefully for evidence of the effects of parental speech. In selecting dependent variables, we have learned to reject measures of the child's performance in favor of better indicators of the child's grammatical knowledge. We have substantive findings on the independent variables of expansion, modeling, and production of occasional questions.

GRAMMATICAL KNOWLEDGE VERSUS PERFORMANCE. In certain facts about construction frequency there lies a major trap for the student of child speech who is interested in the development of knowledge of grammar: the first fact is that in mother-to-child speech the various constructions that English grammar permits are of grossly unequal frequency; the second is that the frequencies are astonishingly stable across mothers; and the third is that frequencies in child speech, within the limits of the child's competence, tend to match adult frequencies. We have examined frequencies on many levels, from major types of sentence all the way down to the several allomorphs of *be*, and the story is always the same: rank order correlations among the mothers and between each mother and her child ranging from .65 to .90.

Some of the stable inequalities one might have guessed: active affirmative, declarative sentences are much more common than negatives, yes-no interrogatives, or wh interrogatives, and well-formed passives are almost nonexistent.

Others are easy to understand but are not likely to have occurred to anyone who has not counted: the impersonal pronouns *it*, *this*, and *that* as sentence subjects almost always have their allomorph of *be* (*is*) as verb, whereas the personal pronouns *I*, *you*, *he*, and so forth as subjects have a main verb much more often than an allomorph of *be*; *where* questions are very much more frequent than *when* or *how* or *why* questions; catenative semi-auxiliaries like *wanna* and *gonna* are much more frequent than the modal auxiliaries *will* or *can*, and *may* and *must* are seldom heard; the progressive inflection *-ing* is much more frequent than the regular past *-ed*, and irregular pasts (e.g., *ran*, *saw*, *did*) are more frequent than regular pasts; and so on. The important general fact is that there seems to be something like a standard frequency profile for mother-to-child English, a profile that children match within their competence at any given time, and in this profile great inequalities exist even among very simple and familiar constructions.

Consider two examples in detail: major sentence types and expressions of possession. If we set an arbitrary frequency in child speech as a criterion of emergence—for example, the occurrence of three instances of a given type of sentence in each of three consecutive samples of seven hundred utterances—we find a high rank order correlation between parental frequencies and order of emergence in the child for twenty-four types of sentence—affirmatives, declaratives, negatives, yes-no interrogatives, and wh interrogatives using, respectively, lexical verbs or *have* or *be* or *will* or *can* or *may*. Lexical and *be*-verbs in declarative sentences are the most common in all three mothers and appear first in the speech of all three children. But suppose we entertain the extreme hypothesis that all twenty-four types enter the child's competence simultaneously. Because the probability that a given construction will attain an arbitrary criterion varies with its standard frequency in mother-to-child English, and because these frequencies are grossly unequal, lexical and *be*-verbs would appear first on a strict probability basis. The student of child speech might then conclude that the hypothesis of simultaneous development was false when it could indeed still be true. Highly stable orders of construction emergence, in terms of an arbitrary frequency criterion, are not inconsistent with the possibility that the children in question know how to form all the constructions from the start but produce them with unequal frequency.

The same misleading performance match appears when we relate individual differences in construction frequencies among the children to differences in their mothers' speech. For instance, one of the first individual differences we noted was Eve's tendency to use N+N constructions far more often than Adam or Sarah did. At I, the frequencies of N+N in 700 utterances were: Eve, 66; Adam, 40; Sarah, 10, of which 8 were imitations. In looking for an explanation, we thought it possible that the speech of the three mothers might differ in the frequency with which sentences were spoken from which N+N constructions might be telegraphically derived. The best match to the rank order of the children was the particular subset of parental N+N constructions that express possession, such as *Daddy's chair*. In the first 1,253 utterances of each mother, these frequencies were: Eve's mother, 31; Adam's mother, 24; Sarah's mother, only 6. This is an extremely interesting relation. One can hypothesize that territoriality and property rights are more important in homes where father is a graduate student, and that this is related to the child's tendency to use the N+N construction. But it is not sufficient evidence that greater frequency in parent speech produces earlier learning in the child. It is the antecedents of grammatical *knowledge* we are seeking, not influences on performance.

There are various ways out of the trap, all involving data that are better indexes of knowledge or competence than is an arbitrary frequency of production. One can consider child frequencies against a background of known stable adult frequencies and so set frequency criteria that are not entirely arbitrary; one can consider frequencies of forms in contexts that make them obligatory; one can consider the pattern of omissions in the total distributional range of a form; one can consider the adequacy of the child's responses to adult questions and assertions; and above all, one can use the child's analogical errors of commission. In analyses of the relation of child speech to parental speech, the frequency of forms in contexts that make them obligatory has proved an especially useful measure. Each of these contexts in the child's speech can be considered a learning trial, and we can compute the proportion of times in which the child performs appropriately as that proportion changes over time.

FURTHER EVIDENCE ON EXPANSIONS AND MODELING. Because we considered the manipulative experiment inconclusive, we have probed further into the effect of expansions and modeling on the growth of specific aspects of grammatical knowledge in our three subjects. We have charted the emergence of prepositions in Eve's speech and of appropriate answers to four kinds of wh questions and five noun and verb inflections in all three children.

Table 6–8. Eve's Performance in Supplying Various Prepositions in Samples 7–12 Compared with Eve's Mother's Modeling Frequencies and Expansions in Samples 1–6

Preposition	Mother's Modeling Frequencies 1–6	Mother's Proportion of Expansions 1–6	Proportion Correct in Eve 7–12
On	157	.57 (25/44)	.90 (82/92)
In	142	.61 (20/33)	.92 (147/159)
With	54	.64 (7/11)	.67 (29/43)
Of	33	.50 (1/2)	.70 (14/20)
For	32	.40 (2/5)	.69 (11/16)
To	31	.00 (0/3)	.78 (7/9)

Table 6–8 presents the data for the emergence of Eve's prepositions. Two findings are of interest: First, for any given preposition, both the frequency with which it is modeled and the frequency (but not proportion) of expansions are strongly related to the point at which that preposition is regularly supplied by the child in all the phrases requiring it. In Samples 1–6, Eve's mother uses *in* and *on* approximately three times as often as she uses *with*, *of*, *for*, or *to*. In Samples 7–12, Eve

supplies *in* and *on* correctly at least 90 per cent of the time, and the proportion correct for each of the other four prepositions is between .67 and .77.

Second, there is no relation at all between modeling frequency of particular phrases—*in there* versus *in the wastebasket*—and the point at which the child produces that phrase with the preposition in place. A given preposition appears in all the phrases requiring it at about the same time, and it does not matter whether the particular phrase has been often modeled by the mother or not. This is a good example of how parental speech aids the induction of general rules but does not provide models for imitation as such.

With wh questions, we can determine what proportion of a given type elicits semantically and grammatically appropriate answers from the child. Four wh-adverbial questions are rather well matched in grammatical (though probably not in semantic) complexity, but they differ greatly in parental frequency. For all three mothers at II, the order of frequency is locatives first (about three fourths of the total), then causal, manner, and time—in other words, *where, why, how,* and *when*. This rank order matches the rank order of proportion of appropriate responses from the children at V except for questions about time, for which the data are too few to be reliable. Pooled data for the three mothers and children are presented in the following table.

	Frequency of Mother's Questions	Proportion of Children's Appropriate Responses
Locative	228	.64 (29/45)
Causal	29	.40 (14/35)
Manner	18	.11 (1/9)
Time	7	.50 (1/2)

Before turning to the emergence of inflections, another comment on method is in order. For relating child behaviour to parental behavior in a sample of more than one child, two approaches are possible. The child's language can be related to antecedents in his parent's speech, and this relation then compared across the dyads; no direct comparison of the children is made. The preceding analysis of twenty-four verb forms, prepositions, and answers to wh questions were of this type. Alternatively, differences in the language of the children can be related to differences in the language of their parents. The preceding analysis of N+N constructions was of this type. Here, direct comparison of the children is required, and the experimenter faces the question of a metric for that comparison. We have analyzed the emergence of inflections in both ways.

The five regular inflections which emerge between I and V are the plural and possessive inflections on the noun and the present progressive, regular past, and present indicative inflections on the verb. For this analysis we used as a criterion of emergence the first sample of three, such that, in all three, the child supplies the inflection in at least ninety per cent of the contexts in which they are clearly required. The charting of this aspect of development is a long story in itself and will be reported in detail elsewhere. We shall describe here only the data for the correlations between the sequence of emergence and three features of the child's linguistics environment: the proportion of times in which his omitted inflections are expanded by the parent during the entire period I–V, the absolute frequency of those expansions, and the frequency with which the inflections are modeled in four samples of seven hundred parental utterances which immediately precede Levels II, III, IV, and V of the children's speech.

First, we computed rank-order correlations for each child separately. For all three children, order of emergence within the child's language system is more strongly related to the frequency with which the inflection is modeled by the parent than it is to the proportion or frequency of expansions. The only statistically significant positive correlation is with frequency of modeling for Sarah, $\rho = .90$ $(p > .05)$.

We have also looked for relations between differences among the children and differences among their parents. It is here that a metric for comparing the children is required. In the above analysis of N+N constructions, the three children were compared at II; the metric, therefore, was mean length of utterance. A more conventional metric is age. We have analyzed individual differences in the order of emergence of inflections on both bases of comparison—the contrast in outcomes is itself informative.

When we compare the children on the basis of age, the order of development is what one would expect from Figure 6–1: Eve way out in front, Adam second, and Sarah third. But when we ignore age and compare the children on the basis of mean length, the rank order of the children changes sharply. At II, when all three children have a mean length of 2.25 morphemes, only Sarah has reached the 90 per cent criterion on any inflection (plurality). By IV, when mean length has increased to 3.50 morphemes, she has reached criterion on five inflections, Eve has on four, and Adam on two. Data tabulated independently for the percentage of missing functors (everything except nouns, verbs, adjectives, and adverbs) at II and V yield the same relation: for Eve, 81 per cent of the functors were missing at II and 43 per cent at V; for Adam, 83 per cent at II, 20 per cent at V; and for Sarah, 74 per cent at II, 15 per cent at V.

Looked at in this way, the relative position of Eve and Sarah is reversed. At any given mean length value for utterances, Sarah is handling inflections and functors in general more successfully than Eve. Conversely, since Eve's speech contains proportionately more content words than Sarah's, her utterances are more informative. Eve had undoubtedly caught up in the provision of functors by the time she reached Sarah's age, probably well before. The point is that Sarah is less benind in the provision of obligatory functors than in what she is trying to say.

Table 6–9 shows the relation between order of emergence of the five inflections on these two bases of comparison (age and mean length) and proportion and frequency of expansions and frequency of modeling in parent speech.

As one would expect from the previous discussion of mother-child communication patterns, the difference in modeling frequency among the parents is small. But the difference in proportion and frequency of expansions is considerable: Sarah's telegraphic utterances omitting inflections are fol-

Table 6–9. Emergence of Inflections and Two Features of Parental Speech

Child's Speech	Eve	Adam	Sarah
Inflections			
Order of emergence,[a] by age	5	12.5	12.5
Order of emergence,[a] by mean length	11	12	7
Proportion of parental expansions	.45	.51	.29
	(191/427)	(348/679)	(86/294)
Frequency of parental models	499	576	471

[a] Order of emergence is given in summed ranks which range from 5 to 15— first to last of the three children on the five inflections combined.

lowed much less frequently by a parent utterance including the appropriate inflection than are Adam's and Eve's. This we expected from our observation of differential expansion rates at the beginning of our work. What is surprising is the negative relation between expansion rate and order of emergence in terms of mean length of utterance. Sarah receives the lowest density of expansions, yet her language system is relatively the most advanced in the provision of inflections. It is hard to reconcile this finding with our original hypothesis that expansions should provide the most usable information for the acquisition of all types of functors.

INTERACTION ROUTINES WITH OCCASIONAL QUESTIONS. In describing the relations that underlie the grammar of wh questions, we introduced in Table 6–5 the forms called occasional questions because we believe they are a great help in making those relations clear in explicit form to adults. We naturally wonder, therefore, whether the occasional questions also help make the relations clear in implicit form to children. The mothers of Adam, Eve, and Sarah produced such questions in two circumstances, which may be represented as follows: First, *say constituent again*—(a) Child, "I want milk," Mother, "You want what?" Child, "Milk." or (b) Child, "Put milk in glass." Mother, "Put milk where?" Child, "In glass." Second, *constituent prompt*—(a) Mother, "What do you want?" Child, no answer. Mother, "You want what?"

or (b) Mother, "Where will I put it?" Child, no answer. Mother, "I will put it where?"

The *say-constituent-again* interaction occurred when mother found a part of a child's utterance unintelligible. She then repeated what she had understood and replaced the constituent which was the locus of unintelligibility with the right kind of wh word. Since the wh word appeared in the sentence position of a constituent, the result was an occasional question. The occasion was unintelligibility in a constituent, and the child's response was repetition of the constituent displaced. The mother's question is essentially a request to say the constituent again and that is the name we have given to this kind of interaction. What should such exchanges be able to teach the child? Perhaps, the membership of each type of sentence constituent—members of NP, for example, are just those terms, of whatever complexity, that can be replaced by *what*.

The *constituent-prompt* interaction was initiated by the mother. She asked a question in the normal form—"What do you want?"—and received no answer. She then reformulated the question as "You want what?" which is, incidentally, an occasional question. She was, in effect, turning the question into a sentence completion item, and since the mothers usually resorted to this prompting form when the normal form had failed, they must have felt that it was easier to process. In our materials, the occasional form was, in fact, more likely to elicit an appropriate answer than was the normal form. What should exchanges of this type be able to teach the child? Fundamentally, the equivalence of particular normal and occasional questions—equivalents are questions that replace one another when no answer is forthcoming.

A large amount of structural information is revealed in these two interactions with unusual clarity because of the use of the occasional question. It must be possible to discover the systematic relations that underlie the grammar of wh questions without the benefit of the occasional question, since many children who learn English do not have attentive mothers around to echo and prompt them. However, it may be easier to discover the relations if the middle term is often heard. It may be accidental, but in our records, the occasional form was used much more frequently by the mothers of the two children whose grammatical understanding developed more rapidly, Adam and Eve. In samples of seven thousand parental utterances, Adam's mother produced occasional questions at the rate of 1 in 57 utterances; Eve's mother at the rate of 1 in 80; Sarah's mother at the rate of only 1 in 146.

Whether or not the occasional questions prove to be helpful for the discovery of wh grammar, it seems likely that the many kinds of grammatical exchange in discourse will prove to be the richest data available to the child in his search for a grammar. It may be as difficult to derive a grammar from hearing unconnected static sentences as it would be to derive the invariance of quantity and number from simply looking at liquids in containers and objects in space. The changes produced by pouring back and forth and by gathering together and spreading apart are the data that most strongly suggest the conservation of quantity and number. We suspect that the changes sentences undergo as they shuttle between persons in conversation are, similarly, the data that most clearly expose the underlying structure of language.

We have examined the effect on the child's development of grammatical knowledge of two aspects of the speech he hears: variation in the frequency with which particular constructions are modeled and variation in the frequency of particular parental responses—expansions and occasional questions. There is a small amount of evidence that modeling frequency does affect the acquisition of knowledge. With regard to the parental response of expansion, the present evidence is that it has no effect on the development of grammatical knowledge. The role of occasional questions is still unknown. Our own interest in isolated training variables is giving way to an interest in the structural information latent in various forms of linguistic interaction. Perhaps we shall someday find that linguistic environments at home do vary significantly in structural richness but that any single form of response is an unreliable index of this variation, even as age of weaning has proved an unreliable index of something more important— general child-rearing attitudes.

References

BROWN, R. The development of wh questions in child speech. *J. verb Learn. verb. Behav.*, 1968, 7, 277–290.

BROWN, R., and BELLUGI, URSULA. Three processes in the child's acquisition of syntax. *Harvard Educational Review*, 1964, 34, 133–151.

BROWN, R., and FRASER, C. The acquisition of syntax. In C. N. Cofer & Barbara S. Musgrave (Eds.), *Verbal behavior and learning: Problems and processes.* New York: McGraw-Hill, 1963.

CAZDEN, COURTNEY B. *Environmental assistance to the child's acquisition of grammar.* Unpublished doctoral dissertation, Harvard University, 1965.

CHOMSKY, N. *Syntactic Structures.* The Hague: Mouton, 1957.

CHOMSKY, N. *Aspects of the theory of syntax.* Cambridge, Mass.: M.I.T. Press, 1965.

FODOR, J. A. How to learn to talk: Some simple ways. In F. Smith and G. A. Miller (Eds.), *The genesis of language.* Cambridge, Mass.: M.I.T. Press, 1966.

GLEASON, H. A., JR. *An Introduction to descriptive linguistics.* (Rev. ed.) New York: Holt, Rinehart & Winston, 1961.

HARRIS, Z. S. Morpheme alternates in linguistic analysis. *Language*, 1942, 18, 169–180.

HARRIS, Z. S. *Methods in structural linguistics.* Chicago: University of Chicago Press, 1951.

HEFFNER, R. M. S. *General phonetics.* Madison: University of Wisconsin Press, 1949.

HOCKETT, C. F. Problems of morphemic analysis. *Language*, 1947, 23, 321–43.

KATZ, J. J., and POSTAL, P. M. *An integrated theory of linguistic descriptions.* Cambridge, Mass.: M.I.T. Press, 1964.

KLIMA, E. S. Negation in English. In J. A. Fodor & J. J. Katz (Eds.), *The structure of language: Readings in the philosophy of language.* Englewood Cliffs, N. J.: Prentice-Hall, 1964.

McNEILL, D. Developmental psycholinguistics. In F. Smith and G. A. Miller (Eds.), *The genesis of language.* Cambridge, Mass.: M.I.T. Press, 1966.

MILLER, G. A., and McNEILL, D. Psycholinguistics. In G. Lindzey

& E. Aronson (Eds.), *Handbook of social psychology*, Vol. III. Reading, Mass.: Addison-Wesley, 1969.

NIDA, E. S. The identification of morphemes. *Language*, 1948, 24, 414–441.

SLOBIN, D. I. The acquisition of Russian as a native language. In F. Smith and G. A. Miller (Eds.), *The genesis of language*. Cambridge, Mass.: M.I.T. Press, 1966.

SPITZ, R. A. *No and yes: On the genesis of human communication.* New York: International Universities Press, 1957.

[7]

Derivational Complexity and Order of Acquisition in Child Speech[1]

The publication of Chomsky's *Syntactic Structures* initiated two lines of psycholinguistic research: experimental studies of sentence processing by adults and naturalistic studies of grammar acquisition by children. The experimental studies were very successful and seemed, in the early 1960's, to have established a general conclusion: the psychological complexity of sentences, as measured by difficulty in remembering them or understanding them, is closely related to their grammatical (or "derivational") complexity as defined in Chomsky's theory. Which seemed to mean that the theory of transformational grammar had "psychological reality." However, in the mid-1960's exceptions were found to the rule relating psychological and grammatical complexity, and it became clear that the relation between the two could not be so

The paper was prepared for the 1968 Carnegie-Mellon Symposium on Cognitive Psychology and appears in *Cognition and the Development of Language* (Wiley, 1970) under the editorship of John R. Hayes. Camille Hanlon was co-author. Reprinted by permission of the authors.

[1] This investigation was supported by PHS, Grant HD–02908 from the National Institute of Child Health and Development.

simple and general as had been supposed. Not for adult sentence processing at any rate.

The present paper explores the role of grammatical complexity in child speech. Are constructions mastered in an order of increasing complexity? The answer turns out to be "yes"—for the set of sentence-types studied here. One year later, with more knowledge of the facts of acquisition, I find that I can make quite a long list of exceptions to the rule. It seems now possible to me that the rule works particularly well for the sentences studied in the paper because some of those sentences have a rather special property.

The derivation of a sentence in a generative grammar is intended to be a formal representation of everything that native speakers know about the structure of that sentence: the way it breaks up into sub-wholes, the way in which some lexical items constrain others, the ways in which the sentence under derivation is related to other sentences in the language. Ordinarily when a sentence is spoken there is nothing that compels one to suppose that the speaker has had to *use* all or even any substantial part of the knowledge the derivation represents. But for some sentences there *is* reason to suppose that a good part of the speaker's knowledge of structure has been called into play. For instance, with a tag question like: *Can't you?*

In actual discourse the tag *Can't you?* would follow a declarative sentence such as, for instance: *You can drive.* How does the speaker arrive at the tag which must have exactly the form indicated and could not have any other form. It could not be *Isn't it?* or *Didn't you?* or *Won't he?* but must be *Can't you?* The tag is potentially derivable in an entirely mechanical way from the antecedent sentence—by interrogation and negation and cutting off the predicate after *can*. Furthermore, it is difficult, perhaps impossible, to see how the tag could be created without operating on the antecedent. But these operations on the antecedent involve a large part of the *knowledge* of the structure of the tag that would be formally represented in its derivation. In short, in the case of tags, and certain other sentences treated in this paper, *performance* comes more than ordinarily close to *competence*. That may be why the relation between complexity and order of acquisition is, in turn, as close as it is here. It makes one wonder whether, if we had good indices of competence for all the constructions a child acquires, the exceptions that currently plague the rule would disappear.

FODOR AND GARRETT (1966) have made a useful retrospective analysis of the experiments done in the past five years to test the "psychological reality" of transformational grammar. It seems to Fodor and Garrett that investigators in this tradition have been testing the proposition that the complexity of derivation of a sentence, measured by the number of optional transformational rules applied, corresponds with the psychological complexity of processing the sentence. The idea that derivational complexity ought to correspond with psychological complexity derives, Fodor and Garrett suggest, from a notion that the grammar of a language might function as an actual component of the psychological programs involved in understanding sentences. The grammar could be a literal component if, at one implausible extreme, a listener assigned a structural description to a received sentence by synthesizing all possible sentences up to the point (some months later) at which he generated a match. The grammar could also be a literal component if, somewhat more plausibly, a received sentence were assigned a structure by rewriting less general symbols into more general symbols utilizing a set of reversed phrase structure rules in reverse order.

The early experiments on the psychological reality of transformational grammar seemed to provide impressive evidence for a rather direct relation between derivational and psychological complexity. Later on, the grammar moved from beneath these early experiments changing the character of the derivational complexities involved and calling attention to the fact that changes of meaning were also involved. In the early experiments complexity was often confounded with sentence length, frequency, and naturalness as well as with meaning; replications controlling for one or more of these variables have generally yielded results in which the importance of derivational complexity seems much reduced.

The early experiments stayed nervously close to a small family of sentences: the simple, active, affirmative, declarative (SAAD), the negative (N), the question (Q), the passive (P), and such compounds of these as passive-negative (PN), negative question (NQ) and so on. Later experiments broadened the range of sentences studied and, at the same time, complicated the idea of derivational complexity. When separable verbs in transformed position (*Put your coat on*) are compared with separable verbs in non-transformed position (*Put on your coat*) we have a difference of one optional, singulary, meaning-preserving, transformation. When the negative (*I don't see it*) is compared with a corresponding SAAD (*I see it*) we have a difference in the morphemes generated by the phrase structure rules as well as a difference of obligatory transformations (T*do*) and optional transformations (T*not*). When verbal auxiliaries of varying complexity are compared (e.g., *He was going* and *He would have been going*) we have, among other things, a difference in the number of times a particular obligatory transformation must be applied in a single derivation. The only cases in which an increase in derivational complexity is at all reliably associated with an increase in psychological difficulty seem to be those in which meaning is also changed.

The very earliest experiments in the tradition (those George Miller did with McKean and Slobin, 1962) undertook to assess complexity by measuring the time required to transform sentences of one type into sentences of another type. Later on, other indices of psychological complexity were utilized: time to understand a sentence well enough to judge it true or false; ability accurately to recall sentences in a free recall situation and in a single-sentence, immediate recall situation with buffer material added to make it possible to measure the storage space required for the sentence. For this range of tasks it is not surprising that a difference of derivational complexity, even when it is of a single fixed type, does not show a stable relationship to psychological complexity. With respect to an SAAD and its corresponding and Negative (N) Passive (P), for instance, it takes more time to transform from SAAD to P than from SAAD to N but the N takes longer to comprehend than the P.

Fodor and Garrett draw the one general conclusion that it

is now possible to draw from this literature: derivational complexity, in the sense of the number of rules applied in deriving a sentence, does not correspond in any simple way to the psychological complexity involved in understanding and retaining the sentence. Fodor and Garrett also accept the one clear implication of their conclusion: transformational grammars are not actual components of the routines by which sentences are processed; the relation between the formalization of the native speaker's presumed competence (the grammar) and his psycholinguistic performances must be less direct than had been imagined. The Fodor and Garrett conclusions are the ones the experimental literature now justifies but probably these conclusions are not the last or the most interesting things that will be said about these results. The complex pattern of evidence that says nothing to us now that is not negative may find an affirmative voice in the future.

In this paper we propose to ask whether derivational complexity is related to the order in which constructions emerge in child speech. In view of the outcome of the experimental literature on adult processing of sentences it is necessary to say why any relation of the kind described should be expected in child speech.

We shall, in the first place, limit ourselves to relations of derivational complexity of the type we call cumulative. When the derivation of a sentence "Y" applies all the rules applied in the derivation of a sentence "X" plus at least one rule not applied in X, then Y has greater cumulative derivational complexity than X (X < Y). The negative passive sentence in English stands in a relation of greater cumulative derivational complexity to both its negative active counterpart and its affirmative passive counterpart. However, the negative passive does not stand in this relation to the *yes–no* question even though more rules are applied in deriving the former than in deriving the latter. The crucial point is that the negative–passive utilizes some rules not utilized in the question but the question also utilizes at least one rule not utilized in the negative passive.

Some of the experimenters who have studied adult processing of sentences have explicitly limited their predictions to the cumulative case (e.g., Savin and Perchonock, 1965) but others have simply calculated derivational complexity in terms of the number of rules applied, not requiring the rules to stand in a cumulative relation. The difference is, of course, that when psychological complexity is predicted to follow derivational complexity calculated in terms simply of the number of rules there is an assumption that any one rule equals any other in adding a constant increment of psychological complexity. That is a pretty improbable assumption even looking no further than the fact that one rule may employ just one of the elementary transformations (deletion, substitution, adjunction, and permutation) while another rule employs several. When psychological complexity is predicted from *cumulative* derivational complexity there is no assumption that one rule equals another. The suggestion is simply that when the derivation of one sentence involves everything that the derivation of another involves, plus something more, then the something-more sentence will be more complex psychologically.

But why should derivations, which are more like proofs in geometry than like programs for speaking or understanding, have anything to do with the order in which children begin to understand and speak sentences of various kinds? A generative grammar is intended to represent the linguistic knowledge of the native speaker even though it does not represent the *manner* in which such knowledge is brought to bear in speaking and understanding. The native speaker's feeling for the way that a sentence cracks into a hierarchy of sub-wholes is represented by the phrase-structure rules and these also represent his feeling for such relations in a sentence as are called subject–predicate and verb–object. The native speaker's sense that large sets of sentences are related to one another in such a way that, for each member of one set, there is a specific counterpart in the other set is represented by transformational rules. One sometimes has the feeling, as generative grammars undergo their own historical transformations, that the powerful systematic requirements of the whole structure are moving the formalization rather a long way from "untrained" intuition. Still, through 1965 at least (Chomsky, 1965; Katz and Postal, 1964; Klima, 1964) the main lines of M.I.T. intuition check with our own.

Since a grammar formalizes adult knowledge it is reasonable to hypothesize that the child's knowledge of the structure of his language grows from that which is, in the grammar, derivationally less complex to that which is derivationally more complex; the hypothesis is reasonable and not necessarily true. To test the hypothesis we should have good experimental techniques for inquiring about the young child's knowledge of the structure of sentences. We do not have such techniques and so we propose to infer—with much uncertainty—the points at which grammatical knowledge emerges, from the study of naturally-occurring linguistic interaction between child and mother. We propose to treat the child's production of a construction, in quantity and over a good part of its proper range, together with evidence that he understands the construction when others use it, as *signs* that he has the grammatical knowledge represented formally by the derivation of that construction in the adult grammar. It seems possible to us that the order of emergence of such knowledge would reflect derivational complexity even when the *speed* and *accuracy* with which such knowledge is employed in understanding and retaining sentences does not.

Probably the derivation is no nearer to being a description of performance for the child than it is for the adult. There may be all kinds of strategies of speaking and understanding which, from the first, make the relation between grammar and performance an indirect one. We do not mean to suggest otherwise but rather to suggest that when performance over a range of sentences and situations attains a near-adult level of excellence the performance may be taken as a sign of the acquisition of knowledge. Between knowledge and the grammar there may be a fairly direct relation.

There is reason to think that among the sentence types on which we shall report are some for which it is more than ordinarily reasonable to treat performance as a sign of the acquisition of structural knowledge. The total set comprises:

yes-no questions (Q), negatives (N), truncated predicates (Tr), truncated questions (TrQ), negative questions (NQ), truncated negatives (TrN), and truncated negative questions (TrNQ). Although there are some knotty derivational problems (discussed at a later point), the sentences in this set may be partially-ordered in terms of cumulative derivational complexity. The most complex in the set are the truncated negative questions, which are such negative tags as: *The old man drives well, doesn't he?* One of the more complex types in the set is the truncated question, which is an affirmative tag like: *The old man doesn't drive well, does he?* With respect to these tags, in particular, the inference from performance to structural knowledge seems strong.

INTRODUCTION TO TAG QUESTIONS

The boy we call Adam when he was four years and seven months old produced thirty-two tags in a two-hour sample of conversation. Included among them were the following:

Ursula's my sister, isn't she?
I made a mistake, didn't I?
Me and Diandros are working, aren't we?
He can't beat me, can he?
He doesn't know what to do, does he?

The truncated questions at the ends of these all seem to have the same semantic; they are requests for confirmation. There is one minor variation. The negative questions, appended to affirmative propositions, convey a presumption that the answer will be affirmative and, in fact, the most common answers to these were *Yes* and *That's right.* The affirmative questions, appended to negative propositions convey a presumption that the answer will be negative and *No* was the most common answer.

There are simpler mechanisms than the tag question for requesting confirmation. English speakers can use *huh?* or *right?* and the children we have studied used these forms much earlier than they used the tags.[1] In some languages even the mature tags are, like *huh*?, forms that do not vary with the structure of the sentences to which they are appended; the Germans can always ask *nicht wahr*? and the French *n'est-ce pas*? We could suppose that forms like these could be learned as fixed routines but mature English tags cannot be. Adam requests confirmation with *isn't she*? and *didn't I*? and *does he*? and *aren't you*? and in many other ways. This variation of form occurs with no appreciable variation of semantic but it is not a free variation; the form of the tag is fixed by the structure of the declarative.

Suppose, now, that we had, from Adam, the sentence *Me and Diandros are working* without the question and, on a different occasion, as an independent utterance, the question *Aren't we*? and we wondered how much the child knew of the structure of these sentences. Did he know that the subject of the first was *Me and Diandros* and that this subject was plural in number? Did he know, about his second sentence, that it could be derived from a declarative counterpart (*We aren't*) by interchanging the subject and the first member of the auxiliary (plus *n't*)? Did he know, of this same sentence, that it could be derived from an affirmative counterpart (*Are we*?) by adjunction of the negative morpheme? In the record itself there would be nothing to go on but the fact that the sentences were produced. Even if there had been time to prepare experimental tests to inquire about Adam's knowledge it is doubtful that such tests could have been invented. Suppose that we imagine the situation changed to the actual case in which the two sentences were produced as one, as the tag question *Me and Diandros are working, aren't we*? The fact of production now offers fairly powerful evidence of grammatical knowledge.

The negative truncated question in the tag is a complex derivative of the antecedent declarative. It may be said, in

[1] Professor Dwight Bolinger has pointed out to me that the child's *huh*? has a rise-fall intonation quite unlike that of the adult's form. It is an intonation that sounds so very "childish" when an adult does it that I suspect adults never do.

loose terms, that the question is derived by the following processes: pronominalization, negation, interrogation, and truncation. Still speaking loosely, the processes go like this. It is the subject that must be pronominalized, and so the child must know that *Me and Diandros* constitutes the subject. This is the kind of knowledge one would represent in the tree structure of the sentence by showing that *Me and Diandros* constitutes a "NP" directly dominated by "S." Clearly the subject of a sentence cannot, in the few examples from Adam, let alone in English generally, be identified with any surface feature of the sentence such as the first word in the sentence or the first noun. To select the correct pronoun *we* it is necessary to know that the subject is plural and inclusive of the speaker. In other cases it would be necessary to know the gender of the subject. From *Me and Diandros are working*, by the process of pronominalization alone, the sentence *We are working* is obtained and that is still a long way from the ultimate tag form.

Negation can be said (roughly) to adjoin *n't* to the first member of the auxiliary. To do that Adam must have had the auxiliary properly bracketed and labelled. In deriving *didn't I?* from *I made a mistake*, Adam seems to have known something like the fact that the first member of the auxiliary was the morpheme "Past," which requires *do* support in the absence of any other auxiliary. Adding negation to pronominalization we arrive at *We aren't working*.

Interrogation interchanges the first member of the auxiliary plus *n't* with the subject and so yields *Aren't we working?* Predicate truncation deletes all of the predicate except the first member of the auxiliary plus *n't* and so at length we obtain the truncated negative question *Aren't we?* This loose derivation is summarized as follows:

Sentence	Grammatical Change
Diandros and me are working.	Pronominalization
We are working.	Negation
We aren't working.	Interrogation
Aren't we working?	Truncation
Aren't we?	

The structure of English sentences is so obvious to the native speaker that he can scarcely realize how difficult it would be to derive truncated questions from declaratives without knowledge of sentence structure. Consider the following numerical parallel in which the string of digits following the comma can be derived from the string before the comma by using a constant function.

321118596,6210
95617,5227
2242139128746,6224
34229997,____?

Is there anyone who feels able to complete the last utterance? The rule is:

1. Consider the subject to be the first set of digits summing to 5 or more. To pronominalize, if the subject is exactly 5, double it. If more than 5, triple it.
2. The first member of the auxiliary is the first set of numbers following the subject that sums to 3 or more. To adjoin the negative insert the number "2" following the first member of the auxiliary.
3. The interrogative is created by interchanging the subject and the first member of the auxiliary together with the negative "2." If the first member of the auxiliary sums to exactly 3, double it (for *do* support).
4. Truncate the predicate by deleting the string after the subject. The step-by-step derivation of the last tag is shown in Table 7–1.

Table 7–1. Derivation of Interrogative Tag

Sentence	Grammatical Change
34229997	Pronominalization
21229997	Negation
212229997	Interrogation
222219997	Truncation
22221	

165

It is difficult to see how Adam could produce the variety of tags that he does if he did not have all the structural knowledge described, which is a large part of the knowledge formally represented in the derivation of tags. To be sure, one could argue that since the form of the truncated question is fixed by the form of the declarative Adam could have learned all his thirty-two sentences in the one sample as fixed routines. However, this is unlikely on the face of it and grows more so as you look at more and more tags and see that practically all of them are one-time occurrences.

For tags, both negative and affirmative, the fact of production is rather strong evidence of grammatical knowledge. For the other kinds of sentences to be considered one cannot feel as sure that correct production and evidence of comprehension are signs that the child has all the knowledge represented by the derivations in the adult grammar. The evidence is unevenly strong across sentence types and situations. A truncated negative declarative (TrN) like *I can't* produced in response to a parental sentence like *You can lift it* strongly suggests knowledge of the negation and truncation rules as well as correct bracketing of the verbal auxiliary. With respect to *yes-no* questions (Q) one can get fairly convincing evidence of comprehension since these sentences, produced by others, tend to elicit responses from the child. For a full discussion of all the evidence, readers will have to consult the full grammatical work-ups prepared by the project. In this paper we propose simply to present production figures for sentence types since that is the aspect of the evidence that is easily made public. For all the sentence types there is evidence of comprehension which appears in advance of production.

SENTENCE DERIVATIONS AND THE ORDER OF COMPLEXITY

It will help the authors to keep their bearing if we start with an advance overview of the loose grammatical conception guiding the study. We will then introduce formal rules as refinements of this conception.

An Overview

The kinds of sentences to be considered are as follows:

1. Simple, active, affirmative, declarative (SAAD). For example: *We had a ball.*
2. Simple, active, affirmative, interrogative (Q). For example: *Did we have a ball?*
3. Simple, active, negative, declarative (N). For example: *We didn't have a ball.*
4. Simple, active, affirmative, declarative, truncated (Tr). For example: *We did.*
5. Simple, active, negative, interrogative (NQ). For example: *Didn't we have a ball?*
6. Simple, active, affirmative, interrogative, truncated (TrQ). For example: *Did we?* (Also used as affirmative tag.)
7. Simple, active, negative, declarative, truncated (TrN). For example: *We didn't.*
8. Simple, active, negative, interrogative, truncated (TrNQ). For example: *Didn't we?* (Also used as negative tag.)

Examining the above scheme a reader may wonder why we did not rotate sentence types in all the slots, including, for instance, passives as well as actives and complex sentences as well as simple ones. In the case of passives the answer is that well-formed passives, not truncated but complete with agents had only just begun to appear at the point where our records presently terminate—about five years of age. In the case of complex sentences, which include the various kinds of embeddings and conjoinings, the problems of analysis and interpretation are so complicated as to call for an independent study.

The cumulative derivational complexity of the seven types of sentences named and exemplified above works out roughly like this.

$$\text{SAAD} < Q < NQ, TrQ, TrNQ \qquad \text{4 predictions}$$
$$\text{SAAD} < N < NQ, TrN, TrNQ \qquad \text{4 predictions}$$

167

SAAD < Tr < TrQ,TrN,TrNQ	4 predictions
SAAD < NQ < TrNQ	2 predictions
SAAD < TrQ < TrNQ	2 predictions
SAAD < TrN < TrNQ	2 predictions
SAAD < TrNQ	1 prediction

The notation "A<B" means that A is less derivationally complex than B. Sentence symbols separated by commas (e.g., NQ,TrQ,TrNQ) are to be read as not ordered relative to one another in this writing. In the listing above each independent prediction is listed only once; since we have Q<NQ in the first line we do not repeat it in the fourth. It should be noted that the sentence types are not completely ordered in terms of derivational complexity; we do not have an order for the pairs: Q and N, Q and Tr, N and Tr; Q and TrN, N and TrQ, Tr and NQ; NQ and TrQ, NQ and TrN, TrQ and TrN. If the facts of partial ordering are kept in mind, then the following representation of the overall order is helpful:

$$
\begin{array}{lll}
& \text{Q} & \text{NQ} \\
\text{SAAD} & \text{N} \quad \text{TrQ} & \text{TrNQ} \\
& \text{Tr} & \text{TrN}
\end{array}
$$

Why should the complexity order be as we have represented it? SAAD sentences are not, of course, uniform in the number of rules applied in their derivations: there may be a single auxiliary, two, three, or four; and the more auxiliaries there are the more often the obligatory affixation transformation must be applied; noun phrases may have a single determiner or several and predeterminers as well; an SAAD may have none, one, or many adverbials; an SAAD may involve complex selection rules and transformations to accomplish number agreement and it may not. However, for each SAAD there is a Q counterpart which will employ all the rules of the SAAD plus the rule that transposes subject and elements of the auxiliary. For each SAAD similarly there is a negative counterpart which applies the rules of the SAAD and, in addition, at least the rule which accomplishes preverbal placement of the negative morpheme, and sometimes also the rule contracting the negative. For each SAAD finally there is a truncated counterpart which may apply all the rules of the SAAD—if it is derived from a specific full declarative—plus the rule which cuts the predicate back to the first member of the auxiliary. It can then be said that Q, N, and Tr, though not ordered with respect to one another, are all more complex than SAAD. The increments of derivational complexity are clearly not uniform. The added rules are all different, and negatives often involve contraction when the others do not. In addition, however, there is a difference of meaning between SAAD and either N or Q but not between SAAD and Tr. The deep structures of N and Q contain morphemes missing from otherwise corresponding SAAD sentences.

This is perhaps the right point at which to call attention to an important difference between the naturalistic study of child speech and the experimental studies mentioned at the start of this paper. In an experimental study of derivational complexity, sentences that are exact counterparts of one another can be compared; for example: *The boy hit the ball*; *Did the boy hit the ball? The boy didn't hit the ball*; etc. To simplify our description above of the sentence types that concern us we carried a single example *We had a ball* across all types. In fact, however, only one of these sentences actually came within the empirical compass of the study; the little girl we call Sarah did produce the tag *We had a ball, didn't we?* It is not possible to study exact counterpart sentences in a naturalistic study in the way that one can in an experiment. We shall be comparing frequencies of sentences of any one type (e.g., negatives) with frequencies of entirely different specific sentences of other types. We must, therefore, make a large assumption. The assumption is that the population of sentences of one type (e.g., negatives), with respect to all grammatical features except those defining the type, is of the same average complexity as the population of sentences of each other type.

The sentence types N, Q, and Tr are more complex than SAAD sentences because each of them adds at least one new rule not only to particular sentences but to the grammar as a whole. The rules are Tnot, Tq, and Ttr. According to our rough general conception, the remaining differences of complexity arise from the laying on of additional rules in particular derivations but not from the addition of new rules to the grammar. We think of NQ, TrQ, and TrN as combinations of two rules employed one at a time in N, Q, and Tr. We think of TrNQ as a triadic combination from the same set. There is then a qualitative difference between the predictions of the first level (comparing Q, N, and Tr with SAAD) and those of the later levels, and it will be interesting to see if this qualitative line can be seen in the data. In addition, some of the comparisons of the later levels, like some of those on the first level, involve semantic changes (e.g., Q and NQ) whereas others do not (Q and TrQ).

Formal Rules and Problems

In general our discussion of rules operates with the assumptions of transformational generative grammar of 1965 and draws upon such works as Chomsky (1965), Katz and Postal (1964), and Klima (1964). We are working at the level of what might be called the second generation version of transformational grammar, which differs from the first generation version (Chomsky, 1957) in many respects: rules of semantic interpretation are conceived to apply only to underlying P-markers (deep structures) and transformations are written so as not to change meaning; selection restrictions are represented by the expansion of complex symbols and the use of syntactic features, etc. Of course, the grammatical frontier has moved on since 1965. A lag of about five years seems always to exist between linguistics and psycholinguistics. In so laborious an undertaking as the longitudinal study of child speech it is inevitable.

Unluckily for us there is considerable disagreement even among transformationalists publishing around 1965 and, still more unluckily, nowhere in the writings of this period can we find a consistent and fully satisfactory set of rules covering the range of constructions with which we are concerned. We offer, in Table 7-2, a single set of rules based on what we have learned from what has been written and on what we have been able to work out on our own. The rules are imperfect.

Table 7–2. Transformational Rules for Negation, Interrogation, Truncation, and Tagging

TI. Tag-question formation (opt.)

(a)
$$\begin{bmatrix} Q-NP-Tn-V-W \\ Q-NP-Tn-M-V-W \\ Q-NP-Tn-be-W \end{bmatrix} \Rightarrow \begin{bmatrix} NP-Tn-V-W-Q-neg-NP+pro-Tn \\ NP-Tn-M-V-W-Q-neg-NP+pro-Tn-M \\ NP-Tn-be-W-Q-neg-NP+pro-Tn-be \end{bmatrix}$$

(b)
$$\begin{bmatrix} Q-neg-NP-Tn-V-W \\ Q-neg-NP-Tn-M-V-W \\ Q-neg-NP-Tn-be-W \end{bmatrix} \Rightarrow \begin{bmatrix} neg-NP-Tn-V-W-Q-NP+pro-Tn \\ neg-NP-Tn-M-V-W-Q-NP+pro-Tn-M \\ neg-NP-Tn-be-W-Q-NP+pro-Tn-be \end{bmatrix}$$

TII. Predicate truncation schema (opt.)

$$\begin{bmatrix} (neg)(Q)NP-Tn-Pro \\ (neg)(Q)NP-Tn-M-Pro \\ (neg)(Q)NP-Tn-be-Pro \end{bmatrix} \Rightarrow \begin{bmatrix} (neg)(Q)NP-Tn \\ (neg)(Q)NP-Tn-M \\ (neg)(Q)NP-Tn-be \end{bmatrix}$$

TIII. Preverbal placement of neg (obl.)

$$\begin{bmatrix} W-neg-X-NP-Tn-Y \\ W-neg-X-NP-Tn-M-Y \\ W-neg-X-NP-Tn-be-Y \end{bmatrix} \Rightarrow \begin{bmatrix} W-X-NP-Tn-neg-Y \\ W-X-NP-Tn-M-neg-Y \\ W-X-NP-Tn-be-neg-Y \end{bmatrix}$$

TIV. Transposition of subject and auxiliary elements in questions (obl.)

$$\begin{bmatrix} Q-W-NP-Tn(neg)-X \\ Q-W-NP-Tn-M(neg)-X \\ Q-W-NP-Tn-be(neg)-X \end{bmatrix} \Rightarrow \begin{bmatrix} Q-W-Tn(neg)-NP-X \\ Q-W-Tn-M(neg)-NP-X \\ Q-W-Tn-be(neg)-NP-X \end{bmatrix}$$

TV. Affixation (obl.)

$Af-v \Rightarrow v+Af$

where v = any verbal element

Af = Tn or -*ing*

TVI. *Do* support

$W-Af-X \Rightarrow W-do+Af-X$

TVII. Negative contraction (opt.)

$$\begin{bmatrix} W-do+Tn-neg-X \\ W-M+Tn-neg-X \\ W-be+Tn-neg-X \end{bmatrix} \Rightarrow \begin{bmatrix} W-do+Tn+neg-X \\ W-M+Tn+neg-X \\ W-be+Tn+neg-X \end{bmatrix}$$

171

The rules of Table 7–2 do not constitute anything like a full set of the rules required to derive the types of sentences with which we are concerned and the sample derivations of Tables 7–3, 7–4, and 7–5 are not complete derivations but only the steps utilizing the rules of Table 7–2. We have not included any phrase structure rules, any of the steps in complex symbol expansion or any morpho-phonemic rules. We have not

Table 7–3. Derivations of SAAD, Q, N, and Tr

String (*We had a ball*)	Rule
we–Pas–have–a–ball	TV
we–have + Pas–a–ball	morpho-phonemic
we–had–a–ball	

String (*Did we have a ball?*)	Rule
Q–we–Pas–have–a–ball	TIV
Q–Pas–we–have–a–ball	TVI
Q–do + Pas–we–have–a–ball	morpho-phonemics
did–we–have–a–ball–?	

String (*We didn't have a ball*)	Rule
neg–we–Pas–have–a–ball	TIII
we–Pas–neg–have–a–ball	TVI
we–do + Pas–neg–have–a–ball	TVII
we–do + Pas + neg–have–a–ball	morpho-phonemics
we–didn't–have–a–ball	

String (*We did*)	Rule
we–Pas–Pro	TII
we–Pas	TVI
we–do + Pas	morpho-phonemics
we–did	

included such transformational rules as accomplish nominalization of subject pronouns, number agreement in predicate nominatives, and NP movement for separable verbs since these involve grammatical features expected to vary from sentence to sentence but not to differentiate between the types involved in our analysis. For the most part, Table 7–2 lists just those transformational rules that account for differences of

Table 7–4. Derivation of Paired Operations from the Set: Interrogation, Negation, Truncation, and Tag

String (*Didn't we have a ball?*)	Rule
neg–Q–we–Pas–have–a–ball	TIII
Q–we–Pas–neg–have–a–ball	TIV
Q–Pas–neg–we–have–a–ball	TVI
Q–do + Pas–neg–we–have–a–ball	TVII
Q–do + Pas + neg–we–have–a–ball	morpho-phonemics
didn't–we–have–a–ball?	

String (*We didn't*)	Rule
neg–we–Pas–Pro	TII
neg–we–Pas	TIII
we–Pas–neg	TVI
we–do + Pas–neg	TVII
we–do + Pas + neg	morpho-phonemics
we–didn't	

String (*Did we?*). Not a tag.	Rule
Q–we–Pas–Pro	TII
Q–we–Pas	TIV
Q–Pas–we	TVI
Q–do + Pas–we	morpho-phonemics
did–we–?	

String (*We didn't have a ball, did we?*) Tag.	Rule
Q–neg–we–Pas–have–a–ball	TI
neg–we–Pas–have–a–ball–Q–we–Pas	TIII
we–Pas–neg–have–a–ball–Q–we–Pas	TIV
we–Pas–neg–have–a–ball–Q–Pas–we	TVI
we–do + Pas–neg–have–a–ball–Q–Pas–we	TVI
we–do + Pas–neg–have–a–ball–Q–do + Pas–we	TVII
we–do + Pas + neg–have–a–ball–Q–do + Pas–we	morpho-phonemics
we–didn't–have–a–ball–did–we?	

derivational complexity between sentence types. The single exception is the pair of rules, TV. "Affixation" and TVI. "*Do* support." The second of these rules is not applied in the derivation of SAAD sentences but is applied in Q, N, and Tr sentences whenever the only auxiliary is "Tense." So TVI is a rule that is added to the child's grammar with Q, N, and Tr. Nevertheless it does not strictly operate so as to make one sentence more complex, cumulatively, than another for the reason that whenever it is not applied TV must be. One or the

Table 7–5. Derivation of Triples from the Set: Interrogation, Negation, Truncation, and Tag

String (*Didn't we ?*). Not a tag.	Rule
Q–neg–we–Pas–Pro	TII
Q–neg–we–Pas	TIII
Q–we–Pas–neg	TIV
Q–Pas–neg–we	TVI
Q–do+Pas–neg–we	TVII
Q–do+Pas+neg–we	morpho-phonemics
didn't–we–?	

String (*We had a ball, didn't we ?*). Tag.	Rule
Q–we–Pas–have–a–ball	TI
we–Pas–have–a–ball–Q–neg–we–Pas	TIII
we–Pas–have–a–ball–Q–we–Pas–neg	TIV
we–Pas–have–a–ball–Q–Pas–neg–we	TV
we–have+Pas–a–ball–Q–Pas–neg–we	TVI
we–have+Pas–a–ball–Q–do+Pas–neg–we	TVII
we–have+Pas–a–ball–Q–do+Pas+neg–we	morpho-phonemics
we–had–a–ball–didn't–we–?	

other rule is obligatory in every sentence but SAAD sentences use only TV. We have included TVI because, through its association with the more complex sentences, it has a certain interest for us. Inclusion of TVI makes it desirable also to include TV so that the derivations of Tables 7–3, 7–4, and 7–5 may all be complete at the same level and so that we shall not mistake the application of TVI, in all sentences except the SAAD, for a strict increment to cumulative complexity.

Looking first at the derivations of Table 7–3 we see that Q,

N, and Tr all differ from SAAD in that they use TVI "Do support" where SAAD uses TV "Affixation." The sentences Q, N, and Tr also all differ from SAAD in that each applies a single additional rule. The respective rules are: TIV "Transposition of subject and auxiliary elements" for Q; TIII "Preverbal placement of neg" for N; TII "Predicate truncation" for Tr. The N sentence, in addition, applies TVII "Negative contraction." Finally Q and N differ from SAAD in their deep structures by virtue of the fact that they include, respectively, the morphemes "Q" and "neg." It is because these morphemes are in the deep structures that the rules TIV and TIII are obligatory (obl.) rather than optional (opt.) as they were in Chomsky's 1957 treatment.

It is worth pausing at this point to notice some profound similarities linking Q, N, and Tr. If you examine the rules TII, TIII, and TIV you will see that they all rely on the same organization of the auxiliary. All three rules organize the first member of the auxiliary as "Tense" (Tn) alone or as "Tense" and "Modal" (M) or as "Tense" and "be" (either as copula or auxiliary). TIV transposes this element; TIII places "neg" just after this element; TII deletes the predicate just back to this element. Closely related to the organization of the auxiliary is the addition of the rule for "Do support" which is applied in just those cases where the auxiliary element consists of "Tense" (Tn) alone. We might expect the learning of Q, N, and Tr to occur at about the same time since a large part of the structure involved is common to all three. We shall see that that is the case. It also seems to be the case that other sentences which utilize this organization of the auxiliary (wh questions and emphatics, for instance) appear at about the same time.

The rule for predicate truncation, TII, involves various problems, the solution of which is beyond us. In our overview we spoke of predicate truncations (or ellipses) as if they were derived from specific sentences containing complete predicates. This is certainly the impression one gets from the study of such sentences in actual discourse. In a typical sort of exchange a parent says: *Eat your peas* and the child responds: *I will.* One is inclined to derive *I will* from *I will (eat my peas)*

175

since that is clearly what the truncation means. To do so, however, involves violating what Katz and Postal (1964) call the requirement of "unique recoverability." From *I will* and a truncation rule one cannot recover the source: *I will eat my peas.* It is perhaps possible to satisfy unique recoverability by deriving *I will* not from a specific full predicate but from a dummy predicate like *I will do something.* We have suggested such a solution in TII by using "PRO" to stand for such a dummy predicate. However, TII involves, in detail, problems we have not solved. For instance, one might hear an exchange like this. Parent: *It is a dog*; Child: *It is.* The dummy in this case would have to stand for a NP and so TII as written, with a single symbol "PRO," does not attain unique recoverability. For these reasons we have called TII a "schema" rather than a "rule." By this we mean to say that while it represents certain aspects of the facts it is not a genuine algorithm as presently formulated. There are additional problems with this rule which arise in connection with tags.

Table 7–4 presents sample derivations for the paired operations: NQ, TrN, and TrQ. Let us defer for two paragraphs the special problems created by tags. We see that the first sentence (NQ) involves all the rules involved in N (III, VI, and VII) plus one that is not (IV) and also all the rules involved in Q (IV and VI) plus two that are not (III and VII). The second sentence (TrN) includes all the rules of Tr (II and VI) plus two others (III and VII) as well as all the rules of N (III, VI, and VII) plus one other (II). The third sentence (TrQ not a tag) includes the rules of Tr (II and VI) plus one other (IV) and the rules of Q (IV and VI) plus one other (II). All of this confirms our overview.

In two minor respects the derivations of Table 7–4 raise problems. The semantic of a NQ like *Didn't we have a ball?* does not seem really to include a negative meaning as the morpheme "neg" suggests it does. It seems to us that we use negative questions when the probabilities of *yes* and *no* answers are not equal, when the presumption is that the answer will be *yes.* The meaning of these questions does not then seem to be a compound of the meanings associated with the morphemes "neg" and "Q" though that is what the underlying string suggests. The second problem is one in connection with adult speech only. The rules of Table 7–2 will generate a negative question with contraction such as *Didn't we have a ball?* but will not generate an uncontracted NQ: *Did we not have a ball?* However, while adults would judge this latter sentence to be grammatical, the uncontracted NQ is not found at all in the speech of the children we have studied.

Finally there is the derivation of the tags themselves, the affirmative tag in Table 7–4 and the negative in Table 7–5. Our TI "Tag Question Formation" is modeled after a rule of Klima's (1964). The rule works like this. The tag question is derived by optional transformation from underlying phrase markers which either contain "Q" alone or else both "Q" and "neg." In the former case, TI leaves the first proposition affirmative but adds "neg" to the question and so the tag question becomes a negative one. In the latter case TI retains "neg" for the first proposition but the tag question itself is affirmative. By these means Klima represents the fact that when the first proposition is affirmative (*We had a ball*) the question must be negative (*didn't we?*) whereas when the first proposition is negative (*We didn't have a ball*) the question must be affirmative (*did we?*). These first aspects of Klima's rule also say, in effect, that the tag question *We had a ball, didn't we?* is equivalent in meaning to the simple *yes-no* question *Did we have a ball?* since both have an underlying phrase marker containing "Q" but not "neg." That seems to us an incorrect claim since the simple *yes-no* question does not presuppose the answer *yes* as does the NQ. Klima's rule, similarly, says that the tag question *We didn't have a ball, did we?* is equivalent in meaning to the NQ *Didn't we have a ball?* since both have "neg" and "Q" in the underlying phrase marker. This claim, too, seems to be incorrect since the affirmative tag presupposes the answer *no* whereas the NQ presupposes *yes*.

To continue with Rule TI: it provides a basis for pronominalization by adding the marker "+pro" to the subject NP. Morpho-phonemic rules would complete the job of pronominalization. In the children's tags we find that pronominalization is not an essential or even usual aspect of tag

177

formation. It often happens, as in *We had a ball, didn't we?* that the subject NP of the first proposition is already a pronoun. The rule could be easily modified to make pronominalization optional.

Rule TI does not truncate the predicate in the underlying phrase-marker but rather repeats it, just through the first auxiliary. Roughly speaking it changes *We had a ball* into *We had a ball we did.* Consequently, when tags are derived using Rule TI, no use at all is made of Rule TII "Predicate truncation" and so the tags in Tables 7–4 and 7–5 are not combinations, respectively, of Tr and Q (Table 7–4) and Tr, Q, and N (Table 7–5). That, however, is the way we represented them in our advance overview.

The problem is complicated further by the fact that we do have, from the children, instances of TrQ not used as a tag (Table 7–4) and also of TrNQ not used as a tag (Table 7–5). They arise in interchanges like this:

Mother: *We had a ball.*   Child: *Did we?*
Mother: *We didn't have a ball.*   Child: *Didn't we?*

Notice that a sentence corresponding to the first proposition of a tag is here produced *by another speaker.* Notice, further, that the questions, sounding like echoes, match the antecedent sentences in that an affirmative antecedent elicits an affirmative question and a negative antecedent elicits a negative question. When antecedent and echo are bound together in a tag question there is an affirmative–negative or negative–affirmative switch. So these echo instances of TrQ and TrNQ do not seem to be the same as proper tags. The echoes are, what the tags were represented to be, in the overview, combinations of the basic operations: Tr, Q, and N.

There is, we think, some possibility that tags should be represented in the way that echoes are, as combinations including truncation. Our Rule TI, modelled after Klima's, is, we have seen, faulty in semantic respects. Furthermore, the effect that Rule TI accomplishes by repeating the underlying predicate through the first auxiliary is essentially the same as the effect accomplished in TII by truncating the predicate back to the first auxiliary. Since a rule like TII is, in any case, needed for truncations that are not tags we should have a simple grammar if we could derive both kinds of sentences with TII. The problem is, how to do it? Presumably we would have to consider the tag to be just the final appended question, *did we* or *didn't we*, and not the complete sentences, *We didn't have a ball, did we?* and *We had a ball, didn't we?* There is something to be said for this approach since in actual discourse the child sometimes breaks the two sentences with an utterance-final intonation. There are even interruptions like this:

Child: *We had a ball.*
Child: *Didn't we?*   Mother: *Yep.*

However, if the tag is identified with the question alone then the perfectly regular affirmative-negative and negative-affirmative switches fall outside the scope of a sentence-generating grammar. It is possible that the switches should fall outside the grammar; that they might better be captured by a rule of discourse. We are just not sure.

What difference do the formal rules make in the ordering of the constructions (presented in the overview) for cumulative derivational complexity? If we substitute the echo forms of TrQ and TrNQ for those called tags in the overview then the ordering there is still exactly correct. Recall that TrQ and TrNQ have the following relations (across all the lines in which they appear):

$$SAAD, Tr, Q < TrQ < TrNQ$$
$$SAAD, Tr, Q, N, TrQ < TrNQ$$

These relations are preserved by the derivations of Tables 7-3, 7-4 and 7-5. TrQ involves all the rules of Tr (II and VI) plus one more (IV) as well as the rules of Q (IV and VI) plus one more (II). TrNQ involves the rules of Tr (II and VI) plus one peculiar to Q (IV) plus two peculiar to N (III and VII).

How is the situation changed with respect to tags which, using Rule TI, are not TrQ and TrNQ but rather TgQ and TgNQ? There is no change at all unless a relation involves both a Tr and either TgQ or TgNQ. The following, for example, still hold:

$$Q < TgQ, TgNQ$$
$$N < TgQ, TgNQ$$
$$NQ < TgNQ$$
$$TgQ < TgNQ$$

All of these (and others) hold because, when tags are derived with TI rather than with the truncation rule TII, the derivations are, in other respects the same. Tags derived with TI still use the Q and the N operations. Consequently TgQ and TgNQ relate to SAAD, Q, N, NQ, and one another exactly as TrQ and TrNQ do. Changes in ordering are limited to the following relations:

Tr cannot be ordered relative to TgQ and TgNQ.
TrN cannot be ordered relative to TgNQ.

These three pairs cannot be ordered within a pair because each member involves something the other does not; either Tr or Tg. Of the original nineteen predictions, then, we lose three. If these three should nevertheless be confirmed for tags that might be taken as evidence that the tags should, after all, not be derived with Rule TI but rather with the truncation rule (TII).

RESULTS

The data come from our longitudinal study of the development of grammar during the preschool years in three children whom we call Adam, Eve, and Sarah. For this study we have transcribed at least two hours of conversation each month between mother and child at home; often we have transcribed more conversation and also done small experiments on one or another aspect of the child's sentence comprehension or production. The principal goal of the study is to describe the growth of grammatical knowledge in the form of a succession of generative grammars.

The developmental period on which our work has focused is defined in terms of a range of values on mean utterance length. The period begins when the mean value is 1.75 morphemes and the longest utterance is 5 morphemes; it ends when the mean is 4.00 and the longest utterance 13 morphemes. Grammars are being written for five points (designated I, II, III, IV, and V) which are evenly spaced across the total interval. At each point we draw a sample of 700 utterances from each child and the grammars are written from these samples. The first versions of Grammars I, II, III, and V but not yet IV have been written for all the three children. For special studies of negatives, wh questions, inflections, forms, coding aspects of time, etc. we and our associates have used more of the data than is included in I–V. This paper reports another such study.

The main data to be reported are frequencies of the constructions with which we are concerned at levels I through V. We have not counted SAAD sentences because simple forms of these are present in good quantity from I on. For negatives (N) and questions (Q) we have simply taken the figures from the 700-utterance grammar samples. For the remaining constructions (Tr, TrN, TrQ, NQ, and TrNQ) it was necessary to take larger samples for the reason that the base output rates for these are much lower than for N and Q in adult speech as well as in child speech. Samples of 700 utterances would yield rather unreliable figures. The size of the samples for the less frequent constructions is 2100 utterances. We simply added on to the basic 700-utterance grammar samples the next 1400 utterances. For Eve at IV and V this procedure ran into difficulty; Eve developed very much more rapidly than Adam and Sarah and her IV and V were so close together that we were able to obtain for IV only about 1500 utterances. The difficulty at V is that Eve left the study just after V (the family moved to Saskatchewan) and so her sample V consists of just the basic 700 utterances. Eve's withdrawal introduces another asymmetry into the report of the data. The transcriptions for Adam and Sarah go right on after V and so we have reported for them on a 2100-utterance sample taken seven months after V; there is no such sample for Eve. We did not bother to count N and Q in this last sample since these constructions had long been fully productive at that point.

The figures in Tables 7–6, 7–7, and 7–8 tell the story pretty well; SAAD sentences were present from I; N, Q, and Tr develop for all the children between III and V; TrQ, TrN, and

NQ tend to develop at least as late as N, Q, and Tr but there is quite a bit of variation from child to child; TrNQ is at least as late as V in all.

The benchmarks, I to V, fall at the same points for all the

Table 7–6. Occurrences Across Time of Seven Sentence Types in Adam

	N*	Q*	Tr†	TrN†	TrQ†	NQ†	TrNQ†
I.	0	0	0	0	0	0	0
II.	1	0	2 b	0	0	0	0
III.	☐13☐	12 a	0	2 c	0	0	0
IV.	19	11 a	4	0	0	0	0
V.	31	☐25☐	☐11☐	☐16☐	5	0	0
7 months later			8	8	0	2	☐10☐

* Based on 700 utterances per sample.
† Based on 2100 utterances per sample.
☐ First occurrence of 6 or more.
a All are questions beginning *D'you want.*
b Both are *I did* and are used inappropriately.
c Both are *I can't.*

Table 7–7. Occurrences Across Time of Seven Sentence Types in Sarah

	N*	Q*	Tr†	TrN†	TrQ†	NQ†	TrNQ†
I.	0	1	1	0	0	0	0
II.	☐7☐	0	5	8	0	0	0
III.	26	1	☐18☐	☐8☐	1	0	0
IV.	28	☐11☐	21	12	4	0	0
V.	33	28	30	16	☐6☐	4	☐7☐
7 months later			29	18	12	3	9

* Based on 700 utterances per sample.
† Based on 2100 utterances per sample except for IV which is based on 1500 and V which is based on 700.
☐ First occurrence of 6 or more.

children in terms of mean length of utterance but not in terms of chronological age. Sarah was somewhat older than Adam at each point and much older than Eve. A comparison of Sarah's table (7–7) with those of Adam and Eve shows that

Table 7–8. Occurrences Across Time of Seven Sentence Types in Eve

	N*	Q*	Tr†	TrN†	TrQ†	NQ†	TrNQ†
I.	0	0	0	0	0	0	0
II.	0	0	0	0	0	0	0
III.	13	0	0	0	0	0	0
IV.	25	2	2	0	0	0	0
V.	35	27	9	3	0	0	0

* Based on 700 utterances per sample.
† Based on 2100 utterances per sample except for IV which is based on 1500 and V which is based on 700.
☐ First occurrence of 6 or more.

Table 7–9. Occurrences in All Samples for Eighteen Months of Five Sentence Types in Adam

Sample	Tr	TrN	TrQ	NQ	TrNQ	Sample	Tr	TrN	TrQ	NQ	TrNQ
19	0	0	0	0	0	35	7	12	0	0	0
20	1	0	0	0	0	36	2	4	1	0	0
21	3	1	0	0	0	37	4	2	3	0	0
22	0	1	0	0	0	38	4	5	0	0	0
23	1	1	0	0	0	39	7	3	3	0	0
24	1	0	0	0	0	40	4	6	2	0	0
25	0	0	0	0	0	41	4	2	1	0	0
26	3	0	0	0	0	42	2	2	3	0	1
27	2	2	0	0	0	43	5	1	2	0	0
28	2	1	0	0	0	44	5	2	1	0	0
29	4	4	2	0	0	45	3	3	0	0	6
30	2	1	0	0	0	46	3	1	0	1	1
31	1	2	2	0	0	47	2	4	0	1	3
32	0	2	1	0	0	48	2	4	1	0	3
33	4	6	4	0	0	49	1	3	1	0	16
34	8	8	0	0	0	50	5	1	0	5	32

in respect of the sentence types with which we are concerned she was ahead of the others relative to the mean length of utterance. From writing the grammars we have learned that the children at a given Roman numeral level will be much alike in terms of those features of grammar that increase utterance length when they are learned—such as obligatory inflections and determiners. In other dimensions we have found that Sarah's age tells and that she knows more, relative to the length of her sentences, than do the other children.

Table 7–9 supplements the partial data of Tables 7–6, 7–7, and 7–8 with complete counts of Tr, TrN, TrQ, NQ, and TrNQ in all samples for Adam from III on. Table 7–9 confirms the impression created by the partial data of Table 7–6 that Tr and TrN occur in quantity before the other constructions, that TrQ follows next but is particularly variable in frequency, and that NQ and TrNQ do not occur at all until near the end of the 18-month period. In the last two samples the TrNQ tags jump from a long-term zero frequency level first to sixteen instances and then to 32. These last output rates are four to eight times adult rates. The children have often shown this kind of brief infatuation with a construction when it was first learned; the frequency typically falls back within a few weeks to a level approximately that of adult speech.

We should like to submit our predictions concerning derivational complexity and order of acquisition to a more explicit test than simple inspection of the data but for that we require a criterion of acquisition. If the criterion becomes complicated, as it sometimes does in the grammars, the possibility of the reader inspecting the evidence becomes remote. The best we can do, therefore, is to adopt a largely arbitrary but not unreasonable criterion and check the data against that. We have counted the sentence types in question in 1400-utterance samples drawn from the three mothers, at times just prior to II and III. We find that the lowest output rate any of these sentence types has in any of the mothers is 6 in 2100 utterances. So we have adopted the value "6" as our threshold of emergence; the first child sample in which a sentence type attains that value or higher is considered to be the sample of emergence. From what we have learned in writing the grammars this value places the emergence points about right. In general the children were giving evidence of understanding the constructions by that point and in general after that point they steadily produced the construction.

There is one case in which we are sure that the frequency

Table 7–10. Predictions Confirmed (+), Disconfirmed (—), and Unsettled (?) for Derivational Complexity and Order of Acquisition

	Adam			Sarah			Eve		
	+	?	—	+	?	—	+	?	—
SAAD < Q	√			√			√		
Q < TrQ	√			√			√		
Q < NQ	√			√			√		
Q < TrNQ	√			√			√		
SAAD < N	√			√			√		
N < TrN	√				√		√		
N < NQ	√			√			√		
N < TrNQ	√			√			√		
SAAD < Tr	√			√			√		
Tr < TrQ*	√			√			√		
Tr < TrN		√			√		√		
Tr < TrNQ*	√			√			√		
SAAD < TrQ	√			√			√		
TrQ < TrNQ......		√			√			√	
SAAD < TrN	√			√			√		
TrN < TrNQ*	√			√				√	
SAAD < NQ	√			√			√		
NQ < TrNQ......		√			√			√	
SAAD < TrNQ ...	√			√			√		
Totals ᵃ	16	1	2	15	2	2	16	3	0
Totals ᵇ	13	1	2	12	2	2	14	2	0

ᵃ Appropriate totals if doubtful cases are TrQ and TrNQ.
ᵇ Appropriate totals if doubtful cases are TgQ and TgNQ.
* Prediction not made for tags (TgQ or TgNQ).

criterion is misleading and in this case we have deserted the criterion. The exception appears in Table 7–6. Adam used a dozen well-formed *yes-no* questions in III and 11 in IV but we have identified V as the sample of emergence. The reason is that all of Adam's well-formed questions in the period from

III through IV began with the fixed form *D'you want*. There were no instances at all of such closely related forms as *Did you want, Does he want, D'you see*, etc. For these and other reasons we do not, in the grammar for III, generate Adam's questions with rules like the rules of the adult grammar. There are other occurrences of sentences which we do not, for one reason or another, take to be adequate evidence that the child knows the underlying structure but in these other cases the frequency does not attain the criterion value of 6.

Using our criterion for emergence we have checked the 19 predictions based on the order of derivational complexity presented in the overview, an order that does not distinguish between TrQ and TgQ or TrNQ and TgNQ. The results appear in Table 7–10. For Adam, 16 predictions are confirmed; 2 are disconfirmed; and 1 is not settled either way by the data. For Sarah, the respective results are 15, 2, and 2. For Eve they are 16 confirmed and 3 unsettled. In arriving at these figures we have assumed that any sentence type which had not attained criterion in the data presented did attain criterion at some point later than the times represented in the data. The prediction that constructions would emerge in the order of derivational complexity described in the overview is supported by the results.

What of the distinction between TrQ and TgQ; TrNQ and TgNQ? As we have seen there are a few cases in which we can define an order of cumulative derivational complexity for TrQ and TrNQ where we have no basis for defining such an order for the tags. The cases (marked with an asterisk in Table 7–10) are these:

$$Tr < TrQ$$
$$Tr < TrNQ$$
$$TrN < TrNQ$$

The first difficulty with this fine-grained analysis is that there are not more than three or four cases of TrNQ in either Adam or Sarah. It is only TgNQ that attains criterion. As it happens, TgNQ appears later than Tr and TrN in all cases. This may mean that TgNQ is cumulatively more complex than Tr and TrN and should, in fact, be derived with the aid of Rule TII

"Predicate truncation." Alternatively, however, it may simply mean that the tags are more complex than Tr and TrN in ways we have not considered. The comparison would have been stronger if we had had a basis for predicting that TgQ would occur before Tr and TrN while TrQ should appear after them. In fact, however, we simply had no basis for ordering TgQ and Tr; TgQ and TrN. Since, however, the cases labelled TrNQ in Table 7–10 are in fact almost all cases of TgNQ we should count confirmations somewhat differently than was done for the first row of "Totals" in Table 7–10. The relations between TgNQ and Tr and TrN are not in fact predicted by cumulative complexity and so their confirmation should not be counted in favor of the hypothesis. The number of confirmations is appropriately reduced in the second line of totals.

With respect to TrQ and TgQ there is a single prediction that applies to one and not the other. TrQ should be later than Tr but for TgQ there is no basis for a prediction. When TrQ and TgQ are separately examined the prediction is confirmed for both and so we are where we were with TrNQ and TgNQ; the result may mean that TgQ should be derived with the aid of Rule TII "Predicate truncation" or it may simply mean that TgQ is, in other ways, more complex than Tr. While a certain number of clear instances of both TrQ and TgQ can be identified there are also many cases in which the identification is not clear. Therefore we have simply added them together in Table 7–10. If we think of the instances as TrQ then the first set of totals is the correct one. If we think of the instances as TgQ then the number of confirmations must be reduced by the number of pairs for which there is no prediction in the case of TgQ. This has been done and is reflected in the second set of totals.

In connection with TgQ there is a point of incidental interest. Both Adam and Sarah made an interesting kind of error in their early use of TgQ; they failed to make the affirmative–negative switch and so, in effect, overgeneralized TgQ. They produced, for instance: *He'll catch cold, will he? But it's all over, is it? This is Boston, is it?* The reciprocal error, which would overgeneralize the negative question, never occurred. There were no instances of sentences such as this: *We didn't have a ball, didn't we?* What should cause this asymmetry? It could, of course, simply result from a difference of derivational complexity. TrNQ is more complex than TrQ. Our guess, however, is that another factor is important.

The children produced TgNQ fairly often and TrNQ not at all whereas they produced (correctly) both TrQ and TgQ. Probably this difference reflects a difference in adult speech. Probably there are fewer occasions calling for the negative echo question (TrNQ) such as *Didn't we?* than there are occasions calling for the affirmative echo question (TrQ) *Did we?* The affirmative echo question does not involve the negative–affirmative switch of the affirmative tag. Since TrQ and TgQ are, except for their relation to an antecedent, identical, it is to be expected that they would interfere with one another. Furthermore, clear cases of TrQ tend to appear before clear cases of TgQ in Adam and Sarah. In Sarah's data, for instance, TrQ sentences begin twenty weeks before TgQ sentences. It seems likely, then, that the child confuses affirmative tags when they first appear with echo questions and so uses them, for a time, without the affirmative–negative switch they require.

SENTENCE LENGTH, FREQUENCY, AND SEMANTIC

What factors other than derivational complexity could account for the order of emergence of SAAD, Q, N, Tr, TrN, TrQ, and TrNQ? Length and frequency are not cognitive variables but we cannot be sure that they will, on that account, fail to influence results obtained by cognitive psychologists. In experimental studies of sentence comprehension and recall, sentence length has often been confounded with complexity, the two increasing together. For example, Savin and Perchonock in their study (1965) of immediate recall made seventeen predictions on the basis of cumulative derivational complexity; thirteen of these seventeen would also be made if one simply used sentence length as an index of complexity. For the wh question in their experiment Savin and Perchonock decide that there are no predictions from cumulative complexity but they fail to note that sentence length makes ten predictions in this case, of which nine are confirmed.

Sutherland (1966) and others have suggested that complexity is likely also to be confounded with frequency in such favorite sets of sentences as: SAAD, Q, N, P (passives), NQ, NP, and NPQ. Since no one seems to have cited any actual counts of sentence types we may as well do so. We have made many such counts in our study for the speech parents use to children. In a sample of 700 sentences the number of SAAD sentences will run between 100 and 200; Q and N will both be something like one-half to one-quarter as frequent as SAAD; of passives, negative questions, negative passives, and the like there will typically be between 0 and 6. Of course we do not know how representative such counts are of adult speech generally but in parent-to-child speech, at any rate, complexity is confounded with frequency for the kinds of sentences that have been most often used in experiments.

Are length and frequency confounded with complexity in the sentences we have studied? Consider length in the following sample set:

SAAD.	*We had a ball.*	(4 words)
Q.	*Did we have a ball?*	(5 words)
N.	*We didn't have a ball.*	(6 words)
Tr.	*We did.*	(2 words)
TrN.	*We didn't.*	(3 words)
TrQ.	*Did we?*	(2 words)
TgQ.	*We didn't have a ball, did we?*	(8 words)
NQ.	*Didn't we have a ball?*	(6 words)
TrNQ.	*Didn't we?*	(3 words)
TgNQ.	*We had a ball, didn't we?*	(7 words)

Of the nineteen predictions from derivational complexity that apply when we have TrQ and TrNQ, rather than complete tags, seven would go the same way if sentence length were used as an index of complexity but twelve would go differently. Of the sixteen predictions from derivational complexity that apply when we have the tags, TgQ and TgNQ, sentence-length predicts the same way in eleven cases and differently in five. So, in our sentences, length and derivational complexity are partially but not completely confounded. Examining the outcomes of the twelve predictions for which length and complexity predict differently (when we have Tr and TrQ) across the three children we find that complexity is correct in thirty-one instances. The outcome is unsettled in four instances and length is correct just once. The results are about the same with tags included. So it does look as if sentence length will not explain the order of emergence even though sentence length is a variable that increases with age. One of the reasons this family of constructions caught our eye in the first place was that we were surprised to find such short utterances as tags and truncations developing quite late in the child's speech.

Frequency turns out to be a more serious variable than length. In order to see whether differential construction frequencies in parental speech could affect order of emergence in child speech we wanted a count of parental frequencies that antedated emergence and was relatively free of influence from the children. So we used two samples of 700 utterances each taken immediately prior to II and III. At III the children were not regularly producing any of the constructions except the SAAD sentences. We counted the eight major constructions in the 2 samples for each of the 3 mothers and used just those sentences of the mother that were neither imitations nor expansions of sentences produced by the children.

As in all the counts we have made for parental speech the frequency profiles of the three mothers were highly correlated. Of the results we will report the average value per 700 utterances, across mothers and samples, for each main sentence type. They are:

	Q(53)	TrQ(2)	
SAAD(139)	N(56)	TrN(2)	TrNQ(4)
	Tr(13)	NQ(4)	

Clearly frequency and derivational complexity are closely related.

The apparently quite general correlation between grammatical complexity and frequency has a certain independent

COMPLEXITY AND ORDER IN CHILD SPEECH

interest. It is not, to begin with, simply an artifact of a system of sentence classification. Potentially there are as many different sentences of one type as of any other type. Any SAAD is susceptible of negation, truncation, interrogation, tagging, etc. Apparently, however, there are many more occasions calling for declaration than interrogation, affirmation than negation; and relatively few occasions calling for truncation and requests for confirmation. One is reminded of Zipf's (1949) empirical law relating word length inversely to word frequency and also of his general idea that the relation exists because of a Principle of Least Effort that causes our frequently used tools to be kept simple and close to hand. The derivationally simple sentence types seem to be those we most often need and the derivationally complex types those we need less often. If psychological complexity is related to derivational complexity then it may not be inappropriate to invoke a Principle of Least Effort.

Of the nineteen main predictions made by derivational complexity, seventeen are also made by frequency and the two predictions that go the other way are based on very small frequency differences in our counts. It is possible then that the order in which the child's knowledge of the sentences develops is determined by the frequency with which parents model the sentences.

We have often before found that parental frequencies predict the order in which constructions will "emerge," in terms of some frequency criterion, in successive samples of child speech. In the early months of our study we had to consider seriously a really radical alternative to the notion that frequent modelling of a sentence type facilitates learning its structure. Suppose the children had known everything from the beginning but emitted constructions according to a frequency profile like the parents. The chance that any particular construction would attain an arbitrary frequency criterion in an early sample would be greater for frequent constructions than for infrequent constructions. So what looked like a pattern of successive "emergences" might simply be a kind of sampling phenomenon. Up to a point that is. But when you have more than two years of zero frequency for something like

191

the negative and affirmative tags you can be confident when they eventually appear that something new has been learned. You can be particularly confident when you see the sudden overproduction we have seen in Adam's sample #50. So we think that at least we need no longer seriously consider the possibility that the children were learning nothing new but we must still consider the possibility that modelling frequency affects the order of learning.

In addition to the differences of length and frequency among sentence types there are semantic differences. Interrogatives, negatives, and tags all differ from SAAD sentences in the meanings they communicate. Is it perhaps the meanings that account for the order of emergence? As it happens the children have primitive ways of asking questions, negating, and requesting confirmation and the primitive forms are present even in I and II. The primitive negative is created by preposing a negative word, *no* or *not*, to a sentence: *No want*, *Not Sarah's*, and the like. Primitive *yes-no* questions are created by using a rising interrogative intonation for any sentence or sentence fragment. Primitive requests for confirmation are chiefly *huh?* and *right?* Of course the mature grammatical forms provide for semantic refinements that the primitive forms miss, the difference, for instance, between *Do you see him?* and *Will you see him?* Still it cannot be the basic semantics of interrogation, negation, and confirmation that defer the acquisition of the mature grammatical structures. The basic meanings have been expressed from the beginning of our records. What has happened developmentally is that immature means of expression have been displaced by mature means.

We must now distinguish between two sorts of order of emergence in child speech. The first sort is an order among constructions which are, all of them, mature adult forms. This is the sort of order with which the present paper has been concerned. We have asked whether the order of emergence of some eight types of well-formed adult sentences reflects the derivational complexity of the types in terms of the adult grammar and found that it does. The second sort of order concerns constructions which are equivalent semantically but which exist in one or more immature or childish forms as well as, eventually, the adult form. The kind of sequence exists for questions, negatives, and tags and for many other constructions. The children we have studied made wh questions with preposed question word but without interposing subject and auxiliary long before they made wh questions that did both. They said *Why you went* and *What he's doing* before they said *Why did you go?* and *What is he doing?* The children combined negation and indeterminates to form sentences like: *I didn't see something* and *It don't have some tapioca in it* before they learned to make indeterminates into indefinites in negative sentences and so to say *I didn't see anything* and *It don't have any tapioca in it.*

With respect to the sort of sequence that moves from immature to mature constructions, it is possible to ask again about the role of derivational complexity. However, the immature forms are not generated by adult grammar, they are ungrammatical from the adult point of view. Consequently the notion of cumulative derivational complexity with which we have thus far operated has no application to the second sort of sequence. The relevant standard of complexity is not the adult grammar but the child's own grammar. What kinds of changes must be made in his system if it is to generate mature negatives, tags, wh questions, indefinites, and the like? Additional rules may be required; old rules may lose some of their generality; rules of an entirely new type may be introduced. This is going to be a long and complicated story and we are not ready in this paper to try to tell it.

There is another interesting question about the progression from immature to mature forms. What causes it to occur at all? Why should the child relinquish old ways? Is it because they are ineffective? Does the necessity of communicating exercise a selection pressure in favor of adult forms? Or are the old ways given up simply because parents express disapproval of them and approval of more mature forms? Is there a pressure toward maturity exerted by contingent approval? Our records offer some information on these questions and we turn to that now.

COMMUNICATION PRESSURE AND CONTINGENT
APPROVAL

The data to be reported in this section flatly contradict what most parents say about their own child-training practices. That may mean that parents do not act as they think they act. It may also mean that the parent-child interaction in our records is simply not representative; probably not representative of parents generally, perhaps not even representative of the parents of Adam, Eve, and Sarah. May not the presence of a psychologist and a tape recorder have altered usual practices? It certainly may have. However, one should not assume that it must have. A single investigator stayed with each child over the course of the study, in one case for three years. The investigator became a family friend and interaction with him and in his presence seems completely unselfconscious after the first couple of weeks.

Communication Pressure

Do ill-formed constructions in child speech give way to well-formed constructions because there is a selection pressure in communication which favors the latter? Child utterances often seem to function as instrumental acts designed to accomplish effects in other persons. Surely the well-formed utterance, since it would be correctly interpreted, is a superior tool to the ill-formed utterance which must often be misunderstood or simply not comprehended. The protocols we have permit a rough test of this proposition with respect to some of the constructions that interest us.

Yes-no question, wh questions, negatives, and tags all occur in child speech in primitive or ill-formed versions before they occur as well-formed constructions. The ill-formed constructions start well in advance of the well-formed versions. Some of the primitive forms are eventually entirely displaced by mature forms (negatives and wh questions). Some primitive forms, the *yes-no* question that does not interpose subject and auxiliary and the *huh?* tag, are acceptable alternatives in adult speech and these are not displaced entirely but rather simply make room for mature forms. In all cases it is possible to find samples in which primitive and mature forms are both present in quantity. What we want to know is whether there is a difference in the quality of response from adult interlocutors to the two kinds of form.

To test the proposition we used (except in the case of tags) two of the samples, corresponding to grammars, for each construction. For *yes-no* questions, samples III and V; for wh questions and also negatives samples III and IV. The samples were selected so as to maximize the numbers of both primitive and well-formed constructions of the type in question for all three children. They represent times when the construction was undergoing change and the child was vacillating between primitive and well-formed versions, times when communication pressure should have operated if it ever does. Tags had to be treated somewhat differently from the other constructions. There were, in Eve's records, no well-formed tags at all; in Sarah's they start at V; in Adam's they do not start until after V. Consequently the study of responses to tags, primitive and well-formed, is limited to Sarah and Adam and is based on just those two-hour samples from each child which contained the largest numbers of tags: Adam's sample 50; Sarah's samples 100–103.

Interlocutor responses to child utterances were classified in the following terms. *Yes-no* questions, wh questions, and tags all request answers and such answers are one sort of comprehending response. Sometimes a response does not directly answer a question but nevertheless clearly shows comprehension and represents a reasonable sort of continuation; for instance, in response to *Where Christmas cookies?* we have *We ate them all.* These two kinds of response to questions are grouped together in Table 7-11 as "Sequiturs" or clearly relevant and comprehending reactions. "Non-Sequiturs" in Table 7-11 represent the conjunction of several different sorts of reactions. Sometimes the interlocutor queries all or some part of the child's question; for instance, in response to *Where my spoon?* we have *Your spoon?* Sometimes the interlocutor responds with a new topic or seeming irrelevancy; for

Table 7-11. Sequiturs and Non-Sequiturs Following Primitive and Well-Formed Constructions

	Yes–No (III and V)		Wh (III and IV)		Tags (Adam 50; Sarah 100–103)		Negatives (III and IV)		Means	
	Primitive	Well-formed	Primitive	Well-formed	Primitive	Well-formed	Primitive	Well-formed	Primitive	Well-formed
Eve										
Sequiturs	.70	.83	.44	.45			.70	.31	.61	.53
Non-Sequiturs	.18	.13	.37	.18			.20	.49	.25	.27
Adam										
Sequiturs	.48	.46	.45	.37	.54	.56	.00	.24	.31	.36
Non-Sequiturs	.50	.43	.50	.52	.42	.44	.86	.52	.62	.49
Sarah										
Sequiturs	.47	.52	.38	.52	.52	.36	.33	.41	.42	.45
Non-Sequiturs	.53	.47	.62	.43	.48	.57	.56	.51	.55	.50
Mean Totals										
Sequiturs									.45	.45
Non-Sequiturs									.47	.42

instance, in response to *Where ice cream?* we find *And the potatoes.* Sometimes a response reveals an actual misunderstanding of the child's question; *What time it is?* elicited *Uh, huh, it tells what time it is.* Sometimes there was simply no response at all to a question. Sometimes there was a response of doubtful classification. Non-Sequiturs then are made up of "Queries" plus "Irrelevancies" plus "Misunderstandings" plus "No Response" plus "Doubtfuls." The Sequiturs and Non-Sequiturs of Table 7–11 do not always sum to 100 per cent because there was a residual category which seemed not to belong with either of the others, a category of "Repeats." Repeats of ill-formed utterances usually contained corrections and so could be instructive; repeats of well-formed utterances would not be corrections. Interlocutor responses to negatives were categorized in the same way as responses to questions, with a single exception. Negatives do not request answers in the way that questions do. Sequiturs are, all of them, simply continuations strongly suggesting comprehension of the child's utterance.

Table 7–11 presents the percentages of Sequiturs and Non-Sequiturs in response to primitive and well-formed constructions of each type for each child. The mean percentages of Sequitur responses to primitive and well-formed constructions are exactly the same (45 per cent). The mean percentage of Non-Sequitur responses is slightly but not significantly higher to primitive constructions than to well-formed constructions; 47 per cent in the former case and 42 per cent in the latter. The obtained difference on Non-Sequiturs should be interpreted in the light of the fact that a great many of the Non-Sequiturs were "No Responses" and it is not clear that these should all be considered unsatisfactory responses. In some cases the child was talking fast and scarcely seemed to expect or leave time for an answer. When "Non-Sequiturs" were counted more narrowly—as instances of genuine misunderstanding—we found precisely one instance (the example given earlier) for all children and all constructions. In general, the results provide no support for the notion that there is a communication pressure favoring mature constructions.

Coding the transcriptions for communication pressure one

forms the impression that the primitive forms were understood perfectly well by adult interlocutors and indeed that they did not notice anything primitive or ill-formed about the constructions. Rising intonation is a fairly good sign of a *yes-no* question, as is the preposed wh word of a wh question, and *no* or *not* for the negative, and *huh*? for the tag. The operations the child fails to perform on these utterances are in fact redundant as far as the meaning of the construction is concerned.

It is possible, of course, that communication pressure plays an important role in speech progression at other seasons of development and with other constructions. It may, for instance, be the force that causes the child to relinquish holophrases in favor of sentences. Unfortunately, there is a kind of paradoxical difficulty in the way of demonstrating such an effect with non-experimental data. In order to prove that a child learns new means of expression because he has messages to communicate which cannot be handled with the means at his command, the investigator must be able to detect such uncommunicated messages. The investigator is not, however, the only person trying to "read" the child and probably not the most expert person; the child's parents or siblings are likely to be the experts. Therefore, it is usually the case that any message the investigator can make out, the family can also make out and so the child will in fact already be communicating any idea that we can be sure he has. In naturalistic studies we usually have to admit that we did not know a child possessed a given refinement of meaning until he started to produce the construction expressing that refinement.

Contingent Approval

It might be supposed that syntactically correct utterances come to prevail over those that are incorrect through the operation of positive reinforcement and punishment on the part of adults. A positive reinforcer is generally defined as any event which, being made contingent upon the emission of an antecedent response, increases the frequency of that response. In this sense reinforcers can never be specified before one has observed their effect. Whether or not an event is a reinforcer waits upon information as to whether or not it has, in fact, reinforced.

The definition of *punishment*, in Skinner's sense, begins with the notion of a "negative reinforcer." An event subsequent to a response is a negative reinforcer of that response when the *withdrawal* of the event, being made contingent on the emission of the response, the response increases in frequence. Shock is often a negative reinforcer. Punishment, finally, involves the *presentation* of a negative reinforcer and while punishment does not seem to extinguish a response it does depress the frequency of its performance.

Strictly speaking there is no way to disconfirm the following proposition: "Syntactically correct utterances become more frequent because of reinforcement and less frequent because of punishment." To disconfirm it one would have to show that there is no event (or better, no way of conceiving events) which increases the frequency of syntactically correct utterances when its presentation is made contingent on such utterances and also no event which increases frequency when its withdrawal is made contingent. Because events subsequent to child speech are indefinitely various (or better, susceptible of being conceived in indefinitely various ways) one can never be sure that there is no event which functions as a reinforcer or punishment.

In practice, of course, we know that certain events are likely to be reinforcers or punishments for a given response because we have seen that they have this effect on many other responses. Money is supposed to be such a conditioned "generalized reinforcer" and social approval is supposed to be another. In *Science and Human Behavior* (1953) Skinner wrote

Another person is likely to reinforce only that part of one's behavior of which he approves, and any sign of his *approval*, therefore, becomes reinforcing in its own right. Behavior which evokes a smile or the verbal response "That's right" or "Good" or any other commendation is strengthened. We use this generalized reinforcer to establish and shape the behavior of others, particularly in education. For example, we teach both children and adults to speak correctly by saying "That's right" when appropriate behavior is emitted (p. 78).

By extension it seems reasonable to think that signs of disapproval would be generalized punishments. The proposition: "Syntactically correct utterances come to prevail over syntactically incorrect utterances through the selective administration of signs of approval and disapproval" is a testable one.

The proposition cannot possibly be true for the natural case of parents and children at home unless parental approval and disapproval are in fact appropriately contingent on syntactical correctness. If the reactions *are* appropriately contingent then they may or may not have the effects proposed. In our materials parental reactions do not even meet the minimal circumstance of appropriate contingency and so the proposition may be discarded without testing its further implications.

The demonstration goes like this. In order to investigate contingencies at different levels of child proficiency we worked with samples II and V. We first listed all of those exchanges in which a parent responded with such signs of approval as: *That's right*, *Correct*, *Very good*, and *Yes* and such signs of disapproval as *That's wrong* or *That's not right* or *No*. We could not, in this analysis, limit ourselves to approval and disapproval following the constructions on which we have focussed in this paper (questions, negatives, tags, etc.) because such exchanges were too infrequent.

The general plan, of course, was to contrast the syntactic correctness of the population of utterances followed by a sign of approval with the population followed by a sign of disapproval. There are some problems about scoring the syntactical correctness of a child's utterance. When an utterance consists of only one word it has no syntax and so cannot be either correct or incorrect. All such were disregarded. Child utterances, like adult utterances, can be well-formed even though they are not complete subject–predicate sentences so we do not want to measure them against some notion of the grammatically complete sentence. The indices we used are not responsive to all aspects of syntax but they are responsive to those that can be confidently scored for spontaneous speech. An error was scored whenever some grammatical marker that was obligatory in terms of the surrounding context of the utterance was missing. For instance, *He not walking* contains an error because *is* is missing. An error was also scored whenever the form of a morpheme required by the context was erroneous; for instance, *Her curl my hair* or *I throwed it,* or *I don't want something.* Finally an error was scored whenever morphemes were not in the correct order: *What he's doing.*

Table 7–12. Relations between Syntactic Correctness of Antecedent Child's Utterance and Approving or Disapproving Parental Response

(a) At II

Sarah			Adam			Eve		
	Correct	Incorrect		Correct	Incorrect		Correct	Incorrect
App.	4	9	App.	4	3	App.	6	19
Dis.	4	6	Dis.	2	0	Dis.	3	5

(b) At V

Sarah			Adam			Eve		
	Correct	Incorrect		Correct	Incorrect		Correct	Incorrect
App.	23	4	App.	13	6	App.	33	29
Dis.	12	2	Dis.	7	1	Dis.	12	15

Only 1 of 6 in right direction. Remaining 1 (Eve at V) is not significant.

The results are summarized in Table 7–12 as a set of frequency tables for which an utterance was simply counted correct or incorrect—whatever the degree of incorrectness. Another analysis scores degrees of correctness and uses mean scores. In neither case is there even a shred of evidence that approval and disapproval are contingent on syntactic correctness.

What circumstances do govern approval and disapproval from parents? Surely they are not emitted without reference to the child's speech. Table 7–13 provides a few examples which suggest the answer. Approval and disapproval are not primarily linked with the grammatical form of the utterance. They are rather linked to the truth value of the proposition which the adult fits to the child's generally incomplete and often deformed sentence. And so, though Eve makes a grammatical error when she expresses the proposition that her mother is a girl with the utterance *he a girl*, the proposition itself is true and since it is the proposition rather than the grammar that governs response, the response is approving. By contrast when Sarah points and says: "There's the animal farmhouse" her syntax is impeccable but the proposition is false and so the reaction is disapproving.

Table 7–13. Examples of Utterances Approved and Disapproved

Approval

Adam. *Draw a boot paper.*	Adam's Mother. *That's right. Draw a boot on the paper.*
Eve. *Mama isn't boy, he a girl.*	Eve's Mother. *That's right.*
Sarah. *Her curl my hair.*	Sarah's Mother. *Um hmm.*

Disapproval

Adam. *And Walt Disney comes on Tuesday.*	Adam's Mother. *No, he does not.*
Eve. *What the guy idea.*	Eve's Mother. *No, that's not right. Wise idea.*
Sarah. *There's the animal farmhouse.*	Sarah's Mother. *No, that's a lighthouse.*

The truth value of a presumed proposition is the most important determinant of approval and disapproval but it is not the only determinant. When Eve says something that may be approximated as *What the guy idea*, she says something that can be neither true nor false; it is a kind of exclamation. The exclamation is identifiable as a poor performance of a familiar routine and mother elects to disapprove phonological aspects of the performance and to model an improved version. While there are several bases for approval and disapproval they are almost always semantic or phonological. Explicit approval or disapproval of either syntax or morphology is extremely rare in our records and so seems not to be the force propelling the child from immature to mature forms.

CONCLUSIONS

What is the significance for child speech of the two sorts of sequence and what is the significance of the negative findings with respect to communication pressure and contingent approval? The fact that some constructions appear in one or more "ungrammatical" forms before they appear in adult form shows that children are learning rules and not simply utterances. A sentence like *I don't see something* has the same force on the syntactic level as *I goed* on the morphological. Both suggest the generalization of rules to cases that ought to be exceptions.

I see smoke.	*It is snowing.*
I don't see smoke.	*It snowed.*
I see something.	*I am going.*
∴ *I don't see something.*	∴ *I goed.*

The fact that some ungrammatical or immature forms have been used by all the children that have been studied shows that children are alike in the innate knowledge, language processing routines, preferences, and assumptions they bring to the problem of language acquisition. One such preference seems to be for a small number of rules of maximal generality (McNeill, in press). The combination of negatives and indeterminate pronouns (e.g., *I don't hear someone*) treats these pronouns as other pronouns and, indeed, noun phrases generally, are treated. The failure to make the affirmative–negative switch on tags, resulting in such sentences as *We can play, can we*? treats the tag question as if it were an echo question given in response to another speaker's production of the first proposition. It is even conceivable that children say *What he wants*? and *Why you went*? because they are trying to use a single rule for wh questions and embedded wh clauses as in: *We know what he wants* and *We know why you went*.

The immature rules for interrogation and negation may arise as McNeill (in press) has suggested because they are much closer to the base structure than are the transformed adult forms. The transformations are certainly language specific and so must be learned. The base structure has a better chance of being universal and innate.

If the negative results for communication pressure and contingent approval are representative of parental practice then these cannot be the forces causing the child to relinquish immature forms and adopt adult forms. In our data the two principles of response (or rule) selection fail to meet the first requirement one can set; they are not contingent in the way that they are required to be. We suspect that the only force toward grammaticality operating on the child is the occasional mismatch between his theory of the structure of the language and the data he receives. Piaget's terms "assimilation" (the present theory), "accommodation" (the impact of the data), and "disequilibrium" (the mismatch) were created to deal with a similar lack of extrinsic motivation in the child for progressing toward operativity. Of course this formulation leaves most questions unanswered. For instance: Why do data have an impact at some times and at other times no effect at all?

The fact that there is a sequence among well-formed constructions from those that are derivationally simple, in terms of the adult grammar, toward those that are derivationally complex rather suggests to us that the adult grammar does, at least roughly, represent what it is that the child is learning. Of course we do not yet know how general the sequence is. It seems to be the case (when a lot of underbrush is hacked away) that control of the base structure precedes control of transformational knowledge and that simple sentences precede conjoinings and embeddings (as these things were understood in the linguistics of 1965). On the other hand, in many points of detail, we do not find a progression from derivational simplicity to complexity. For instance, noun phrases with separable verbs occur in transformed position well before they occur in untransformed position.

Finally there is the relation between parental frequency and order of emergence among well-formed constructions. Our guess is that this is an incidental consequence of the relation between frequency and complexity and that frequency, above some minimum level, does not determine the order in which structural knowledge emerges. What would happen if the parents of a child produced tags at a much higher rate than is normal? We have some basis for a guess.

The parents of Adam, Eve, and Sarah did produce certain wh questions at a very high rate in a period when the children did not understand the structure of wh questions. What happened then? The children learned to produce the two most frequently repeated wh questions, *What's that?* and *What doing?*, on roughly appropriate occasions. Their performance had the kind of rigidity that we have learned to recognize as a sign of incomprehension of structure; they did not produce, as their parents of course did, such structurally close variants as *What are those?* and *Who's that?* and *What is he doing?* When, much later, the children began to produce all manner of wh questions in the preposed form (e.g., *What he wants*) it was interesting to note that *What's that?* and *What are you doing?* were not at first reconstrued in terms of the new analysis. If the children had generated the sentences in terms of their new rules they ought to have said *What that is?* and *What you are doing?* but instead they, at first, persisted with the old forms. One of us (Brown) found himself doing a comparable thing when he studied Japanese at Berlitz. Early in his lessons he learned, and made heavy use of, the form *korewa* meaning "this-one-here." Quite a bit later he learned about the particle *wa* (roughly nominative but see McNeill, in press, for complications) which was added to nouns and pronouns. He did not, however, reanalyze *korewa* into *kore* and *wa* but continued to think of it as a single word. Until one day he heard *kore-no* (genitive) and then *kore-o* (accusative) and thought, "Why it's *kore-wa*!"

We suggest that any form that is produced with very high frequency by parents will be somehow represented in the child's performance even if its structure is far beyond him. He will find a way to render a version of it and will also form a notion of the circumstances in which it is used. The construction will become lodged in his speech as an unassimilated fragment. Extensive use of such an unanalyzed or mistakenly analyzed fragment probably protects it, for a time, from reanalysis when the structure relevant to it is finally learned. Such, we suspect, are the effects of frequency.

205

In closing we would like to express the distaste experimentalists must feel for the assumptions, compromises, and qualifications involved in the use of naturalistic data. We find that naturalistic studies build an appetite for experiment; for controls, complete data, large samples, and statistical analysis. But we also find the reverse. The two kinds of research are complementary activities and complementary forms of evidence. In experimental work one uses the ingenuity he has on advance planning for data collection whereas in naturalistic work little ingenuity goes into the data collection and all that is available goes into data analysis. The history of psychology generally (Rosenthal, 1967) and of psycholinguistics in particular shows that careful experimental work provides no sure path to the truth. Neither does naturalism. There are rich opportunities for error in either method. But, on the whole, the opportunities arise at different points and when the methods are used in combination the truth has a chance to appear.

References

CHOMSKY, N. *Aspects of the theory of syntax.* Cambridge, Mass.: M.I.T. Press, 1965.

CHOMSKY, N. *Syntactic structures.* The Hague: Mouton, 1957.

FODOR, J., and GARRETT, M. Some reflections on competence and performance. In J. Lyons and R. J. Wales (Eds.) *Psycholinguistics papers.* Edinburgh: University Press, 1966.

KATZ, J. J., and POSTAL, P. M. *An integrated theory of linguistic descriptions.* Cambridge, Mass.: M.I.T. Press, 1964.

KLIMA, E. S. Negation in English. In J. A. Fodor and J. J. Katz (Eds.) *The structure of language.* Englewood Cliffs, N. J.: Prentice-Hall, 1964.

MCNEILL, D. The development of language. In P. A. Mussen (Ed.) *Carmichael's manual of child psychology.* In press.

SAVIN, H. B., and ELLEN PERCHONOCK. Grammatical structure and the immediate recall of English sentences. *J. verb. Learn. verb. Behav.*, 4, 348–353, 1965.

SKINNER, B. F. *Science and human behavior.* New York: Macmillan, 1953.

SUTHERLAND, N. S. Discussion of Fodor, J. and Garrett, M. "Some reflections on competence and performance." In J. Lyons and R. J. Wales (Eds.) *Psycholinguistics papers.* Edinburgh: University Press, 1966.

ZIPF, G. K. *Human behavior and the principle of least effort.* Cambridge, Mass.: Addison-Wesley, 1949.

[8]

The First Sentences of Child and Chimpanzee

In 1968–69 several lines of thought about language development came together in an exciting way. Ursula Bellugi and I, in the 1964 paper called "Three Processes in the Acquisition of Syntax," which is included in this volume, had described one sort of common adult response to the telegraphic sentences of very young children, the kind of response called an "expansion." An expansion is essentially a reading of the child's semantic intention. Thus when Eve said, "Mommy lunch" her mother said "That's right, Mommy is having her lunch." Dr. Bellugi and I did not commit ourselves as to the accuracy or "veridicality" of these readings. We were not sure whether children really intended, by their telegraphic sentences, what adults thought they intended, and we could not really see how to find out. Our focus was on the expansion as a potential tutorial mechanism. Whether or not children started out intending what adults attributed to them it seemed to us that expansions would cause them to do so in the end. In 1968 I. M. Schlesinger, working at Hebrew University in Jerusalem, and Lois Bloom, working at Columbia University, independently came to the conclusion that children really did intend certain aspects of the meanings attribu-

---

Some of the research described in this paper was supported by PHS Grant HD–02908 from the National Institute of Child Health and Development.

208

ted to them by adult expansions. They did not intend the meanings expressed in the expansions by grammatical morphemes, by inflections, articles, prepositions, and auxiliary verbs. There was nothing in the child's performance to suggest that they had these things in mind. What they did intend were certain fundamental semantic relations such as Agent-Action, Agent-Object, Action-Object, Possessor-Possessed, and so on. There was, in the child's speech, something to suggest that they intended these relations. This same "something," the aspect of child speech that justified the attribution to them of certain relational meanings, turns out to be missing from the linguistic performance of an important comparison case: the home-raised chimpanzee named Washoe.

Washoe, over a period of more than three years, has been learning the American Sign Language. She now produces many recognizable signs in circumstances that are semantically appropriate. What is more she produces sequences or strings of signs which seem very much like sentences. Does this mean that a chimpanzee has now been shown to have the capacity for linguistic syntax, a capacity we had long thought exlusively human? Perhaps it does. Still there is something missing; the very thing, curiously enough, that justifies the Bloom-Schlesinger semantic approach to the early speech of children.

In this paper the spotlight is on Washoe whose extraordinary feats naturally place her in the center ring. But there are also important events in the other rings. Bloom and Schlesinger are right, I think, and they have increased the power of the analyses we can make of child speech. They also bring to our attention some impressively general and conceivably universal aspects of child speech. As Table 8-2 indicates we begin to have enough analyses of children learning a variety of languages to see what is truly general in language development. And in the months since this paper was written the range has been expanded by dissertations written at Berkeley on the acquisition of Samoan, of Luo (spoken in Kenya) and of Tzeltal (spoken in a region of Chiapas, Mexico).

The present paper, the most recently written of any in the book, has not previously been published. I should like gratefully to acknowledge the courtesy of Dr. R. Allen Gardner and Dr. Beatrice Gardner, who are raising Washoe. They have kindly shown me their films, sent me their diary summaries, and responded to questions I have asked them about this fascinating experiment in comparative psychology.

ONCE AGAIN, and for the third time in this century, psychology has a home-raised chimpanzee who threatens to learn language. Washoe, named for Washoe county in Nevada, has been raised as a child by Allen and Beatrice Gardner of the University of Nevada since June of 1966 when she was slightly under one year old. At this writing the materials available consist of summaries of Washoe's Diary extending to the age of 36 months.

The first of the home-raised chimps was Gua, also a female, raised by the Winthrop Kelloggs nearly 40 years ago. Gua gave some evidence of understanding English utterances, she responded distinctively and appropriately to about 70, but Gua did not speak at all. Viki, the second chimp to be adopted by a human family and also a female, learned to make four sounds that were recognizable approximations to English words. Viki was given intensive training by her foster parents, Keith and Cathy Hayes, but the four word-like sounds seemed to mark the upper limit of her productive linguistic capacity.

Both Viki and Gua were asked to learn one particular form of language—speech—which is not the only form. The essential properties of language can be divorced from articulation. Meaning or "semanticity" and grammatical productivity appear not only in speech but in writing and print and in sign language. There is good reason to believe that the production of vowels and consonants and the control of prosodic features is, simply as a motor performance, something to which chimpanzees are not well adapted. The chimpanzee articulatory apparatus is quite different from the human, and chimpanzees do not make many speech-like sounds either spontaneously or imitatively. It is possible, therefore, that Viki and Gua failed not because of an incapacity that is essentially linguistic but because of a motoric ineptitude that is only incidentally linguistic. The Gardners thought the basic experiment was worth trying again, but with a change that would eliminate the articulatory problem. They have undertaken to teach Washoe the American Sign Language, the language of the deaf in North America. What is required on the motoric level is manual dexterity, and that is something chimps have in abundance. They skillfully manipulate so many of man's inventions that one naturally wonders whether they can also move their fingers in the air—to symbolize ideas.

Why does anyone care? For the same reason, perhaps, that we care about space travel. It is lonely being the only language-using species in the universe. We want a chimp to talk so that we can say: "Hello, out there? What's it like, being a chimpanzee?"

I have always been very credulous about life on other planets and talking animals, and so I have been often disappointed. Remembering the disappointments of Gua and Viki I was slow to take an interest in Washoe. From the beginning of their study the Gardners sent out periodic summaries in diary form to psychologists who might be expected to take an interest. I glanced over the first 4 of these and noticed that Washoe seemed to understand quite a large number of signs and that she was producing a few—in what appeared to be a meaningful way. This much Gua and Viki, between them, had also done, and it seemed likely that Washoe's linguistic progress would soon come to an end, but little advanced beyond that of her forerunners. Then, on the first page of the 5th summary, which covers the period when Washoe was estimated to be between 28 and 32 months old, I read the following: "Since late April, 1967, Washoe has used her signs—at that time there were six—in strings of two or more as well as singly. We have kept records of all occurrences of combinations in the period covered by the previous diary summaries, and found that Washoe used 29 different two-sign combinations and four different combinations of three signs."

It was rather as if the seismometer left on the moon had started to tap out "S-O-S." I got out the earlier diaries and studied them carefully and I read with the greatest interest the subsequent diary installments as they came along, and then the Gardners' article "Teaching Sign Language to a Chimpanzee" which appeared in *Science* in 1969. In the spring of 1969 the Gardners themselves paid us a visit at Harvard for two days, showing films of Washoe and discussing her achievements with a group here that studies the development of language in children. We were particularly interested in comparing Washoe's early linguistic development with that of three children whom we have followed for a number of years. In the literature these children are named: Adam, Eve, and Sarah.

From an evolutionary point of view the important thing about language is that it makes life experiences cumulative; across generations and, within one generation, among individuals. Everyone can know much more than he could possibly learn by direct experience. Knowledge and folly, skills and superstitions, all alike begin to accumulate and cultural evolution takes off at a rate that leaves biological evolution far behind. Among the various defining features of language there are two that are peculiarly important in making experience cumulative. They are semanticity or meaningfulness and productivity or openness.

Semanticity occurs in some degree in the natural communication systems of many kinds of animal society but productivity does not. Productivity is the capacity to generate novel messages for every sort of novel meaning. Languages have this property because they have grammars which are rules for the compositional expression of meaning, rules which create meanings from words and patterns. Signs in sequence suggest grammar, and so it was a momentous day when Washoe began to produce them. For grammar has heretofore been an exclusively human preserve.

WASHOE'S SIGNING PROGRESS

The signs of the American Sign Language (ASL) are described in Stokoe, Casterline, and Croneberg (1965) and a transformational grammar of the language has been written by McCall (1965).

There are two basic forms of ASL: finger-spelling and signing proper. In finger-spelling there is a distinct sign for each letter of the alphabet and the signer simply spells in the air.

This system, like our alphabetic writing, is entirely dependent on knowledge of the spoken language. In signing proper, as opposed to finger-spelling, the configurations and movements produced refer directly to concepts. Some such signs are iconic, which is to say that the sign suggests its sense. The sign for *flower* in American Sign Language is created by holding the fingers of one hand extended and joined at the tips, like a closed tulip, and touching the tip first to one nostril and then another—as if sniffing a flower. That is a good icon. Many other signs are arbitrarily related to their references. Most deaf Americans use some combination of directly semantic signs and finger spelling. The Gardners only attempted to teach Washoe the directly semantic signs.

The Gardners are not deaf and did not know sign language at the start of their experiment. They learned it from books and from a teacher, but do not yet count themselves really fluent. They and their associates, when with Washoe, and someone is with her all day long, sign, as one would with a child, the names of actions and things; they sign questions and requests and they just chatter. In addition to providing this rich opportunity for incidental learning Washoe's human tutors have induced her to imitate signs and have used instrumental conditioning (with tickling as reward) to train her to sign appropriately for objects and pictures in books.

In the first seven months of the project Washoe learned to use four signs with some degree of appropriate semanticity. The *come-gimme* sign was directed at persons or animals and also at objects out of reach. The *more* sign, made by bringing the fingertips together overhead, seemed to ask for continuation or repetition of pleasurable activities and also to ask for second helpings of food. *Up* was used when Washoe wanted to be lifted and *sweet* was used at the end of a meal when dessert was in order. In the next seven months 9 more signs were added, and by the end of 22 months, when Washoe was about three years old, she seemed to control 34 signs.

In the spring of 1969 the Gardners showed a group of us at Harvard a film of Washoe looking at a picture book and making appropriate signs as a tutor pointed and signed "What's this?" On a first showing the performance was rather disappointing. The viewer is not entirely sure that he has seen the signs since there is so much action going on. However, this changes on a second viewing. The signs of sign language are not, at first, perceptual segregates for the uninitiated, but even a single viewing makes them very much more "visible." And, probably because so many of them are iconic, one very rapidly learns about 10–20 of them. I now do not doubt that Washoe produces the signs.

Table 8-1. Some of Washoe's Sign Sequences as Classified by the Gardners

A. Two Signs.

1. Using "emphasizers" (*please, come-gimme, hurry, more*).
   Hurry open.
   More sweet.
   More tickle.
   Come-gimme drink.

2. Using "specifiers."
   Go sweet (to be carried to fruitbushes).
   Listen eat (at sound of supper bell).
   Listen dog (at sound of barking).

3. Using names or pronouns.
   You drink.
   You eat.
   Roger come.

B. Three or More Signs.

1. Using "emphasizers."
   Gimme please food.
   Please tickle more.
   Hurry gimme toothbrush.

2. Using "specifiers."
   Key open food.
   Open key clean.
   Key open please blanket.

3. Using names or pronouns.
   You me go-there in.
   You out go.
   Roger Washoe tickle.

In the diary reports one can trace the semantic generalization of each sign and this generalization, much of it spontaneous, is quite astonishingly childlike. To appreciate the accomplishment it is necessary to recover a certain innocence in connection with some thoroughly familiar abstractions. Consider the notion connected with the English word *more* when it is used as a request. Washoe started out signalling *more* with the specific sense of more tickling. Far from adhering to a particular context the sign rapidly generalized to hairbrushing and swinging and other processes involving Washoe which Washoe enjoyed. And then it generalized further to "second helpings" of dessert and soda pop and the like. And then to performances of another which only involved Washoe as a spectator—acrobatics and somersaults. Human children regularly use the word *more* as a request over just this same range. And when they start to make two-word sentences with *more* they use nouns to request additional helpings (e.g., *More milk, More grapefruit juice*), but also verbs to request that processes and exhibitions be repeated (e.g., *More write, More swing*).

The semantic accomplishments are remarkable, but it is the evidence of syntax that most concerns us. Table 8-1 sets out some of Washoe's strings or sentences; they are drawn from the Gardners' fifth and sixth summaries which appeared in 1968, and I have selected examples which, in English, look very much like sentences. The classification into combinations using "emphasizers," "specifiers," and "names or pronouns" is the Gardners' own. In Table 8-1 we have sign sequences which translate into English as *Hurry open, Go sweet, You eat, Open key clean, You me go-there in*, and so on. How do these multi-sign sequences compare with the first multi-word combinations produced by children learning American English and other languages?

THE AVAILABLE DATA ON CHILD SPEECH

The best index of grammatical development until the age of about three years is simply the mean (or average) length of the child's utterances. When speech begins, of course, all utterances are single words, and the mean-length-of-utterance (MLU) has the value 1.0. As soon as word combining begins the MLU rises above this value. For about 18–24 months almost all grammatical "advances" have the common effect of increasing the MLU. Because these advances tend to occur in the same order for all children learning American English (and perhaps more generally) when two children have the same MLU values the internal grammatical detail of their speech is also quite similar.

It is not the case that two children having the same MLU must be of the same chronological age. Children vary greatly

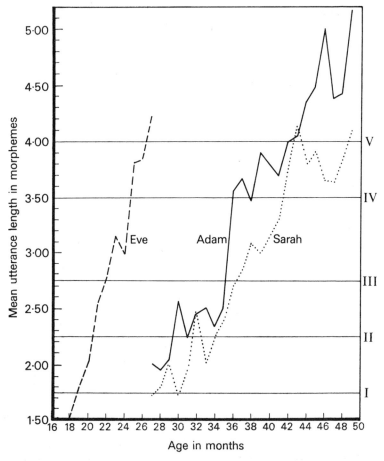

Figure 8–1. Growth in Utterance Length with Age for Adam, Eve, and Sarah.

in the rapidity with which they progress grammatically and, for that reason, chronological age is a poor index of linguistic level. Figure 8–1 plots age against MLU for the three children we have studied. Utterance length was counted in morphemes rather than words so as to give credit for inflections like the -s of plurality, the -s of possession, the -ed for past tense, and the -ing of progressive aspect. As can be seen the utterances of all three children grew steadily longer over this whole period. Eve advanced much more rapidly than Adam and Sarah.

The five straight lines marked with Roman numerals on Figure 8-1 represent points we have arbitrarily selected for intensive analysis in preparing a five-stage description of linguistic progress in this period. At our first stage the MLU values for the three children ranged between 1.68 and 2.06. Many utterances were still single words; most were two or three words long; five words was the longest. Washoe seems to have been at about this point when she was 36 months old.

Adam, Eve, and Sarah at I, and Washoe at 37 months were not at the very beginning of syntax, and it is desirable to have child-speech data for earlier periods to compare with the earlier data for Washoe. There are, in the literature or in progress, longitudinal grammatical studies which include reports for developmental stages lying between an MLU of 1.0 and the level at which our children were first studied. Combining these reports with ours we have information on an initial period which is bounded by an MLU of 1.0, the threshold of syntax, and an MLU of 2.0, the level of the most advanced child in the set—Adam. For the present purpose we shall call this full interval "Stage I." It seems to correspond fairly exactly with the period for which the Gardners have provided data on Washoe: the age of 12 months through the age of 36 months.

The child-speech data include 18 analyses of 13 children which are fully comparable with one another because they are based on large samples of spontaneous speech, tape recorded in the home. These studies are listed in developmental order above the space in Table 8-2. Adam I, Eve I, and Sarah I belong to the set. So, too, do five analyses of the speech of three American children called Gia, Kathryn, and Eric, which appear in the 1968 doctoral dissertation of Lois Bloom. Then there are single analyses for each of three boys, Gregory, Andrew, and Steven, which were published by Martin Braine (1963) and single analyses for two little girls, Susan and

Table 8-2. The Available Data in Developmental Order

Child	MLU	Age at Data	Character of Data	Investigator(s)
Eric I	1.10	1;7	4 hours, tape recorded.	Bloom
Gia I	1.12	1;7	7 hours, tape recorded.	Bloom
Eric II	1.19	1;9	6 hours, tape recorded.	Bloom
Gregory		1;7.5-1;11.5	cumulative inventory.	Braine
Andrew		1;7.5-1;11.5	cumulative inventory.	Braine
Steven		1;11.5-2;0.5	12 play sessions, tape recorded.	Braine
Christy		2;0-2;3	taped weekly 45 minute sessions over 3 months.	Miller, Ervin
Susan		1;9-2;0	taped weekly 45 minute sessions over 3 months.	Miller, Ervin
Kathryn I	1.32	1;9	7½ hours, tape recorded.	Bloom
Gia II	1.34	1;9	7½ hours, tape recorded.	Bloom
Eric III	1.42	1;10	8½ hours, tape recorded.	Bloom
Seppo	1.45	1;11	2 hours taped over 1 month.	Bowerman
Eve I	1.68	1;6	3½ hours taped over 6 weeks.	Brown
Sarah I	1.73	2;3	3 hours taped over 6 weeks.	Brown
Seppo II	1.77*	2;2	2 hours taped over 1 month.	Bowerman
Kathryn II	1.92	1;11	9 hours tape recorded.	Bloom
Rina I	1.95*	2;1	2 hours taped over 1 month.	Bowerman
Adam I	2.06	2;3	2 hours, tape recorded.	Brown
Hildegard		1;0-2;0	parental diary, selectively reported.	Leopold
Charles		1;0-2;0	parental diary, selectively reported.	Grégoire
Edmond		1;0-2;0	parental diary, selectively reported.	Grégoire
Zhenya		?	very selective, interpretative reports.	Gvozdev, Slobin
Canta		2;4	grandfather's diary, selectively reported.	Chao
Washoe		1;0-3;0	foster parental diary, quite fully reported.	Gardners

* MLU is approximation within ±.10 due to special problems in calculating for Finnish.

Christy, published by Miller and Ervin (now Ervin-Tripp) in 1965. To this collection of studies of children learning American English, Melissa Bowerman, a doctoral candidate at Harvard, has recently added three analyses of two children learning a non-Indo-European language. The language is Finnish, and the children are Seppo and Rina. All of these studies concern Stage I speech; the Roman numerals appearing after the names of some of the children were assigned by the investigators in ordering their own analyses. The developmental order is based on the MLU except in five cases for which the MLU was not available. These five (Gregory, Andrew, Steven, Christy, and Susan) were placed in the order on the basis of another simple index.

Beyond the studies described above there is a large literature, mostly American, Russian, French, and German, reporting longitudinal studies of the diary type which are not fully comparable with one another nor with the 18 contemporary analyses we have described above. To represent this large literature and broaden the range of languages considered I have selected four studies: Werner Leopold's (1949) description of the first two years in the grammatical development of his daughter Hildegard who was learning English and German simultaneously; Antoine Gregoire's (1937) account of the first two years of his sons, Charles and Edmond, who were learning French; Dan Slobin's (1966) summary of the detailed account given by the Soviet linguist, A. N. Gvozdev, of the acquisition of Russian by his son, Zhenya; Yuen Ruen Chao's (1951) report on selected aspects of the grammar of his grandson Canta, when Canta, who was learning Mandarin Chinese, was 28 months old. These studies are listed, below the space in Table 8–2, together with the comparison point we never expected to have, the Gardners' study of the first stages in the syntactic development of a chimpanzee, Washoe herself.

MAJOR MEANINGS IN STAGE I

Table 8–3 lists 10 kinds of structural meaning which, among them, characterize the majority of two-word sentences in

Stage I. In the samples for which complete analysis is possible, those of Seppo, Rina, Adam, Eve, and Sarah the structural meanings account for about 75% of all multi-word utterances. The characterization by structural meaning is not all that there is to say about the first sentences, but it is the most important information for present purposes. In the contemporary study of child speech the earliest descriptions published were purely formal, and made little reference to meaning. In 1963 Colin Fraser and I described the first sentences as

Table 8-3. The First Sentences in Child Speech

I. Operations of reference.

Nominations : *That* (or *It* or *There*)+*book, cat, clown, hot, big*, etc.

Notice : *Hi*+*Mommy, cat, belt*, etc.

Recurrence : *More* (or *'Nother*)+*milk, cereal, nut, read, swing, green*, etc.

Nonexistence : *Allgone* (or *No-more*)+*rattle, juice, dog, green*, etc.

II. Relations.

Attributive : Ad+N (*Big train, Red book*, etc.)

Possessive : N+N (*Adam checker, Mommy lunch*, etc.)

Locative : N+N (*Sweater chair, Book table*, etc.)

Locative : N+V (*Walk street, Go store*, etc.)

Agent-Action : N+V (*Adam put, Eve read*, etc.)

Agent-Object : N+N (*Mommy sock, Mommy lunch*, etc.)

Action-Object : V+N (*Put book, Hit ball*, etc.)

"telegraphic" in the sense that they are almost entirely composed of "contentive" words, of nouns, verbs, and adjectives; the little words or grammatical morphemes which are ordinarily omitted from telegrams are also omitted from early child speech. This is a purely descriptive generalization about surface form. As such it is correct and has been confirmed in all studies. The characterization of child speech as telegraphic does not provide for "productivity" or the construction of novel combinations. Martin Braine in 1963 characterized two-word child sentences in terms of a simple but productive grammar involving "Pivot" and "Open" classes. While Braine's description certainly fits his data it does not, as both Lois Bloom and Melissa Bowerman have recently shown, fit all children at I or even all children at the more primitive end of I.

The characterization of two-word sentences in terms of structural meanings was originated in contemporary work by I. M. Schlesinger of the Hebrew University in Jerusalem and by Lois Bloom, both writing in 1968. These researchers differ in the grammatical structures they employ, but they agree on one thing: telegraphic sentences looked at in full linguistic and non-linguistic context can be seen to express certain types of structural meanings. Parents of course have always been of this opinion, and they often will gloss a child's telegraphic utterance as a related English simple sentence. When Eve said "Mommy lunch" her mother said "That's right, Mommy is having her lunch." When Eve said "Fraser coffee" her mother said "Yes, that's Fraser's coffee." The Bloom-Schlesinger approach essentially assumes that such glosses, which the investigator can supply as readily as a parent, are accurate readings insofar as they interpret the child's words as expressing such relations as agent-object or possessor-possessed. They are not assumed to be accurate insofar as they attribute to the Stage I child knowledge of inflections, articles, and other grammatical morphemes for which there is no evidence in his speech. The arguments of Bloom and Schlesinger, as well as the results of our own continuing research, have convinced me that the early sentences are, in fact, expressions of certain structural meanings.

The classification of Table 8–3 is indebted to both Bloom and Schlesinger, but somewhat different from what either proposes. Set I, called "Operations of Reference," is made up of utterance-sets, such that each is defined by one or another constant term appearing in conjunction with various nouns, verbs, and adjectives. Nominative sentences are always used in the presence of a referent which is pointed at, or otherwise singled out for attention, and named. In connection with *hi*, Bloom has noticed that children do not use it as a greeting, do not, that is, use it just when someone hoves in view, but are, rather, likely to "light up" suddenly and say *hi* to someone who has been there all along; to someone, to some-animal, or to some-thing. Kathryn said *Hi, spoon*; Gregory,

Hi, plane, and Adam, *How are you, belt.* These seem to be expressions of attention or notice. Recurrence of a referent (Bloom's category) includes the reappearance of something recently seen, a new instance of the same category, an additional quantity or "helping" of a substance, a new instance of a quality, and repetition of an action. Nonexistence (another of Bloom's categories) means that a referent which has been in the referent field or was expected to appear in it is not now to be seen.

In set II, called "Relations," we have no repeating words to define each class. Both initial and final words are varied, and what defines a set is a certain quite abstract semantic relation. The attributive might be said to take some person or thing (the noun) and "fill in" or "specify" the value of one of its attributes by naming it with an adjective. The possessive identifies, for a given thing, the person having special rights with regard to it. The children's possessive typically divides spaces and objects in the house among family members; it expresses a kind of primitive notion of territoriality and property. The locative (almost always without the preposition that is obligatory in adult speech) names a locus for a movable thing or a locus or terminus of an action. Agent-Action constructions take a verb and specify one of its arguments, the argument naming the (usually animate) initiator or performer of the action. Action-Object constructions name the other argument for two-argument or "transitive" verbs: the recipient or target of action. Agent-Object constructions seem, in context, to be sentences with verbs omitted. Thus *Mommy lunch* means *Mommy is having lunch.* The semantic relations, characterized above, are closely related to the grammatical relations called: modifier of a noun-phrase, subject of a sentence and object of a predicate. However, the grammatical relations are defined in purely formal terms, and while they may, in early child speech, be more or less perfectly coordinated with the semantic rules the two are not the same.

In the course of Stage I certain changes occur. At the lower, more primitive end, operations of reference tend to be more prominent than semantic relations. In the middle stretch operations of reference and two-term relations account for most multi-word utterances. At the end of Stage I, especially in the samples of Adam and Rina, there is a step up in complexity which is manifest in two ways. Several kinds of three-term relations become frequent: agent-action-object; agent-action-locative; agent-object-locative. At the same time one term, the nominal, in two-term relations, which is in the early period always a single noun, begins frequently to be elaborated into a two-word noun phrase. These noun phrases fill all of the positions originally occupied by single nouns. The noun phrases are, furthermore, all expressions of possession, recurrence, or attribution. In fact, then, the elaboration of the noun term is accomplished by filling noun positions with just those two-term operations and relations which are noun phrases and which have been long practised as independent utterances. It is quite wonderful to find that these first structural complications take just the same form in Finnish as they do in English. Finally, while I have omitted any discussion of negative, imperative, and interrogative operations from this discussion all are present in primitive form in Stage I.

The meanings expressed by the sentences of Stage I seem to be extensions of the kind of intelligence that has been called "sensory-motor" by the great developmental psychologist, Jean Piaget. Piaget's studies of the first two years of life (e.g. Piaget, 1937) convinced him that the infant does not at first conceive of objects and persons as permanently existing in a single space which also includes the self. Neither does he recognize that objects and persons are all potential "sources of causality" and potential recipients of force. In the first 18–24 months, in Piaget's view, the infant "constructs" the world of enduring objects and immediate space and time. The meanings of the first sentences pre-suppose the sensory-motor constructions, but they also go beyond them. The aim of sensory-motor intelligence is practical success, not truth; sensory-motor intelligence is *acted* not *thought*. The ability to create propositions which can be expressed in sentences must mature near the end of the sensory-motor period. If the meanings of the first sentences are an extension of sensory-motor intelligence then they are probably universal in mankind. Universal in mankind but not limited to mankind and not innate. Animals may operate with sensory-motor intelligence, and Piaget's work shows that it develops in the infant, over many months, out of his commerce with the animate and inanimate world.

COMPARISON OF WASHOE AND CHILD

How do Washoe's Sign Sequences (Table 8–1) compare with the sentences of Table 8–3? *More sweet* and *More tickle* look like expressions of Recurrence. *Go sweet* (to be carried to the fruit-bushes) seems to be an Action-Locative construction; *You eat* an Agent-Action construction; and *Gimme please food* an Action-Object construction. The sentences with *key* appear to express an Instrumental relation which also occasionally appears in Stage I child speech. Several of Washoe's three-term sequences look like instances of the three-term relations that appear at the end of Stage I for children; *Roger Washoe tickle* could be an Agent-Action-Object sentence and *You out go* an Agent-Action-Locative. In sum, the strings of Table 8–1 look very much the same as a sample of early child speech.

However, there is more to syntax than sequences or strings. The deeper question is whether Washoe was simply making signs distributed in time or whether the signs were *in construction*. What is the difference? As a first approximation, a sequence may simply name a series of ideas which succeed one another in time but do not combine cognitively, whereas a construction puts ideas into one or another structural relation.

In two superficial respects Washoe's combinations seem to be constructions and not simply sequences. Before one can make a grammatical analysis of child speech it must be segmented into utterances which mark off just those words that are "in construction" with one another. Segmentation proves to be very easily done, for the reason that children, when they begin to make combinations, already control several of the prosodic patterns that adults use to mark off sentences. One easily hears in child speech the "declarative" pattern, with high pitch and stress near the end and a final fall and fade, as well as the interrogative pattern that ends with a rising pitch. An adult who uses sign language also has devices for marking off sentences. Stokoe *et al.* (1965) say that in the declarative case the hands of the signer return to the position of repose from which they started when he began to sign. In the interrogative case the hands remain, for a perceptible period, in the position of the last sign or even move out toward the person being interrogated. When we talked with the Gardners we asked whether Washoe used such "terminal" or "juncture" signs. Not having been interested in this particular feature they were not quite sure, but since then Allen Gardner has written to me: "Once we started to look for it, it was very clear that Washoe's segmentation (and our own, of course) is very much the same as that described by Stokoe, *et al.* . . . It is such a natural aspect of signing that we just were not aware that both Washoe and her friends were doing this all along. As in the case of speech contours it is so obvious that you don't notice it until you worry about it."

There is a second surface feature of Washoe's combinations which suggests that they are constructions rather than sequences. In child speech the very slow rise over time in utterance length seems to represent an increase of information-processing power. The fact that the child at I produces subject and object without any verb surely means that he operates under some kind of complexity limitation. Now it also is the case that Washoe's sequences gradually increase. Two signs are common before three and three precede four. Why should that be so if the sign combinations are not constructions? If they were only signs strung out in time and not interacting semantically and grammatically then one would think they might be of any length at all, and that there would be no reason for them to start short and become long.

The presence of terminal contours in child speech suggests that certain words are in construction but not what the constructions are; there are no contours to mark off the various relations and operations of Table 8–3. What is there in child speech to suggest that these structural meanings are being expressed and, specifically to the present point, is there anything not also found in Washoe's sign sequences? What there is in child speech, most generally, is the order of the words. The order, generally, is appropriate to the structural meaning suggested by the non-linguistic situation.

Consider the two drawings of Figure 8–2. An adult might say of the one on the left "A dog is biting a cat" and of the one on the right "A cat is biting a dog." In both pictures just the same creatures and process are involved. The difference is that the arguments of the verb, the agent and object, are coordinated with different nouns in the two cases. It is the structure of the total situation that changes, and in English the changes are expressed by word order, by the order agent-action-object. What would a child of Stage I say in the two cases? Concerning the picture on the left he might say:

Figure 8–2. Pictures Illustrating Agent-Object Relations.

Dog bite (agent-action); *Bite cat* (Action-object), or *Dog-cat* (agent-object). In effect, any two of the three terms in correct relational order. Of the picture on the right he might say: *Cat bite* (agent-action); *Bite dog;* or *Cat-dog.* The two sets of pairs are different; there is no overlap. It is this kind of discriminating response, discriminating with respect to the order of elements, that justifies the inference that the child distinguishes structural meanings. What should we say of a child who in connection with either picture simply produced all possible combinations and permutations of two content words: *Dog bite*; *Bite dog*; *Cat bite*; *Bite cat*; *Dog cat*; and *Cat dog*. We should say that there was no evidence that the structural meanings were understood. This, it turns out, is approximately what Washoe does.

The Gardners have kept careful records of all the occurrences of each combination of signs, and in their 5th and 6th diary summaries they report that the signs in a combination tend to occur in all possible orders. And that order often changes when there is no change in the non-linguistic circumstances. It appears, then, that we do not yet have evidence that Washoe's sequences are syntactic. Because syntax is not just sign-combination but is sign combination employed to express structural meanings. If Washoe does not intend structural meanings, if *Go sweet* and *Sweet go* are not action-object expressions, then what does she intend? What would her stream of ideas be like? It may be that it is a stream of conceptions having no relation beyond order in time. Having thought of "go" she next thinks of "sweet." Washoe's signs may be something like the *leitmotiven* in Richard Wagner's operas. Wagner, especially in the *Ring*, used short musical "motives" with a certain degree of semanticity, enough to enable musicologists to label them with names like *Valhalla*, *Curse of the Ring*, *Nibelungen gold*, *Renunciation of love*, and so on. In given passages the motives succeed one another, and the related ideas may be called to mind in the listener, but they do not enter into relations like agent-object and action-object. They do, of course, enter into musical relationship.

Not every child sentence presents contentives in the appropriate order. There are exceptions such as *Nose blow* (cited by Leopold) and *Balloon throw* (cited by Bloom) and *Apple eat* (cited by Miller and Ervin) and *Suitcase, go get it* (Adam I). Allen Gardner has written to me that he and Mrs. Gardner have not yet made a frequency comparison for the various orders in which each combination is used and, at this point, the possibility is quite open that Washoe has shown a "preference" for the orders that are correct for each relation. It is going to be interesting to learn the outcome of the Gardners' planned frequency comparisons. It must be said, however, that children show something much stronger than a statistical preference for correct order. In the full data of Table 8–2 violations of order are very uncommon; probably fewer than 100 violations in the thousands of utterances quoted. It is definitely not the case that all possible orders of a combination typically occur; they practically never do.

While word order comprises most of the evidence that the child intends structural meanings there is a certain amount of additional evidence. In 1963, Fraser, Bellugi and Brown conducted a test of grammatical comprehension using paired pictures for various constructions with 12 children between 37 and 43 months old. Figure 8–2 is, in fact, taken from that test and is used to inquire into comprehension of the agent and object functions in a sentence. Most of the items in the test are not concerned with the operations and relations of Table 8–3, but there were four test items, in all, concerning agent and object, and the three-year-olds in the experiment were correct on these 85% of the time. The full report appears as the third selection in the present volume.

Of course, even the child of 37 months is well beyond Stage I, often by a year or more. However, in Britain in 1965, Lovell and Dixon administered the same comprehension test to 20 two-year-olds (average age: 2;6) as well as to older children. The two-year-olds showed a significant ability to decode the contrast.

Finally, we have the results of an action test conducted on one of our own children. Ursula Bellugi asked Adam, when he was 30–31 months old, to act out with toys whatever she said. And what she said involved agent-object-contrasts. For example: "Show me, 'the duck pushes the boat' " and, later on, "Show me, 'the boat pushes the duck.' " Adam responded correctly on 11 of 15 such trials, and this result further strengthens the conclusion that Stage I children have the semantic meanings described in Table 8–3.

While I am prepared to conclude that Washoe has not demonstrated that she intends the structural meanings of Table 8–3 I do not conclude that it has been demonstrated that she lacks these meanings. Appropriate word order can be used as evidence for the intention to express structural meanings, but the lack of such order does not establish the absence of such meanings. It does not do so because appropriate word order is not strictly *necessary* for purposes of communication for either the Stage I child or the Stage I chimpanzee. Let us look again at the pictures of Figure 8–2. If the child uses correct orders for the two pictures it is likely that he distinguishes the meanings. But, suppose we were parents in the presence of the action pictures on the left and the child used an inappropriate order: *Cat bite* or *Cat dog* or *Bite dog*. We should still understand him and would mentally make the switches to *Dog bite* and *Dog cat* and *Bite cat* which fit the situation. The structure being supplied by our perception of the situation we can receive the words in any order and understand them as the situation dictates. Even when we are unaquainted with the situation our knowledge of what is possible in the world enables us to set right some sentences such as *Nose blow* and *Balloon throw* and *Garbage empty*. It follows, therefore, that there is little or no communication pressure on either children or Washoe to use the right word order for the meanings they intend. In their world of very simple sentences, which are usually clarified by concurrent circumstances and which often have only one sensible reading in any case, they will be understood whether the order is right or not.

They will be understood, at least, until they begin to want to say things like *I tickle you* and *You tickle me* or *Mommy call Daddy* and *Daddy call Mommy* or *Car hit truck* and *Truck hit car*; and to say these outside of a clarifying action context. In terms of real-world possibilities the paired propositions are on the same footing. If the propositions do not refer to ongoing actions but to actions at another time, then the listener or viewer, if he is to understand the message correctly, must be given structural signals, of order or of some other kind, to indicate who or what is in each semantic role. In general, as sentences become more complex and more varied and become "displaced" in time from their references the need to mark attributives, possessors, locatives, agents, objects, and the like grows greater. The capacity for "displacement" is, like the properties of semanticity and productivity, universal in human languages and we notice now that experience cannot become truly cumulative until it is possible to report on events not concurrent with the act of communication.

My conclusion, therefore, is that the question of Washoe's syntactic capacity is still quite open. If she fails to mark structures distinctively when a real communication-necessity develops then we shall conclude that she lacks real syntactic capacity. If, on the other hand, when her sentences become complex and displaced in reference from the immediate context, Washoe begins to mark structure with whatever means is available to her in the sign language—why then. . . . Then, there is a man on the moon, after all.

References

BLOOM, LOIS. Language development: Form and function in emerging grammars. Unpublished doctoral dissertation, Columbia University, 1968.

BOWERMAN, MELISSA. Brief comparison of Finnish I and English I. Unpublished paper, Harvard University, 1969.

BOWERMAN, MELISSA. The pivot-open class distinction. Unpublished paper, Harvard University, 1969.

BRAINE, M. D. S. The ontogeny of English phrase structure: The first phase. *Language*, 1963, **39**, 1–14.

BROWN, R., and BELLUGI, URSULA. Three processes in the acquisition of syntax. *Harvard educational review*, 1964, **34**, 133–151.

BROWN, R., and FRASER, C. The acquisition of syntax. In C. N. Cofer & Barbara S. Musgrave (Eds.), *Verbal behavior and learning: Problems and processes*. New York: McGraw-Hill, 1963.

CHAO, Y. R. The Cantian idiolect: An analysis of the Chinese spoken by a twenty-eight-months old child. In W. J. Fishel (Ed.), *Semitic and Oriental Studies, University of California Publications in Semitic Philology*, XI. Berkeley and Los Angeles: University of California Press, 1951.

FRASER, C., BELLUGI, URSULA, and BROWN, R. Control of grammar in imitation, comprehension, and production. *J. verb. Learn. verb. Behav*, 1963, **2**, 121–135

GARDNER, R. A., and GARDNER, BEATRICE T. Teaching sign language to a chimpanzee. *Science*, 1969, **165**, 664–672.

GRÉGOIRE, A. *L'Apprentissage du langage; Les deux premières années*. Paris: Librairie E. Droz, 1937.

HAYES, K. J., and HAYES, CATHERINE. The intellectual development of a home-raised chimpanzee. *Proceedings of the American philosophical society*, 1951, **95**, 105–109.

KELLOGG, W. N., and KELLOGG, LOUISE A. *The ape and the child.* New York: McGraw-Hill, 1933.

LEOPOLD, W. F. *Speech development of a bilingual child; a linguist's record,* Vol. III, *Grammar and general problems in the first two years.* Evanston, Ill.: Northwestern University Press, 1949.

LOVELL, K., and DIXON, E. M. The growth of the control of grammar in imitation, comprehension, and production. *Journal of child psychology and psychiatry,* 5, 1965, 1–9.

MCCALL, ELIZABETH A. A generative grammar of sign. Unpublished master's dissertation, University of Iowa, 1965.

MILLER, W., and ERVIN, SUSAN. The development of grammar in child language. In Ursula Bellugi & R. Brown (Eds.), *The acquisition of language. Mongr. Soc. Res. Child Developm.,* 1964, 29, No. 1, 9–34.

PIAGET, J. *The construction of reality in the child.* (1st ed., 1937). New York: Basic Books, 1954.

SCHLESINGER, I. M. Production of utterances and language acquisition. In D. Slobin (Ed.), *The ontogenesis of grammar: Some facts and several theories.* In press.

SLOBIN, D. Acquisition of Russian as a native language. In G. A. Miller & F. Smith (Eds.), *The genesis of language.* Cambridge, Mass.: M.I.T. Press, 1966.

STOKOE, W. C., CASTERLINE, DOROTHY, and CRONEBERG, C. G. *A dictionary of American sign language.* Washington, D. C.: Gallaudet College Press, 1965.

PART TWO

PSYCHOLINGUISTIC PROCESSES IN ADULT LIFE

Researches start in all kinds of ways. Some are even done to test hypotheses deduced from theories. Some are done because there is a method or a piece of apparatus to be exercised. Most of the researches in this section started with phenomena. Since life is filled with phenomena it is necessary to say why some should attract research while most do not. Usually I think it is the phenomena that contradict accepted ideas that attract us.

The basic datum in the phonetic symbolism experiment is that people enjoy better-than-chance success guessing the meanings of words from a foreign language of which they believe themselves to be completely ignorant. This should not happen if, as is generally supposed, word forms are arbitrarily related to word meanings. The datum rather suggests the heretical position that the form of a word tends to be appropriate to its sense.

The paper called "A Study in Language and Cognition" starts with the fact that some languages have words for which other languages have no equivalents, a fact that challenges the view that languages are simply alternative codes for expressing some universal set of conceptions. It seems rather to be possible that languages represent quite distinct world views. The paper on the pronouns of address starts from the same kind of thing; the major European languages all have two forms of address where English has only one. The French may say *tu* or *vous*, the Germans *du* or *Sie*, the Italians *tu* or *Lei*, but we have only *you*. What is the distinction among persons that so many languages code but that English seems not to code?

In the "tip of the tongue" state one is unable to recall a word that is, however, quite well known. The surprising thing is that, though the target word itself is missing, other words when they come to mind can be confidently sorted into those that resemble the target in meaning and those that resemble it in form; those that resemble it closely and those that resemble it little. Common sense would have it that judgments like these involve comparison against a standard but in the "tip of the tongue" where is the standard? It seems to be a kind of disembodied presence, a grin without the Cheshire Cat.

The phenomenon from which the "Personality and Style" paper begins is different from the rest. It is not a mental state but rather an exceptional research opportunity. In the late nineteenth century, in the little town of Concord, Massachusetts lived two writers, Emerson and Thoreau, who were perhaps uniquely well-matched, among great writers, in respect of time, place, education, genre, subject matter, and philosophy. The match provides an almost-experimental opportunity for the study of style in relation to personality and the research exploits that opportunity.

As for Nabokov and his novel *Lolita*, clearly they too are phenomena.

234

[9]

A Study in Language and Cognition

A graduate student from Germany recently talked with me about some American English words which seem to him to have no German equivalents. One of these is the verb *appreciate*, in the sense of "John appreciates classical music; he doesn't appreciate rock." Obviously one easily says in German the equivalents of "John likes classical music," or "John enjoys classical music," but *appreciate* is not quite the same as *enjoy* or *like* or *admire* or *take an interest in*. Notice that if someone invites you to listen to a recording of *Tristan and Isolde* the effect of "I don't like Wagner" is very different from "I don't appreciate Wagner." To appreciate *x* is to be attuned to real virtues *x* is presumed to have and not to appreciate is to fail to be attuned; it is not to deny that *x* has virtues. In short, *appreciate* seems to presuppose in the object qualities deserving admiration in a way that *like*, *admire*, and so on do not. It is a verb that enables Americans to talk about differences of taste in a minimally abrasive and rather democratic manner; everything may be presumed deserving of interest but individuals differ in the interests they happen to have developed.

Differences of this kind in the lexicons of languages are always

---

The paper was first published in *The Journal of Abnormal and Social Psychology*, Vol. 49, No. 3 (July 1954), 454–462. Eric H. Lenneberg was the co-author. Reprinted by permission of the authors.

fascinating. If one language has a gap where the other language has a word, does the first language lack also the idea that is the word's meaning? So long as the ideas concern social life we are not surprised that cross-language differences exist. However, the differences extend also to terms that make reference to the physical world; for example, to the names for colors.

In many languages, for instance, there is a single word for both green and blue. This term is also often the name given the sea. But then we begin to understand. Surely the word was used first for the sea and then, by abstraction, for just that range of colors which the sea passes through: the greens and the blues. In a similar way our color terms *orange* and *rose* and *olive* were first object names but have come to be names for the colors the objects exemplify. We can see how differences in the scope of particular color terms might arise in this way. But what we cannot tell, from the linguistic evidence alone, is what such differences signify about the thought and perception of the people who use them. To find that out experiments are needed and this paper describes one such.

IT IS WIDELY THOUGHT that reality exists in much the same form to all men of sound mind. There are objects like a house or a cat and qualities like red or wet and events like eating or singing and relationships like near to or between. Languages are itemized inventories of this reality. They differ, of course, in the sounds they employ, but the inventory is always the same. The esthetic predilections of the Italian lead him to prefer euphonious vowels, while the German is addicted to harsh consonant groupings, but the things and events named are the same in both tongues. We are confirmed in this view by our linguistic education, which requires us to memorize lists of French or German or Latin words and their exact English equivalents.

There are, of course, poetic persons who claim to find in each language some special genius that peculiarly fits it for the expression of certain ideas. But the majority of us are at a loss to understand how this can be, since there is apparently a relationship of mutual translatability among the languages we learn. To be sure, we can see that one language might contain a few items more than another. If the Germans were to invent a new kind of automobile and we had not yet thought of such a machine, their dictionary would have one entry more than ours until we heard of the discovery and named it for ourselves. But these inequalities are in the lexical fringe. They do not disturb the great core of common inventory.

THE WHORF THESIS

This linguistic ethnocentrism will be seriously disturbed by the study of languages that lie outside the Indo-European group. It has not prepared us for finding that there is a language in which noun and verb categories apparently do not exist, or that there is another in which the colors gray and brown are called by the same name. Such data from the study of American Indian tongues led Whorf (1950) to reject the usual view of the relationship between language and thought. He suggested that each language embodies and perpetuates a particular world view. The speakers of a language are partners to an agreement to see and think of the world in a certain way—not the only possible way. The world can be structured in many ways, and the language we learn as children directs the formation of our particular structure. Language is not a cloak following the contours of thought. Languages are molds into which infant minds are poured. Whorf thus departs from the common sense view in a) holding that the world is differently experienced and conceived in different linguistic communities and b) suggesting that language is causally related to these psychological differences.

Other authors have believed that the relationship between language and thought is somewhat as proposed by Whorf. Cassirer (1953), maintained that language is the direct manifestation of knowledge; he explicitly denied a form-content relationship between words or language structure and isolates of knowledge. In this he was in agreement with such other German writers as Wundt (1900) and Bühler (1934).

Orwell (1949) in his novel *Nineteen Eighty-Four* describes a totalitarian England of the future. The really efficient dictatorship of that day invents a language—Newspeak—in which it is impossible not only to express, but even to think, a rebellious thought. An equally great faith in the causal efficacy of language lies behind the General Semantics movement. Korzybski (1951), for instance, holds that clear thinking and social progress are to be attained through the reform of language.

Cognitive Differences between Linguistic Communities

The first tenet of the Whorf thesis is that the world is differently experienced and conceived in different linguistic communities. The evidence presented in support of this claim is entirely linguistic. It will be helpful to distinguish between the conclusions based on lexical features of two languages and those based on structural features.

Lexical Features. In the Eskimo lexicon there are three words to distinguish three varieties of snow. There are no single-word equivalents for these in English. The word "snow" would be used to describe all three. What psychological conclusions can be drawn from these data? Does the Eskimo see differences and similarities that we are unable to see?

Psychologists ordinarily infer perceptual discrimination when a subject is consistently able to respond differently to distinctive stimulus situations. The subject may be rat, dog, or man. The response may be running, salivation, or—speech. Words are used meaningfully when they are selectively employed with reference to some kind of environment—whether physical, social, or linguistic. The linguist in the field may discover the referent of a term by noting the pattern of its usage. The Eskimo's three "snows" are sufficient evidence from which to infer that he discriminates three varieties of snow. These selective verbal responses satisfy the conditions for inferring perceptual discrimination.

What can be said of the English speaker's ability to distinguish the same three kinds of snow? When different stimuli do not elicit differential responses, the stimuli may or may not be discriminated. A subject may be perfectly able to distinguish two situations and still not care to do anything about it. Consequently the fact that English speakers do not have different names for several kinds of snow cannot be taken to mean that they are *unable* to see the differences. It would seem, then, that all such comparisons are psychologically inconclusive. The Eskimo and American may or may not see the world differently.

There is, however, other evidence to indicate that the speaker of English can classify snows as the Eskimo does. If we listen to the talk of small boys, it is clear that they perceive at least two kinds of snow—good-packing snow and bad-packing snow. This is a distinction of the greatest importance to anyone interested in making snowballs. This discrimination is evidenced by differential response—not distinct lexical items but combinations of items—*good-packing snow* and *bad-packing snow*. Whorf himself must have been able to see snow as the Eskimos did since his article describes and pictures the referents for the words. Since both Eskimo and American are able to make differential responses to snows, we must conclude that both are able to see differences. This seems to lead us to the conclusion that the Eskimo and American world views do not differ in this regard.

Although the three kinds of snow are namable in both Eskimo and English, each of them requires a phrase in ordinary English, whereas single words will do it for the Eskimo. Zipf (1935) has shown that there exists a tendency in Peiping Chinese, Plautine Latin, and American and British English for the length of a word to be negatively correlated with its frequency of usage. This is true whether word length is measured in phonemes or syllables. It is not difficult to find examples of this relationship in English. New inventions are usually given long names of Greek or Latin derivation, but as the products become widely known and frequently used in conversation the linguistic community finds shorter tags for them. Thus the *automobile* becomes the *car* and *television* shrinks to *video* and eventually to *TV*. Three-dimensional movies are predictably described as *3-D*.

Doob (1952) has suggested that this principle bears on Whorf's thesis. Suppose we generalize the findings even beyond Zipf's formulation and propose that the length of a verbal expression provides an index of its frequency in speech and that this, in turn, is an index of the frequency with which the relevant perceptual judgments of difference and equivalence are made. If this is true, it would follow that the Eskimo distinguishes his three kinds of snow more often than Americans do. It would mean—to cite another example—that the Hopi is less often called upon to distinguish airplanes, aviators, and butterflies than is the American, since the Hopi has but a single name for all three of these. Such conclusions are, of course, supported by extralinguistic cultural analysis, which reveals the importance of snow in the Eskimo's life and the comparative indifference of the Hopi to airplanes and aviators.

We will go further and propose that increased frequency of a perceptual categorization will mean a generally greater "availability" of that category. In the experimental study of memory we are accustomed to think of the methods of recall, recognition, and relearning as increasingly sensitive indices of retention. In the experimental study of categorizing behavior there are two principal methods: (a) Goldstein's (1948) technique of presenting a subject with an array of objects and asking him to group them, and (b) Hull's (1920) discrimination learning technique. Hull's method seems to be the more sensitive of the two. We should guess that when the Eskimo steps from his igloo in the morning and is confronted by a snowy world, these snows will fall into named categories for him in a way that they will not for the American. If however, the American were subjected to a discrimination learning experiment, or if the perceptual structure were otherwise made worth his while, he could see snow as does the Eskimo. We think, really, that more namable categories are nearer the top of the cognitive "deck."

Structural Features. Members of structural categories have no phonetic common denominator. They are grouped together because they have the same structural relations with other forms in the language. In English, nouns constitute a structural category; its members can appear with definite and indefinite articles, can form plurals in certain ways, etc. In French all nouns of the feminine gender belong to one structural category since they all require the feminine articles and suffixes.

Whorf generally assumes that structural categories are also symbolic categories. When he finds structural differences in languages he concludes that there are parallel cognitive differences. There are in Hopi two structural categories showing some similarity to our verb and noun categories, with the difference that one of the Hopi classes includes only the names for such short-term events as lightning, flame, and spasm, while the other includes only such long-term events as man, house, and lifetime. Whorf concludes that the Hopi organizes his world on a dimension we usually overlook. When the structural class has such obvious semantic properties, Whorf's conclusions have a kind of plausibility.

However, very few structural classes have such clear and consistent meanings. In the languages we know best, those of the Indo-European family, there are many structural categories with no discernible meaning. In French, for instance, it is not clear that the gender of a form signifies anything to a speaker. Certainly it is difficult to find any common attributes in the references for French nouns of feminine gender. Not even the majority of them manifest feminine sexuality—even in the extended sense of Freud. The French speak of *le balcon* in spite of their saying, "Elle a du balcon." The linguist Charles Fries (1952) has shown how difficult it is to describe a semantic for the English "parts of speech." If the noun can be defined as "the name of a person, place, or thing," this is only because "thing" is left unexplicated. It serves handily to designate whatever is nominalized and yet neither person nor place.

Even where the ethnolinguist can discover consistent structural meanings, it does not follow that these meanings are present to the native speakers of a language. Suppose that a subject in the laboratory were required to signal his recognition of each of ten different musical chords by raising that one of his ten fingers which has been designated for each chord. If all extraneous sensory information were excluded, his ability to pattern correctly the movements of his fingers would be evidence of his ability to identify the chords. The experimenter might introduce a potential structural meaning by ruling that the fingers of the right hand would always be raised for chords in the major mode and the fingers of the left hand for minor chords. The subject's responses might follow this pattern and yet he need never have detected the major and minor modes. Similarly, even if there were some semantic to French gender, one could speak the language without detecting it. *La fille* and *la femme* could be learned without noticing that both are in the feminine mode. No safe inferences about cognition can be made on the basis of the simple existence of the structural classes described by Whorf. The structural evidence is extremely difficult to interpret, and it seems clear that psychological data are needed to supplement those of the linguist.

Language in Causal Relation to Cognition

The second major tenet of Whorf's thesis is that language causes a particular cognitive structure. In what way can this occur? There seem to be two possibilities. Suppose that the colors red and green are not "given" categories but must be learned. A father who has formed these categories may play a game with his child that will teach the categories. The green blocks are to be used for building a house and the red ones for a barn. The child cannot properly pattern the blocks without learning to make the visual distinctions involved. Notice that the barn and house are not essential here. A father could ask his child to tell him whether each block is red or green. In learning this game, too, the child necessarily would learn to perceive the colors. Because words have symbolic properties, because their usage is patterned with reference to the total environment, language can cause a cognitive structure. To the degree that children are motivated to speak a language as it is spoken in their community they are motivated to share the world view of that community. To be sure, linguistic training is not the only means of procuring cognitive socialization; the house-barn game demonstrates that. The word game has the tremendous advantage that it can be played constantly and concurrently with many other activities. The child and his adult tutor can chatter together whether they are walking or riding, playing or working. In this chatter more is taught than a simple motor skill involving the muscles of articulation. A total culture is internalized.

There is a second, more dubious, avenue for the influence of language on thought. If life is a river, speech is a babbling brook whose course parallels that of the river. The brook is smaller and simpler than the river. A child can learn the phonemic structure of his language fairly easily. He will also realize that as the phonemic patterns he hears spoken change there are important changes in the nonlinguistic world. There is, for instance, an important difference that goes with the shift of speech from *father* to *mother*. When, on the other hand, combinations of phonemes are repeated, two situations are equivalent in some important way. Consider the "strike" and the "ball" in baseball. These are rather difficult categories. The differences between them are subtle and complex. A naive observer of a baseball game would have a difficult time learning these categories by simply observing the game. It makes a great difference that the umpire calls out *strike!* each time a member of that category occurs and *ball!* to identify an instance of the other category. The umpire's shout directs us to look here and now to discover something of importance. The word spotlights a moment of consciousness and puts it in connection with other events similarly spotlighted. The various "strikes" are equivalent in some way and distinct as a category from the events labelled *ball*. The babbling brook can, then, be a guide to the structure of the more complex but also more interesting river.

All of our reasoning cannot be said to prove the validity of any set of psychological conclusions. It does, however, point the direction for such a proof and suggests empirical steps that will advance our knowledge of this problem. We have made a small beginning in this work.

Our findings bear on only one of the claims made by Whorf—

that there are cognitive differences correlated with lexical differences. We have developed lexical differences into the variable of "codability" and attempted to determine the relationship between this variable and a single cognitive performance—recognition.

THE EXPERIMENT

Sensory psychologists have described the world of color with a solid using three psychological dimensions: hue, brightness, and saturation. The color solid is divisible into millions of just noticeable differences; *Science of Color* (1953) estimates 7,500,000. The largest collection (Evans, 1948; Maerz and Paul, 1930) of English color names runs to less than 4,000 entries, and of these only about 8 occur very commonly (Thorndike and Lorge, 1944). Evidently there is considerable categorization of colors. It seems likely to us that all human beings with normal vision will be able to make approximately the same set of discriminations. This ability appears to depend on the visual system, which is standard equipment for the species. Whatever individual differences do exist are probably not related to culture, linguistic or extralinguistic. It does not follow that people everywhere either see or think of the color world in the same way. Cultural differences probably operate on the level of categorization rather than controlled laboratory discrimination.

Our explorations in the Yale Cross-Cultural Index turned up many reports of differences on this level. Seroshevskii (1896), for instance, has reported that in the Iakuti language there is a single word for both green and blue. This is the kind of language difference discussed in the first section of this paper. A region of experience is lexically differentiated in one culture but undifferentiated in another. Color categories differ from such categories as snows in that they have boundaries that can be plotted on known dimensions. Color categories, furthermore, are continuous with one another, sharing their boundaries. Consider for a moment the single dimension of hue taken at a high level of saturation and brightness. Native speakers of English could be shown various shades and asked to give the usual color name for each stimulus presented. For each common color name there would be some shades invariably called by that name. There would be other shades sometimes associated with one name, sometimes with another. When the responses are divided about equally between two or more names, we should have boundaries between categories. If a native speaker of Iakuti were asked to provide the usual color names for the various shades, we should anticipate a somewhat different pattern. English speakers would have trouble naming the hues in the boundary region between green and blue. Probably they would hesitate, disagree among themselves, and sometimes use phrases or such combination names as *greenish blue*. For the Iakuti, on the other hand, this region is right in the center of a category and would be named with great ease.

Of course, our example is greatly simplified over the actual case since we have dealt with the single dimension of hue whereas the color lexicon is actually patterned with respect to all of the three dimensions of visual experience. When these are considered, the range of applicability of a color term is a space within the color solid rather than a distance along a line. The simplification was for expository purposes and does not alter the logic of the argument.

This example of a cultural difference serves to introduce the variable *codability*. Certain colors are differentially codable in the Iakuti and English languages. So long as the data collected are of the usual linguistic variety, this difference of codability will be manifest in only one way—environmental distinctions expressed lexically in one language are expressed with word combinations in another language. Our reasoning led us to expect differential availability of reference categories in such a case. We undertook experimental work to discover additional behavioral indices of codability, and hoped to find one more sensitive than that which can be teased out of linguistic data. If we found such an index, we would go on to explore the behavioral consequences of differential availability of cognitive categories.

There are differences of codability within English itself.

Some shades fall safely within the province of a given name while others lie within boundary regions. Here it is a matter of comparing the English codability of one region of visual experience with another region, whereas the ethnolinguist has usually compared the codability of one region of experience in several languages. If we explore the codability variable in English, it seems likely that our discoveries will apply to the cultural differences with which the inquiry began. If a general law can be found relating codability to availability, individual cultures may conform to the law though they differ among themselves in the values these variables assume in particular regions of experience.

Measurement of Codability

The entire series of Munsell colors for the highest level of saturation ("chroma" as Munsell calls it) was mounted on cards in systematic fashion. Five judges were asked to pick out the best red, orange, yellow, green, blue, purple, pink, and brown from these 240 colors. These names are the most frequently appearing color terms in English (Thorndike and Lorge, 1944). For each name the color chip most often selected was added to our test list. Agreement among judges was high, and it is quite clear, therefore, that there is in this series one particular color chip with the best claim to each color name. The number of colors was then raised to 24 by adding chips that would, in combination with the first 8, provide as even a coverage of the color space as practicable. These colors are specified in Table 9-1. One set of the 24 chips was mounted on white 3 × 5 cards, one chip to a card. Another set was arranged randomly on a single large card.

To expose the single small cards a drop shutter was mounted in a 3 × 2-foot gray (Munsell neutral value 6, reflectance 30 per cent) board. The board was about three feet from the subject's eyes and was illuminated from above and behind by a General Electric standard daylight fluorescent lamp.

The subjects were 24 Harvard and Radcliffe students who spoke English as a native language and had no particular training in distinguishing colors. They were screened for color blindness with the standard Pseudo-Isochromatic Plates. The subjects were first shown the 24-color random chart for about five minutes. After the chart was removed they were

Table 9–1. The Munsell Notation and Scores for Discriminability, Codability, and Recognition for the 24 Test Colors

Munsell Notation*	Discriminability		Codability		Recognition (Group C Table 9–3)	
	Score	Rank	Score	Rank	Score	Rank
2.5R 7/8	38	2	18	9.5	.875	8
2.5R 5/10	27.5	6	7	18.5	.694	11
5R 4/14	23	10.5	19	7.5	1.020	5
7.5R 8/4	18	15	7	18.5	.236	18
2.5YR 6/14	38	2	29	1.5	1.499	2
5YR 3/4	24	9	26	3	.972	7
7.5YR 5/8	26	7.5	8	16	.736	9
2.5Y 7/10	12	19	3	24	.486	13
5Y 8/12	37	4	25	4	2.450	1
7.5Y 6/8	13	17	4	23	.250	17
3GY 7.5/11.2	23	10.5	14	12	1.222	4
7.5GY 3/4	9.5	23	14	12	0.000	23.5
2.5G 5/8	18.5	14	23	6	.986	6
7.5G 8/4	17.5	16	19	7.5	.167	19
5BG 3/6	4.5	24	12	15	.111	22
10BG 6/6	21	12	7	18.5	.458	14
8.5B 3/6.8	38	2	13	14	0.000	23.5
2.5PB 7/6	19	13	18	9.5	.436	16
5PB 4/10	10.5	21	29	1.5	.695	10
10PB 5/10	12	19	7	18.5	.125	20.5
5P 8/4	12	19	14	12	.547	12
10P 3/10	10	22	24	5	.444	15
5RP 6/10	26	7.5	6	21.5	.125	20.5
8RP 3.4/12.1	31	5	6	21.5	1.464	3

*For conversion to C.I.E. Tristimulus values and Source C, C.I.E. chromaticity coordinates see Nickerson, Tomaszewski, and Boyd (1953).

told that each of the colors on the chart would appear individually in the tachistoscope and that the subject's task was to give the name of each as it appeared. "Name" was defined as the word or words one would ordinarily use to describe the color to a friend. The subjects were urged to be both quick and accurate.

The 24 colors were presented in a predetermined random order for each subject. No order was repeated. Each color was exposed until the subject had named it. In our trial procedure we used a voice key and chronoscope to measure the reaction time. The scope was activated by the opening shutter of the tachistoscope and stopped by the subject's first vocalization. This method proved to be unsuitable since subjects would frequently burst out with something other than a color name, which, of course stopped the undiscriminating chronoscope. Consequently, we abandoned this technique and used the stop watch. The watch was started as the experimenter dropped the shutter and stopped at first mention of a color name.

The variable of codability was measured in five ways. (a) The average length of naming response to each color was obtained by counting syllables. (b) The average length was also obtained by counting words. (c) The average reaction time for each color was obtained by ranking all of the reaction times of an individual subject and taking the mean rank across subjects for every color. (d) The degree to which subjects agreed with one another in naming a color was assessed as follows: We counted the total number of different responses to a color (DR) and also the number of subjects who agreed on whatever response was most often given to a particular color (CR). The first value was subtracted from the second and a constant of 20 added to keep the results positive (CR – DR + 20). Color 18, for example, was given the following eight different names: *gray-blue, blue, light gray-blue, light blue, very pale blue, light blue-gray, pale blue,* and *powder blue.* Of these, the single-word response *blue* occurred most often—six times. Color 18, then, scored 6 – 8 + 20, or 18. (e) The degree to which subjects agreed with themselves from one time to another in naming a color was calculated as follows: Five subjects were recalled after a period of one month and subjected to a repetition of the naming procedure. When a subject gave identical responses to a color on the two occasions, we counted one agreement. We determined the number of agreements for each subject and considered that to be unity. Each individual agreement was then given the appropriate fractional value. Suppose a subject had eight agreements. If he agreed in his name for Color 11, he would add $\frac{1}{8}$ to the score for that color. The agreement score is, then, the sum of the individual performances weighted for each individual's overall tendency to agreement.

In Table 9–2 the intercorrelations of scores on these five measures appear. All correlations are in the predicted direction and most of them are significant, with .355 the smallest.

Table 9–2. Correlation Matrix for Five Indices of Codability

Measure	1	2	3	4	5
Number of syllables					
Number of words	.425*				
Reaction time	.387	.368			
Interpersonal agreement	.630*	.486*	.864*		
Intrapersonal agreement	.355	.537*	.649*	.773*	
k from second factoring	.589	.587	.787	.976	.795
Communality from					
first factoring	.403	.378	671	.873	.653

* $p \leqslant .05$.

With a single iteration this matrix yielded a general factor which we call *codability*. No correlations over .113 remain after the extraction of this single factor. Our fourth index, the degree of agreement between subjects, has by far the largest factor loading. It was selected as the measure of codability for the second phase of the experiment. The obtained codability values for the 24 colors are listed in Table 9–1.

Codability and Recognition

Once the codability variable suggested by Whorf's ethnolinguistic observations had been operationalized, it remained to relate this variable to some nonlinguistic behavior which might be considered an index of availability. We selected the recognition of colors.

From the 240 Munsell chips taken at highest saturation we

selected out alternate chips, taking care to include the 24 colors for which codability data had been collected. The resultant collection of 120 colors was systematically mounted on a white card. Hue varied along the vertical dimension of the card and brightness on the horizontal dimension. Since there were 20 steps of hue and only 6 of brightness, we divided the total colors in half and mounted one half above the other so as to make a more manipulable display.

New subjects were screened, as before, for color blindness and language background. The basic procedure was to expose simultaneously 4 of the 24 colors, remove them, and ask subjects to point to the colors just seen, on the large chart of 120. Neither the experimenter nor the subject mentioned any color name during the session. The recognition score for a color was computed as follows: We determined the number of correct identifications made by each subject and considered this number to be unity. Each individual correct identification was given the appropriate fractional value. Suppose for instance, that a subject who correctly identified a total of six colors recognized Color 24. This recognition would have counted as $\frac{1}{6}$ on the total recognition score for that color. Another subject for whom Color 24 was one of eight correctly identified colors would have contributed $\frac{1}{8}$ to the score for Color 24. In other words, the recognition score for a color is the sum of the individual performances weighted for each subject's over-all ability to recognize colors. The scores for the 24 colors appear in Table 9-1.

In trial runs, subjects were asked how they managed to retain the four colors in memory after they were removed from sight. Most subjects reported that they named the colors when they were exposed and "stored" the names. It seemed likely, therefore, that those colors that are quite unequivocally coded would be most likely to be recognized. When a color elicits a considerable range of names, the chances of recovering the color from the name would be reduced. This expectation was fulfilled by a rank-order correlation of .415 between codability and recognition scores.

There is, however, another variable that influenced recognition. The 120 colors used are not perceptually perfectly equidistant. The manufacture of equidistant color chips is technically difficult and expensive and, indeed, above a certain level of saturation, impossible. Since we were unable to control experimentally the variable "discriminability," we must ask whether or not our findings were due to a positive correlation between codability and discriminability. Could it be that our codable colors were so distant, perceptually, from their nearest neighbors that their superior recognizability was actually due to these better discrimination conditions? To obtain an answer to this question we determined the true perceptual distance between each of the colors used from the Newhall, Nickerson, and Judd (1943) charts. These charts convert every Munsell book notation into a renotation which is the specification of a true perceptual locus of each color within the Munsell coordinate system. The difference between two renotations expresses quantitatively the perceptual distance between the colors.

For each of the 24 test colors we computed a discriminability score which describes its distinctiveness from the colors surrounding it. The difference between two renotations yields three numbers, one for each dimension. To make these numbers perceptually commensurable (i.e., to reduce them to a common denominator), the Optical Society of America Subcommittee on the Spacing of the Munsell Colors suggests the values 3, 2, and 1 for hue, chroma, and value, respectively. Since every color has two neighbors on each of the three dimensions, a total of six numbers will express, in a rough way, the discriminability of that color. The sum of these yields the unadjusted discriminability score. Adjustments of this score are necessary (a) because if a color appears on the margin of our chart it has a lower chance of being recognized correctly and (b) because a color that has a very close neighbor on one side and distant neighbors on three others might come out with a good discriminability score although the close contiguity on one side would hinder correct recognition considerably. Consequently, colors appearing on the margin of our chart had the constant 3 subtracted from their unadjusted discriminability score, and colors with a close neighbor had the constant 6 subtracted.

Our scoring method is to a certain degree arbitrary, to be sure, but since the equation of perceptual distances on different visual dimensions is an unsolved problem, there seems to be no more objective method available. In addition, of course, all decisions were made without knowledge of recognition scores.

Since we were unable to control discriminability experimentally, we controlled it statistically. The partial correlation between codability and recognition, with discriminability constant, is .438. Furthermore, the correlation between codability and discriminability is .074, which is not significant. Evidently the relation between codability and recognition is not a consequence of variations in discriminability.

Table 9–3. Recognition Procedures

Group	N	Number of Colors Originally Exposed	Length of Interval	Content of Interval
A	9	1	7 seconds	
B	9	4	7 seconds	
C	16	4	30 seconds	
D	9	4	3 minutes	Tasks

Note.—Exposure time for all groups was 3 seconds.

Since the reports of our early subjects indicated that colors were stored in linguistic code, it seemed likely that color codability would increase in importance as the storage factor was maximized in the recognition situation. Discriminability, on the other hand, should remain at the same level of importance or possibly decline somewhat. If, for example, a single color were exposed, removed, and then identified with minimal delay, subjects might retain some direct memory of the color, perhaps as a visual image. In this situation discriminability would be a determinant of recognition but codability would not be. However, when the number of colors is increased and the interval prolonged and filled with activity, the importance of linguistic coding should increase. Table 9–3 describes the experimental variations we used. Groups A, B, C, and D are arranged in what we believed to be an order of increasingly difficult storage of colors. Group C is our major group, for which results have already been described. The tasks which filled the interval for Group D were simple but absorbing—the kind of thing often used in experiments on the Zeigarnik phenomenon.

It can be seen from the data in Table 9–4 that the correlation between recognition and codability scores does increase as the importance of storage in the recognition task increases. The particular order obtained would occur by chance only once in 24 times.

Table 9–4. Correlations Involving Scores on Codability (C), Discriminability (D), and Recognition (R) with Four Experimental Conditions for Recognition

Group	C with R	D with R	C with R, D constant
A	.248	.540*	.248
B	.411	.460*	.426*
C	.415	.503*	.438*
D	.487*	.505*	.523*

* $p \leqslant .05$.

Table 9–4 also shows that discriminability is most closely related to recognition in Group A, for which the possibility of some direct memory of the color is maximized. The importance of discriminability declines slightly but not significantly as the recognition is made more difficult. Our expectations with regard to both codability and discriminability are generally confirmed.

In the first section of this paper we concluded our discussion of lexical differences between languages with the prediction that a given set of cognitive categories will be more available to the speakers of a language that lexically codes these categories than to the speakers of a language in which the categories are not represented in the lexicon. Lexical differences have been expanded into the variable of codability, and category availability has been operationalized as a recognition score. We found that differences in the English codability of colors are related to differences in the recognition of these colors. We expected these results to apply to the cross-cultural case, and some confirmation of this expectation is available in the results of a study by Lenneberg and Roberts (1953). This study of Zuni Indians used a field adaptation of our methods and apparatus. The Zuni color lexicon codes the colors we call orange and yellow with a single term. Monolingual Zuni subjects in their recognition task frequently confused the orange and yellow colors in our stimulus set. Our English-speaking subjects never made this error. It is a distinction which is highly codable in English and highly uncodable in Zuni. Interestingly, bilingual Zunis who knew English fell between the monolingual Zuni and the native speaker of English in the frequency with which they made these errors.

The Whorf thesis claims more than a simple relationship between language and cognition; language is held to be causally related to cognitive structure. Our correlational evidence does not, of course, establish the direction of causality. If we may be permitted a guess it is that in the history of a culture the peculiar features of the language and thought of a people probably develop together.

In the history of an individual born into a linguistic community the story is quite different. The patterned responses are all about him. They exist before he has the cognitive structure that will enable him to pattern his behavior in the approved fashion. Simple exposure to speech will not shape anyone's mind. To the degree that the unacculturated individual is motivated to learn the language of a community, to the degree that he uses its structure as a guide to reality, language can assume a formative role.

SUMMARY

The Whorf thesis on the relationship between language and thought is found to involve the following two propositions: (a) Different linguistic communities perceive and conceive reality in different ways. (b) The language spoken in a community helps to shape the cognitive structure of the individuals speaking that language. The evidence for the first proposition derives from a comparison of the lexical and structural characteristics of various languages. The linguistic comparisons alone do not establish the proposition. They need to be complemented with psychological data. The second proposition is not directly supported by any data. However, it is clear that language can be described as a molder of thought since speech is a patterned response that is learned only when the governing cognitive patterns have been grasped. It is also possible that the lexical structure of the speech he hears guides the infant in categorizing his environment. These matters require empirical exploration.

An experiment is described which investigates a part of proposition *a*—the idea that lexical differences are indicative of cognitive differences. Whorf reports many cases in which a given range of experience is lexically differentiated in one language whereas the same discriminations can only be described with phrases in another language. Rather than compare members of different linguistic communities, we chose to work with native speakers of English and to compare their linguistic coding of two regions of experience. Within the realm of color vision there are colors that can be named with a single word and others that require a phrase. This kind of linguistic difference in the length of name (measured by words or syllables) was found to be correlated with the latency of the naming response and the reliability of the response from person to person within the linguistic community and from time to time in one person. A factor analysis of these measures yielded a single general factor—codability. The measure carrying the largest factor loading was the reliability of naming response between individuals who speak the same language. This variable—the codability of a color—proved to be related to the subjects' ability to recognize colors. Codability accounted for more variance in the recognition task as the task was delayed and complicated to increase the importance of the storage factor. Data obtained from the Zuni Indians show a similar relationship between codability and recognition. It is suggested that there may be general laws relating codability to cognitive processes. All cultures could conform to these laws although they differ among themselves in the values the variables assume in particular regions of experience.

References

BÜHLER, K. *Sprachtheorie*. Jena: G. Fischer, 1934.

CASSIRER, E. *The philosophy of symbolic forms*. Vol. 1. *Language*. New Haven: Yale University Press, 1953.

DOOB, L. W. *Social psychology*. New York: Holt, 1952.

EVANS, R. M. *An introduction to color*. New York: Wiley, 1948.

FRIES, C. C. *The structure of English*. New York: Harcourt, Brace, 1952.

GOLDSTEIN, K. *Language and language disturbances*. New York: Grune & Stratton, 1948.

HULL, C. L. Quantitative aspects of the evolution of concepts. *Psychol. Monogr.*, 1920, **28**, No. 1 (Whole No. 123).

KORZYBSKI, A. The role of language in the perceptual processes. In R. R. Blake & G. V. Ramsey (Eds.), *Perception; an approach to personality*. New York: Ronald, 1951.

KURTZ, K. H., and HOVLAND, C. I. The effect of verbalization during observation of stimulus objects upon accuracy of recognition and recall. *J. exp. Psychol.*, 1953, **45**, 157–164.

LENNEBERG, E. H., and ROBERTS, J. M. The denotata of color terms. Paper read at Linguistic Society of America, Bloomington, Indiana, August, 1953.

MAERZ, A., and PAUL, M. R. *A dictionary of color*. New York: McGraw-Hill, 1930.

NEWHALL, S. M., NICKERSON, D., and JUDD, D. B. Final report of the OSA subcommittee on the spacing of the Munsell colors. *J. opt. Soc. Amer.*, 1943, **33**, 385–418.

NICKERSON, D., TOMASZEWSKI, J. J., and BOYD, T. F. Colorimetric specifications of Munsell repaints. *J. opt. Soc. Amer.*, 1953, **43**, 163–171.

OPTICAL SOCIETY OF AMERICA, COMMITTEE ON COLORIMETRY. *The science of color*. New York: Crowell, 1953.

ORWELL, G. *Nineteen eighty-four.* New York: Harcourt, Brace, 1949.

SEROSHEVSKII, V. R. *Iakuti.* St. Petersburg: Royal Geographical Society, 1896.

THORNDIKE, E. L., and LORGE, I. *The teacher's word book of 30,000 words.* New York: Teachers College, Columbia University, 1944.

WHORF, B. L. *Four articles on metalinguistics.* Washington: Foreign Service Institute, 1950.

WUNDT, W. *Völkerpsychologie.* Vol. 1. *Die Sprache.* Leipzig: Engelmann, 1900.

ZIPF, G. K. *The psycho-biology of language.* Boston: Houghton Mifflin, 1935.

[10]

Phonetic Symbolism in Natural Languages

The experiment described in this paper has been repeated very many times with many languages, and so far as I can remember the effect has never failed. One asks native speakers of English to listen to pairs of antonyms from a language unrelated to English and then to try to guess, given the English equivalents, which foreign word translates which English word. They are to do it by attending to the sounds of the foreign words and letting the sounds suggest meanings. Suppose the words were *ch'ing* and *chung* and the English equivalents, not necessarily in this order, *light* and *heavy*. About 90 per cent of English-speakers guess correctly that *ch'ing* means light. Of course this is a particularly striking pair; a more usual result would be between 55 per cent and 60 per cent correct. But if the choices were simply guesses based on no knowledge at all the results should center on 50 per cent. In the published studies that I know, and also in five or six unpublished studies involving various African and Oriental languages, the outcome has always been significantly more successful than chance. What does this result mean?

This paper was first published in *The Journal of Abnormal and Social Psychology* in 1955 (pages 388–393). Abraham H. Black and Arnold E. Horowitz were co-authors. Reprinted by permission of the authors.

One meaning is indisputable: speakers of English share certain notions about the meanings that are suggested by various speech contrasts. For example, the lower-pitched back vowels such as are heard in *who, how, hoe,* and *haw* suggest what is heavy, dark, slow, blunt, and male while the higher-pitched front vowels such as are heard in *heat, hit,* and *hat* suggest what is light, bright, fast, sharp, and female. One can think of several not very interesting ways in which English speakers might come by these notions. Perhaps, for example, such correlations are ultimately arbitrary and accidental but happen, in the course of history, to have been built into the English lexicon, with the result that speakers of the language have unwittingly extracted them and will use them in guessing the sense of strange words. But this does not account for the fact that those guesses are correct more often than they should be by chance. And, of course, it is the correctness that is the surprising result. What it suggests is contrary to long accepted views. It suggests that words and meanings are not associated in an altogether arbitrary way in natural languages. It suggests that, however it has come about, there is a thread of sound symbolism in languages, a thread conceivably universal. What is still lacking to establish this thesis is evidence that speakers of languages other than English, and unrelated to English, have the same notions about phonetic symbolism as we do. Unfortunately it is still the case today that although the languages used as sources for antonym pairs are wonderfully diverse, the subjects have almost always been speakers of English.

IN OUR EXPERIMENTS native speakers of English guessed the meanings of words from unfamiliar languages. The subjects agreed very well on the meanings likely to be attached to these strange phonetic sequences. This agreement suggests a culturally acquired phonetic symbolism derived from experience with a common native language. However, the semantic judgments of our subjects were also correct more often than would be expected by chance, and this suggests that there may be some features of phonetic symbolism which have a universal validity. It is possible that speech originated in symbols imitative or somehow suggestive of their meanings and that traces of these "appropriate" linkages survive in all languages today.

NONLINGUISTIC PHONETIC SYMBOLISM

In 1929 Sapir conducted experiments using pairs of "nonlinguistic words" built on the CVC model. Within a pair the two words were matched for the initial and final consonants while the vowels were varied in the range from *a* to *i* (e.g., *Mal–Mil*). Sapir asked his subjects to judge which member of a pair symbolized the larger reference. He found a strong tendency to consider the reference larger for the word that included a vowel nearer the *a* end of the scale.

In 1933 Newman further analyzed Sapir's data and discovered systematic relationship between the size judgments and such factors as the position of the tongue in forming the vowels, the frequencies of the principal acoustic formants, and the size of the oral cavity created in pronunciation. Newman also discovered the magnitude implications of English consonants and investigated the symbolic values of the vowels and consonants for the dimension "bright to dark."

Bentley and Varon (1933) used nonlinguistic words like those of Sapir and Newman together with some English words and standard nonsense syllables. Their subjects were simply asked to come up with a free associate for each item on a mixed list of such materials. The authors report no tendency to match reference magnitudes with nonlinguistic words in the manner that we should anticipate from the work of Sapir and Newman. From experimental variations Bentley and Varon learned that the reference value had to be forced out of the words by the suggestion of a scale of magnitude.

Bentley and Varon questioned the relevance of all of this work to the study of language. Both volume and brightness were known to be among the attributes of pure tones. Sapir and Newman might be said to have demonstrated that these same dimensions could be applied to complex vocal tones. Where in all this was there any justification for speaking of the "symbolic" value of "nonlinguistic words"? It had not been demonstrated that phonetic symbolism actually occurred in natural languages.

PHONETIC SYMBOLISM IN NATURAL LANGUAGES

In 1934 Tsuru wrote an unpublished paper called "Sound and Meaning,"[1] in which he described an experiment in phonetic symbolism. Tsuru compiled a list of thirty-six pairs of Japanese antonyms. His subjects were fifty-seven Harvard and Radcliffe undergraduates who spoke English as their native language and disclaimed any knowledge of Japanese.

Table 10–1. Percentages of Correct Translations in Three Studies

Author	Languages	N	% Correct
Tsuru	Japanese	57	69
Allport	Hungarian	68	56.6
Rich	Japanese	44	57.2*
Rich	Polish	44	64.8*

* Reported to be significantly larger than chance ($p < .005$).

Seated in a group, the subjects first saw a pair of Japanese words printed in Romish characters. The English equivalent pair was then written on the board, the order of the words within the pair being randomly related to the order within the Japanese pair. From the back of the room a native Japanese pronounced the words twice, reversing the order the second time. The subjects then attempted to match English–Japanese synonyms with one minute allowed for each pair. Table 10–1 indicates that they were able to average 69 per cent correct guesses.

Tsuru had demonstrated that someone who knows both English and Japanese can find Japanese words whose meanings will be correctly guessed in a single alternative situation by subjects who know English but not Japanese. Although

[1] The paper was written for a psychology course with Professor Gordon W. Allport, who has kindly made it available to us.

261

English and Japanese are believed to be historically unrelated, it would surely be possible to find some synonyms which sound alike. Tsuru's findings, then, could be consistent with the view that symbols are arbitrarily assigned in natural languages. If his subjects had learned in childhood to connect certain sounds in English with their arbitrary meanings they would be able to translate correctly Japanese words if these words were selected for their resemblance to the English. Tsuru's list does not appear to have been selected in this fashion, but the fact that he made his selection with full knowledge of both languages leaves this possibility uncontrolled. The work of Müller (1935) with words from Swahili and Bantu suffers from the same difficulty.

Gordon Allport made the necessary improvement in an unpublished experiment. He had a native speaker of Hungarian translate Tsuru's list into that language. This Finno-Ugric tongue is historically unrelated to either English or Japanese. Because the translator simply translated the list he was given, there was no opportunity to select words in the foreign language for their resemblance to English equivalents. The results appear in Table 10–1. Subjects performed somewhat less well than Tsuru's original group but were still above the chance level of fifty per cent.

In 1953 Susannah Rich, an undergraduate at Radcliffe College, wrote a senior honors thesis which bears in part on our problem. She used twenty-five pairs of words and had them translated into Japanese and Polish. Native speakers of the two languages recorded their pronunciations of the words. The subjects were forty-four Radcliffe girls. The results appear in Table 10–1 and again are above the level to be expected by chance.

Neither Tsuru nor Allport conducted a test for the significance of the departure from chance represented by their results. Rich reported the mean percentages correct for both Polish and Japanese to be significantly better than chance ($p \leq .005$). In general the results in Table 10–1 encourage the belief that there are significant traces of phonetic symbolism in natural languages.

THE EXPERIMENT

English antonyms were selected from the Thorndike-Lorge word list with two considerations in mind. *a*) The words should name sense experiences (e.g., warm–cool, heavy–light). *b*) The members of a pair should both fall in the frequency range of 100 or over per million. The final list of 21 pairs consisted of those on which the three authors could agree. We were all completely ignorant of the languages into which the list was to be translated—Chinese, Czech, and Hindi.

The English lists were presented for translation to native speakers or scholars of the particular languages.[1] None of the translators was aware of the purpose of the study. They were asked to render the list into the familiar foreign equivalents—preserving the opposition within a pair. They then recorded their pronunciation of the pairs with five seconds between words and ten seconds between pairs.

The subjects were eighty-six Harvard and Radcliffe students in an undergraduate laboratory in social psychology. They participated in sections of about twenty students each. Our subjects were told that they were to take part in a study of sound symbolism in which meanings of foreign words were to be guessed from the sounds. Ranged down one side of a page were pairs of English antonyms. On the other side appeared foreign language antonyms matched pair by pair with the English. Words within a pair were randomly arranged so that while subjects knew that a given English word translated into one or the other of two foreign words he could not tell from the arrangement which of the two it was. The subjects heard the words pronounced in the same order as they appeared on the sheet and were then allowed ten seconds in which to match the two English words with their foreign language equivalents. The languages were presented in five random orders. All subjects were asked to describe their previous experience with

---

[1] The Czech was translated by Rose Adamek McGee, the Chinese by Dr. Bernard Solomon of the Harvard-Yenching Institute, and the Hindi by Dr. Surenda K. Srivastava.

the three languages. One subject was disqualified by his knowledge of Chinese.

Preliminary analysis convinced us that the men and women did not show any significant differences in performance and consequently we combined their data. The results are presented in Table 10–2 in a form comparable to that used by earlier authors and summarized in Table 10–1. The mean percentages all depart significantly from chance. This calculation is made with reference to the binomial distribution. From these statistics we cannot tell whether all pairs on the list are judged with somewhat better than chance success or whether the average result is produced by combining a few words that are nearly always translated correctly with many that are at the chance level or below.

Table 10–2. Percentages of Correct Translations for Three Languages in Experimental Condition A

Language	No. of Ss.	% Correct	Significance of Departure from Chance
Chinese	86	58.9	.001
Czech	86	55.7	.001
Hindi	85	59.6	.001

The results have therefore been computed in a different fashion. The performance on each pair of words for each language has been separately determined. We can then ask concerning each item whether more subjects answered it correctly than would be expected by chance. These findings are summarized in Tables 10–3 and 10–4 as experimental condition A. On a given pair when there is agreement on 64 per cent of the judgments this result is significant at the .01 level. The great majority of the words in all three languages meet this criterion. It is clear that subjects shared a conception of the more appropriate meaning for most of the words presented. We are interested in knowing how often this conception was correct. There must be 64 per cent correct judgments to reach the .01 level of significance. There are at least nine such pairs in all languages. There are only half as many significant

Table 10–3. Percentage of Correct Translations for Each Pair in Three Languages for Experimental Conditions A and B

English	Chinese	% Correct A	% Correct B	Czech	% Correct A	% Correct B	Hindi	% Correct A	% Correct B
1. beautiful	meǐ	88*	70	krása	57	31	khubsurat	64*	50
ugly	ch'oǔ			ošklivost			badsurat		
2. blunt	tuǹ	78*	70	tupý	81*	83*	gothil	68*	83*
sharp	k'uài			špičatý			tez		
3. bright	liang	67*	90*	svetlý	64*	77	chamakdar	51	90*
dark	aǹ			tmavý			dhundhala		
4. coarse	ts'u	65*	70	hrubý	21†	44	mota	48	31
fine	hsi			drobný			achha		
5. down	hsià	10†	31	dolů	56	50	niche	75*	83*
up	shàng			nahoru			upar		
6. drunk	tsuì	66*	50	opilý	21†	70	nashemen	80*	77
sober	hsǐng			střízlivý			sanjida		
7. dry	kān	72*	70	suchý	44	50	sukha	42	44
wet	shih			mokrý			bhiga		
8. fast	k'uai	83*	83*	rychlý	87*	83*	tez	27†	57
slow	màn			pomalý			sust		
9. fat	feí	31†	57	tlustý	69*	77	mota	66*	57
thin	shoù			tenký			patala		
10. gold	chīn	57	57	zlato	19†	57	sona	42	64
iron	t'iēh			železo			loha		

(Table continues on following page)

265

Table 10–3. Percentage of Correct Translations for Each Pair in Three Languages for Experimental Conditions A and B

English	Chinese	% Correct A	% Correct B	Czech	% Correct A	% Correct B	Hindi	% Correct A	% Correct B
11. bad	huài	34†	64	zlý	62	57	kharab	64*	31
good	haǒ			hodný			achha		
12. happy	huān	38	50	radostný	57	64	khush	17†	38
sad	peī			smutný			ranjida		
13. hard	kāng	97*	83*	tvrdý	76*	96*	sakht	61	64
soft	joú			měkký			narm		
14. light	ch'ing	93*	90*	lehký	66*	77	halka	36†	57
heavy	chuǐg			těžký			wazani		
15. long	ch'áng	55	44	dlouhý	80*	70	lamba	93*	70
short	tuǎn			kratký			chhota		
16. many	tō	73*	57	mnoho	55	25	bahut	88*	90*
one	yī			jeden			ek		
17. strong	ch'iáng	37	64	silný	28†	64	mazbut	34†	31
weak	jò			slabý			kamzor		
18. sweet	t'ién	58	51	sladký	24†	25	mitha	88*	70
sour	suān			kyselý			khatta		
19. thunder	leí	23†	31	hrom	92*	96*	garaj	62	77
lightning	tieǹ			blesk			chamak		
20. warm	nǔan	73*	50	teplý	69*	77	garam	66*	77
cool	liáng			chladný			thanda		
21. wide	k'uān	37	90*	široký	43	57	chaura	76*	51
narrow	chaǐ			úzký			tang		

* Choices are correct with $p \leqq .01$. † Choices are incorrect with $p \leqq .01$.

results in the wrong direction. In other words our subjects' conceptions of the proper translation were right twice as often as they were wrong.

Table 10–4. Summary Data of Translations for 21 Pairs of Words in Three Languages in Experimental Conditions A and B

Language and Experimental Condition	No. of Subjects	Mean % Correct	No. of Pairs Significantly Correct	No. of Pairs Significantly Incorrect
Chinese				
A	86	58.9	11	4
B	16	61.9	5	0
Czech				
A	86	55.7	9	5
B	16	61.9	4	0
Hindi				
A	85	59.6	11	4
B	16	60.7	4	0

Table 10–5. Frequency Distribution of Percentages of Correct Translations for Three Languages in Experimental Condition A

	No. of Subjects		
% Correct	Chinese	Czech	Hindi
88			1
83	1	1	2
78	3	2	8
73	11	3	5
68	8	9	15
63	18	12	14
58	20	24	7
53	9	11	15
48	7	12	10
43	7	6	5
38	2	5	1
33		1	2

The foregoing analysis describes the performance on each pair of words but it does not tell us how the performances of individual subjects were distributed. Table 10–5 shows that most subjects correctly translated over half the words in a given list. There were 70 subjects for Chinese, 61 for Czech, and 67 for Hindi who had scores of 11 or better out of 21.

Allport's data have been subjected to the same kinds of analyses. Of his 36 pairs of Hungarian words 16 showed positive results significant at the .01 level; 53 of the 68 subjects correctly translated over half of the words.

Possible Causes of the Obtained Results

How are subjects able to arrive at so many correct translations? We suspect that the ability derives from a suggestive power in the phonetic sequences, but there are two other possibilities to be considered.

DIFFERENTIAL LENGTH OF WORDS WITHIN A PAIR. Zipf (1935) has demonstrated for samples of English, Plautine Latin, Peipingese Chinese, and several American Indian tongues that word frequency is related to word length, with the more common words tending to be shorter. It is possible that English words are correlated with their foreign language counterparts in both frequency and length. If this were so, a subject need only match the longer English word with the longer foreign language word in each pair to achieve better than chance results. As a first precaution against this possibility we equated our English words for frequency range in the Thorndike-Lorge list. This step does not equate members of all pairs in length. Examining the data we find no indications that performance is better when the words differ in length, and, furthermore, we find that performance with the Chinese language, where the translations are all monosyllables of almost exactly equivalent length, is superior to performance on Czech, where the words vary in length.

THE EXPRESSIVE QUALITY OF THE SPEAKER'S VOICE. Our translators did not know the purpose of the study but were aware of the meanings of the words they pronounced. How can we be sure that the correct translations of our subjects were not made possible by some expressive quality in the

recorded voices? May they not have introduced some sharp-
ness into their enunciation of "sharp," some haste into their
versions of "fast"? Since these are sensory words it would
be possible to adjust the quality of speech so as directly to
produce the sense quality in question.

To check this possibility we asked a control group of
subjects (experimental condition B) to match words without
the recorded pronunciation, using only the printed versions.
These suggest a roughly correct pronunciation to most native
speakers of English. The expressive quality of the voice is
eliminated since subjects do not know the meanings of the
words when they pronounce to themselves. The results for
condition B, which appear in Tables 10–3 and 10–4, show that
over-all performance in this control group was slightly more
successful than in the experimental group. Correlating performances on individual items for the two groups we obtain
an r of .59 for Chinese, .61 for Czech, and .55 for Hindi. All of
these are significant ($p \leq .02$), and it seems to be clear that the
words we have used have stable semantic implications which
are not a consequence of expressive, nonphonetic aspects of
pronunciation.

Interpretation of the Results

Since speech originated in prehistory, long before writing,
there can be no record of the act or acts of origination. Traditional speculation on this subject has been trivialized with
such titles as the "ding-dong theory" and the "bow-wow
theory." The stale whimsy of this language has helped to
make the subject distasteful. We shall avoid passing the
standard theories in review, but will make one distinction
among them. Some theories (especially Thorndike (1933))
suppose that symbols are arbitrarily assigned to their references. It is then only necessary to assume the random emission
of vocalization and some such learning principles as the
familiar "contiguity" and "reinforcement" to explain the
perpetuation and social diffusion of particular vocalizations.
Other theories assume that the earliest speech, like the earliest
writing (Gelb, 1952), was "representational." There are

269

three subvarieties of the representational position. The first two of these assume some kind of imitation. The onomatopoeia theory holds that vocal sound can suggest nonvocal sound. The gestural theory holds that motion and contour described by articulatory muscles can suggest motion and contour in the external world. Sir Richard Paget (1930) has contended that human communication began with such gestural imitation of the external world. The third theory holds that vocalization falling on the auditory sense will naturally arouse meanings associated with other modalities. Hornbostel wrote of the "unity of the senses." Students of synesthesia have claimed (Kouwer, 1949) that perception is not an act involving only a particular receptor but is an affair of the whole body. Of course hearing does not involve all parts of the organism in equal degree but reducing hearing to audition alone means ignoring essential components. We doubt that this third variety of representational vocalization should be assimilated to synesthesia for the reason that studies of synesthetic response have typically yielded large individual differences. We prefer to use Werner's (1948) term "physiognomic language" to name these universal, unlearned intersensory connections.

All of these speculations must be supplemented with a learning theory. They share, however, a belief that some sound-meaning connections begin with a little boost in habit strength that elevates them above the level of arbitrary connections. If languages all began by making use of these associations our data might be explained by the survival of some of these associations in modern languages.

The existence of onomatopoeia in modern, natural languages is widely accepted though it is considered to be far too infrequent to account for the origin of language. If we had selected our words for onomatopoeic possibilities no one would have been surprised at positive results. It would not be very interesting, for example, to demonstrate that subjects could distinguish the word for the cry of the rooster from the word for the cry of the cat in many languages. However, none of our words names an auditory experience and therefore onomatopoeia cannot account for our correct results. It is possible, however, that the origin of speech in gestural imitation and physiognomic language has left a residue of roughly translatable words in all languages and that we have tapped this residue in Chinese, Czech, and Hindi, while Allport tapped it in Hungarian, and Rich in Japanese and Polish.

The uniformity of performance among our subjects might alternatively be explained by the fact that they are all native speakers of English who naturally share a cultural conception of the sounds likely to express a given meaning. The fact that our subjects showed a significant amount of agreement in both incorrect as well as correct choices tends to substantiate this view. If the connections between linguistic sounds and meanings are arbitrary, however, the English speaker's cultural conception of phonetic symbolism should lead him to make correct translations of languages historically related to his native tongue but not to make correct translations of totally unrelated languages. Of the languages studied three are Indo-European (Czech, Hindi, and Polish) while three are not (Chinese, Japanese, and Hungarian). The Indo-European tongues should show a closer resemblance to English than the languages outside the family. However, there is no clear tendency favoring the Indo-European tongues. We are inclined to believe that most of our subjects did not usually translate an English word with the foreign word bearing the closer resemblance, but rather responded in terms of principles of phonetic symbolism imperfectly realized in all languages. The words *light* and *heavy*, for instance, translate into Chinese *ch'ing̅* and *chung̀*. As we might predict from the work of Sapir and Newman, 93 per cent of our subjects were correct on that pair.

Even if we assume a phonetic symbolism which is not a cultural acquisition, it does not necessarily follow that the presence of such symbolism in natural languages must be explained by the origin of speech in representational vocalization. Speech might have begun with the arbitrary association of sounds and meanings and then moved toward phonetic symbolism. A given speech form might have been aided in the struggle for survival if it chanced to be representational. Instead of assuming that speech has fallen away from a golden age of phonetic symbolism we may come to believe that, in the evolution of languages, speech forms have been selected for symbolism and that we are moving toward a golden millennium of physiognomic speech. Work is under way which we hope will decide between these interpretations.

SUMMARY

Three separate investigations, using three lists of English words and six foreign languages, have shown superior to chance agreement and accuracy in the translation of unfamiliar tongues. The agreement can be explained as the result of a "cultural conception" of the symbolic values attached to various phonetic combinations. This hypothesis does not explain the accuracy of translation. The accuracy can be explained by the assumption of some universal phonetic symbolism in which speech may have originated or toward which speech may be evolving. For the present we prefer to interpret our results as indicative of a primitive phonetic symbolism deriving from the origin of speech in some kind of imitative or physiognomic linkage of sounds and meanings. We forsake conservatism on this occasion for the excellent reason that the thesis proposed is so alien to most thinking in psycholinguistics that it needs to be brought forward strongly so that we may see that its unpopularity has not been deserved.

References

BENTLEY, M. and VARON, EDITH J. An accessory study of phonetic symbolism. *Amer. J. Psychol.*, 1933, **45,** 78–86.

GELB, I. J. *A study of writing.* Chicago: University of Chicago Press, 1952.

KOUWER, B. J. *Colors and their character.* The Hague: Nijhoff, 1949

MÜLLER, H. *Experimentelle Beiträge zur Analyse des Verhältnisses von Laut und Sinn.* Berlin: Müller & I. Kiepenheuer, 1935.

NEWMAN, S. S. Further experiments in phonetic symbolism. *Amer. J. Psychol.*, 1933, **45,** 53–75.

PAGET, R. *Human speech.* New York: Harcourt, Brace, 1930.

RICH, SUSANNAH. The perception of emotion. Unpublished honors thesis, Radcliffe College, 1953.

SAPIR, E. A study in phonetic symbolism. *J. exp. Psychol.*, 1929, **12,** 225–239.

THORNDIKE, E. L. The origin of language. *Science*, 1933, **77,** 173–175.

TSURU, S. Sound and meaning. Unpublished manuscript on file with Gordon W. Allport, Harvard University, 1934.

WERNER, H. *Comparative psychology of mental development.* Chicago: Follett, 1948.

ZIPF, G. K. *The psycho-biology of language.* Boston: Houghton Mifflin, 1935.

[11]

The "Tip of the Tongue" Phenomenon

This research may have been more fun than any other I have
done. That is partly because in the "tip of the tongue" state the
mind swims excitingly close to the surface. Everyone knows the
state—you cannot recall a word, even though you know it perfectly
well, and a kind of intensive search is set up in your brain, a
search that tosses up a succession of words which are not the one
sought but are quite tantalizingly close. It is like fumbling in a file
cabinet for a particular card when you know the approximate, but
not the exact, location. You come up with a fistful of cards—all
wrong but all obviously out of the right drawer. The general idea
of the experiment is that by examining the words that come to mind
when searching for one that does not we should be able to discover
the principles governing the classification system utilized in our
memory.

Since this paper was written, we have used the "tip of the
tongue" experiment as a regular exercise in the large introductory
course in Social Relations at Harvard. Data have been obtained
from nearly a thousand subjects and all the main effects reported
in the first paper have been fully confirmed. Other possible effects

This paper first appeared in the *Journal of Verbal Learning and Verbal
Behavior*, Vol. 5, No. 4 (August 1966), 325–337. David McNeill was co-
author. Reprinted by permission of the authors.

have been suggested by these data but never demonstrated at a significant level. For instance, one finds a certain number of errors of a kind that we call "sound-stuff" or "letter-stuff" errors. A subject trying to find the word *ambergris* thinks of *Seagram*. The usual sorts of resemblance that constitute the main effects of the experiment (short strings of identical letters at the beginning and ends of the words) are absent. Still there is a resemblance that can hardly be accidental. All of the letters of *Seagram* are contained in *ambergris*. The word found seems to utilize the same letter-stock or sound-stock as the word sought but without regard for order. This is a fascinating outcome because it corresponds with one kind of rather common reading mistake and, together with the reading mistakes, it suggests that order may be a feature of a word that is stored independently of letters.

The "tip of the tongue" experiment has also become for some of us a kind of parlor game. As you grow older and retrieval gets less efficient, the opportunities to play this game become richer. Sometimes the game turns up an effect that would be hard to demonstrate experimentally. One evening, a group was trying to recall the name of the well-known philosopher *Nelson Goodman*. Everyone knew the name but at first no one could recall it. In the end someone did. The names proposed during the search showed the usual main effects; for example, someone thought the first name might be *Nathan*. However, when we had finished and looked back over the record we found an unexpected effect. The names proposed by those present who were Jewish were all Jewish names; the names proposed by non-Jews were not all Jewish. What does that mean? It may mean that the Jews present had in their memories an ethnic tag "Jewish" on the lexical entry for Nelson Goodman, a tag missing from the memories of the non-Jews, and a tag that was accessible when the name was not.

In this paper an effort is made to invent a semi-mechanical model for the "tip of the tongue" phenomenon and that effort gave us particular pleasure. Psychologists find it exciting when a complex mental phenomenon—something intelligent and slippery—seems about to be captured by a mechanical model. We yearn to see the model succeed. But when, at the last minute, the phenomenon proves too much for the model and darts off on some uncaptureable tangent there is something in us that rejoices at the defeat.

WILLIAM JAMES wrote, in 1893: "Suppose we try to recall a forgotten name. The state of our consciousness is peculiar. There is a gap therein; but no mere gap. It is a gap that is intensely active. A sort of wraith of the name is in it, beckoning us in a given direction, making us at moments tingle with the sense of our closeness and then letting us sink back without the longed-for term. If wrong names are proposed to us, this singularly definite gap acts immediately so as to negate them. They do not fit into its mould. And the gap of one word does not feel like the gap of another, all empty of content as both might seem necessarily to be when described as gaps" (p. 251).

The "tip of the tongue" (TOT) state involves a failure to recall a word of which one has knowledge. The evidence of knowledge is either an eventually successful recall or else an act of recognition that occurs, without additional training, when recall has failed. The class of cases defined by the conjunction of knowledge and a failure of recall is a large one. The TOT state, which James described, seems to be a small subclass in which recall is felt to be imminent.

For several months we watched for TOT states in ourselves. Unable to recall the name of the street on which a relative lives, one of us thought of *Congress* and *Corinth* and *Concord* and then looked up the address and learned that it was *Cornish*. The words that had come to mind have certain properties in common with the word that had been sought (the "target word"): all four begin with *Co*; all are two-syllable words; all put the primary stress on the first syllable. After this experience we began putting direct questions to ourselves when we fell into the TOT state, questions as to the number of syllables in the target word, its initial letter, etc.

Woodworth (1934), before us, made a record of data for naturally occurring TOT states and Wenzl (1932, 1936) did the same for German words. Their results are similar to those we obtained and consistent with the following preliminary characterization. When complete recall of a word is not presently possible but is felt to be imminent, one can often correctly recall the general type of the word; *generic* recall may succeed when particular recall fails. There seem to be two common varieties of generic recall. (a) Sometimes a part of the target word is recalled, a letter or two, a syllable, or affix. Partial recall is necessarily also *generic* since the class of words defined by the possession of any *part* of the target word will include words other than the target. (b) Sometimes the abstract form of the target is recalled, perhaps the fact that it was a two-syllable sequence with the primary stress on the first syllable. The whole word is represented in *abstract form recall* but not on the letter-by-letter level that constitutes its identity. The recall of an abstract form is also necessarily *generic*, since any such form defines a class of words extending beyond the target.

Wenzl and Woodworth had worked with small collections of data for naturally occurring TOT states. These data were, for the most part, provided by the investigators; were collected in an unsystematic fashion; and were analyzed in an impressionistic non-quantitative way. It seemed to us that such data left the facts of generic recall in doubt. An occasional correspondence between a retrieved word and a target word with respect to number of syllables, stress pattern or initial letter is, after all, to be expected by chance. Several months of "self-observation and asking-our-friends" yielded fewer than a dozen good cases and we realized that an improved method of data collection was essential.

We thought it might pay to "prospect" for TOT states by reading to a subject definitions of uncommon English words and asking him to supply the words. The procedure was given a preliminary test with nine subjects who were individually interviewed for 2 hrs each.[1] In 57 instances a subject was, in fact, "seized" by a TOT state. The signs of it were unmistakable; he would appear to be in a mild torment, something like the brink of a sneeze, and if he found the word his relief was considerable. While searching for the target a subject told us all the words that came to his mind. He volunteered the information that some of them resembled the target in sound but not in meaning; others he was sure were similar in meaning but not in sound. The experimenter intruded on a subject's agony with two questions: (a) How many syllables has the

[1] We wish to thank Mr. Charles Hollen for doing the pretest interviews.

target word? (b) What is its first letter? Answers to the first question were correct in 47 per cent of all cases and answers to the second question were correct in 51 per cent of the cases. These outcomes encouraged us to believe that generic recall was real and to devise a group procedure that would further speed up the rate of data collection.

METHOD

Subjects

Fifty-six Harvard and Radcliffe undergraduates participated in one of three evening sessions; each session was 2 hrs long. The subjects were volunteers from a large General Education Course and were paid for their time.

WORD LIST. The list consisted of 49 words which, according to the Thorndike-Lorge *Word Book* (1952) occur at least once per four million words but not so often as once per one million words. The level is suggested by these examples: *apse*, *nepotism*, *cloaca*, *ambergris*, and *sampan*. We thought the words used were likely to be in the passive or recognition vocabularies of our subjects but not in their active recall vocabularies. There were 6 words of 1 syllable; 19 of 2 syllables; 20 of 3 syllables; 4 of 4 syllables. For each word we used a definition from *The American College Dictionary* (Barnhart, 1948) edited so as to contain no words that closely resembled the one being defined.

RESPONSE SHEET. The response sheet was laid off in vertical columns headed as follows:
    Intended word (+ *One I was thinking of*).
    (− *Not*).
    Number of syllables (1–5).
    Initial letter.
    Words of similar sound. (1. *Closest in sound*)
                     (2. *Middle*)
                     (3. *Farthest in Sound*)

Words of similar meaning.
Words you had in mind if not intended word.

Procedure

We instructed subjects to the following effect.

In this experiment we are concerned with that state of mind in which a person is unable to think of a word that he is certain he knows, the state of mind in which a word seems to be on the tip of one's tongue. Our technique for precipitating such states is, in general, to read definitions of uncommon words and ask the subject to recall the word.

(1) We will first read the definition of a low-frequency word.

(2) If you should happen to know the word at once, or think you do, or, if you should simply not know it, then there is nothing further for you to do at the moment. Just wait.

(3) If you are unable to think of the word but feel sure that you know it and that it is on the verge of coming back to you then you are in a TOT state and should begin at once to fill in the columns of the response sheet.

(4) After reading each definition we will ask whether anyone is in the TOT state. Anyone who is in that state should raise his hand. The rest of us will then wait until those in the TOT state have written on the answer sheet all the information they are able to provide.

(5) When everyone who has been in the TOT state has signalled us to proceed, we will read the target word. At this time, everyone is to write the word in the leftmost column of the response sheet. These of you who have known the word since first its definition was read are asked not to write it until this point. Those of you who simply did not know the word or who had thought of a different word will write now the word we read. For those of you who have been in the TOT state two eventualities are possible. The word read may strike you as definitely the word you have been seeking. In that case please write ' + ' after the word, as the instructions at the head of the column direct. The other possibility is that you will not be sure whether the word read is the one you have been seeking or, indeed, you may be sure that it is not. In this case you

are asked to write the sign ' − ' after the word. Sometimes when the word read out is not the one you have been seeking your actual target may come to mind. In this case, in addition to the minus sign in the leftmost column, please write the actual target word in the right-most column.

(6) Now we come to the column entries themselves. The first two entries, the guess as to the number of syllables and the initial letter, are required. The remaining entries should be filled out if possible. When you are in a TOT state, words that are related to the target word do almost always come to mind. List them as they come, but separate words which you think resemble the target in sound from words which you think resemble the target in meaning.

(7) When you have finished all your entries, but before you signal us to read the intended target word, look again at the words you have listed as 'Words of similar sound.' If possible, rank these, as the instructions at the head of the column direct, in terms of the degree of their seeming resemblance to the target. This must be done without knowledge of what the target actually is.

(8) The search procedure of a person in the TOT state will sometimes serve to retrieve the missing word before he has finished filling in the columns and before we read out the word. When this happens please mark the place where it happens with the words "Got it" and *do not provide any more data.*

RESULTS

Classes of Data

There were 360 instances, across all words and all subjects, in which a TOT state was signalled. Of this total, 233 were positive TOTs. A positive TOT is one for which the target word is known and, consequently, one for which the data obtained can be scored as accurate or inaccurate. In those cases where the target was not the word intended but some other word which subjects finally recalled and wrote in the rightmost column his data were checked against that word, his effective target. A negative TOT is one for which the subject judged the word read out not to have been his target and, in addition, one in which the subject proved unable to recall his own functional target.

The data provided by the subject while he searched for the target word are of two kinds: explicit guesses as to the number of syllables in the target and the initial letter of the target; words that came to mind while he searched for the target. The words that came to mind were classified by the subject into 224 words similar in sound to the target (hereafter called "SS" words) and 95 words similar in meaning to the target (hereafter called "SM" words). The subject's information about the number of syllables in, and the initial letter of the target may be inferred from correspondences between the target and his SS words as well as directly discovered from his explicit guesses. For his knowledge of the stress pattern of the target and of letters in the target, other than the initial letter, we must rely on the SS words alone since explicit guesses were not required.

To convey a sense of the SS and SM words we offer the following examples. When the target was *sampan* the SS words (not all of them real words) included: *Saipan*, *Siam*, *Cheyenne*, *sarong*, *sanching*, and *sympoon*. The SM words were: *barge*, *houseboat*, and *junk*. When the target was *caduceus* the SS words included: *Casadesus*, *Aeschelus*, *cephalus*, and *leucosis*. The SM words were: *fasces*, *Hippocrates lictor*, and *snake*. The spelling in all cases is the subject's own.

We will, in this report, use the SM words to provide baseline data against which to evaluate the accuracy of the explicit guesses and of the SS words. The SM words are words produced under the spell of the positive TOT state but judged by the subject to resemble the target in meaning rather than sound. We are quite sure that the SM words are somewhat more like the target than would be a collection of words produced by subjects with no knowledge of the target. However, the SM words make a better comparative baseline than any other data we collected.

General Problems of Analysis

The data present problems of analysis that are not common in psychology. To begin with, the words of the list did not reliably precipitate TOT states. Of the original 49 words, all but *zither* succeeded at least once; the range was from one success to nine. The subjects made actual targets of 51 words not on the original list and all but five of these were pursued by one subject only. Clearly none of the 100 words came even close to precipitating a TOT state in all 56 subjects. Furthermore, the subjects varied in their susceptibility to TOT states. There were nine who experienced none at all in a 2-hr period; the largest number experienced in such a period by one subject was eight. In our data, then, the entries for one word will not usually involve the same subjects or even the same number of subjects as the entries for another word. The entries for one subject need not involve the same words or even the same number of words as the entries for another subject. Consequently for the tests we shall want to make there are no significance tests that we can be sure are appropriate.

In statistical theory our problem is called the "fragmentary data problem."[1] The best thing to do with fragmentary data is to report them very fully and analyze them in several different ways. Our detailed knowledge of these data suggests that the problems are not serious for, while there is some variation in the pull of words and the susceptibility of subjects there is not much variation in the quality of the data. The character of the material recalled is much the same from word to word and subject to subject.

Number of Syllables

As the main item of evidence that the subject in a TOT state can recall with significant success the number of syllables in a target word he has not yet found we offer Table 11–1. The entries on the diagonal are instances in which guesses were

---

[1] We wish to thank Professor Frederick Mosteller for discussing the fragmentary data problem with us.

correct. The order of the means of the explicit guesses is the same as the order of the actual numbers of syllables in the target words. The rank order correlation between the two is 1.0 and such a correlation is significant with a $p < .001$ (one-tailed) even when only five items are correlated. The modes of the guesses correspond exactly with the actual numbers of syllables, for the values one through three; for words of four and five syllables the modes continue to be three.

When all TOTs are combined, the contributions to the total effects of individual subjects and of individual words are unequal. We have made an analysis in which each word counts but once. This was accomplished by calculating the mean of the guesses made by all subjects for whom a particular word precipitated a TOT state and taking that mean as the score for that word. The new means calculated with all words equally weighted were, in order: 1.62; 2.30; 2.80; 3.33; and 3.50. These values are close to those of Table 11–1 and *rho* with the actual numbers of syllables continues to be 1.0.

Table 11–1. Actual Numbers of Syllables and Guessed Numbers for All TOTs in the Main Experiment

| | | Guessed Numbers | | | | | | |
		1	2	3	4	5	No Guess	Mode	Mean
Actual Numbers	1	9	7	1	0	0	0	1	1.53
	2	2	55	22	2	1	5	2	2.33
	3	3	19	61	10	1	5	3	2.86
	4	0	2	12	6	2	3	3	3.36
	5	0	0	3	0	1	1	3	3.50

We also made an analysis in which each subject counts but once. This was done by calculating the mean of a subject's guesses for all words of one syllable, the mean for all words of two syllables, etc. In comparing the means of guesses for words of different length one can only use those subjects who made at least one guess for each actual length to be compared. In the present data only words of two syllables and three syllables precipitated enough TOTs to yield a substantial number of such matched scores. There were 21 subjects who made guesses for both two-syllable and three-syllable words. The simplest way to evaluate the significance of the differences in these guesses is with the Sign Test. In only 6 of 21 matched scores was the mean guess for words of two syllables larger than the mean for words of three syllables. The difference is significant with a $p = .039$ (one-tailed). For actual words that were only one syllable apart in length, subjects were able to make a significant distinction in the correct direction when the words themselves could not be called to mind.

The 224 SS words and the 95 SM words provide supporting evidence. Words of similar sound (SS) had the same number of syllables as the target in 48% of all cases. This value is close to the 57% that were correct for explicit guesses in the main experiment and still closer to the 47% correct already reported for the pretest. The SM words provide a clear contrast; only 20% matched the number of syllables in the target. We conclude that the subject in a positive TOT state has a significant ability to recall correctly the number of syllables in the word he is trying to retrieve.

In Table 11–1 it can be seen that the modes of guesses exactly correspond with the actual numbers of syllables in target words for the values one through three. For still longer target words (four and five syllables) the means of guesses continue to rise but the modes stay at the value three. Words of more than three syllables are rare in English and the generic entry for such words may be the same as for words of three syllables; something like "three or more" may be used for all long words.

Initial Letter

Over all positive TOTs, the initial letter of the word the subject was seeking was correctly guessed 57% of the time. The pretest result was 51% correct. The results from the main experiment were analyzed with each word counting just once by entering a word's score as "correct" whenever the most common guess or the only guess was in fact correct; 62% of words were, by this reckoning, correctly guessed. The SS words had initial letters matching the initial letters of the target words in 49% of all cases. We do not know the chance level of success for this performance but with 26 letters and many words that began with uncommon letters the level must be low. Probably the results for the SM words are better than chance and yet the outcome for these words was only 8% matches.

We did an analysis of the SS and SM words, with each subject counting just once. There were 26 subjects who had at least one such word. For each subject we calculated the proportion of SS words matching the target in initial letter and the same proportion for SM words. For 21 subjects the proportions were not tied and in all but 3 cases the larger value was that of the SS words. The difference is significant by Sign Test with $p = .001$ (one-tailed).

The evidence for significantly accurate generic recall of initial letters is even stronger than for syllables. The absolute levels of success are similar but the chance baseline must be much lower for letters than for syllables because the possibilities are more numerous.

Syllabic Stress

We did not ask subjects to guess the stress pattern of the target word but the SS words provide relevant data. The test was limited to the syllabic location of the primary or heaviest stress for which *The American College Dictionary* was our authority. The number of SS words that could be used was limited by three considerations. (a) Words of one syllable had to be excluded because there was no possibility of variation. (b) Stress locations could only be matched if the SS word had the same number of syllables as the target, and so only such matching words could be used. (c) Invented words and foreign words could not be used because they do not appear in the dictionary. Only 49 SS words remained.

As it happened all of the target words involved (whatever their length) placed the primary stress on either the first or the second syllable. It was possible, therefore, to make a 2×2 table for the 49 pairs of target and SS words which would reveal the correspondences and noncorrespondences. As can be seen in Table 11–2 the SS words tended to stress the same syllable as the target words. The χ^2 for this table is 10.96 and that value is significant with $p < .001$. However, the data do not meet the independence requirement, so we cannot be sure

Table 11–2. Syllables Receiving Primary Stress in Target Words and SS Words

		Target Words	
		1st Syllable	2nd Syllable
SS Words	1st Syllable	25	6
	2nd Syllable	6	12

that the matching tendency is significant. There were not enough data to permit any other analyses, and so we are left suspecting that the subject in a TOT state has knowledge of the stress pattern of the target, but we are not sure of it.

Letters in Various Positions

We did not require explicit guesses for letters in positions other than the first, but the SS words provide relevant data. The test was limited to the following positions: first, second, third, third-last, second-last, and last. A target word must have at least six letters in order to provide data on the six positions; it might have any number of letters larger than six and still provide data for the six (relatively defined) positions. Accordingly we included the data for all target words having six or more letters.

Figure 11–1 displays the percentages of letters in each of six positions of SS words which matched the letters in the same positions of the corresponding targets. For comparison purposes these data are also provided for SM words. The SS curve is at all points above the SM curve; the two are closest together at the third-last position. The values for the last three positions of the SS curve quite closely match the values for the first three positions. The values for the last three positions of the SM curve, on the other hand, are well above the values for the first three positions. Consequently the *relative* superiority of the SS curve is greater in the first three positions.

The letter-position data were also analyzed in such a way as to count each target word just once, assigning each position in the target a single score representing the proportion of matches across all subjects for that position in that word.

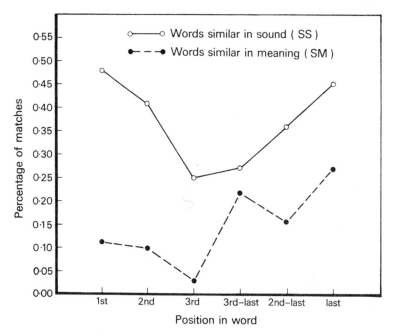

Figure 11–1. Percentages of Letter Matches between Target Words and SS Words for Six Serial Positions.

The order of the SS and SM points is preserved in this finer analysis. We did Sign Tests comparing the SS and SM values for each of the six positions. As Fig. 11–1 would suggest the SS values for the first three positions all exceeded the SM values with p's less than .01 (one-tailed). The SS values for the final two positions exceeded the SM values with p's less than .05 (one-tailed). The SS values for the third-last position were greater than the SM values but not significantly so.

The cause of the upswing in the final three positions of the SM curve may be some difference in the distribution of information in early and late positions of English words. Probably there is less variety in the later positions. In any case the fact that the SS curve lies above the SM curve for the last three positions indicates that the subject in a TOT state has knowledge of the target in addition to his knowledge of English word structure.

Chunking of Suffixes

The request to the subject that he guess the initial letter of the target occasionally elicited a response of more than one letter; e.g., *ex* in the case of *extort* and *con* in the case of *convene*. This result suggested that some letter (or phoneme) sequences are stored as single entries having been "chunked" by long experience. We made only one test for chunking and that involved three-letter suffixes.

It did not often happen that a subject produced an SS word that matched the target with respect to all of its three last letters. The question asked of the data was whether such three-letter matches occurred more often when the letters constituted an English suffix than when they did not. In order to determine which of the target words terminated in such a suffix, we entered *The American College Dictionary* with final trigrams. If there was an entry describing a suffix appropriate to the grammatical and semantic properties of the target we considered the trigram to be a suffix. There were 20 words that terminated in a suffix, including *fawning, unctuous*, and *philatelist*.

Of 93 SS words produced in response to a target terminating in a suffix, 30 matched the target in their final three letters. Of 130 SS words supplied in response to a target that did not terminate in a suffix only 5 matched the target in their final three letters. The data were also analyzed in a way that counts each subject just once and uses only subjects who produced SS words in response to both kinds of target. A Sign Test was made of the difference between matches of suffixes and matches of endings that were not suffixes; the former were more common with $p = .059$ (one-tailed). A comparable Sign Test for SM words was very far from significance. We conclude that suffix-chunking probably plays a role in generic recall.

Proximity to the Target and Quality of Information

There were three varieties of positive TOT states: (1) Cases in which the subject *recognized* the word read by the experimenter as the word he had been seeking; (2) Cases in which the subject *recalled* the intended word before it was read out; (3) Cases in which the subject *recalled* the word he had been seeking before the experimenter read the intended word and the recalled word was not the same as the word read. Since the subject in a TOT state of either type 2 or type 3 reached the target before the intended word was read and the subject in a TOT state of type 1 did not, the TOTs of the second and third types may be considered "nearer" the target than TOTs of the first type. We have no basis for ordering types 2 and 3 relative to one another. We predicted that subjects in the two kinds of TOT state that ended in recall (types 2 and 3) would produce more accurate information about the target than subjects in the TOT state that ended in recognition (type 1).

The prediction was tested on the explicit guesses of initial letters since these were the most complete and sensitive data. There were 138 guesses from subjects in a type 1 state and 58 of these, or 42%, were correct. There were 36 guesses from subjects in a type 2 state and, of these, 20 or 56%, were correct. There were 59 guesses from subjects in a type 3 state and of these 39, or 66%, were correct. We also analyzed the results in such a way as to count each word only once. The percentages correct were: for type 1, 50%; type 2, 62%; type 3, 63%. Finally, we performed an analysis counting each subject just once but averaging together type 2 and type 3 results in order to bring a maximum number of subjects into the comparison. The combining action is justified since both type 2 and type 3 were states ending in recall. A Sign Test of the differences showed that guesses were more accurate in the states that ended in recall than in the states that ended in recognition; one-tailed $p < .01$. Supplementary analyses with SS and SM words confirmed these results. We conclude that when a subject is nearer his target his generic recall is more accurate than when he is farther from the target.

Special interest attaches to the results from type 2 TOTs. In the method of our experiment there is nothing to guarantee that when the subject said he recognized a word he had really done so. Perhaps when the experimenter read out a word the subject could not help thinking that that was the word he had in mind. We ourselves do not believe anything of the sort happened. The single fact that most subjects claimed fewer than five positive TOT's in a 2-hr period argues against any such effect. Still it is reassuring to have the 36 type 2 cases in which the subject recalled the intended word *before* it was read. The fact that 50% of the guesses of initial letters made in type 2 states were correct is hard-core evidence of generic recall. It may be worth adding that 65% of the guesses of the number of syllables for type 2 cases were correct.

Judgments of the Proximity of SS Words

The several comparisons we have made of SS and SM words demonstrate that when recall is imminent a subject can distinguish among the words that come to mind those that resemble the target in form from those that do not resemble the target in form. There is a second kind of evidence which shows that a subject can tell when he is getting close (or "warm").

In 15 instances subjects rated two or more SS words for comparative similarity to the target. Our analysis contrasts those rated "most similar" (1) with those rated next most similar (2). Since there were very few words rated (3) we attempted no analysis of them. Similarity points were given for all the features of a word that have now been demonstrated to play a part in generic recall—with the single exception of stress. Stress had to be disregarded because some of the words were invented and their stress patterns were unknown.

The problem was to compare pairs of SS words, rated 1 and 2, for overall similarity to the target. We determined whether each member matched the target in number of syllables. If one did and the other did not, then a single similarity point was assigned the word that matched. For each word, we counted, beginning with the initial letter, the number of consecutive letters in common with the target. The word having the longer sequence that matched the target earned one similarity point. An exactly comparable procedure was followed for sequences starting from the final letter. In sum, each word in a pair could receive from zero to three similarity points.

We made Sign Tests comparing the total scores for words rated most like the target (1) and words rated next most like the target (2). This test was only slighly inappropriate since only two target words occurred twice in the set of 15 and only one subject repeated in the set. Ten of 12 differences were in the predicted direction and the one-tailed $p = .019$. It is of some interest that similarity points awarded on the basis of letters in the middle of the words did not even go in the right direction. Figure 11–1 has already indicated that they also do not figure in subjects' judgments of the comparative similarity to the target of pairs of SS words. Our conclusion is that a subject at a given distance from the target can accurately judge which of two words that come to mind is more like the target and that he does so in terms of the features of words that appear in generic recall.

Conclusions

When complete recall of a word has not occurred but is felt to be imminent there is likely to be accurate generic recall. Generic recall of the *abstract form* variety is evidenced by the subject's knowledge of the number of syllables in the target and of the location of the primary stress. Generic recall of the *partial* variety is evidenced by the subject's knowledge of letters in the target word. This knowledge shows a bowed serial-position effect since it is better for the ends of a word than for the middle and somewhat better for beginning positions than for final positions. The accuracy of generic recall is greater when the subject is near the target (complete recall is imminent) than when the subject is far from the target. A person experiencing generic recall is able to judge the relative similarity to the target of words that occur to him and these judgments are based on the features of words that figure in partial and abstract form recall.

DISCUSSION

The facts of generic recall are relevant to theories of speech perception, reading, the understanding of sentences, and the organization of memory. We have not worked out all the implications. In this section we first attempt a model of the TOT process and then try to account for the existence of generic memory.

A Model of the Process

Let us suppose (with Katz and Fodor, 1963, and many others) that our long-term memory for words and definitions is organized into the functional equivalent of a dictionary. In real dictionaries, those that are books, entries are ordered alphabetically and bound in place. Such an arrangement is too simple and too inflexible to serve as a model for a mental dictionary. We will suppose that words are entered on keysort cards instead of pages and that the cards are punched for various features of the words entered. With real cards, paper ones, it is possible to retrieve from the total deck any subset punched for a common feature by putting a metal rod through the proper hole. We will suppose that there is in the mind some speedier equivalent of this retrieval technique.

The model will be described in terms of a single example. When the target word was *sextant*, subjects heard the definition: "A navigational instrument used in measuring angular distances, especially the altitude of sun, moon and stars at sea." This definition precipitated a TOT state in 9 subjects of the total 56. The SM words included: *astrolabe, compass, dividers* and *protractor*. The SS words included: *secant, sextet*, and *sexton*.

The problem begins with a definition rather than a word and so the subject must enter his dictionary backwards, or in a way that would be backwards and quite impossible for the dictionary that is a book. It is not impossible with keysort cards, providing we suppose that the cards are punched for some set of semantic features. Perhaps these are the semantic "markers" that Katz and Fodor (1963) postulate in their account of the comprehension of sentences. We will imagine that it is somehow possible to extract from the definition a set of markers and that these are, in the present case: "navigation, instrument, having to do with geometry." Metal rods thrust into the holes for each of these features might fish up such a collection of entries as: *astrolabe*, *compass*, *dividers*, and *protractor*. This first retrieval, which is in response to the definition, must be semantically based and it will not, therefore, account for the appearance of such SS words as *sextet* and *sexton*.

There are four major kinds of outcome of the first retrieval and these outcomes correspond with the four main things that happen to subjects in the TOT experiment. We will assume that a definition of each word retrieved is entered on its card and that it is possible to check the input definition against those on the cards. The first possible outcome is that *sextant* is retrieved along with *compass* and *astrolabe* and the others and that the definitions are specific enough so that the one entered for *sextant* registers as matching the input and all the others as not matching. This is the case of correct recall; the subject has found a word that matches the definition and it is the intended word. The second possibility is that *sextant* is not among the words retrieved and, in addition, the definitions entered for those retrieved are so imprecise that one of them (the definition for *compass*, for example) registers as matching the input. In this case the subject thinks he has found the target though he really has not. The third possibility is that *sextant* is not among the words retrieved, but the definitions entered for those retrieved are specific enough so that none of them will register a match with the input. In this case, the subject does not know the word and realizes the fact. The above three outcomes are the common ones and none of them represents a TOT state.

In the TOT case the first retrieval must include a card with the definition of *sextant* entered on it but with the word itself incompletely entered. The card might, for instance, have the following information about the word: two-syllables, initial s, final t. The entry would be a punchcard equivalent of S__ __T. Perhaps an incomplete entry of this sort is James's "singularly definite gap" and the basis for generic recall.

The subject with a correct definition, matching the input, and an incomplete word entry will know that he knows the word, will feel that he almost has it, that it is on the tip of his tongue. If he is asked to guess the number of syllables and the initial letter he should, in the case we have imagined, be able to do so. He should also be able to produce SS words. The features that appear in the incomplete entry (two-syllables, initial s, and final t) can be used as the basis for a second retrieval. The subset of cards defined by the intersection of all three features would include cards for *secant* and *sextet*. If one feature were not used then *sexton* would be added to the set.

Which of the facts about the TOT states can now be accounted for? We know that subjects were able, when they had not recalled a target, to distinguish between words resembling the target in sound (SS words) and words resembling the target in meaning only (SM words). The basis for this distinction in the model would seem to be the distinction between the first and second retrievals. Membership in the first subset retrieved defines SM words and membership in the second subset defines SS words.

We know that when a subject had produced several SS words but had not recalled the target he could sometimes accurately rank-order the SS words for similarity to the target. The model offers an account of this ranking performance. If the incomplete entry for *sextant* includes three features of the word then SS words having only one or two of these features (e.g., *sexton*) should be judged less similar to the target than SS words having all three of them (e.g., *secant*).

When an SS word has all of the features of the incomplete entry (as do *secant* and *sextet* in our example) what prevents its being mistaken for the target? Why did not the subject who produced *sextet* think that the word was "right"? Because of the definitions. The forms meet all the requirements of the incomplete entry but the definitions do not match.

The TOT state often ended in recognition; i.e., the subject failed to recall the word but when the experimenter read out *sextant* the subject recognized it as the word he had been seeking. The model accounts for this outcome as follows. Suppose that there is only the incomplete entry S_ _T in memory, plus the definition. The experimenter now says (in effect) that there exists a word *sextant* which has the definition in question The word *sextant* then satisfies all the data points available to the subject; it has the right number of syllables, the right initial letter, the right final letter, and it is said to have the right definition. The result is recognition.

The proposed account has some testable implications. Suppose that the experimenter were to read out, when recall failed, not the correct word *sextant* but an invented word like *sekrant* or *saktint* which satisfies the incomplete entry as well as does *sextant* itself. If the subject had nothing but the incomplete entry and the experimenter's testimony to guide him then he should "recognize" the invented words just as he recognizes *sextant*.

The account we have given does not accord with intuition. Our intuitive notion of recognition is that the features which could not be recalled were actually in storage but less accessible than the features that were recalled. To stay with our example, intuition suggests that the features of *sextant* that could not be recalled, the letters between the first and the last, were entered on the card but were less "legible" than the recalled features. We might imagine them printed in small letters and faintly. When, however, the experimenter reads out the word *sextant*, then the subject can make out the less legible parts of his entry and, since the total entry matches the experimenter's word, the subject recognizes it. This sort of recognition should be "tighter" than the one described previously. *Sekrant* and *saktint* would be rejected.

We did not try the effect of invented words and we do not know how they would have been received but among the outcomes of the actual experiment there is one that strongly favors the faint-entry theory. Subjects in a TOT state, after all, sometimes recalled the target word without any prompting. The incomplete entry theory does not admit of such a possibility. If we suppose that the entry is not S___T but something more like S*ex tan*T (with the italicized lower-case letters representing the faint-entry section) we must still explain how it happens that the faintly entered, and at first inaccessible, middle letters are made accessible in the case of recall.

Perhaps it works something like this. The features that are first recalled operate as we have suggested, to retrieve a set of SS words. Whenever an SS word (such as *secant*) includes middle letters that are matched in the faintly entered section of the target then those faintly entered letters become accessible. The match brings out the missing parts the way heat brings out anything written in lemon juice. In other words, when *secant* is retrieved the target entry grows from S*ex tan*T to SE*x t*ANT. The retrieval of *sextet* brings out the remaining letters and the subject recalls the complete word—*sextant*.

It is now possible to explain the one as yet unexplained outcome of the TOT experiment. Subjects whose state ended in recall had, before they found the target, more correct information about it than did subjects whose state ended in recognition. More correct information means fewer features to be brought out by duplication in SS words and so should mean a greater likelihood that all essential features will be brought out in a short period of time.

All of the above assumes that each word is entered in memory just once, on a single card. There is another possibility. Suppose that there are entries for *sextant* on several different cards. They might all be incomplete, but at different points, or some might be incomplete and one or more of them complete. The several cards would be punched for different semantic markers and perhaps for different associations so that the entry recovered would vary with the rule of retrieval. With this conception we do not require the notion of faint entry. The difference between features commonly recalled, such as the first and last letters, and features that are recalled with difficulty or perhaps only recognized, can be rendered in another way. The more accessible features are entered on more cards or else the cards on which they appear are punched for more markers; in effect, they are wired into a more extended associative net.

The Reason for Generic Recall

In adult minds words are stored in both visual and auditory terms and between the two there are complicated rules of translation. Generic recall involves letters (or phonemes), affixes, syllables, and stress location. In this section we will discuss only letters (legible forms) and will attempt to explain a single effect—the serial position effect in the recall of letters. It is not clear how far the explanation can be extended.

In brief overview this is the argument. The design of the English language is such that one word is usually distinguished from all others in a more-than-minimal way, i.e., by more than a single letter in a single position. It is consequently *possible* to recognize words when one has not stored the complete letter sequence. The evidence is that we do not store the complete sequence if we do not have to. We begin by attending chiefly to initial and final letters and storing these. The order of attention and of storage favors the ends of words because the ends carry more information than the middles. An incomplete entry will serve for recognition, but if words are to be produced (or recalled) they must be stored in full. For most words, then, it is eventually necessary to attend to the middle letters. Since end letters have been attended to from the first they should always be more clearly entered or more elaborately connected than middle letters. When recall is required, of words that are not very familiar to the subject, as it was in our experiment, the end letters should often be accessible when the middle are not.

In building pronounceable sequences the English language, like all other languages, utilizes only a small fraction of its combinatorial possibilities (Hockett, 1958). If a language used all possible sequences of phonemes (or letters) its words could be shorter, but they would be much more vulnerable to misconstruction. A change of any single letter would result in reception of a different word. As matters are actually arranged most changes result in no word at all; for example: *textant*, *sixtant*, *sektant*. Our words are highly redundant and fairly indestructible.

Underwood (1963) has made a distinction for the learning of nonsense syllables between the "nominal" stimulus which is the syllable presented and the "functional" stimulus which is the set of characteristics of the syllable actually used to cue the response. Underwood reviews evidence showing that college students learning paired-associates do not learn any more of a stimulus trigram than they have to. If, for instance, each of a set of stimulus trigrams has a different initial letter, then subjects are not likely to learn letters other than the first, since they do not need them.

Feigenbaum (1963) has written a computer program (EPAM) which simulates the selective-attention aspect of verbal learning as well as many other aspects. ". . . EPAM has a *noticing order for letters of syllables*, which prescribes at any moment a letter-scanning sequence for the matching process. Because it is observed that subjects generally consider end letters before middle letters, the noticing order is initialized as follows: first letter, third letter, second letter" (p. 304). We believe that the differential recall of letters in various positions, revealed in Fig. 11–1 of this paper, is to be explained by the operation in the perception of real words of a rule very much like Feigenbaum's.

Feigenbaum's EPAM is so written as to make it possible for the noticing rule to be changed by experience. If the middle position were consistently the position that differentiated syllables, the computer would learn to look there first. We suggest that the human tendency to look first at the beginning of a word, then at the end and finally the middle has "grown" in response to the distribution of information in words. Miller and Friedman (1957) asked English speakers to guess letters for various open positions in segments of English text that were 5, 7, or 11 characters long. The percentages of correct first guesses show a very clear serial position effect for segments of all three lengths. Success was lowest in the early positions, next lowest in the final positions, and at a maximum in the middle positions. Therefore, information was greatest at the start of a word, next greatest at the end, and least in the middle. Attention needs to be turned where information is, to the parts of the word that cannot be guessed. The Miller and Friedman segments did not necessarily break at word boundaries but their discovery that the middle positions of continuous text are more easily guessed than the ends applies to words.

Is there any evidence that speakers of English do attend first to the ends of English words? There is no evidence that the eye fixations of adult readers consistently favor particular parts of words (Woodworth and Schlosberg, 1954). However, it is not eye fixation that we have in mind. A considerable stretch of text can be taken in from a single fixation point. We are suggesting that there is selection within this stretch, selection accomplished centrally; perhaps by a mechanism like Broadbent's (1958) "biased filter."

Bruner and O'Dowd (1958) studied word perception with tachistoscopic exposures too brief to permit more than one fixation. In each word presented there was a single reversal of two letters and the subject knew this. His task was to identify the *actual* English word responding as quickly as possible. When the *actual* word was AVIATION, subjects were presented with one of the following: VAIATION, AVITAION, AVIATINO. Identification of the actual word as AVIATION was best when the subject saw AVITAION, next best when he saw AVIATINO, and most difficult when he saw VAIATION. In general, a reversal of the two initial letters made identification most difficult, reversal of the last two letters made it somewhat less difficult, reversal in the middle made least difficulty. This is what should happen if words are first scanned initially, then finally, then medially. But the scanning cannot be a matter of eye movements; it must be more central.

Selective attention to the ends of words should lead to the entry of these parts into the mental dictionary, in advance of the middle parts. However, we ordinarily need to know more than the ends of words. Underwood has pointed out (1963), in connection with paired-associate learning, that while partial knowledge may be enough for a stimulus syllable which need only be recognized it will not suffice for a response item which must be produced. The case is similar for natural language. In order to speak one must know all of a word. However, the words of the present study were low-frequency words, words likely to be in the passive or recognition vocabularies of the college-student subjects but not in their active vocabularies; stimulus items, in effect, rather than response items. If knowledge of the parts of new words begins at the ends and moves toward the middle we might expect a word like *numismatics*, which was on our list, to be still registered as NUM_ _ICS. Reduced entries of this sort would in many contexts serve to retrieve the definition.

The argument is reinforced by a well-known effect in spelling. Jensen (1962) has analyzed thousands of spelling errors for words of 7, 9, or 11 letters made by children in the eighth and tenth grades and by junior college freshmen. A striking serial position effect appears in all his sets of data such that errors are most common in the middle of the word, next most common at the end, and least common at the start. These results are as they should be if the order of attention and entry of information is first, last, and then, middle. Jensen's results show us what happens when children are forced to produce words that are still on the recognition level. His results remind us of those bluebooks in which students who are uncertain of the spelling of a word write the first and last letters with great clarity and fill in the middle with indecipherable squiggles. That is what should happen when a word that can be only partially recalled must be produced in its entirety. End letters and a stretch of squiggles may, however, be quite adequate for recognition purposes. In the TOT experiment we have perhaps placed adult subjects in a situation comparable to that created for children by Jensen's spelling tests.

There are two points to clarify and the argument is finished. The subjects in our experiment were college students, and so in order to obtain words on the margin of knowledge we had to use words that are very infrequent in English as a whole. It is not our thought, however, that the TOT phenomenon occurs only with rare words. The absolute location of the margin of word knowledge is a function of the subject's age and education, and so with other subjects we would expect to obtain TOT states for words more frequent in English. Finally the need to produce (or recall) a word is not the only factor that is likely to encourage registration of its middle letters. The amount of detail needed to specify a word uniquely must increase with the total number of words known, the number from which any one is to be distinguished. Consequently the growth of vocabulary, as well as the need to recall, should have some power to force attention into the middle of a word.

References

BARNHART, C. L. (Ed.) *The American college dictionary*. New York: Harper, 1948.

BROADBENT, D. E. *Perception and communication*. New York: Macmillan, 1958.

BRUNER, J. S., AND O'DOWD, D. A note on the informativeness of words. *Language and Speech*, 1958, **1,** 98–101.

FEIGENBAUM, E. A. The stimulation of verbal learning behavior. In E. A. Feigenbaum and J. Feldman (Eds.) *Computers and thought*. New York: McGraw-Hill, 1963.

HOCKETT, C. F. *A course in modern linguistics*. New York: Macmillan, 1958.

JAMES, W. *The principles of psychology*, Vol. I. New York: Holt, 1893.

JENSEN, A. R. Spelling errors and the serial-position effect. *J. educ. Psychol.*, 1962, **53,** 105–109.

KATZ, J. J., AND FODOR, J. A. The structure of a semantic theory. *Language*, 1963, **39,** 170–210.

MILLER, G. A., AND FRIEDMAN, ELIZABETH A. The reconstruction of mutilated English texts. *Inform. Control.*, 1957, **1,** 38–55.

THORNDIKE, E. L., AND LORGE, I. *The teacher's word book of 30,000 words*. New York: Columbia Univer., 1952.

UNDERWOOD, B. J. Stimulus selection in verbal learning. In C. N. Cofer and Barbara S. Musgrave (Eds.) *Verbal behavior and learning: problems and processes.* New York: McGraw-Hill, 1963.

WENZL, A. Empirische und theoretische Beiträge zur Erinnerungs-arbeit bei erschwerter Wortfindung. *Arch. ges. Psychol.*, 1932, **85**, 181–218.

WENZL, A. Empirische und theoretische Beiträge zur Erinnerungs-arbeit bei erschwerter Wortfindung. *Arch. ges. Psychol.*, 1936, **97**, 294–318.

WOODWORTH, R. S. *Psychology.* (3rd ed.). New York: Holt, 1934.

WOODWORTH, R. S., AND SCHLOSBERG, H. *Experimental psychology.* (Rev. ed.). New York: Holt, 1954.

[12]

The Pronouns of Power and Solidarity

Instead of "power" in this article, we ought to have said "social status." The facts are correct as given: pronominal address is sometimes non-reciprocal, with one person, the older, nobler, or wealthier, using a condescending form and the other using a deferential form. The differences of lineage, caste, class, sex, race, age, and occupation that are found in such dyads suggest both power and status. In life the two variables are usually confounded, with the person of higher social "value" or "status," as reckoned in his culture, having the greater real control over the positive and negative outcomes and ultimately the behavior of the person of lower status. Sometimes, however, the variables diverge—as when a servant actually "bosses" his master, a minister his king, or a child his parent. In such cases the forms of address follow conventional status rather than real relative power. So status rather than power is the concept that best explains the non-reciprocal pattern of address.

This paper was prepared for a Conference on Style held at Indiana University, in Bloomington, in April of 1958. I think I enjoyed that conference more than any other I have ever attended. Much of the pleasure came from meeting and listening to the great

This paper was first published in the report of the Conference on Style (*Style and Language*, M.I.T., 1960) edited by Thomas A. Sebeok. Albert Gilman was co-author of the paper. Reprinted by permission of the authors.

scholar, I. A. Richards. Professor Richards gave an evening lecture in which he analyzed his own poetic processes in the composition of a poem called:

> Harvard Yard in April
> April in Harvard Yard

Asked to explain the reversed phrases of his title he said: "Harvard Yard in April is just a temporal and locating phrase, no more. But when we reverse it it seems to me that April, in slight personification, has changed its function. It is no longer mere location. It's what she's up to and April has become a she instead of a month. What she's up to in Harvard Yard has something to do with the nostalgia of the persona, the mask for the speaker." It was a wonderful lecture.

MOST OF US in speaking and writing English use only one pronoun of address; we say *you* to many persons and *you* to one person. The pronoun *thou* is reserved, nowadays, to prayer and naive poetry, but in the past it was the form of familiar address to a single person. At that time *you* was the singular of reverence and of polite distance and, also, the invariable plural. In French, German, Italian, Spanish, and the other languages most nearly related to English there are still active two singular pronouns of address. The interesting thing about such pronouns is their close association with two dimensions fundamental to the analysis of all social life—the dimensions of power and solidarity. Semantic and stylistic analysis of these forms takes us well into psychology and sociology as well as into linguistics and the study of literature.

This paper is divided into five major sections. The first three of these are concerned with the semantics of the pronouns of address. By semantics we mean covariation between the pronoun used and the objective relationship existing between speaker and addressee. The first section offers a general description of the semantic evolution of the pronouns of address in certain European languages. The second section describes semantic differences existing today among the

303

pronouns of French, German, and Italian. The third section proposes a connection between social structure, group ideology, and the semantics of the pronoun. The final two sections of the paper are concerned with expressive style by which we mean covariation between the pronoun used and characteristics of the person speaking. The first of these sections shows that a man's consistent pronoun style gives away his class status and his political views. The last section describes the ways in which a man may vary his pronoun style from time to time so as to express transient moods and attitudes. In this section it is also proposed that the major expressive meanings are derived from the major semantic rules.

In each section the evidence most important to the thesis of that section is described in detail. However, the various generalizations we shall offer have developed as an interdependent set from continuing study of our whole assemblage of facts, and so it may be well to indicate here the sort of motley assemblage this is. Among secondary sources the general language histories (Baugh, 1935; Brunot, 1905; Diez, 1874; Grimm, 1822–1837; Jespersen, 1905; Meyer-Lübke, 1900) have been of little use because their central concern is always phonetic rather than semantic change. However, there are a small number of monographs and doctoral dissertations describing the detailed pronoun semantics for one or another language—sometimes throughout its history (Gedike, 1794; Grand, 1930; Johnston, 1904; Schliebitz, 1886), sometimes for only a century or so (Kennedy, 1915; Stidston, 1917), and sometimes for the works of a particular author (Byrne, 1936; Fay, 1920). As primary evidence for the usage of the past we have drawn on plays, on legal proceedings (Jardine, 1832–1835), and on letters (Devereux, 1853; Harrison, 1935). We have also learned about contemporary usage from literature but, more importantly, from long conversations with native speakers of French, Italian, German, and Spanish both here and in Europe. Our best information about the pronouns of today comes from a questionnaire concerning usage which is described in the second section of this paper. The questionnaire has thus far been answered by the following numbers of students from abroad who were visiting in Boston in 1957–

1958: fifty Frenchmen, twenty Germans, eleven Italians, and two informants, each, from Spain, Argentina, Chile, Denmark, Norway, Sweden, Israel, South Africa, India, Switzerland, Holland, Austria, and Yugoslavia.

We have far more information concerning English, French, Italian, Spanish, and German than for any other languages. Informants and documents concerning the other Indo-European languages are not easily accessible to us. What we have to say is then largely founded on information about these five closely related languages. These first conclusions will eventually be tested by us against other Indo-European languages and, in a more generalized form, against unrelated languages.

The European development of two singular pronouns of address begins with the Latin *tu* and *vos*. In Italian they became *tu* and *voi* (with *Lei* eventually largely displacing *voi*); in French *tu* and *vous*; in Spanish *tu* and *vos* (later *usted*). In German the distinction began with *du* and *Ihr* but *Ihr* gave way to *er* and later to *Sie*. English speakers first used *thou* and *ye* and later replaced *ye* with *you*. As a convenience we propose to use the symbols *T* and *V* (from the Latin *tu* and *vos*) as generic designators for a familiar and a polite pronoun in any language.

THE GENERAL SEMANTIC EVOLUTION OF *T* AND *V*

In the Latin of antiquity there was only *tu* in the singular. The plural *vos* as a form of address to one person was first directed to the emperor and there are several theories (Byrne, 1936; Châtelain, 1880) about how this may have come about. The use of the plural to the emperor began in the fourth century. By that time there were actually two emperors; the ruler of the eastern empire had his seat in Constantinople and the ruler of the west sat in Rome. Because of Diocletian's reforms the imperial office, although vested in two men, was administratively unified. Words addressed to one man were, by implication, addressed to both. The choice of *vos* as a form of address may have been in response to this implicit plurality.

An emperor is also plural in another sense; he is the summation of his people and can speak as their representative. Royal persons sometimes say *we* where an ordinary man would say *I*. The Roman emperor sometimes spoke of himself as *nos*, and the reverential *vos* is the simple reciprocal of this.

The usage need not have been mediated by a prosaic association with actual plurality, for plurality is a very old and ubiquitous metaphor for power. Consider only the several senses of such English words as "great" and "grand". The reverential *vos* could have been directly inspired by the power of an emperor.

Eventually the Latin plural was extended from the emperor to other power figures. However, this semantic pattern was not unequivocally established for many centuries. There was much inexplicable fluctuation between T and V in Old French, Spanish, Italian, and Portuguese (Schliebitz, 1886), and in Middle English (Kennedy, 1915; Stidston, 1917). In verse, at least, the choice seems often to have depended on assonance, rhyme, or syllable count. However, some time between the twelfth and fourteen centuries (Gedike, 1794; Grand, 1930; Kennedy, 1915; Schliebitz, 1886), varying with the language, a set of norms crystallized which we call the nonreciprocal power semantic.

The Power Semantic

One person may be said to have power over another in the degree that he is able to control the behavior of the other. Power is a relationship between at least two persons, and it is nonreciprocal in the sense that both cannot have power in the same area of behavior. The power semantic is similarly nonreciprocal; the superior says T and receives V.

There are many bases of power—physical strength, wealth, age, sex, institutionalized role in the church, the state, the army, or within the family. The character of the power semantic can be made clear with a set of examples from various languages. In his letters, Pope Gregory I (590–604) used T to his subordinates in the ecclesiastical hierarchy and they invariably said V to him (Muller, 1914). In medieval Europe, generally, the nobility said T to the common people and received V; the master of a household said T to his slave, his servant, his squire, and received V. Within the family, of whatever social level, parents gave T to children and were given V. In Italy in the fifteenth century penitents said V to the priest and were told T (Grand, 1930). In Froissart (late fourteenth century) God says T to His angels and they say V; all celestial beings say T to man and receive V. In French of the twelfth and thirteenth century man says T to the animals (Schliebitz, 1886). In fifteenth century Italian literature Christians say T to Turks and Jews and receive V (Grand, 1930). In the plays of Corneille and Racine and Shakespeare, the noble principals say T to their subordinates and are given V in return.

The V of reverence entered European speech as a form of address to the principal power in the state and eventually generalized to the powers within that microcosm of the state—the nuclear family. In the history of language, then, parents are emperor figures. It is interesting to note in passing that Freud reversed this terminology and spoke of kings, as well as generals, employers, and priests, as father figures. The propriety of Freud's designation for his psychological purposes derives from the fact that an individual learning a European language reverses the historical order of semantic generalization. The individual's first experience of subordination to power and of the reverential V comes in his relation to his parents. In later years similar asymmetrical power relations and similar norms of address develop between employer and employee, soldier and officer, subject and monarch. We can see how it might happen, as Freud believed, that the later social relationships would remind the individual of the familial prototype and would revive emotions and responses from childhood. In a man's personal history recipients of the nonreciprocal V are parent figures.

Since the nonreciprocal power semantic only prescribes usage between superior and inferior, it calls for a social structure in which there are unique power ranks for every individual. Medieval European societies were not so finely structured as that, and so the power semantic was never the only rule for the use of T and V. There were also norms of address for persons of roughly equivalent power, that is, for members of a common class. Between equals, pronominal address was reciprocal; an individual gave and received the same form. During the medieval period and for varying times beyond, equals of the upper classes exchanged the mutual V and equals of the lower classes exchanged T.

The difference in class practice derives from the fact that the reverential V was always introduced into a society at the top. In the Roman Empire only the highest ranking persons had any occasion to address the emperor, and so at first only they made use of V in the singular. In its later history in other parts of Europe the reverential V was usually adopted by one court in imitation of another. The practice slowly disseminated downward in a society. In this way the use of V in the singular incidentally came to connote a speaker of high status. In later centuries Europeans became very conscious of the extensive use of V as a mark of elegance. In the drama of seventeenth century France the nobility and bourgeoisie almost always address one another as V. This is true even of husband and wife, of lovers, and of parent and child if the child is adult. Mme. de Sévigné in her correspondence never uses T, not even to her daughter the Comtesse de Grignan. Servants and peasantry, however, regularly used T among themselves.

For many centuries French, English, Italian, Spanish, and German pronoun usage followed the rule of nonreciprocal T–V between persons of unequal power and the rule of mutual V or T (according to social-class membership) between persons of roughly equivalent power. There was at first no rule differentiating address among equals but, very gradually, a distinction developed which is sometimes called the T of intimacy and the V of formality. We name this second dimension *solidarity*, and here is our guess as to how it developed.

The Solidarity Semantic

The original singular pronoun was T. The use of V in the singular developed as a form of address to a person of superior power. There are many personal attributes that convey power. The recipient of *V* may differ from the recipient of *T* in strength, age, wealth, birth, sex, or profession. As two people move apart on these power-laden dimensions, one of them begins to say *V*. In general terms, the *V* form is linked with differences between persons. Not all differences between persons imply a difference of power. Men are born in different cities, belong to different families of the same status, may attend different but equally prominent schools, may practice different but equally respected professions. A rule for making distinctive use of *T* and *V* among equals can be formulated by generalizing the power semantic. Differences of power cause *V* to emerge in one direction of address; differences not concerned with power cause *V* to emerge in both directions.

The relations called *older than*, *parent of*, *employer of*, *richer than*, *stronger than*, and *nobler than* are all asymmetrical. If *A* is older than *B*, *B* is not older than *A*. The relation called *more powerful than*, which is abstracted from these more specific relations, is also conceived to be asymmetrical. The pronoun usage expressing this power relation is also asymmetrical or nonreciprocal, with the greater receiving *V* and the lesser *T*. Now we are concerned with a new set of relations which are symmetrical; for example, *attended the same school* or *have the same parents* or *practice the same profession*. If *A* has the same parents as *B*, *B* has the same parents as *A*. Solidarity is the name we give to the general relationship and solidarity is symmetrical. The corresponding norms of address are symmetrical or reciprocal with *V* becoming more probable as solidarity declines. The solidary *T* reaches a peak of probability in address between twin brothers or in a man's soliloquizing address to himself.

Not every personal attribute counts in determining whether two people are solidary enough to use the mutual *T*. Eye color does not ordinarily matter nor does shoe size. The similarities that matter seem to be those that make for like-mindedness or similar behavior dispositions. These will ordinarily be such things as political membership, family, religion, profession, sex, and birthplace. However, extreme distinctive values on almost any dimension may become significant. Height ought

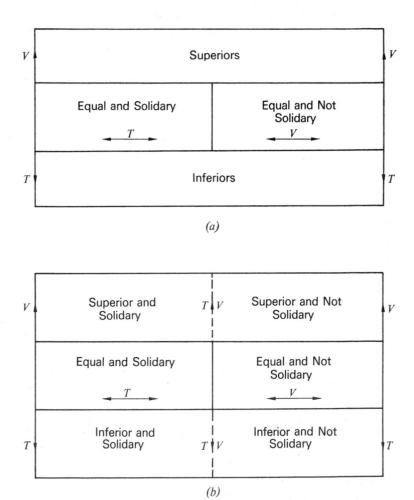

Figure 12–1. The Two-Dimensional Semantic (*a*) in Equilibrium and (*b*) under Tension.

to make for solidarity among giants and midgets. The T of solidarity can be produced by frequency of contact as well as by objective similarities. However, frequent contact does not necessarily lead to the mutual T. It depends on whether contact results in the discovery or creation of the like-mindedness that seems to be the core of the solidarity semantic.

Solidarity comes into the European pronouns as a means of differentiating address among power equals. It introduces a second dimension into the semantic system on the level of power equivalents. So long as solidarity was confined to this level, the two-dimensional system was in equilibrium (see Figure 12–1a), and it seems to have remained here for a considerable time in all our languages. It is from the long reign of the two-dimensional semantic that T derives its common definition as the pronoun of either condescension or intimacy and V its definition as the pronoun of reverence or formality. These definitions are still current but usage has, in fact, gone somewhat beyond them.

The dimension of solidarity is potentially applicable to all persons addressed. Power superiors may be solidary (parents, elder siblings) or not solidary (officials whom one seldom sees). Power inferiors, similarly, may be as solidary as the old family retainer and as remote as the waiter in a strange restaurant. Extension of the solidarity dimension along the dotted lines of Figure 12–1b creates six categories of persons defined by their relations to a speaker. Rules of address are in conflict for persons in the upper left and lower right categories. For the upper left, power indicates V and solidarity T. For the lower right, power indicates T and solidarity V.

The abstract conflict described in Figure 12–1b is particularized in Figure 12–2a with a sample of the social dyads in which the conflict would be felt. In each case usage in one direction is unequivocal but, in the other direction, the two semantic forces are opposed. The first three dyads in Figure 12–2a involve conflict in address to inferiors who are not solidary (the lower right category of Figure 12–1b), and the second three dyads involve conflict in address to superiors who are solidary (the upper left category in Figure 12–1b).

Well into the nineteenth century the power semantic

311

prevailed and waiters, common soldiers, and employees were called *T* while parents, masters, and elder brothers were called *V*. However all our evidence consistently indicates that in the past century the solidarity semantic has gained supremacy. Dyads of the type shown in Figure 12–2a now reciprocate the pronoun of solidarity or the pronoun of nonsolidarity. The

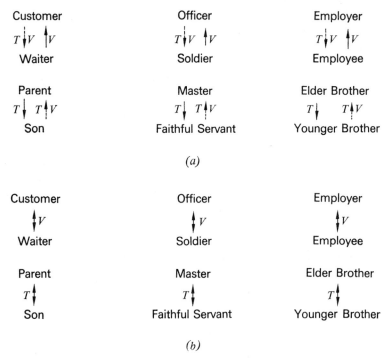

Figure 12–2. Social Dyads Involving (*a*) Semantic Conflict and (*b*) their Resolution.

conflicted address has been resolved so as to match the unequivocal address. The abstract result is a simple one-dimensional system with the reciprocal *T* for the solidary and the reciprocal *V* for the nonsolidary.

It is the present practice to reinterpret power-laden attributes so as to turn them into symmetrical solidarity attributes. Relationships like *older than*, *father of*, *nobler than*, and *richer than* are now reinterpreted for purposes of *T* and *V* as relations of *the same age as, the same family as, the same kind of ancestry as,* and *the same income as.* In the degree that these relationships hold, the probability of a mutual *T* increases and, in the degree that they do not hold, the probability of a mutual *V* increases.

There is an interesting residual of the power relation in the contemporary notion that the right to initiate the reciprocal *T* belongs to the member of the dyad having the better power-based claim to say *T* without reciprocation. The suggestion that solidarity be recognized comes more gracefully from the elder than from the younger, from the richer than from the poorer, from the employer than from the employee, from the noble than from the commoner, from the female than from the male.

In support of our claim that solidarity has largely won out over power we can offer a few quotations from language scholars. Littré (1882), writing of French usage, says: "Notre courtoisie est meme si grande, que nous ne dédaignons pas de donner du vous et du monsieur a l'homme de la condition la plus vile." Grand (1930) wrote of the Italian *V*: "On commence aussi à le donner aux personnes de service, à qui on disait tu autrefois." We have found no authority who describes the general character of these many specific changes of usage: a shift from power to solidarity as the governing semantic principle.

The best evidence that the change has occurred is in our interviews and notes on contemporary literature and films and, most importantly, the questionnaire results. The six social dyads of Figure 12–2 were all represented in the questionnaire. In the past these would have been answered in accordance with asymmetrical power. Across all six of these dyads the French results yield only eleven per cent non-reciprocal power answers, the German twelve per cent, the Italian twenty-seven per cent. In all other cases the usage is reciprocal, as indicated in Figure 12–2b. In all three of the languages, address between master and servant retains the greatest power loading. Some of the changes toward solidarity are very recent. Only since the Second World War, for instance, has the French Army adopted a regulation requiring officers to say V to enlisted men.

Finally, it is our opinion that a still newer direction of semantic shift can be discerned in the whole collection of languages studied. Once solidarity has been established as the single dimension distinguishing T from V the province of T proceeds to expand. The direction of change is increase in the number of relations defined as solidary enough to merit a mutual T and, in particular, to regard any sort of camaraderie resulting from a common task or a common fate as grounds for T. We have a favorite example of this new trend given us independently by several French informants. It seems that mountaineers above a certain critical altitude shift to the mutual T. We like to think that this is the point where their lives hang by a single thread. In general, the mutual T is advancing among fellow students, fellow workers, members of the same political group, persons who share a hobby or take a trip together. We believe this is the direction of current change because it summarizes what our informants tell us about the pronoun usage of the "young people" as opposed to that of older people.

CONTEMPORARY DIFFERENCES AMONG FRENCH, ITALIAN, AND GERMAN

While T and V have passed through the same general semantic sequence in these three languages, there are today some differences of detailed usage which were revealed by the questionnaire data. Conversations with native speakers guided us in the writing of questionnaire items, but the conversations themselves did not teach us the characteristic semantic features of the three languages; these did not emerge until we made statistical comparison of answers to the standard items of the questionnaire.

The questionnaire is in English. It opens with a paragraph informing the subject that the items below all have reference to the use of the singular pronouns of address in his native

language. There are twenty-eight items in the full questionnaire for French students:

1. (a) Which pronoun would
    you use in speaking to
    your mother?

      T (definitely) ———
      T (probably) ———
Possibly T, possibly V ———
      V (probably) ———
      V (definitely) ———

1. (b) Which would she use
    in speaking to you?

      T (definitely) ———
      T (probably) ———
Possibly T, possibly V ———
      V (probably) ———
      V (definitely) ———

The questionnaire asks about usage between the subject and
his mother, his father, his grandfather, his wife, a younger
brother who is a child, a married elder brother, that brother's
wife, a remote male cousin, and an elderly female servant
whom he has known from childhood. It asks about usage
between the subject and fellow students at the university at
home, usage to a student from home visiting in America, and
usage to someone with whom the subject had been at school
some years previously. It asks about usage to a waiter in a
restaurant, between clerks in an office, fellow soldiers in the
army, between boss and employee, army private and general.
In addition, there are some rather elaborate items which ask
the subject to imagine himself in some carefully detailed
social situation and then to say what pronoun he would use.
A copy of the full questionnaire may be had on application to
the authors.

    The most accessible informants were students from abroad
resident in Boston in the fall of 1957. Listings of such students
were obtained from Harvard, Boston University, M.I.T., and
the Office of the French Consul in New England. Although we
have data from a small sample of female respondents, the
present analysis is limited to the males. All the men in the
sample have been in the United States for one year or less;
they come from cities of over 300,000 inhabitants, and these
cities are well scattered across the country in question. In
addition, all members of the sample are from upper-middle-
class, professional families. This homogeneity of class mem-

bership was enforced by the factors determining selection of students who go abroad. The occasional informant from a working-class family is deliberately excluded from these comparisons. The class from which we draw shows less regional variation in speech than does the working class and, especially, farmers. At the present time we have complete responses from fifty Frenchmen, twenty Germans, and eleven Italians; many of these men also sent us letters describing their understanding of the pronouns and offering numerous valuable anecdotes of usage. The varying numbers of subjects belonging to the three nationalities result from the unequal representation of these nationalities among Boston students rather than from national characterological differences in willingness to answer a questionnaire. Almost every person on our lists agreed to serve as an informant.

In analyzing the results we assigned the numbers 0–4 to the five response alternatives to each question, beginning with "Definitely V" as 0. A rough test was made of the significance of the differences among the three languages on each question. We dichotomized the replies to each question into: a) all replies of either "Definitely T" or "Probably T"; b) all replies of "Definitely V" or "Probably V" or "Possibly V, possibly T." Using the chi-squared test with Yates's correction for small frequencies we determined, for each comparison, the probability of obtaining by chance a difference as large or larger than that actually obtained. Even with such small samples, there were quite a few differences significantly unlikely to occur by chance ($p = .05$ or less). Germans were more prone than the French to say T to their grandfathers, to an elder brother's wife, and to an old family servant. The French were more prone than the Germans to say T to a male fellow student, to a student from home visiting in America, to a fellow clerk in an office, and to someone known previously as a fellow student. Italians were more prone than the French to say T to a female fellow student and also to an attractive girl to whom they had recently been introduced. Italians were more prone than the Germans to say T to the persons just described and, in addition, to a male fellow student and to a student from home visiting in America. On no question did either the French or the Germans show a significantly greater tendency to say T than did the Italians.

The many particular differences among the three languages are susceptible of a general characterization. Let us first contrast German and French. The German T is more reliably applied within the family than is the French T; in addition to the significantly higher T scores for grandfather and elder brother's wife there are smaller differences showing a higher score for the German T on father, mother, wife, married elder brother, and remote male cousin. The French T is not automatically applied to remote relatives, but it is more likely than the German pronoun to be used to express the camaraderie of fellow students, fellow clerks, fellow countrymen abroad, and fellow soldiers. In general it may be said that the solidarity coded by the German T is an ascribed solidarity of family relationships. The French T, in greater degree, codes an acquired solidarity not founded on family relationship but developing out of some sort of shared fate. As for the Italian T, it very nearly equals the German in family solidarity and it surpasses the French in camaraderie. The camaraderie of the Italian male, incidentally, is extended to the Italian female; unlike the French or German student the Italian says T to the co-ed almost as readily as to the male fellow student.

There is a very abstract semantic rule governing T and V which is the same for French, German, and Italian and for many other languages we have studied. The rule is that usage is reciprocal, T becoming increasingly probable and V less probable as the number of solidarity-producing attributes shared by two people increases. The respect in which French, German, and Italian differ from one another is in the relative weight given to various attributes of persons which can serve to generate solidarity. For German, ascribed family membership is the important attribute; French and Italian give more weight to acquired characteristics.

SEMANTICS, SOCIAL STRUCTURE, AND IDEOLOGY

A historical study of the pronouns of address reveals a set

of semantic and social psychological correspondences. The nonreciprocal power semantic is associated with a relatively static society in which power is distributed by birthright and is not subject to much redistribution. The power semantic was closely tied with the feudal and manorial systems. In Italy the reverential pronoun *Lei* which has largely displaced the older *voi* was originally an abbreviation for *la vostra Signoria*"your lordship"and in Spanish *vuestra Merced*"your grace" became the reverential *usted*. The static social structure was accompanied by the Church's teaching that each man had his properly appointed place and ought not to wish to rise above it. The reciprocal solidarity semantic has grown with social mobility and an equalitarian ideology. The towns and cities have led the way in the semantic change as they led the way in opening society to vertical movement. In addition to these rough historical correspondences we have made a collection of lesser items of evidence favoring the thesis.

In France the nonreciprocal power semantic was dominant until the Revolution when the Committee for the Public Safety condemned the use of V as a feudal remnant and ordered a universal reciprocal T. On October 31, 1793, Malbec made a Parliamentary speech against V: "Nous distinguons trois personnes pour le singulier et trois pour le pluriel, et, au mépris de cette regle, l'esprit de fanatisme, d'orgueil et de féodalité, nous a fait contracter l'habitude de nous servir de la seconde personne du pluriel lorsque nous parlons à un seul" (quoted in Brunot, 1926). For a time revolutionary "fraternitè" transformed all address into the mutual *Citoyen* and the mutual *tu*. Robespierre even addressed the president of the Assembly as *tu*. In later years solidarity declined and the differences of power which always exist everywhere were expressed once more.

It must be asked why the equalitarian ideal was expressed in a universal T rather than a universal V or, as a third alternative, why there was not a shift of semantic from power to solidarity with both pronouns being retained. The answer lies with the ancient upper-class preference for the use of V. There was animus against the pronoun itself. The pronoun of the "*sans-culottes*" was *T*, and so this had to be the pronoun of the Revolution.

Although the power semantic no longer governs pronominal address in France today, native speakers are still aware of it. In part they are aware of it because it prevails in so much of the greatest French literature. Awareness of power as a potential factor in pronoun usage was revealed by our respondents' special attitude toward the saying of *T* to a waiter. Most of them felt that this would be shockingly bad taste in a way that other norm violations would not be, apparently because there is a kind of seignorial right to say *T* to a waiter, an actual power asymmetry, which the modern man's ideology requires him to deny. In French Africa, on the other hand, it is considered proper to recognize a caste difference between the African and the European, and the nonreciprocal address is used to express it. The European says *T* and requires *V* from the African. This is a galling custom to the African, and in 1957 Robert Lacoste, the French Minister residing in Algeria, urged his countrymen to eschew the practice.

In England, before the Norman Conquest, *ye* was the second person plural and *thou* the singular. *You* was originally the accusative of *ye*, but in time it also became the nominative plural and ultimately ousted *thou* as the usual singular. The first uses of *ye* as a reverential singular occur in the thirteenth century (Kennedy, 1915), and seem to have been copied from the French nobility. The semantic progression corresponds roughly to the general stages described in the first section of this paper, except that the English seem always to have moved more freely from one form to another than did the continental Europeans (Jesperson, 1905).

In the seventeenth century *thou* and *you* became explicitly involved in social controversy. The Religious Society of Friends (or Quakers) was founded in the middle of this century by George Fox. One of the practices setting off this rebellious group from the larger society was the use of Plain Speech, and this entailed saying "thou" to everyone. George Fox explained the practice in these words:

"Moreover, when the Lord sent me forth into the world, He forbade me to put off my hat to any, high or low; and I was required to

Thee and Thou all men and women, without any respect to rich or poor, great or small" (quoted in Estrich and Sperber, 1946).

Fox wrote a fascinating pamphlet (1660), arguing that *T* to one and *V* to many is the natural and logical form of address in all languages. Among others he cites Latin, Hebrew, Greek, Arabick, Syriack, Aethiopic, Egyptian, French, and Italian. Fox suggests that the Pope, "in his vanity," introduced the corrupt and illogical practice of saying *V* to one person. Farnworth, another early Friend, wrote a somewhat similar pamphlet (1657), in which he argued that the Scriptures show that God and Adam and God and Moses were not too proud to say and receive the singular *T*.

For the new convert to the Society of Friends the universal *T* was an especially difficult commandment. Thomas Ellwood has described (1714) the trouble that developed between himself and his father:

But whenever I had occasion to speak to my Father, though I had no Hat now to offend him; yet my language did as much: for I durst not say YOU to him, but THOU or THEE, as the Occasion required, and then would he be sure to fall on me with his Fists.

The Friends' reasons for using the mutual *T* were much the same as those of the French revolutionaries, but the Friends were always a minority and the larger society was antagonized by their violations of decorum.

Some Friends use *thee* today; the nominative *thou* has been dropped and *thee* is used as both the nominative and (as formerly) the accusative. Interestingly many Friends also use *you*. *Thee* is likely to be reserved for Friends among themselves and *you* said to outsiders. This seems to be a survival of the solidarity semantic. In English at large, of course, *thou* is no longer used. The explanation of its disappearance is by no means certain; however, the forces at work seem to have included a popular reaction against the radicalism of Quakers and Levelers and also a general trend in English toward simplified verbal inflection.

In the world today there are numerous examples of the association proposed between ideology and pronoun semantics. In Yugoslavia, our informants tell us, there was, for a short time following the establishment of Communism, a universal mutual *T* of solidarity. Today revolutionary *esprit* has declined and *V* has returned for much the same set of circumstances as in Italy, France, or Spain. There is also some power asymmetry in Yugoslavia's "Socialist manners." A soldier says *V* and *Comrade General*, but the general addresses the soldier with *T* and surname.

It is interesting in our materials to contrast usage in the Afrikaans language of South Africa and in the Gujerati and Hindi languages of India with the rest of the collection. On the questionnaire, Afrikaans speakers made eight nonreciprocal power distinctions; especially notable are distinctions within the family and the distinctions between customer and waiter and between boss and clerk, since these are almost never power-coded in French, Italian, German, etc., although they once were. The Afrikaans pattern generally preserves the asymmetry of the dyads described in Figure 12–2, and that suggests a more static society and a less developed equalitarian ethic. The forms of address used between Afrikaans-speaking whites and the groups of "coloreds" and "blacks" are especially interesting. The Afrikaaner uses *T*, but the two lower castes use neither *T* nor *V*. The intermediate caste of "coloreds" says *Meneer* to the white and the "blacks" say *Baas*. It is as if these social distances transcend anything that can be found within the white group and so require their peculiar linguistic expressions.

The Gujerati and Hindi languages of India have about the same pronoun semantic, and it is heavily loaded with power. These languages have all the asymmetrical usage of Afrikaans, and, in addition, use the nonreciprocal *T* and *V* between elder brother and younger brother and between husband and wife. This truly feudal pronominal pattern is consistent with the static Indian society. However, that society is now changing rapidly and, consistent with that change, the norms of pronoun usage are also changing. The progressive young Indian exchanges the mutual *T* with his wife.

In our account of the general semantic evolution of the pronouns, we have identified a stage in which the solidarity rule was limited to address between persons of equal power.

This seemed to yield a two-dimensional system in equilibrium (see Figure 12–1a), and we have wondered why address did not permanently stabilize there. It is possible, of course, that human cognition favors the binary choice without contingencies and so found its way to the suppression of one dimension. However, this theory does not account for the fact that it was the rule of solidarity that triumphed. We believe, therefore, that the development of open societies with an equalitarian ideology acted against the nonreciprocal power semantic and in favor of solidarity. It is our suggestion that the larger social changes created a distaste for the face-to-face expression of differential power.

What of the many actions other than nonreciprocal T and V which express power asymmetry? A vassal not only says V but also bows, lifts his cap, touches his forelock, keeps silent, leaps to obey. There are a large number of expressions of subordination which are patterned isomorphically with T and V. Nor are the pronouns the only forms of nonreciprocal address. There are, in addition, proper names and titles, and many of these operate today on a nonreciprocal power pattern in America and in Europe, in open and equalitarian societies.

In the American family there are no discriminating pronouns, but there are nonreciprocal norms of address. A father says "Jim" to his son but, unless he is extraordinarily "advanced," he does not anticipate being called "Jack" in reply. In the American South there are no pronouns to mark the caste separation of Negro and white, but there are nonreciprocal norms of address. The white man is accustomed to call the Negro by his first name, but he expects to be called "Mr. Legree." In America and in Europe there are forms of nonreciprocal address for all the dyads of asymmetrical power; customer and waiter, teacher and student, father and son, employer and employee.

Differences of power exist in a democracy as in all societies. What is the difference between expressing power asymmetry in pronouns and expressing it by choice of title and proper name? It seems to be primarily a question of the degree of linguistic compulsion. In face-to-face address we can usually avoid the use of any name or title but not so easily the use of a pronoun. Even if the pronoun can be avoided, it will be implicit in the inflection of the verb. "Dites quelque chose" clearly says *vous* to the Frenchman. A norm for the pronominal and verbal expression of power compels a continuing coding of power, whereas a norm for titles and names permits power to go uncoded in most discourse. Is there any reason why the pronominal coding should be more congenial to a static society than to an open society?

We have noticed that mode of address intrudes into consciousness as a problem at times of status change. Award of the doctoral degree, for instance, transforms a student into a colleague and, among American academics, the familiar first name is normal. The fledgling academic may find it difficult to call his former teachers by their first names. Although these teachers may be young and affable, they have had a very real power over him for several years and it will feel presumptuous to deny this all at once with a new mode of address. However, the "tyranny of democratic manners" (Cronin, 1958) does not allow him to continue comfortable with the polite *Professor X.* He would not like to be thought unduly conscious of status, unprepared for faculty rank, a born lickspittle. Happily, English allows him a respite. He can avoid any term of address, staying with the uncommitted *you*, until he and his addressees have got used to the new state of things. This linguistic *rite de passage* has, for English speakers, a waiting room in which to screw up courage.

In a fluid society crises of address will occur more frequently than in a static society, and so the pronominal coding of power differences is more likely to be felt as onerous. Coding by title and name would be more tolerable because less compulsory. Where status is fixed by birth and does not change each man has enduring rights and obligations of address.

A strong equalitarian ideology of the sort dominant in America works to suppress every conventional expression of power asymmetry. If the worker becomes conscious of his unreciprocated polite address to the boss, he may feel that his human dignity requires him to change. However, we do not feel the full power of the ideology until we are in a situation that gives us some claim to receive deferential address. The American professor often feels foolish being given his title, he almost certainly will not claim it as a prerogative; he may take pride in being on a first-name basis with his students. Very "palsy" parents may invite their children to call them by first name. The very President of the Republic invites us all to call him "Ike." Nevertheless, the differences of power are real and are experienced. Cronin has suggested in an amusing piece (1958) that subordination is expressed by Americans in a subtle, and generally unwitting, body language. "The repertoire includes the boyish grin, the deprecatory cough, the unfinished sentence, the appreciative giggle, the drooping shoulders, the head-scratch and the bottom-waggle."

GROUP STYLE WITH THE PRONOUNS OF ADDRESS

The identification of style is relative to the identification of some constancy. When we have marked out the essentials of some action—it might be walking or speaking a language or driving a car—we can identify the residual variation as stylistic. Different styles are different ways of "doing the same thing," and so their identification waits on some designation of the range of performances to be regarded as "the same thing."

Linguistic science finds enough that is constant in English and French and Latin to put all these and many more into one family—the Indo-European. It is possible with reference to this constancy to think of Italian and Spanish and English and the others as so many styles of Indo-European. They all have, for instance, two singular pronouns of address, but each language has an individual phonetic and semantic style in pronoun usage. We are ignoring phonetic style (through the use of the generic T and V), but in the second section of the paper we have described differences in the semantic styles of French, German, and Italian.

Linguistic styles are potentially expressive when there is covariation between characteristics of language performance and characteristics of the performers. When styles are "interpreted," language behavior is functionally expressive. On that abstract level where the constancy is Indo-European and the styles are French, German, English, and Italian, interpretations of style must be statements about communities of speakers, statements of national character, social structure, or group ideology. In the last section we have hazarded a few propositions on this level.

It is usual, in discussion of linguistic style, to set constancy at the level of a language like French or English rather than at the level of a language family. In the languages we have studied there are variations in pronoun style that are associated with the social status of the speaker. We have seen that the use of V because of its entry at the top of a society and its diffusion downward was always interpreted as a mark of good breeding. It is interesting to find an organization of French journeymen in the generation after the Revolution adopting a set of rules of propriety cautioning members against going without tie or shoes at home on Sunday and also against the use of the mutual T among themselves (Perdiguier, 1914). Our informants assure us that V and T still function as indications of class membership. The Yugoslavians have a saying that a peasant would say T to a king. By contrast, a French nobleman who turned up in our net told us that he had said T to no one in the world except the old woman who was his nurse in childhood. He is prevented by the dominant democratic ideology from saying T to subordinates and by his own royalist ideology from saying it to equals.

In literature, pronoun style has often been used to expose the pretensions of social climbers and the would-be elegant. Persons aping the manners of the class above them usually do not get the imitation exactly right. They are likely to notice some point of difference between their own class and the next higher and then extend the difference too widely, as in the use of the "elegant" broad [a] in *can* and *bad*. Molière gives us his *"précieuses ridicules"* saying V to servants whom a refined person would call T. In Ben Jonson's *Everyman in his Humour* and *Epicoene* such true gallants as Wellbred and Knowell usually say *you* to one another but they make frequent expressive shifts between this form and *thou*, whereas such fops as John Daw and Amorous-La-Foole make unvarying use of *you*.

Our sample of visiting French students was roughly homogeneous in social status as judged by the single criterion of paternal occupation. Therefore, we could not make any systematic study of differences in class style, but we thought it possible that, even within this select group, there might be interpretable differences of style. It was our guess that the tendency to make wide or narrow use of the solidary *T* would be related to general radicalism or conservatism of ideology. As a measure of this latter dimension we used Eysenck's Social Attitude Inventory (1957). This is a collection of statements to be accepted or rejected concerning a variety of matters—religion, economics, racial relations, sexual behavior, etc. Eysenck has validated the scale in England and in France on members of Socialist, Communist, Fascist, Conservative, and Liberal party members. In general, to be radical on this scale is to favor change and to be conservative is to wish to maintain the status quo or turn back to some earlier condition. We undertook to relate scores on this inventory to an index of pronoun style.

As yet we have reported no evidence demonstrating that there exists such a thing as a personal style in pronoun usage in the sense of a tendency to make wide or narrow use of *T*. It may be that each item in the questionnaire, each sort of person addressed, is an independent personal norm not predictable from any other. A child learns what to say to each kind of person. What he learns in each case depends on the groups in which he has membership. Perhaps his usage is a bundle of unrelated habits.

Guttman (Stouffer, Guttman, *et al.*, 1950) has developed the technique of Scalogram Analysis for determining whether or not a collection of statements taps a common dimension. A perfect Guttman scale can be made of the statements: *a*) I am at least 5' tall; *b*) I am at least 5' 4" tall; *c*) I am at least 5' 7" tall; *d*) I am at least 6' 1" tall; *e*) I am at least 6' 2" tall. Endorsement of a more extreme statement will always be associated with endorsement of all less extreme statements. A person can be assigned a single score—*a*, *b*, *c*, *d*, or *e*—which represents the most extreme statement he has endorsed and, from this single score all his individual answers can be reproduced. If he scores *c* he has also endorsed *a* and *b* but not *d* or *e*. The general criterion for scalability is the reproducibility of individual responses from a single score, and this depends on the items being interrelated so that endorsement of one is reliably associated with endorsement or rejection of the others.

The Guttman method was developed during World War II for the measurement of social attitudes, and it has been widely used. Perfect reproducibility is not likely to be found for all the statements which an investigator guesses to be concerned with some single attitude. The usual thing is to accept a set of statements as scalable when they are ninety per cent reproducible and also satisfy certain other requirements; for example, there must be some statements that are not given a very one-sided response but are accepted and rejected with nearly equal frequency.

The responses to the pronoun questionnaire are not varying degrees of agreement (as in an attitude questionnaire) but are rather varying probabilities of saying *T* or *V*. There seems to be no reason why these bipolar responses cannot be treated like yes or no responses on an attitude scale. The difference is that the scale, if there is one, will be the semantic dimension governing the pronouns, and the scale score of each respondent will represent his personal semantic style.

It is customary to have 100 subjects for a Scalogram Analysis, but we could find only fifty French students. We tested all twenty-eight items for scalability and found that a subset of them made a fairly good scale. It was necessary to combine response categories so as to dichotomize them in order to obtain an average reproducibility of eighty-five per cent. This coefficient was computed for the five intermediate items having the more-balanced marginal frequencies. A large number of items fell at or very near the two extremes. The solidarity or *T*-most end of the scale could be defined by father, mother, elder brother, young boys, wife, or lover quite as well as by younger brother. The remote or *V*-most end could be defined by "waiter" or "top boss" as well as by "army general." The intervening positions, from the T-end to the V-end, are: the elderly female servant known since childhood, grandfather, a male fellow student, a female fellow student, and an elder brother's wife.

For each item on the scale a T answer scores one point and a V answer no points. The individual total scores range from 1 to 7, which means the scale can differentiate only seven semantic styles. We divided the subjects into the resultant seven stylistically homogeneous groups and, for each group, determined the average scores on radicalism-conservatism. There was a set of almost perfectly consistent differences.

Table 12–1. Scores on the Pronoun Scale in Relation to Scores on the Radicalism Scale

Group Pronoun Score	Group Mean Radicalism Score
1	5.50
2	6.66
3	6.82
4	7.83
5	6.83
6	8.83
7	9.75

In Table 12–1 appear the mean radicalism scores for each pronoun style. The individual radicalism scores range between 2 and 13; the higher the score the more radical the person's ideology. The very striking result is that the group radicalism scores duplicate the order of the group pronoun scores with only a single reversal. The rank-difference correlation between the two sets of scores is .96, and even with only seven paired scores this is a very significant relationship.

There is enough consistency of address to justify speaking of a personal-pronoun style which involves a more or less wide use of the solidary T. Even among students of the same socio-economic level there are differences of style, and these are potentially expressive of radicalism and conservatism in ideology. A Frenchman could, with some confidence, infer that a male university student who regularly said T to female fellow students would favor the nationalization of industry, free love, trial marriage, the abolition of capital punishment, and the weakening of nationalistic and religious loyalities.

What shall we make of the association between a wide use of T and a cluster of radical sentiments? There may be no "sense" to it at all, that is, no logical connection between the linguistic practice and the attitudes, but simply a general tendency to go along with the newest thing. We know that left-wing attitudes are more likely to be found in the laboring class than in the professional classes. Perhaps those offspring of the professional class who sympathize with proletariat politics also, incidentally, pick up the working man's wide use of T without feeling that there is anything in the linguistic practice that is congruent with the ideology.

On the other hand perhaps there is something appropriate in the association. The ideology is consistent in its disapproval of barriers between people: race, religion, nationality, property, marriage, even criminality. All these barriers have the effect of separating the solidary, the "in-group," from the nonsolidary, the "out-group." The radical says the criminal is not far enough "out" to be killed; he should be re-educated. He says that a nationality ought not to be so solidary that it prevents world organization from succeeding. Private property ought to be abolished, industry should be nationalized. There are to be no more out-groups and in-groups but rather one group, undifferentiated by nationality, religion, or pronoun of address. The fact that the pronoun which is being extended to all men alike is T, the mark of solidarity, the pronoun of the nuclear family, expresses the radical's intention to extend his sense of brotherhood. But we notice that universal application of the pronoun eliminates the discrimination that gave it a meaning and that gives particular point to an old problem. Can the solidarity of the family be extended so widely? Is there enough libido to stretch so far? Will there perhaps be a thin solidarity the same everywhere but nowhere so strong as in the past?

329

THE PRONOUNS OF ADDRESS AS EXPRESSIONS OF
TRANSIENT ATTITUDES

Behavior norms are practices consistent within a group. So long as the choice of a pronoun is recognized as normal for a group, its interpretation is simply the membership of the speaker in that group. However, the implications of group membership are often very important; social class, for instance, suggests a kind of family life, a level of education, a set of political views, and much besides. These facts about a person belong to his character. They are enduring features which help to determine actions over many years. Consistent personal style in the use of the pronouns of address does not reveal enough to establish the speaker's unique character, but it can help to place him in one or another large category.

Sometimes the choice of a pronoun clearly violates a group norm and perhaps the customary practice of the speaker. Then the meaning of the act will be sought in some attitude or emotion of the speaker. It is as if the interpreter reasoned that variations of address between the same two persons must be caused by variations in their attitudes toward one another. If two men of seventeenth century France properly exchange the *V* of upper-class equals and one of them gives the other *T*, he suggests that the other is his inferior since it is to his inferiors that a man says *T*. The general meaning of an unexpected pronoun choice is simply that the speaker, for the moment, views his relationship as one that calls for the pronoun used. This kind of variation in language behavior expresses a contemporaneous feeling or attitude. These variations are not consistent personal styles but departures from one's own custom and the customs of a group in response to a mood.

As there have been two great semantic dimensions governing *T* and *V*, so there have also been two principal kinds of expressive meaning. Breaking the norms of power generally has the meaning that a speaker regards an addressee as his inferior, superior, or equal, although by usual criteria, and according to the speaker's own customary usage, the addressee is not what the pronoun implies. Breaking the norms of solidarity generally means that the speaker temporarily thinks of the other as an outsider or as an intimate; it means that sympathy is extended or withdrawn.

The oldest uses of T and V to express attitudes seem everywhere to have been the T of contempt or anger and the V of admiration or respect. In his study of the French pronouns Schliebitz (1886) found the first examples of these expressive uses in literature of the twelfth and thirteenth centuries, which is about the time that the power semantic crystallized in France, and Grand (1930) has found the same thing for Italian. In saying T, where V is usual, the speaker treats the addressee like a servant or a child and assumes the right to berate him. The most common use of the expressive V, in the early materials, is that of the master who is exceptionally pleased with the work of a servant and elevates him pronominally to match this esteem.

Racine, in his dramas, used the pronouns with perfect semantic consistency. His major figures exchange the V of upper-class equals. Lovers, brother and sister, husband and wife—none of them says T if he is of high rank, but each person of high rank has a subordinate confidante to whom he says T and from whom he receives V. It is a perfect nonreciprocal power semantic. This courtly pattern is broken only for the greatest scenes in each play. Racine reserved the expressive pronoun as some composers save the cymbals. In both *Andromaque* and *Phèdre* there are only two expressive departures from the norm, and they mark climaxes of feeling.

Jespersen (1905) believed that English *thou* and *ye* (or *you*) were more often shifted to express mood and tone than were the pronouns of the continental languages, and our comparisons strongly support this opinion. The *thou* of contempt was so very familiar that a verbal form was created to name this expressive use. Shakespeare gives it to Sir Toby Belch (*Twelfth Night*) in the lines urging Andrew Aguecheek to send a challenge to the disguised Viola: "Taunt him with the license of ink, if thou thou'st him some thrice, it shall not be amiss." In life the verb turned up in Sir Edward Coke's attack on Raleigh at the latter's trial in 1603 (Jardine, 1832–1835):

"All that he did, was at thy instigation, thou viper; for I thou thee, thou traitor."

The *T* of contempt and anger is usually introduced between persons who normally exchange *V* but it can, of course, also be used by a surbordinate to a superior. As the social distance is greater, the overthrow of the norm is more shocking and generally represents a greater extremity of passion. Sejanus, in Ben Jonson's play of that name, feels extreme contempt for the emperor Tiberius but wisely gives him the reverential *V* to his face. However, soliloquizing after the emperor has exited, Sejanus begins: "Dull, heavy Caesar! Wouldst thou tell me . . . ." In Jonson's *Volpone* Mosca invariably says *you* to his master until the final scene when, as the two villains are about to be carted away, Mosca turns on Volpone with "Bane to thy wolfish nature."

Expressive effects of much greater subtlety than those we have described are common in Elizabethan and Jacobean drama. The exact interpretation of the speaker's attitude depends not only on the pronoun norm he upsets but also on his attendant words and actions and the total setting. Still simple enough to be unequivocal is the ironic or mocking *you* said by Tamburlaine to the captive Turkish emperor Bajazeth. This exchange occurs in Act IV of Marlowe's play:

Tamburlaine: Here, Turk, wilt thou have a clean trencher?
Bajazeth: Ay, tyrant, and more meat.
Tamburlaine: Soft, sir, you must be dieted; too much eating will make you surfeit.

Thou is to be expected from captor to captive and the norm is upset when Tamburlaine says *you*. He cannot intend to express admiration or respect since he keeps the Turk captive and starves him. His intention is to mock the captive king with respectful address, implying a power that the king has lost.

The momentary shift of pronoun directly expresses a momentary shift of mood, but that interpretation does not exhaust its meaning. The fact that a man has a particular momentary attitude or emotion may imply a great deal about his characteristic disposition, his readiness for one kind of feeling rather than another. Not every attorney general, for instance, would have used the abusive *thou* to Raleigh. The fact that Edward Coke did so suggests an arrogant and choleric temperament and, in fact, many made this assessment of him. When Volpone spoke to Celia, a lady of Venice, he ought to have said *you* but he began at once with *thee*. This violation of decorum, together with the fact that he leaps from his sick bed to attempt rape of the lady, helps to establish Volpone's monstrous character. His abnormal form of address is consistent with the unnatural images in his speech. In any given situation we know the sort of people who would break the norms of address and the sort who would not. From the fact that a man does break the norms we infer his immediate feelings and, in addition, attribute to him the general character of people who would have such feelings and would give them that kind of expression.

With the establishment of the solidarity semantic a new set of expressive meanings became possible—feelings of sympathy and estrangement. In Shakespeare's plays there are expressive meanings that derive from the solidarity semantic as well as many dependent on power usage and many that rely on both connotations. The play *Two Gentlemen of Verona* is concerned with the Renaissance ideal of friendship and provides especially clear expressions of solidarity. Proteus and Valentine, the two Gentlemen, initially exchange *thou*, but when they touch on the subject of love, on which they disagree, their address changes to the *you* of estrangement. Molière (Fay, 1920) has shown us that a man may even put himself at a distance as does George Dandin in the soliloquy beginning: "George Dandin! George Dandin! Vous avez fait une sottise . . ."

In both French and English drama of the past, *T* and *V* were marvelously sensitive to feelings of approach and withdrawal. In terms of Freud's striking amoeba metaphor the pronouns signal the extension or retraction of libidinal pseudopodia. However, in French, German, and Italian today this use seems to be very uncommon. Our informants told us that the *T*, once extended, is almost never taken back for the reason that it would mean the complete withdrawal of esteem. The only modern expressive shift we have found is a rather chilling one. Silverberg (1940) reports that in Germany in 1940 a prostitute and her client said *du* when they met and while they were together but when the libidinal tie (in the narrow sense) had been dissolved they resumed the mutual distant *Sie*.

We have suggested that the modern direction of change in pronoun usage expresses a will to extend the solidary ethic to everyone. The apparent decline of expressive shifts between *T* and *V* is more difficult to interpret. Perhaps it is because Europeans have seen that excluded persons or races or groups can become the target of extreme aggression from groups that are benevolent within themselves. Perhaps Europeans would like to convince themselves that the solidary ethic once extended will not be withdrawn, that there is security in the mutual *T*.

References

BAUGH, A. C. *A history of the English language.* New York: Appleton-Century, 1935.

BRUNOT, F. *Histoire de la langue française des origines à 1900.* Paris: Colin, 1905.

BRUNOT, F. *La pensée et la langue; Méthode, principes et plan d'une théorie nouvelle du langage appliquée au Français,* 2nd ed. Paris: Masson, 1926.

BYRNE, SISTER ST. GERALDINE. Shakespeare's use of the pronoun of address; Its significance in characterization and motivation. Unpublished doctoral dissertation. The Catholic University of America, 1936.

CHÂTELAIN, É. Du pluriel de respect en Latin. *Revue de philologie,* 1880. 4, 129–139.

CRONIN, M. The tyranny of democratic manners. *The new republic,* 1958, 137, 12–14.

DEVEREUX, W. B. *Lives and letters of the Devereux, earls of Essex, in the reigns of Elizabeth, James I, and Charles I, 1540–1646.* London: Murray, 1853.

DIEZ, F. *Grammaire des langue romanes*. Paris: Franck, 1874.

ELLWOOD, T. *The history of the life of Thomas Ellwood*. London: Sowle, 1714.

ESTRICH, R. M., and SPERBER, H. *Three keys to language*. New York: Rinehart, 1946.

EYSENCK, H. J. *Sense and nonsense in psychology*. Harmondsworth, Middlesex: Penguin, 1957.

FARNWORTH, R. *The pure language of the spirit of truth* . . . . London, 1657.

FAY, P. B. The use of "tu" and "vous" in Molière. *University of California publications in modern philology*, 1920, 8, 227–286.

FOX, G. *A battle-door for teachers and professors to learn plural and singular*. London: Wilson, 1660.

GEDIKE, F. *Über du und sie in der deutschen Sprache*. Berlin: Unger, 1794.

GRAND, C. *Tu. voi. lei; Étude des pronoms allocutoires Italien*. Ingenbohl, Switzerland: P. Theodose, 1930.

GRIMM, J. *Deutsche Grammatic*, 4 vol. Göttingen: Dieterichsche, 1822–1837.

JARDINE, D. *Criminal trials*. Vols. 1–2. London: Knight, 1832–1835.

JESPERSEN, O. *Growth and structure of the English language*. Leipzig: Teubner, 1905.

JOHNSTON, O. M. The use of "ella," "lei," and "la" as polite forms of address in Italian. *Modern philology*, 1904, 1, 469–475.

KENNEDY, A. G. *The pronoun of address in English literature of the thirteenth century*. Stanford, Calif.: The University, 1915.

LITTRÉ, É. *Dictionnaire de la langue française*. Vol. 4. Paris: Ploetz, 1882.

MEYER-LUBKE, W. *Grammaire des langues romanes*. Vol. 3, Paris: Welter, 1900.

MULLER, H. F. The use of the plural of reverence in the letters of Pope Gregory I. *The romantic review*, 1914, 5, 68–89.

PERDIGUIER, A. *Mémoires d'un compagnon*. Moulins, 1914.

SCHLIEBITZ, V. *Die Person der Anrede in der französischen Sprache*. Breslau, 1886.

SILVERBERG, W. V. On the psychological significance of "du" and "sie." *Psychoanalytic quarterly*, 1940, 9, 509–525.

STIDSTON, R. O. *The use of ye in the function of thou: a study of grammar and social intercourse in fourteenth-century England*. Stanford, Calif.: The University, 1917.

STOUFFER, S. A., GUTTMAN, L., *et al.*, *Measurement and prediction*. Princeton: Princeton University Press, 1950.

[13]

Personality and Style in Concord

By *style* we always mean a *way* of doing *something* and so any conception of style presupposes some conception of constancy or invariance, a *something* which can be done in various ways. In certain non-linguistic cases the invariance with reference to which style should be defined has a quite natural definition. In music the printed score is the constant that may be interpreted in various ways. For any action that has a well-defined goal—clothing the body, serving a dinner, answering the telephone—the goal of the action is a constant that may be attained in various ways. When it comes to speech and writing and especially to literature, however, it is not at all clear how the invariance should be defined that leaves style as a residual.

In certain cases, contrived for psychological purposes, style does have a clear sense. For the Rorschach test individuals are asked to interpret a fixed set of inkblots and for the TAT test to tell stories about a fixed set of pictures. This is like asking painters to work from the same live model. There is a constant task that renders

This paper was written for a collection made in honor of the great American literary scholar Austin Warren. Albert Gilman, who was one of Professor Warren's students, was co-author. The book itself is called *Transcendentalism and Its Legacy*; it was edited by Myron Simon and Thornton H. Parsons and published by the University of Michigan Press in 1966. Reprinted by permission of the authors.

individual productions roughly comparable and makes it reasonable to treat the remaining variance as stylistic and, in the psychological cases, diagnostic. But people speaking spontaneously and literary men writing plays, novels, and essays do not start from the same imposed task. Nevertheless we freely speak of styles in all these cases and we must mean something by it.

What we usually mean surely is that certain sentences or passages have the same meaning even though they differ in form or styles. But a great many critics have argued very convincingly that no two distinguishable sentences ever mean exactly the same thing. Consider a pair that I. A. Richards has discussed: "Socrates is wise" and "Wisdom belongs to Socrates." They are close certainly but when you think about it the first would be used in answer to a question like "What kind of man is Socrates?" whereas the second would be responsive to a question like "What do you mean by wisdom?" Surely there is some difference of meaning that corresponds to this difference of function. Any pair proposed seems just to be a temporary challenge to interpretive ingenuity; eventually one discovers some difference of meaning. I think the point must be granted that distinguishable sentences never have *exactly* the same sense. Well then, must we not settle on some *kind* or *degree* of semantic identity that will constitute the invariance with which a definition of style can begin? Various suggestions have been made: identity in "cognitive" meaning or "propositional" meaning. Richard Ohmann, in an interesting paper,* has started from transformational linguistics and suggested that sentences with the same deep structure but different surface structures are the only ones that should be said to differ in style. All of these attempts involve difficulties: some are simply not well-defined; some, like Ohmann's are reasonably well-defined but isolate a class for which it is difficult to find useful instances. How often do two literary men create sentences with identical deep structures and different surface structures? Practically never.

My position is that there are indefinitely many possible levels at which meaning might be held constant and an equal number of possible definitions of linguistic style. I suspect that there is no natural and general definition comparable to the definitions

* Ohmann, R. Generative grammars and the concept of style. *Word*, 20, 1964, 423–439.

available for music and for explicitly instrumental actions. The problem is not to find the right level but a level or levels that prove revealing for the works and for their creators. The present paper starts with what are frankly subjective judgments of approximate propositional equivalence in works of Emerson and Thoreau and then attempts to show that the residual variance is revealing and consistent.

IS IT POSSIBLE to distinguish the styles of two writers living in the same time and place, educated at the same school, writing in the same genre, on the same topic, voicing the same opinion, with nothing but their personalities to keep them apart? Emerson and Thoreau provide the almost experimental contrast that is required. They are, to begin with, very well matched in respect of all the historical and demographic factors that can cause one man's writing to differ from that of another. Both lived in the nineteenth century, Thoreau's shorter lifetime being encompassed by that of Emerson. Both lived most of their lives in the village of Concord, Massachusetts, and both were educated at Harvard. Whatever differences there may be in the styles of the two men cannot be attributed to membership in distinct census groupings.

Because the various genres of literature set distinct problems and have distinct conventions, it is desirable to hold genre constant in looking for features of style that are determined by personality. Although Emerson and Thoreau both wrote some poetry, the present study is limited to their prose. Both men wrote personal journals, essays, and Lyceum lectures. The three forms stand in the same relation to one another for the two authors: the journals were source books from which essays and lectures were mined. The passages we will consider are drawn from these shared forms.

Style is to some extent dictated by topic. Between an essay on the Over-Soul and an accounting of the cost of food consumed in eight months beside Walden Pond some differences of diction and grammar are to be expected. However, one need not look to personality for an explanation; the differences would be there if both passages had a single author. Since topical effects tend to obscure personality effects, we have tried to hold topic constant. That is easy to do with Emerson and Thoreau because their topical range is about the same. The great subjects of both writers include Nature, self-reliance, conscience, the state, poetry, friendship, manners, possessions, and Slavery. It is not only the topics that match but the opinions, the arguments, the general philosophies. There are even short passages that approach propositional equivalence, and we will restrict our study to these.[1] In these passages we will find some sentences, even paragraphs, that either Emerson or Thoreau might have written. We will even find passages actually written by one that would be taken for the work of the other. On most passages, however, we will discover that Emerson and Thoreau have left their stylistic fingerprints.

Of course, a man's style, unlike his fingerprint, may be as it is because he has undertaken to make it so. A difference of style, produced by intention, to correspond with an ideal, is an expression of personality but not an expression of the most interesting aspects of personality. The significance of the Emerson–Thoreau contrast is heightened by the fact that they had very similar ideals of style. Both, for example, valued compression, vitality, and straight-line direction. Emerson wrote of the good style (No. 10): "It is a shower of bullets . . ." (*J*, *V*, 420). Thoreau wrote: "The *art* of composition is as simple as the discharge of a bullet from a rifle" ("The Last Days of John Brown," *W*, IV, 447). The ideals are similar, but even in these phrases we notice that "a shower of bullets" has not the compression, force, and direction of "the discharge of a bullet from a rifle." And, a few sentences further on, Thoreau, suppressing his predicates, creates the rhythm of bullets thudding into a target: "This first, this second, this third; pebbles in your mouth or not" (p. 448). Emerson's next clause begins with "whilst" and has a compound subject and a compound predicate. There was something that kept the styles apart, something other than education, genre, topic, or stylistic ideal.

THE PERSONALITIES

The differences in the personalities of Emerson and Thoreau, for the most part, lie in temperament and intelligence. In temperament Thoreau was more aggressive than Emerson, more *aggressive* in two senses: more *combative* and also more *vigorous*. Vigor and combativeness are distinguishable characteristics, and it may be that the two are bundled together by the English word "aggression" for accidental and arbitrary reasons. It is more likely, however, that the lexicon reflects an actual association in human and animal nature. At any rate, they were associated in Thoreau.

The difference of temperament is rather well attested by contemporaries of the two men, by incident in their lives, and by self report. John Gardner, a friend of Emerson's in Latin School days, speaks of Ralph Waldo's rather overpowering "equanimity"; Gardner though Emerson could do with "a few harsher traits & perhaps more Masculine vigor" (Rusk, 1949, p. 67). Emerson himself wrote in early adult years of his "sore uneasiness in the company of most men and women, a frigid fear of offending" (Rusk, 1949, p. 104). Comparing himself with his brilliant brother Edward, Emerson said: "My own manner is sluggish; my speech sometimes flippant, sometimes embarrassed and ragged; my actions (if I may say so) are of a passive kind" (Rusk, 1949, p. 128).

Emerson's transcendental philosophy inspired his friends to vigorous social action, to the creation of the experimental communities, Brook Farm and Fruitlands. Emerson did not join either community. After one evening of excited talk, at his home, about Brook Farm, Emerson wrote in his diary: "Not once could I be inflamed but sat aloof and thoughtless; my voice faltered and fell" (Rusk, 1949, p. 289).

In 1869 Emerson found himself temporarily a member of the Harvard faculty and scheduled to give a series of eighteen lectures which were to form a theoretical unit. He seems to have found the university lectures a serious strain and to have announced to his class a defensively modest aspiration; he would make no attempt at formulating a system but "wanted only to dot a little curve of personal observation." Emerson wrote more than once of his distaste for debate with tough-minded opponents. "The men of strong understanding are a menacing rapid trenchant race—they cut me short—they drive me into a corner" (Rusk, 1949, p. 235).

Thoreau, fourteen years younger than Emerson, became a disciple when he read the essay *Nature*. The two men were well acquainted all their adult lives and in 1841–43 and 1847–49 Thoreau lived in the Emerson household. Emerson is a good authority on Thoreau's temperament: "He has muscle, and ventures on and performs feats which I am forced to decline" (*J*, IX, 522). Emerson here referred to moral and intellectual muscle, but Thoreau also had physical muscle. He was in his early life much stronger and healthier than Emerson, but he contracted tuberculosis and died at the age of forty-five, whereas Emerson lived to the age of seventy-eight. Emerson testifies to Thoreau's combativeness as well as to his vigor (No. 14): "If I knew only Thoreau, I should think cooperation of good men impossible. . . . Always some weary captious paradox to fight you with, and the time and temper wasted" (*J*, IX, 15–16).

Thoreau conducted his own experiments in living. He never married and is not known ever to have been in love. He did not smoke, would not drink wine, coffee or tea, and was, from time to time, vegetarian. He refused to pay his poll tax and on that account spent a single night in jail. Above all, of course, he lived for two years alone in his cabin by Walden Pond. The Walden experiment was not done to show that man could live in the woods. The Walden years and all of Thoreau's life were intended to show that a man can live as he wants to live, that he can have what he truly values if he will find out what that is and single-heartedly insist upon it.

A man's temperament is often revealed in his choice of heroes. Thoreau's greatest hero was one whom comfortable folk thought a fanatic—Captain John Brown. When Brown was jailed and threatened with hanging, Thoreau called his townsmen together and delivered a plea for John Brown's life. From that plea it would appear that Thoreau took Brown for a bolder, and therefore more admirable, version of himself.

"He was a man of Spartan habits. . . . A man of rare common sense and directness of speech, as of action" ("A Plea for Captain John Brown," *W*, IV, 413). And "He did not recognize unjust human laws, but resisted them as he was bid. For once we are lifted out of the trivialness and dust of politics into the region of truth and manhood" (pp. 424–25). "Read his admirable answers to Mason and others. . . . On the one side, half-brutish, half-timid questioning; on the other, truth, clear as lightning, crashing into their obscene temples" (p. 426). And (No. 20): "Think of him,—of his rare qualities!—such a man as it takes ages to make, and ages to understand; no mock hero, nor the representative of any party. A man such as the sun may not rise upon again in this benighted land. To whose making went the costliest material, the finest adamant" (p. 437).

The second difference between Emerson and Thoreau is one of intelligence. It is not a question of intellectual power, but of intellectual (or conceptual) style. Thoreau's is a more analytic mind and Emerson's a more synthetic. Thoreau gives us a world well-differentiated, the experience of concrete particulars. Emerson gives us a world processed by abstraction with similarities seen everywhere. It is the difference really between a bean patch and the Over-Soul.

In explaining his poem "The Sphinx" Emerson champions his own synthetic conceptual style. "The perception of identity unites all things and explains one by another, and the more rare and strange is equally facile as the most common. But if the mind live only in particulars, and see only differences (wanting the power to see the whole—all in each), then the world addresses to this mind a question it cannot answer, and each new fact tears it in pieces, and it is vanquished by the distracting variety" (Rusk, 1949, p. 313). To put Emerson's statement in balance one is obliged to add that synthesis without analysis is seldom compelling. If Emerson saw identity everywhere, it was partly because he had a tendency to smear.

Thoreau's analytic, conceptual style put him in some danger of contributing to natural science. Channing wrote of Thoreau: "But his habit of mind demanded complete accuracy, the utmost finish, and that nothing should be taken on hearsay he had his gauges on the river, which he consulted winter and summer; he knew the temperature of all the springs in the town; he measured the snows when remarkable" (Krutch, 1948, p. 141). Thoreau interested himself in botany and zoology and in his will he left to the Boston Society of Natural History a collection of plants and of Indian relics. Emerson's attitude toward science and disciplined study seems to have been a little different. As a sophomore at Harvard he said: "Mathematics I hate." Shortly before his twenty-first birthday he wrote: "My reasoning faculty is proportionably weak" and spoke of Locke and Hume as "Reasoning Machines." Later in life he confessed that "he generally felt himself repelled by physicists" (Rusk, 1949, p. 457).

The fourteen volumes of Thoreau's *Journal* are replete with descriptions and measurements that are something like scientific data. It is not imprecision that prevents them from being data but rather their scientific aimlessness. They were not recorded for the purpose of inducing or testing empirical generalizations. In the absence of scientific aim Thoreau's data would suggest a mindless compulsion to inventory Nature if we did not know that he had extra-scientific aims. As Krutch (1948) says, Thoreau always sought to experience the natural world and to transmit that experience. The generalizations he sought were metaphysical, moral, and poetic, rather than scientific.

The characterization of Thoreau as analytic and aggressive does not prepare us for his apparent chastity. There is some evidence that analytic intelligence, in this society at least, tends to be a masculine characteristic (Kagan, Moss, and Sigel, 1963), and among primate species in general a high level of aggressiveness in the mature male is associated with a high level of sexual activity.[2] But, of course, a personality is not just a profile of dimensional values; it is an organized system, and the principles of organization are in part peculiarly human. We cannot now hope to discover the cause of Thoreau's chastity, but there are passages which suggest an exaggerated physical squeamishness, a squeamishness which his philosophy did not approve.[3] "We discourse freely without shame of one form of sensuality, and are silent about another. We are so degraded that we cannot speak simply of the necessary functions of human nature. In earlier ages, in some countries, every function was reverently spoken of and regulated by law. Nothing was too trivial for the Hindoo law-giver, however offensive it may be to modern taste. He teaches how to eat, drink, cohabit, void excrement and urine, and the like, elevating what is mean, and does not falsely excuse him-self by calling these things trifles" (*Walden*, *W*, II, 244–45).

We can feel more confident of the *consequences* of Thoreau's chastity than of its causes. He himself offers an explicit sublimation theory. "The generative energy, which, when we are loose, dissipates and makes us unclean, when we are continent invigorates and inspires us. Chastity is the flowering of man; and what are called Genius, Heroism, Holiness, and the like, are but various fruits which succeed it" (p. 243). The simple hydraulics implied by this statement and also by Freud's libido theory are probably wrong. And yet Thoreau's chastity did help to make possible his extraordinary achieve-ments. Not for dynamic reasons, not by way of the diversion of libido, we would guess, but by keeping him free of the affec-tional ties that would have compromised his life of principle. To put it simply, a man without family is freer to follow his conscience than is a man with family, freer to live at Walden Pond, to spend a night in jail, to give his time to the study of Nature, to speak out strongly for John Brown. If Thoreau's absolute and uncompromising idealism has a certain adoles-cent quality, it is because adolescence is an age of mature intelligence and underdeveloped responsibilities, and so an age when morality is clear and absolute.

In time, the friendship between Thoreau and Emerson, which began so warmly, became strained and unsatisfying to both. We do not believe that the differences of personality alone foredoomed the friendship. A dominant, vigorous person of analytic intelligence and a less aggressive, less analytic, younger disciple compose a familiar sort of symbiotic pair. The difficulty in the case of Emerson and Thoreau was that the roles of leader and follower defined by the differences of age and reputation were fitted to the wrong personalities.

The less aggressive, less analytic Emerson could not effectively play the sage with Thoreau for very long. But the dignity of Emerson's years, the extent of his fame, and the recollected pleasure of having had a disciple would not permit him to play any other role.

Both men testify to the difficulties. Thoreau wrote in 1853: "Talked, or tried to talk, with R. W. E. Lost my time—nay, almost my identity" (J, V, 188). And in 1856 he wrote of Emerson (No. 14): "He would not meet me on equal terms, but only be to some extent my patron. He would not come to see me, but was hurt if I did not visit him" (J, VIII, 199). In that same year Emerson said of Thoreau (No. 14): "Must we always talk for victory, and never once for truth, for comfort, and joy?" (J, IX, 15).

THE STYLES

Are there specific features in the styles of Emerson and Thoreau which express their differences of temperament and intelligence? In order to hold constant the many sources of stylistic variation other than personality we thought it desirable to work with passages matched, as nearly as possible, for content. The statistical analysis we planned to make required that the passages be matched as pairs, one from each author, and the fact that Emerson and Thoreau manifest a degree of stylistic overlap directed us to look for a substantial number of pairs. We found thirty-two of them.

There is no mechanical procedure that will select from the works of Emerson and Thoreau just those paired passages that are, in context, maximally close to identity. The trouble with nonmechanical procedures involving human judgment is the possibility that the judgments will not be sensitive to content alone but also to style. Nevertheless, judgment had to do the job. We looked for closely similar passages, attempting to disregard style, and at a time when the specific features to be counted had not yet been identified.

Passages were judged to constitute a matched pair when it seemed to us that a single proposition would convey the main point of both. Because this kind of propositional equivalence does not extend over long sequences, no passage is longer than about five hundred words. As far as possible, we made up the pairs with single continuous passages from each author. Sometimes, however, in an effort to maximize propositional equivalence, discontinuous selections from one or more works have been combined. In several instances the combination was made in order to bring into the corpus a single sentence, detached from the main body of one author's passage, which made an especially close match with something from the other author. The sources of the thirty-two passages are listed in Table 13–1 together with the abstract propositions in virtue of which each pair is equivalent.[4]

Table 13–1. Paired Passages and the Propositions they Express

1. Not only thought but action also is valuable.
   Em. "The American Scholar," *W*, I, 95–96. "I do . . . . splendid products"
   Th. *Walden*, *W*, II, 56. "The student . . . . to end"
2. Actual friendship involves many difficulties.
   Em. "Friendship," *W*, II, 199. "We are . . . . by solitude"
   Th. *A Week*, *W*, I, 294–95. "The only . . . . not understood"
3. One should not accept tradition unthinkingly.
   Em. "The American Scholar," *W*, I, 105–6. "Yes, we . . . . the moon"
   Th. *Walden*, *W*, II, 9–10. "It is . . . . nothing about"
4. One should not imitate others.
   Em. "Self-Reliance," *W*, II, 46. "There is . . . . has tried"
   "Self-Reliance," *W*, II, 83. "Insist on . . . . exhibited it"
   Th. *Walden*, *W*, II, 78–79. "One young . . . . true course"
5. One should live in the present.
   Em. "Self-Reliance," *W*, II, 67. "These roses . . . . above time"
   "Self-Reliance," *W*, II, 76. "He walks . . . . lives already"
   Th. *Walden*, *W*, II, 59. "This spending . . . . at once"
   "Walking," *W*, V, 245–46. "Above all . . . . this moment"
6. Nature has great value for a city man.
   Em. *Nature*, *W*, I, 16. "To the . . . . finds himself"
   Th. *Walden*, *W*, II, 349–50. "Our village . . . . ground"
   Walden, *W*, II, 350. "We must . . . . produces freshets"
7. I have no genius for philanthropy.
   Em. "Self-Reliance," *W*, II, 51–52. "If malice . . . . to withhold"
   Th. *Walden*, *W*, II, 80–81. "But all . . . . they will"

8. A man should set his own conscience above all conventional standards.
   Em. "Self-Reliance," *W*, II, 74. "The populace....one day"
   Th. *Walden*, *W*, II, 355. "This was....with such"

9. Personal possessions are not important to the great soul.
   Em. "Heroism," *W*, II, 252. "Yet the....earnest nonsense"
       "Heroism," *W*, II, 255. "The heroic....its loss"
   Th. *Walden*, *W*, II, 25. "Old shoes....them do"
       Walden, *W*, II, 26. "I say....of clothes"
       Walden, *W*, II, 32. "I used....be free"
       Walden, *W*, II, 72. "Thank God....furniture warehouse"
       Walden, *W*, II, 74. "When I....to carry"

10. The language of the street is strong and agreeable.
    Em. "The Superlative," *W*, X, 169. "I am....and agreeable"
        Journals, V, 419–20. "The language....half sentence"
    Th. *A Week*, *W*, I, 109. "We are....the pine"
        A Week, *W*, I, 110. "A sentence....the end"
        Journal, I, 237. "There is....quite cheap"
        Journal, I, 237. "The scholar....high art"
        Journal, I, 237. "I like....of nature"

11. A good style is a concentrated one.
    Em. *Journals*, X, 302–3. "All writing....a surprise"
        Journals, V, 213. "There is....of surface"
    Th. *Journal*, II, 418–19. "It is....without digesting"

12. I dislike easy familiarity, lack of reserve and of self-reliance.
    Em. "Manners," *W*, III, 136–37. "I prefer....much acquainted"
        "Manners," *W*, III, 139. "The love....to flight"
        "Friendship," *W*, II, 208–9. "Let me....unites them"
        "Behaviour," *W*, VI, 186–87. "The basis....its members"
    Th. *Journal*, V, 263–65. "Here have....beautiful reserve"

13. Temperance in food and drink is admirable.
    Em. "Heroism," *W*, II, 254–55. "The temperance....before it"
    Th. *Walden*, *W*, II, 236–37. "Before, there....me essentially"
        Walden, *W*, II, 240. "I believe....of tea"

14. My friendship with Thoreau (Emerson) was a difficult one.
    Em. *Journals*, VIII, 303. "Thoreau gives....set aside"
        Journals, IX, 15–16. "If I....temper wasted"
    Th. *Journal*, III, 250. "I doubt....comprehensive character"
        Journal, VIII, 199. "I had....our affection"

15. Self-culture is more important than traveling.
    Em. "Self-Reliance," *W*, II, 80. "It is....educated Americans"
        "Self-Reliance," *W*, II, 81–82. "Our first....fled from"
    Th. *Walden*, *W*, II, 352–53. "The other....be after"
        Walden, *W*, II, 353. "Be rather....higher latitudes"

Walden, W, II, 353. "Nay, be. . . . of thought"

16. An ideal friendship is a relation of love, truth, and equality.
    Em. "Friendship," *W*, II, 205–6. "I wish. . . . was drudgery"
    Th. *A Week, W*, I, 283–85. "A Friend. . . . for us"

17. Fine clothing is not necessary to the great spirit.
    Em. "Social Aims," *W*, VIII, 87–88. "To pass. . . . to bestow"
    Th. *Walden, W*, II, 23–24. "As for. . . . clothes on"
    Walden, W, II, 25–26. "A man. . . . of clothes"

18. The personal conscience is a higher standard than government or law.
    Em. "John Brown: Speech at Boston," *W*, XI, 271–73. "The state. . . . of paper"
    Th. "A Plea for Captain John Brown," *W*, IV, 437–38. "Any man. . . . from that"

19. Slavery now impinges on my life.
    Em. "The Fugitive Slave Law," *W*, XI, 228–29. "I said. . . . not exist"
    Th. "Slavery in Massachusetts," *W*, IV, 405–6. "I have. . . . see it"

20. John Brown should not hang.
    Em. "John Brown: Speech at Boston," *W*, XI, 269–70. "It is. . . . poor prisoner"
    Th. "A Plea for Captain John Brown," *W*, IV, 437. "Who is. . . . of men"

21. Regrets and pangs of conscience are of little value.
    Em. "Self-Reliance," *W*, II, 78–79. "Another sort. . . . are swift"
    Th. *A Week, W*, I, 75. "Men have. . . . no milk"

22. Few men understand the art of walking.
    Em. "Country Life," *W*, XII, 142. "Few men. . . . a dog"
    "Country Life," *W*, XII, 158–59. "Dr Johnson. . . . call professors"
    Th. "Walking," *W*, V, 205–6. "I have. . . . a walk"

23. My vicinity offers many good walks.
    Em. "Country Life," *W*, XII, 143–44. "For walking. . . . a park"
    Th. "Walking," *W*, V, 211–12. "My vicinity. . . . to you"

24. Through books there is community of mind.
    Em. "The American Scholar," *W*, I, 91–92. "Undoubtedly there. . . never see"
    Th. *Walden, W*, II, 119–20. "It is. . . . the board"

25. Our houses are no credit to us.
    Em. "Domestic Life," *W*, VII, 110–11. "I am. . . . dearly bought"
    Th. *Walden, W*, II, 31. "From the. . . . mausoleum instead"
    Walden, W, II, 32. "I used. . . . as this"

26. The less government the better.
    Em. "Politics," *W*, III, 215–16. "Hence the. . . . and flowers"
    Th. "Civil Disobedience," *W*, IV, 356. "I heartily. . . . standing government"
    "Civil Disobedience," *W*, IV, 356–67. "This American. . . . the railroads"

"Civil Disobedience," *W*, IV, 358. "But a . . . . the right"

27. There is poetry in the primitive sense of words.
    Em. "The Poet," *W*, III, 21–22. "The poets . . . . a tree"
    Th. "Walking," *W*, V, 232. "Where is . . . . surrounding Nature"
28. Thought and spirit are more important than form in true poetry.
    Em. "The Poet," *W*, III, 9–10. "Our poets . . . . its poet"
    Th. *A Week*, *W*, I, 400. "A true . . . . always divine"
29. All nature and all experience feed the true poet.
    Em. "The Poet," *W*, III, 42. "And this . . . . or ignoble"
    Th. *A Week*, *W*, I, 101–2. "At least . . . . and then"
30. America awaits her poet.
    Em. "The Poet," *W*, III, 37–38. "Banks and . . . . for metres"
    Th. "Walking," *W*, V, 232. "I do . . . . than anything"
    "Walking," *W*, V, 233. "The West . . . . American mythology"
31. It is possible to find contentment in the simple things of life.
    Em. "Experience," *W*, III, 61–62. "The fine . . . . by analysis"
    Th. *Walden*, *W*, II, 361. "However mean . . . . a palace"
    Walden, *W*, II, 361. "Do not . . . . about me"
32. There is nothing in history that is not also in the present.
    Em. "Works and Days," *W*, VII, 174–75. "The world . . . . is Doomsday"
    Th. *A Week*, *W*, I, 160–61. "In every . . . . the researched"

We will begin by comparing the passages qualitatively and will find that the propositional equivalence attained is never perfect, that temperament and conceptual style always intervene to make one author express something the other does not. While these qualitative comparisons are often persuasive, they are both selective and subjective, and so one cannot be confident that they establish real differences characteristic of the two authors. We will then compare the passages quantitatively, showing that there are formally defined features, interpretable as expressions of temperament and intelligence, which appear with statistically significant differential frequency in Emerson and Thoreau.

QUALITATIVE COMPARISONS

The thirty-two propositions of Table 13–1 convey fairly well the philosophy, social attitudes, and cranky opinions that Emerson and Thoreau had in common. The statements of Table 13–1 are a rather banal set. Only our reverence for the two authors deterred us from phrasing No. 31 as "The best things in life are free," and No. 32 as "History repeats itself." In part the banality of the statements in Table 13–1 is explained by the fact that they are encapsulations of the longer original passages. In part the paraphrases seem banal, whereas the sources do not because, for both writers, it is the way the thing is said that chiefly matters. Emerson and Thoreau are nearer to being poets than to being systematic philosophers or psychologists. But they are poets with distinct personalities. The same idea has never the same overtones for the two.

Consider first the difference of vigor between Emerson and Thoreau. Here is Emerson describing the benefits that Nature offers to a city man (No. 6): "To the body and mind which have been cramped by noxious work or company, nature is medicinal and restores their tone. The tradesman, the attorney comes out of the din and craft of the street and sees the sky and the woods, and is a man again. In their eternal calm, he finds himself" (*Nature*, *W*, I, 16). Here is Thoreau on the same subject: "Our village life would stagnate if it were not for the unexplored forests and meadows which surround it. We need the tonic of wildness. . . . We must be refreshed by the sight of inexhaustible vigor, vast and titanic features, the seacoast with its wrecks, the wilderness with its living and its decaying trees" (*Walden*, *W*, II, 349–50). For both men nature is medicinal, but Emerson craves a healing balm and Thoreau "the tonic of wildness."

Emerson, thinking of the importance of living in the present (No. 5), preaches a sermon on "These roses under my window. . . . There is no time to them. There is simply the rose; it is perfect in every moment of its existence" ("Self-Reliance," *W*, II, 67). Perfect the rose certainly is but also rather bland by comparison with "the cock crow in every barn-yard within our horizon," which is what comes to mind in a similar connection for Thoreau. "That sound commonly reminds us that we are growing rusty and antique in our employments and habits of thought. His philosophy comes down to a more recent time than ours" ("Walking," *W*, V, 246).

Emerson, comparing travel unfavorably with selfculture

(No. 15), exposes a shadow of melancholy: "I pack my trunk, embrace my friends, embark on the sea and at last wake up in Naples, and there beside me is the stern fact, the sad self, unrelenting, identical, that I fled from" ("Self-Reliance," *W*, II, 81–82). Thoreau, advising us not to travel to the "other side of the globe," adds the exhortation: "Be rather the Mungo Park, the Lewis and Clark and Frobisher, of your own streams and oceans; explore your own higher latitudes. . . . Nay, be a Columbus to whole new continents and worlds within you, opening new channels, not of trade, but of thought" (*Walden*, *W*, II, 353).

Again and again Thoreau sounds the more vigorous note. For example, in No. 26: "I heartily accept the motto,—'That government is best which governs least' " ("Civil Disobedience," *W*, IV, 356). Emerson's near equivalent is: "Hence the less government we have the better" ("Politics," *W*, III, 215). Emerson on the subject of wine (No. 13) quotes John Eliot, the Indian Apostle: " 'It is a noble, generous liquor and we should be humbly thankful for it, but, as I remember, water was made before it' " ("Heroism," *W*, II, 254–55). Thoreau's related sentence has more athletic spring: "I believe that water is the only drink for a wise man; wine is not so noble a liquor; and think of dashing the hopes of a morning with a cup of warm coffee, or of an evening with a dish of tea!" (*Walden*, *W*, II, 240).

Consider next the manifestations of combativeness. Here is Emerson telling an audience that John Brown ought not to be hanged (No. 20): "Nothing can resist the sympathy which all elevated minds must feel with Brown, and through them the whole civilized world. . . . Indeed, it is the *reductio ad absurdum* of Slavery, when the governor of Virginia is forced to hang a man whom he declares to be a man of the most integrity, truthfulness and courage he has ever met. Is that the kind of man the gallows is built for?" ("John Brown," *W*, XI, 269–70). We have already seen some of Thoreau's lines in defense of John Brown, but here are a few others. "Who is it whose safety requires that Captain Brown be hung? . . . If you do not wish it, say so distinctly. . . . A man . . . sent to be the redeemer of those in captivity; and the only use to which you can put him is to hang him at the end of a rope!" ("A Plea for Captain John Brown," *W*, IV, 437). Emerson is measured, stately, a little remote with his *reductio ad absurdum*. Thoreau is passionately and personally combative: "If you do not wish it," "the only use to which *you* can put him" (italics added). Emerson did not have the stomach for this sort of face-to-face accusation.

It is regularly the case in the thirty-two pairs of passages we have studied that Thoreau is more concerned than Emerson with destroying his opposition. Both advise us not to follow tradition unthinkingly (No. 3); Emerson in the mild words: "It is a mischievous notion that we are come late into nature; that the world was finished a long time ago" (*Nature*, *W*, I, 105). Thoreau is more challenging and abrupt: "What old people say you cannot do, you try and find that you can. Old deeds for old people, and new deeds for new. . . . I have lived some thirty years on this planet, and I have yet to hear the first syllable of valuable or even earnest advice from my seniors" (*Walden*, *W*, II, 9–10). With Emerson it is usually possible to feel that an attack is not leveled against anyone in particular. With Thoreau one generally feels that there is someone who will take offense.[5]

Emerson expresses his taste in manners (No. 12) as follows: "I prefer a tendency to stateliness to an excess of fellowship. Let the incommunicable objects of nature and the metaphysical isolation of man teach us independence. Let us not be too much acquainted" ("Manners," *W*, III, 136–37). Thoreau expresses the same taste in connection with a particular acquaintance and in strongly personal terms: "I wanted that he should straighten his back, smooth out those ogling wrinkles of benignity about his eyes, and, with a healthy reserve, pronounce something in a downright manner. It was difficult to keep clear of his slimy benignity, with which he sought to cover you before he swallowed you and took you fairly into his bowels" (*J*, V, 264).

When Thoreau blazes away in his most aggressive vein he reminds us of a writer with whom he is not often compared— George Bernard Shaw. The points of resemblance between Shaw and Thoreau are numerous: iconoclasm, impatience, extravagance, a taste for paradox. Both men attempted to found every action, even trivial ones, on principle. Both eschewed alcohol and tobacco, both were vegetarians, both admired fanatical men. There was a certain coolness in the private lives of both; both are under grave suspicion of chastity.

When Thoreau is least like Emerson he is most like Shaw (No. 5):

This spending of the best part of one's life earning money in order to enjoy a questionable liberty during the least valuable part of it reminds me of the Englishman who went to India to make a fortune first, in order that he might return to England and live the life of a poet. He should have gone up garret at once. "What!" exclaim a million Irishmen starting up from all the shanties in the land, "is not this railroad which we have built a good thing?" Yes, I answer, *comparatively* good, that is, you might have done worse; but I wish, as you are brothers of mine, that you could have spent your time better than digging in this dirt.

The passage is from *Walden* (*W*, II, 59–60), but the impatience, the vigor, the extravagance, the paradox, are very Shavian. And so are they in this sentence from *Walden*: "As for the Pyramids, there is nothing to wonder at in them so much as the fact that so many men could be found degraded enough to spend their lives constructing a tomb for some ambitious booby, whom it would have been wiser and manlier to have drowned in the Nile, and then given his body to the dogs" (*W*, II, 64).

The difference of conceptual style between Emerson and Thoreau appears, in extreme form, in their remarks on the subject of housing (No. 25). Emerson advises: "His house ought to show us his honest opinion of what makes his well-being when he rests among his kindred, and forgets all affectation, compliance, and even exertion of will. He brings home whatever commodities and ornaments have for years allured his pursuit, and his character must be seen in them" ("Domestic Life," *W*, VII, 110–11). Thoreau is rather more concrete. "I used to see a large box by the railroad, six feet long by three wide, in which the laborers locked up their tools at night; and it suggested to me that every man who was hard pushed might get such a one for a dollar, and, having bored a few auger holes in it, to admit the air at least, get into it when it rained and at night, and hook down the lid, and so have freedom in his love, and in his soul be free" (*Walden*, *W*, II, 32).

A contrast in level of abstraction appears in many of the paired passages including some that we have already cited to illustrate the difference of temperament. For example, Emerson lists as benefits of Nature for the city man (No. 6), the sky and the woods. Thoreau's list is more fully itemized: the bittern, the meadow-hen, the snipe, the whispering sedge, decaying trees, the thundercloud, etc. (*Nature*, *W*, I, 16; *Walden*, *W*, II, 349–50).

The association between concrete, analytic concepts and a combative tone is not entirely arbitrary. Other things equal, it is easier to disagree with a concrete statement than with an abstract generalization. On the highest level of abstraction men tend either to agree or to be unable to determine whether they do or do not agree. But when someone advises you to sleep in a box, six feet long by three wide, you know where you are.

QUANTITATIVE COMPARISONS

With matched passages it is possible to use a simple test for the statistical significance of obtained differences, the Sign Test (Siegel, 1956). Probably everyone who makes a count in connection with a study of style feels the force of the question: How large and consistent must a difference be before it is taken seriously? The question is ordinarily answered with intuitions of probability: "A difference of only 5 words in passages 1000 words long may be meaningless." Intuition does not necessarily set easier tasks than the theory of probability, but it is more partial than that theory to the investigator's hypotheses and in that respect less trustworthy.

In testing any particular hypothesis about differences in the styles of Emerson and Thoreau, we propose to treat the thirty-two matched samples as if they were thirty-two tosses of a coin. In essence we shall be asking whether the coin is an unbiased one for which the two outcomes, heads and tails, are equally probable or a biased one for which one outcome is more probable than the other. There will be in our count two outcomes corresponding to the heads and tails of coin tossing: a difference that favors Emerson will be the one outcome and a difference that favors Thoreau the other. We shall be asking of each stylistic feature whether the outcomes are equally probable across the passages or whether we should consider that the tosses are biased and the styles therefore truly distinctive with regard to the feature in question.

With a coin that is really unbiased *any* obtained sequence of outcomes is *possible*—even, for instance, thirty-two successive cases of heads. However, the probability of obtaining so discrepant an outcome with an unbiased coin is astronomically small. A reasonable man who obtained such an outcome would conclude that the coin was not in fact unbiased but biased in favor of heads. What would he conclude for various less extreme outcomes, for 30 heads and 2 tails, 28 heads and 4 tails, 26 heads and 6 tails? As the outcomes approach equality they become more and more compatible with the conclusion that the coin is actually unbiased. Mathematical theory (the expansion of the binomial) assigns exact probabilities to each sequence of results on the assumption that the coin is unbiased. However, the drawing of the line where one will begin to believe that the coin is biased is a partially arbitrary decision. It is conventional in the use of tests of significance of this kind to treat results which have a probability of occurrence no greater than 5 times in 100 ($p = .05$) as significant results, as evidence that the outcomes are not equally likely.

As an example let us apply this statistical model to one count. The hypothesis is that Thoreau makes greater use of the first-person, singular pronouns, "I", "me," and "my," than does Emerson. Because the first selection of such a pronoun in a sentence tends to constrain subsequent selections in that sentence, we decided to count each sentence just once—as containing a first-person singular pronoun or as not containing one. The count was made for each passage and expressed as a ratio with the number of sentences containing a pronoun as the numerator and the total number of sentences in the passage as the denominator. Expression as a ratio is necessary because the paired passages are not exactly matched in length.

In No. 3 Emerson used no first-person singular pronouns in his 11 sentences (0/11), whereas Thoreau used pronouns of this type in 4 sentences from his total of 14 (4/14). The Sign Test of significance directs us to ignore the size of a difference of this kind and simply to record its direction. The difference is given a plus sign if, as in the present instance, it is in the predicted direction and a minus sign if it goes contrary to the prediction. In short, the outcomes are dichotomized into heads and tails. With the numerical data, of course, one sometimes gets a tie; there were 7 ties in the present comparison. A tie is like the case in which a coin rolls down the register and cannot be read. The outcome does not count either way and the number of tosses is reduced by 1.

Of the 25 pairs of passages usable for the pronoun analysis, Thoreau exceeded Emerson 19 times and Emerson exceeded Thoreau 6 times. A table of probabilities for the expansion of the binomial tells us that an outcome as extreme as this would not happen more than 7 times in 1000 (p = .007) if the two writers really used the first-person singular pronoun equally often in passages of matched content. Being reasonable men we conclude that the coin is biased, the styles in this respect distinct, and the hypothesis confirmed. Of course, careful readers of Thoreau and Emerson have known all along that Thoreau made greater use of "I," but our tests will demonstrate that some other things which careful readers believe are probably not true. Since not all of our impressions will survive the test, we can feel more confident of those that do.

Aggressiveness

The difference in the tendency to use the first-person singular pronoun is one of the form features that we consider to be expressions of differential aggressiveness. It is so because it occurs with another set of features, the negative forms "not," "none," "no," and the like.[6] Negatives were counted only once per sentence and the ratio of negative to affirmative sentences counted for each sample. There were no matches in the entire set of 32 pairs. In 24 pairs Thoreau had the greater proportion of negatives, whereas Emerson had the greater proportion in only 8 pairs. A difference as large as this would be obtained by chance less often than once in a thousand times ($p < .001$) if there were really no difference in the styles of Emerson and Thoreau. We also counted sentences marked by the conjunction of a first-person singular pronoun and a negative. There were 16 untied cases, and Thoreau led Emerson in 14 of them; a difference significant with $p = .002$.

Why should negatives in conjunction with the first-person singular pronoun be considered an index of aggressiveness? Why, for instance, is it aggressive of Thoreau to write (No. 4): "I would not have any one adopt *my* mode of living on any account" (*Walden*, *W*, II, 78)? The sentence is aggressive because it implies the existence of another mind that holds to the affirmative form of the proposition being negated. One does not negate propositions that no one is entertaining. We say, "It is not sunny out," only if someone thinks it is, and "It will not fly," only if someone thinks it will. Thoreau's sentence, "I would not have any one adopt *my* mode of living on any account," implies the existence of someone who believes that Thoreau *would* have him adopt *his* mode of living. And indeed Thoreau refers to "one young man of my acquaintance" (p. 78) who did think just that.

The development of an argument by means of a succession of negative propositions represents a preoccupation with the mistaken ideas that must be set aside before the truth can be established. Thoreau consistently attempted to get at the false propositions in the mind of the opposition so that he might strike them down. The use of the first-person singular pronoun made the combat a personal one, Thoreau against the conventional ideas of his time.

Our impression of a temperamental affinity between Thoreau and Shaw is strengthened by the finding for negatives. Richard M. Ohmann, in his study of Shaw (1962), considers the "posture of opposition" to be one of the most characteristic features of Shaw's style. Ohmann supported his qualitative impressions with word counts, comparing passages from Shaw with a control set of passages from Chesterton, Wilde, the Webbs, Yeats, and Bertrand Russell. Ohmann made no tests of statistical significance, but he counts many more negatives in the passage from Shaw than in the other passages.

There are formal features other than the negative that reveal Thoreau's combativeness. The logical structure of discourse in English is sometimes explicitly marked with such connectives as "because," "if"–"then," "therefore," "though," "but," and "yet." Thoreau uses more of such connectives than does Emerson, and the difference is significant, though only barely so. The logical connectives in general are not clearly related to combativeness, but one subvariety, the contrasting conjunction, does seem to be.

Contrasting conjunctions like "but," "though," and "yet" encode a relation of negative implication linking two propositions or two modifiers of a single head word (which commonly transform into two propositions). One says, in English: "There was thunder and lightning *but* no rain"; "I liked her *even though* she hated me"; "She was beautiful *but* dumb, poor *but* happy." In each of these constructions an expectancy is generated and then violated. Negative implication is a kind of conflict, and the writer who develops his argument through the use of negative implication—as, for instance, does John Donne—sounds more combative than one who does not. Thoreau uses a larger number of contrastive conjunctions than does Emerson in 20 passages; Emerson uses more in 9 passages. The difference is significant with $p < .05$.

The passages from Emerson and Thoreau listed as No. 1 illustrate the contrast between argument by positive implication and argument by negative implication. Emerson begins with the general assertion that he does not see how any man can afford "to spare any action in which he can partake." This assertion implies that action is valuable, and the remaining sentences of the passage assert that it is so indeed and list the ways. It is "pearls and rubies" to his discourse; it is an instructor "in eloquence and wisdom"; it is the "raw material out of which the intellect moulds her splendid products" ("The American Scholar," *W*, I, 95–96). The entire paragraph is a harmonious unfolding of the implications of the first sentence.

Thoreau's way is different. His first sentence asserts that the student who foregoes action and experience makes a mistake. This sentence, like Emerson's first sentence, implies that action is valuable. Instead, however, of listing the various ways in which it is valuable, Thoreau throws up a challenge to the implication. " 'But,' says one, 'you do not mean that the students should go to work with their hands instead of their heads?' " And then a challenge to the challenge: "I do not mean that exactly, but I mean something which he might think a good deal like that." The conclusion which fights its way through the several challenges is: the student should not "*play* life" or "*study* it merely" but "earnestly *live* it from beginning to end" (*Walden*, *W*, II, 56).

Conceptual style

As one index of the synthetic-analytic contrast of conceptual style, we have used a ratio of abstract nouns to concrete nouns. The noun form that seems to us to convey the strongest sense of abstraction is the singular common noun without any determiner (Long, 1961). Emerson uses six of them in the following sentence (No. 1): "Drudgery, calamity, exasperation, want, are instructors in eloquence and wisdom" ("The American Scholar," *W*, I, 95). The addition of a determiner (*a calamity* or *this calamity* or *some wisdom*) would limit the abstraction. Pluralization seems to fragment it (*calamities*, *wants*). There is one sort of singular noun without determiner, the mass noun referring to a physical substance (e.g., *sand*, *water*), that does not convey a strong sense of abstraction. These latter we counted as concrete, along with all plurals, all proper nouns, and all singular nouns with determiners. The differences between Emerson and Thoreau are large and consistent. Emerson was more abstract in twenty-three cases and Thoreau in eight, a difference significant at better than the .001 level. Emerson knew of this difference between himself and Thoreau: "In reading him, I find the same thought, the same spirit that is in me, but he takes a step beyond, and illustrates by excellent images that which I should have conveyed in a sleepy generality" (*J*, IX, 522).[7]

As a second index of conceptual style we have used a ratio of sensory-and-motor verbs to the total words in a passage. Sensory verbs are those that make reference to sensation in a particular modality, such verbs as "see," "hear," "smell," and "feel." Motor verbs are those that make reference to some definite picturable activity, such words as "walk," "run," "cut," "stand up," "pluck," and "bounce." It seemed to us that this count would capture the difference between Thoreau's tendency to render concrete experience and Emerson's tendency to abstract and synthesize. The quantitative difference turned out to be a very large one. In twenty-one cases Thoreau uses more sensory and motor verbs than does Emerson, while Emerson uses more of them in just two cases (p < .001).

The common sensory and motor verbs in English all have multiple meanings including usually several abstract meanings. One can *see* the sky or—the point of an argument; one can see a client, see that something is done, see someone home, etc. Thoreau and Emerson do not differ significantly in the raw frequencies with which they use the *words* in question; their differences are with respect to the sensory and motor meanings of the words. Thus Emerson uses "see" in No. 17 ("Social Aims," *W*, VIII, 87) and uses it again in No. 18 ("John Brown, *W*, XI, 271), but the object of the verb in the former passage is "moral benefit" and in the latter "the use of a judge." In Emerson's No. 16 ("Friendship," *W*, II, 205) we have the verb "vaults" but with "friendship" as subject; in his No. 10 (*J*, V, 420) we have "walk" and "run" but with "words" as subject. On the other hand, when Thoreau uses "see" in No. 9 (*Walden*, *W*, II, 32) it is with himself as subject and "a large box" as object. In No. 5 ("Walking," *W*, V, 246) he "hears" the "cock crow" and in No. 6 (*Walden*, *W*, II, 350) "smells" the "whispering sedge." In No. 32 his "thrust" (*A Week*, *W*, I, 160) is of a "stick"; in No. 6 it is "the mink" that "crawls" (*Walden*, *W*, II, 350) and in No. 9 "an immigrant" who is seen "tottering under a bundle" (*Walden*, *W*, II, 74). In sum, Thoreau's sensory verbs are likely to name physical sensations and his motor verbs are likely to name physical actions, whereas Emerson's sensory and motor verbs are likely to be used with extended metaphorical meanings. It is a count of meanings rather than words that distinguishes the writers.

Indirection, archaism, and other features

Not everything we counted served to distinguish Emerson from Thoreau, and not everything that distinguished them can be interpreted in terms of conceptual style or temperament. We had thought it likely that Emerson would make a higher score for the use of "elevated" diction (such words as "firmament," "poetry," "divine"). We have expected Thoreau to use more superlatives, more negative affixes (for example "un-," "dis-"), more all-or-nothing words (for example, "all," "each," "nobody"), and more imperative constructions, to italicize more often, and to use the exclamation point more liberally. The absolute frequencies were in the anticipated direction in almost all cases, but the differences were not consistent enough to be judged significant. Some of these features would almost certainly register as significantly different if one were to compare passages selected at random. It should be remembered that the design of the present study demands more than is usual of stylistic features; they are required to demonstrate diagnostic power in passages matched with respect to everything but the personalities of the authors.

There are, finally, two features that do distinguish Emerson from Thoreau and do certainly contribute to the reader's perception of the two styles but which seem to be related to both personality dimensions rather than to either one alone. One of the features is the balance between direct constructions and indirect constructions. We mean by a direct construction a declarative sentence (identified by the author's own end punctuation) in which the main subject, verb, and predicate object (or predicate adjective or predicate nominative) occur in that order. An indirect construction is any declarative that breaks this order; for example, Emerson's (No. 14): "Centrality he has, and penetration" (*J*, IX, 15) and his (No. 21): "Welcome evermore to gods and men is the self-helping man" and "For him all doors are flung wide; him all tongues greet," both from "Self-Reliance" (*W*, II, 78). The difference between the two authors is again significant, though not quite so consistent as others we have reported. In eighteen cases Emerson uses a larger proportion of indirect constructions, while Thoreau does so but nine times (p about .05).

Many readers have noted that Emerson often used archaisms.[8] In our passages we find quite a few of these. In No. 1 an inanimate object is assigned gender: "the intellect moulds her splendid products" ("The American Scholar," *W*, I, 95–96). In No. 7 we find the archaic negative: "Expect me not" ("Self-Reliance," *W*, II, 52). The archaic use of "be" with the intransitive verb "come" occurs in No. 3 ("The American Scholar," *W*, I, 105). Archaic subjunctives appear in many passages; for example, No. 20: "It were bold" ("John Brown," *W*, XI, 270). The archaic pronoun "thou" is used and the associated archaic verbal inflections ("shouldst," "couldst"), and "very" is used in the archaic sense of "truly." In eleven passages Emerson used a larger proportion of archaisms than Thoreau, whereas Thoreau used a larger proportion in only two passages.[9] The numbers are small, but the disproportion is great enough to be significant with p about .01.

The one frequent archaism in the Thoreau passages is the word "perchance" and, in the nineteenth century, this term was archaic in only some of its uses. What is interesting is the fact that Thoreau uses "perchance" in six different passages whereas Emerson does not use it at all. This is the sort of word that would be useful if we were studying style in order to fix the authorship of doubtful works. It is this sort of word, in conjunction with a statistical model, that has enabled Mosteller and Wallace (1964) to establish the authorship of the disputed *Federalist* papers.

When indirection, abstraction, impersonality, and archaism come together, we have Emerson's extreme manner, the stately, "composed" style that is farthest removed from Thoreau's tart, personal, concrete manner. We have quoted examples of Thoreau's extreme; here now are some lines from

Emerson (No. 3) that Thoreau could not have written. "It is a mischievous notion that we are come late into nature; that the world was finished a long time ago. As the word was plastic and fluid in the hands of God, so it is ever to so much of his attributes as we bring to it. To ignorance and sin, it is flint. They adapt themselves to it as they may; but in proportion as a man has any thing in him divine, the firmament flows before him and takes his signet and form" ("The American Scholar," *W*, I, 105).

SELF-REPRESENTATION

Heredity and childhood endowed Emerson and Thoreau with unlike temperaments and conceptual styles. Probably endowments like these are not alterable in adult years, but their effects are nevertheless not fully determined for the reason that a man may or may not recognize that he has them, may value them or regret them, may accept them or struggle against them. One of us (Albert Gilman) remembers hearing Austin Warren say in 1949 that there was a difference between Emerson and Thoreau on the level of self-representation and self-acceptance. It seemed to Professor Warren that Emerson had the stronger sense of personal deficiency, the greater need to wrestle with his own nature.

Very early in this paper we quoted passages to show that Emerson and Thoreau had similar ideals of style, but even in those few phrases there were signs that the ideal was more easily realized by Thoreau than by Emerson. That impression is confirmed by other closely matched sentences on the subject of style. Emerson wrote (No. 10): "I am daily struck with the forcible understatement of people who have no literary habit. The low expression is strong and agreeable" ("The Superlative," *W*, X, 169). Thoreau's very similar sentence is: "We are often struck by the force and precision of style to which hard working men, unpracticed in writing, easily attain when required to make the effort" (*A Week*, *W*, I, 109). We notice that Emerson in praising plain, honest speech says something not strictly true: he cannot have been *daily* "struck with the forcible understatement of people who have no literary habit." In praising the style of people with "no literary habit" he employs the very literary phrase, "I am daily struck," and he characterizes the stylists he admires in terms they would never use, as persons "who have no literary habit" and who are given to the "low expression." They would be more likely to describe themselves in Thoreau's terms as "hard-working men, unpracticed in writing." The shared ideal of style seems to have corresponded more closely with Thoreau's natural inclinations than with Emerson's.

The central ideal in the philosophy shared by Emerson and Thoreau was self-reliance or independence. A man should find his own way of life and insist upon it for himself, whether or not it is approved by tradition and convention. Both writers were perfectly clear that the claims of personal conscience are superior to those of any law or any social pressure. This sure morality, independent of the present consensus, made it possible for them to oppose the Fugitive Slave Law and to champion the imprisoned John Brown.

Though Emerson first articulated the philosophy of self-reliance, it was more congenial to Thoreau. Thoreau, like the salmon whose migration upstream is guaranteed by a seasonal need to push against pressure, felt himself only in opposition. Thoreau makes on us the compact impression of a man whose natural inclinations agree with his convictions. Emerson seems more dispersed, the line he describes less clear.

Independence and self-reliance were values that Emerson chose rather than values that directly expressed his temperament. He was not fond of combat but was rather inclined to compliance. However, having adopted a creed of independence, he struggled with his own nature and, at important points, did what his conscience required. He resigned from Second Church in 1832 because he could not in conscience continue to administer communion. He knew that his Divinity School Address in 1838 would bring obloquy upon him, but he was not deterred.

When conscience required it, Emerson could act against his inclinations, but he knew what his inclinations were and knew that they were fundamentally unalterable. Most impressively he saw that the philosophy of self-reliance required that he choose his own nature (No. 4). "Insist on yourself; never imitate. Your own gift you can present every moment with the cumulative force of a whole life's cultivation; but of the adopted talent of another you have only an extemporaneous half possession" ("Self-Reliance," *W*, II, 83).

William James in his address at the Emerson centenary in Concord especially praised the philosopher-poet for knowing and accepting his own nature.

This duty of spiritual seeing and reporting determined the whole tenor of his life. It was to shield this duty from invasion and distraction that he dwelt in the country, that he consistently declined to entangle himself with associations or to encumber himself with functions which, however he might believe in them, he felt were duties for other men and not for him. (Konvitz and Whicher, 1962).

Even on the issue of slavery, which strongly engaged his conscience, Emerson concluded: "I have quite other slaves to free than those negroes."

The United States in the early 1960's creates an appetite for leaders of sure morality and uncompromising conscience. Morality has been so thoroughly displaced by consensus that even our liberal statesmen are willing to call extremism an evil. It has become possible to talk as if departure from the great central stream—in whatever direction—were necessarily bad. That is the way things are, but it is not the way they have always been. We all know that there is an honorable American tradition of extremism in a good cause, and we feel some yearning for the moral confidence that made that tradition honorable. In these circumstances Thoreau's clear, confident voice is extremely impressive.

But there is more than one standard by which to judge a man's thought and style and personality. If we take account of the complexity of the problem solved, the integration of Emerson's personality is the more impressive achievement. His experience was richer than Thoreau's—he lived in the American South and traveled in Europe and Africa; he had talked with Coleridge, Wordsworth, Carlyle, and other great men of the age. Thoreau had little direct acquaintance with the world outside of Concord and Boston. Emerson had a more refractory temperament, more extended sympathies, and loyalties necessarily more divided. The problem life set him was more like the problem life now sets us. "I am always insincere, as always knowing there are other moods" ("Nominalist and Realist," *W*, III, 247).

Emerson's experience was more comprehensive and so was his understanding. We have repeatedly quoted him on himself, on Thoreau, on their styles, and on their friendship. Not so often Thoreau, since he seems not to have seen so far round their lives. This present paper is no more than an expansion of such exact Emersonian observations as this one concerning Thoreau and himself: " 'T is as if I went into a gymnasium, and saw youths leap, climb, and swing with a force unapproachable,—though their feats are only continuations of my initial grapplings and jumps" (*J*, IX, 522).

Thoreau is the uncompromising idealist. Only perfect friendship is worthwhile; alcohol, meat, and even a dish of tea must be eschewed since they do not accord with principle; no law is too trivial to be disobeyed if it is morally wrong. Emerson is more compromising—or temperate. He thinks it (No. 13) not worth his while to denounce "flesh-eating or wine-drinking" ("Heroism," *W*, II, 254). He sees (No. 16) that "friendship should have feet, as well as eyes and eloquence" ("Friendship," *W*, II, 205), that there is some value in "the municipal virtues of justice, punctuality, fidelity and pity" (p. 205). If we ask which man is the rarer type today, the more striking and invigorating, the answer is Thoreau. If we ask which man we would prefer to trust with power, today and over ourselves, the answer is Emerson.

Notes

1. All references to these passages will be indicated by the number assigned to them in Table 13–1 and by the appropriate volume and page reference to the standard edition in the parentheses

following the quotation. For Emerson: *The Complete Works of Ralph Waldo Emerson*, 12 vols. (Boston, 1903–4) and *The Journals of Ralph Waldo Emerson*, 10 vols. (Boston, 1909–14). For Thoreau: *The Writings of Henry David Thoreau*, 6 vols. (Boston, 1906), and *The Writings of Henry David Thoreau* [*Journal*], 14 vols. (Boston, 1906). A passage from Emerson or Thoreau quoted but not given a number is a passage that was not used by us in the stylistic analysis and for which Table 13–1 does not give a reference.

2. There is even some evidence that among mature males differences of aggressiveness are related to differences in the production of the male sex hormone. Males of many species have an organized dominance order such that the higher ranking animals have rights of precedence to space, food, and females. Several studies have shown that when a male animal who is low in the dominance order is given injections of male hormone he will fight his way up to a higher position. See, for instance, Scott (1958) and Clark and Birch (1945, 1946).

3. Raymond Gozzi in his doctoral dissertation, "Tropes and Figures: A Psychological Study of David Henry Thoreau [sic]" (New York University, 1957), has attempted a psychoanalytic study of Thoreau's personality. It seems to us that his case is not convincing because the data are too few and their relevance too remote. For a summary of the dissertation see Bode (1962).

4. To facilitate location of the passages we have given the title of the work, volume, and page, and the first two and last two words of the passage.

5. O. W. Firkins (1915) has shown that Emerson's tone is on occasion brusque, rough, even coarse. It is our impression, nevertheless, that combativeness and vigor are more *characteristic* of Thoreau, characteristic in two senses: the qualities are frequent and also unstudied. On the infrequent occasions when Emerson is rough he seems to be so from principle rather than temperament—perhaps in a deliberate effort to "invigorate" his style. This is, of course, only an impression, but the case does not chiefly rest on the impressions reported in this section of the paper but rather on the quantitative comparisons of the next section.

6. We were here guided by a discussion of negation in the terms of transformational grammar by Klima (1964).

7. For a discussion of Emerson's use of abstractions from another point of view, see Lauter, 1960.

8. See, for instance, Firkins (1915) and Célières (1936).
9. In his master's thesis, "A Formal Study of H. D. Thoreau" (University of Iowa, 1948), William Drake states that such poetic archaisms as "o'er," "e'er," "yon," "methinks," "ye," "oft" make a "negligible appearance" in *Walden*. He also points out that in working over journal material for *A Week*, Thoreau "modernized" the "archaic form" "o'er" to "over." Portions of the thesis are reprinted in Paul (1962).

References

BODE, C. The half-hidden Thoreau. *The Massachusetts Review*, 1962, IV, 68–80.

CÉLIÈRES, A. *The prose style of Emerson.* Paris: Impressions. Pierre André, 1936.

CLARK, G., and BIRCH, H. G. Hormonal modification of social behavior, *Psychosomatic medicine*, 1945, VII, 321–329 and 1946, VII, 320–31.

FIRKINS, O. W. *Ralph Waldo Emerson.* Boston: Houghton Mifflin, 1915.

KAGAN, J., MOSS, H. A., and SIGEL, I. Psychological significance of styles of conceptualization. In J. C. Wright & J. Kagan (Eds.), *Basic cognitive processes in children.* Monographs of the Society for Research in Child Development, 1963, XXVIII, No. 2.

KLIMA, E. S. Negation in English. In J. A. Fodor & J. J. Katz (Eds.), *The structure of language: Readings in the philosophy of language.* Englewood Cliffs, N. J.: Prentice-Hall, 1964.

KONVITZ, M. R., AND WHICHER, S. E. *Emerson: A collection of critical essays.* Englewood Cliffs, N. J.: Prentice-Hall, 1962.

KRUTCH, J. W. *Henry David Thoreau.* New York: W. Sloane, 1948.

LAUTER, P. Truth and nature: Emerson's use of two complex words. *English Literary History*, 1960, XXVII, 66–85.

LONG, R. B. *The sentence and its parts.* Chicago: University of Chicago Press, 1961.

MOSTELLER, F., AND WALLACE, D. L. *Inference and disputed authorship: "The Federalist."* Reading, Mass.: Addison-Wesley, 1967.

PAUL, S. *Thoreau; A collection of critical essays.* Englewood Cliffs, N. J.: Prentice-Hall, 1962.

RUSK, R. L. *The life of Ralph Waldo Emerson.* New York: Scribner's 1949.

SCOTT, J. P. *Aggression.* Chicago: University of Chicago Press, 1958.

SIEGEL, S. *Nonparametric statistics for the behavioral sciences.* New York: McGraw-Hill, 1956.

[14]

A Review of Nabokov's Lolita

Edwin G. Boring, the distinguished historian of psychology, became the first editor of the journal *Contemporary Psychology* when he was almost seventy years old. As S. S. Stevens has said ". . . seldom has a man derived so much delight from so much hard work in the eighth decade of a distinguished career." Boring created a fine journal of reviews of books in psychology.

When Nabokov's novel *Lolita* came out I enjoyed it so much that I kept telling people about it. Not quite seriously I asked editor Boring whether he could use a review of *Lolita* in *Contemporary Psychology*. The journal did not cover fiction but Boring was so open to ideas and interested in keeping things lively that I thought it was worthwhile asking. He said he could use such a review if it had a psychological aspect, and that is how this review was written.

How can a novelist give to a reader the impression of participation in a consciousness not ordinarily his

This review appeared in *Contemporary Psychology* (June 1959), pages 172–174. Reprinted by permission of the author.

own? The consciousness functioning in *Lolita* has more variety in more dimensions than the novelistic standard; it is a slippery, self-observant, sardonic mind operating under the dominion of a quaint passion. The author gives us the feel of this consciousness by means of an exceptionally deliberate use of the resources of the printed language.

Lolita is about a man who is sexually attracted to girls of nine to fourteen years or at least to certain fey specimens within this range whom he calls *nymphets*. The book purports to be the confession of this man whose name is Humbert Humbert and, in the main, it concerns his relations with an American girl whose name is Dolores Haze but whom he calls Lolita. Humbert marries Mrs. Haze, a widow, in order to get close to Lolita and, when Mrs. Haze is accidentally killed, he carries off her daughter on a long motel-to-motel tour of America. Eventually Lolita runs away from Humbert with another nympholept, Clare Quilty, and several years pass before Humbert finds her again. Her abductor has deserted her long since, and Lolita is now married to an everyday young man and is carrying his child. Humbert obtains from her the name of his first rival, seeks him out, and kills him.

For the greater part of his life the primary force in Humbert's mind was his obsessive lust, and it operates in these memoirs as a force shaping the language. Its power is most apparent in the selection of metaphors. For Humbert, a telephone has a "a sudden discharge of coins," a "spasmodic refund"; the alarm of a clock is forestalled by "pressing home its nipple." A clerk, in a store selling clothing for little girls, recites a list of fashion's hues: "Dream pink, frosted aqua, glans mauve. . . ." Metaphors in a novel are often apt only in a general sort of way (e.g., *a shower of coins* from a telephone) and so convey nothing of the point of view of the protagonist. The objects and events of Humbert's world are not allowed to remind him of just anything; they are always selected by a state of mind and serve to place us in that state of mind.

Humbert's passion also operates on words, rummaging through their natural polysemy to find a congenial sense. For example, Papa-Lecher Humbert is at one point reluctant to allow Lolita to take part in a school play, and he tells her teacher that he will not grant permission unless "the male parts are taken by female parts." He does not say *unless the male parts are taken by females*, though the teacher apparently hears it so. The extra *parts* reminds us that this word means *privates* as well as *roles in a play*. This is a use of language particularly well adapted to Nabokov's purpose. The "appended" *parts* is an unexpected addition to a phrase already conventionally complete, and so it conveys the alien intrusive quality of Humbert's passion. Not being detected by the teacher, it retains the privacy of obsessive thought. The language here is wonderfully witty in its concentration and in its mockery of Humbert playing the "part" of an Old-Fashioned Papa who hesitates to let his little daughter participate in coeducational dramatics. Nor is it to be understood as the unconscious wit of a linguistic lapse but rather as the sly, outrageous joke of an extraordinarily self-conscious mind.

Humbert's desire, finally, accomplishes a sort of lexical fission in which words are fragmented into meaningful parts, many of which are not true structural units but are pseudomorphemes created by Humbert's obsession. He notices, for instance, that a change of spacing transforms *therapist* into *the rapist* and that *fiends* is contained in *friends*. The reader soon picks up this habit and perceives, for instance, that an exchange of initial syllables in the names of the two English teachers, Miss Lester and Miss Fabian, is informative. Perhaps we should take this ability to shatter words as a measure of the force of Humbert's desire, but, probably, this particular feature owes more to Nabokov's history than to Humbert's. The author's native language is Russian and Russian is a language of much greater morphological complexity than English. Russian words can usually be analyzed into two or more meaningful components and Russian children, we know, regularly create words by recombining morphemes. A Russian-born novelist should see morphemes in English that a native speaker misses, and there are examples of this splitting in other works of Nabokov where his style is otherwise very unlike that of Humbert.

It is a paradox of Humbert's style that his words are most directly sexual where the manifest events are not sexual at all. When there is something carnal to be described, Humbert's language is likely to go elaborately metaphorical, as when he writes: "The conjurer had poured milk, molasses, foaming champagne into a young lady's new white purse; and lo, the purse was intact." What has happened, in vulgar fact, is that Humbert, the fastidious literary gentleman, has contrived to have a playful romp with his landlady's daughter Dolores and this romp, which was only that to the child, has excited him to secret orgasm. For the most part, sexual events and sexual language are separated so that we regularly get simultaneous views from above and from below. This displacement spoils the book as pornography because, in pornography, as the author writes in his appendix to *Lolita*, "every kind of aesthetic enjoyment has to be entirely replaced by simple sexual stimulation which demands the traditional word for direct action upon the patient." Humbert's story is seldom titillating because it is seldom wholeheartedly sexual.

The important figures in Humbert's mind do not have fixed values or meanings. Like ambiguous figure-ground drawings they keep executing unwilled perceptual flip-flops. Nabokov suggests these changes of perceived character by changes of proper name. The assignment of appropriate names to fictional people is used to familiar comic effect in Jacobean and Restoration drama, e.g., *Sir Epicure Mammon*, *Sir Politic Would-Be*, *Doll Tearsheet*, and *Lady Wishfort*. Modern writers seldom construct names from morphemes in this obvious way, though they generally do select from existent proper names those of roughly appropriate connotation, e.g., *Rodney* for the rich-and-spoiled young man. In the ordinary novel, names, once assigned, are not changed, but in *Lolita* each major figure has a nest of names and these are used to suggest the varied ways in which that figure can be conceived. Humbert sometimes even names himself in the third person, an appropriate shift, since a Life Space does indeed sometimes contain an "objective" Perceived Self. Humbert's Self does not always look the same to him and so the name shifts among Edgar H.

Humbert, Humbug, Hamburger, Humbert the Small, Humbert le Bel, and many others.

The most elaborate word game is played with the name of Lolita. She has many names and these represent her various incarnations in Humbert's mind. The trail begins with Humbert's childhood when he fell in love with his first nymphet. This girl-child's name was Annabel Leigh, a homophone of Poe's *Annabel Lee* which we cannot suppose to be an accident in view of Poe's lines: "*I* was a child and *she* was a child, In this Kingdom by the sea;" and of Humbert's sentences: "In point of fact, there might have been no Lolita at all had I not loved, one summer, a certain initial girl-child. In a princedom by the sea." Humbert sometimes spells *Lolita* phonetically as *Lo-lee-ta* and, in this form, it is clear that his later love reminds him of the earlier. Once, when he thinks she is lost to him, Humbert echoes Poe a second time, calling her *Lenore*. Sometimes, when she is thought of as a small child, he calls her *Lo*; as an odious bobby-soxer, all potato chips and juke boxes, she may be *Lola*; but in Humbert's arms her name is always *Lolita*, the affectionate, doting diminutive, providing the perfect expression of his desire. At the end of the book, married and "with that baby, dreaming already in her of becoming a big shot and retiring around 2020 A.D.," her name is *Dolly*. The *lee* syllable is still there but moved from its central position and deprived of stress. *Dolly* is a blowsy no-longer-young name suitable to "her ruined looks and her adult rope-veined narrow hands."

Always, of course, Lolita's real name is *Dolores*, and *Dolores* means *pain* or *sorrow*. That this is not an accident is clear from Nabokov's frequent use of the word *dolor*. The principal development in the novel is Humbert's increasing awareness of the sorrowful side of his Lolita. At first his involvement with her is only sensual; she is his love *object* and he actually plans to enjoy her sexually while she sleeps under heavy Humbert-administered narcosis. Because our response is not tuned to the objective facts of the story but to their representation in Humbert's consciousness, we, with Humbert, have at first little compassion for Lolita. However, Humbert's consciousness is transformed in the final section of the book.

He loses his detachment and fills up with pity and guilt. His awareness loses most of its variety because his involvement serves to fix values and meanings as cool reflection has not. Perhaps it is not too far afield to suggest that Lolita reverses the Undine romance in that a mortal acquires a soul through love of a nymph.

The word *nymph* refers, most familiarly, to a class of lesser Greek divinities but, also to the pupal or chrysalis stage in development. When a *nymphet* reaches the age of 14 years she must be transformed into a young woman, "the coffin of coarse female flesh within which my nymphets are buried alive." Some part of Humbert's frenzy must be attributed to his dread of this transformation which he expects to destroy his love (at one point he speculates on the possibility of breeding himself a supply of nymphets with Lolita as co-genitor). However, when the metamorphosis has been accomplished and Lolita is Dolly, a greater metamorphosis has been accomplished in Humbert: "and I looked and looked at her and knew as clearly as I know I am to die that I loved her more than anything I had ever seen or imagined on earth, or hoped for anywhere else."

What Humbert is depends on what Lolita is; his vileness is a corollary of her humanity. Once his love has hydrated Lolita into full life, Humbert is left with remorse. Clare Quilty is Humbert's brother stylist and nympholept. Like Humbert he quotes French phrases and plays with words and even over-acts his own death agony. There is much to indicate that Humbert shucks off his own chrysalis, his humbug self, his umbra, in killing guilty Quilty.

Certainly the reader of *Lolita* is a very active participant. He is kept on the *qui vive* by the necessity of working out all the allusions and anagrams, taking in the metaphors, correctly registering the unexpected words, and keeping track of the metamorphoses of proper names. The curious thing is that all of this elaborate, vaguely Freudian, cryptanalysis teaches him nothing that he cannot learn from Humbert's explicit, self-descriptive statements. For everything about Humbert that is revealed by indirection is, in addition, "verbalized." This is a rather neat technique for representing a mind with insight. The indirect expressive channel from which we might expect to learn secrets of the Unconscious delivers messages that are wholly congruent with the character's self-reports. We appear to be participating in a mind that has no true Unconscious.

Lolita is, I think, a genuinely startling novel. It has been assumed that this is because of the theme—a passion for little girls and a suggestion of incest. Certainly this is not an everyday theme, but twentieth-century readers have accepted topics fully as shocking and treatments far more lurid. Perhaps it is not so much the theme that startles and puzzles as the thoroughgoing violation of the conventions of the modern psychological novel. Humbert's troubles are not caused by an unwillingness to be aware of disagreeable truths. His self-perception is accurate and complete. But his state of psychic grace does not have the consequences we have been taught to take for granted. Fully aware though Humbert is, he does not understand why he should be what he is; nor can he accept what he is; and he cannot change. No flood of therapeutic insight will help Humbert. In fact, there is no help for him except the gratification of making art from his plight. In these respects the novel challenges the axioms of the Age of Psychology.

INDEXES

AUTHOR INDEX

SUBJECT INDEX

"It is now 18 years since the Social Science Research Council brought together three linguists and three psychologists for an interdisciplinary conference that led quite directly to the creation of the field of psycholinguistics. If the interaction of two kinds of specialists is to result in the creation of a new field, the field must combine the two specialties in one way or another....I think psycholinguistics is one of the very few hybrids in all of behavioral science that has penetrated to the hard truth that a dilettante interest in another field is not enough to support interdisciplinary work."

—from the *Preface*